MODERNIZATION
AND THE STRUCTURE
OF SOCIETIES

MODERNIZATION
AND THE STRUCTURE
OF SOCIETIES

A SETTING
FOR INTERNATIONAL AFFAIRS

BY MARION J. LEVY, JR.

VOLUME ONE

PRINCETON, NEW JERSEY

PRINCETON UNIVERSITY PRESS

1966

FOR

CLARENCE E. AYRES

TALCOTT PARSONS

AND THE LATE

FRANK W. TAUSSIG

FROM WHOM ONE COULD ALWAYS LEARN

WITHOUT HAVING TO AGREE

ACKNOWLEDGMENTS

I owe a large debt to the National Science Foundation which made possible two years of part-time release from teaching plus secretarial aid, which in turn made it possible for me to do more work along several lines, including this one, than I have ever been able to do before or since in comparable time. I cannot overstate the admiration I have for the pleasant conditions which the Foundation made possible.

I owe a badly unpaid debt to a previous grant from the Ford Foundation which made possible my repeated references to Japanese materials though this in no way completes that bulky study of Japan which stares me down daily—which is my old man of the sea.

I owe a general debt to my university community which still makes individual research possible. My indebtedness to the Woodrow Wilson School of Public and International Affairs is especially great. Three of her mid-career students, Mr. David Munson, Dr. Kenneth E. Ogren, and Mr. Donald A. Wehmeyer, furnished valuable criticism when this manuscript was in its infancy. In general my graduate students were helpfully rebellious.

Professor M. Stanley Kelley, Jr. of the Politics Department here and Dr. Roger S. Pinkham of the Bell Laboratories helped in ways that defy identification. Indeed, they bear a certain responsibility for what appears here since our discussions were so incessant that much of what I present may properly be theirs.

I am beholden to the Princeton University Research Committee for making available the services of Mrs. Elsa Granade to edit this essay in hypotheses and for Mrs. Lorna R. Harvey's help with the index, and to Princeton's Bureau of Student Aid, which furnished the invaluable assistance of Messrs. G. Sumida and T. Mira in the preparation of the index.

I shall be most indebted of all to those who read and criticize this work. Essays in hypotheses are risky and questionable at best. Their one possible payoff is in fruitfulness for further developments, and critical scrutiny from many different points of view is the minimal prerequisite for estimating that.

Marion J. Levy, Jr.
Woodrow Wilson School of Public and International Affairs
Princeton University, Princeton, New Jersey

CONTENTS

· ix ·

MODERNIZATION
AND THE STRUCTURE
OF SOCIETIES

INTRODUCTION

I

THE POINT OF VIEW

This book had its beginnings in a course designed for graduate students resolved on professional careers in public and international affairs. So broad a subject is a distillation of concerns ranging from puristic scholarship and science to casual comments—cutting across all of the disciplines of social analysis. Since this large book attempts much, it may be useful to say first what it does not attempt. It makes no attempt to deal with the history of international affairs in general or with diplomatic history in particular. Although comparative, it makes no attempt to go into any of the details of operation of conventional distinctions among governments or economies. It is not, for example, concerned with the contrasts between the British Parliamentary System and the United States Congressional System or with the differences between the economic aspects of French and German social structure. It makes no attempt to deal with either the nature or the mechanisms of the conventional organizations oriented to international affairs. It is not at all concerned with either the structure or the operations associated with the United Nations Organization, the World Court, the International Bank, the International Monetary Fund, etc. It does not concern itself with the subject of international trade directly. It pays little or no attention to problems of geography or of international communications as those are ordinarily treated. Finally, it does not attempt to go into any of the details of leadership and relations in international affairs in any particular or general case. Questions of the "British hegemony," Bismarck's leadership, the balance-of-power system, bipolarity, neutral nations, and third men are not discussed at all directly.

These are all matters of the greatest importance. What is offered here is no substitute for the voluminous writing on these matters, or for the classics of history, which form the general background of the competent and literate in this field. Whoever is not deeply acquainted with them would do well to steep himself in them before reading this. In the field of international affairs they are indispensable.

This book does attempt something highly relevant to the problems of international affairs. First, it attempts to sensitize one to the social background—to a setting—for international affairs. It discusses, on very general levels, the relevance of the varied social backgrounds of the members of different societies for the kind of relationships they are likely to have in the international field. Second, it attempts to show the interdependencies of societies as wholes in matters that are relevant for international affairs. A great deal is said about societies from the economic point of view, from the political point of view, or from the point of view of one of the many organizations that characterize societies. Nevertheless, I never intentionally concentrate on one of these points of view for its own sake; all such treatments are undertaken to show how the different elements of social structure fit together. Any attempt at such a holistic approach is in part elusory. A complete picture of how elements of even a single society fit together as a whole would entail final knowledge, not only about it and all its members, but also about everything else with which it and they were interrelated. Still, I wish to emphasize how members act in terms of their society rather than in terms of their governments, their business firms, their class positions, etc., considered as things apart from one another.[1]

Third, this book attempts to distinguish different types of societies. After brief discussion of various classifications of this sort, I use a distinction between relatively nonmodernized societies and relatively modernized societies. I judge this distinction to be not only highly relevant to general questions of social analysis but also particularly relevant to the analysis of problems of international affairs today.

Fourth, the book attempts to show something of the common elements in all societies. Fifth, it attempts to show something of

[1] One of the special bits of jargon used throughout distinguishes between units such as societies, social systems, organizations, etc., and the individual(s) involved in them. For technical reasons, I define all such units "as various sets of structures [i.e., patterns] of social action involving a plurality of interacting individuals" rather than as various sets of individuals or groups. Given such usage it is improper to speak of such units "doing" anything. Individuals or members of various sorts do things in terms of the structures of action that constitute those units. Thus the members or office holders of a government *do* things but the government does not *do* anything. To speak of a society or government in this sense as doing anything is to commit the pathetic fallacy in social analysis. I justify the more cumbersome phrasing of this usage by asserting that it avoids: (1) begging questions by substituting a phrase like the government decided for an analysis of the decision making process, (2) confusing individuals with organizations and hence obscuring the extent to which unofficial elements may be relevant to official actions, (3) the anthropomorphism or organismic analogy of referring to organizations as though they were men or other biological entities, and (4) the possibility of obscuring common elements among different organizations by constant reference to them as separate and more or less isolated entities. *States* are never *actors* here. Society *does* nothing to people; people do things to one another in terms of some society(ies).

the main variations among societies. For hundreds of years two saws have bestridden the field of social analysis in general and that of international affairs in particular as a paradox. One holds human nature to be the same everywhere. The other holds no two human beings to be alike. The pair is not paradoxical. Both views are correct, and, stated correctly, they are not contradictory. In extremely general respects, people and societies everywhere *are* alike. The more detailed our interest in people and societies, the greater is the amount of variation we must be prepared to handle. Finally, this book attempts to show something of the way in which the main lines of similarity *underlie* the main lines of variation treated.

Pursuit of these six objectives is in terms of three principal comparative analyses. The first is a comparative analysis of relatively nonmodernized and relatively modernized societies. Although there are difficulties about these concepts, I believe the distinction to be the most generally relevant breakdown of societies, not only for present purposes but also for the purposes of analysis of societies in general. I can illustrate this by an extreme assertion. In terms of social structure highly relevant for problems of international affairs in particular, and social analysis in general, any two cases well on either side of this classification have more in common with one another than any one of them has with a case well on the other. Despite the fact that modern English society clearly developed out of thirteenth-century English society, thirteenth-century English society has more in common with the society of the Trobriand Islanders in more respects relevant both to international affairs and general social analysis than thirteenth-century English society has in common with modern English society. One may disagree with this assertion, this example, and the point of view exemplified, but this work attempts to show where they lead.

The second comparative analysis is a comparison of those things that all societies have in common with the major lines of variation among societies. The third comparative analysis focuses on two matters that I think contain the heart of the general problem of international affairs in the present world. The first of these is the problem of modernization of the relatively nonmodernized societies; the second is the problem of stability of the relatively modernized [and especially of the most highly modernized] societies. I do not think there is any escaping the former problem, and I am not sure that there is any satisfactory solution to the latter. There are few problems of international affairs today—including the problems of the implications of nuclear weapons—that do not hinge heavily on either the modernization of the relatively nonmodernized societies or on stability among the members of highly modernized societies, such as the United States and the Soviet Union.

Before turning to the organization of this work and the basic distinctions used, two further points of view should be stressed explicitly. The first has to do with jargon and the second with the kind of statements and evidence on which this effort rests.

A great deal of jargon is used throughout this work. Some takes the form of special usage already referred to in the first footnote of this work, and much takes the form of specialized terminology of various sorts. Jargon, in the sense of a technical language used for subject matter treated in a specialized way by adepts, develops about any subject—whether it be sociology, theology, music, baseball, or physics—that becomes a focus of great attention. There is no getting away from it—especially as a field begins to get somewhere. It is, however, possible to distinguish between *justifiable* and *unjustifiable* jargon. *Justifiable* jargon is any that improves the brief expression of precise ideas that are used frequently. Most of us are thoroughly addicted to jargon, and if it is justifiable enough, we are frequently unaware of it as jargon. The sports section of any good United States newspaper is full of justifiable jargon [e.g., "filly takes dash with stretch run," "with *Columbia's* skipper pinned firmly under his lee and astern," etc.].

I have tried to use only justifiable jargon, but I have not hesitated to use quite cumbersome jargon if I could not make a passage unambiguous without it. Authors vary widely in their abilities to combine easy-to-read with clarity. In a work like this I feel the choice must go to the latter if the writer's limitations force a sacrifice of one or the other. In the presence of sin, I have tried to sin bravely—and carefully.

The ideas and materials presented throughout this work are presented primarily to stimulate, sensitize, and inform. The focus of this work is so broad and important that any approach to definitive treatment, either theoretically or empirically, is well beyond present knowledge. I have tried to present as many relevant general propositions on this subject as I can and to illustrate them by empirical examples. The examples used are taken largely from the historical materials with which I am most familiar, i.e., those on traditional China, Japan, and the United States. They are not given as demonstrations, only as illustrations.

I have not knowingly presented propositions or allegations about the facts that are false or misleading—but many of the propositions are questionable, and few, if any of them, can be considered definitively demonstrated. *Therefore,* the propositions asserted throughout this work—no matter how smugly or dogmatically I assert them—should be regarded as hypotheses, that is, as unconfirmed propositions. The references to empirical data or evidence should always be regarded as *hypotheses about the facts* and not as any definitive presentation of the facts themselves.[2] In scientific work it is more important to be fruitful for further work than to be right. I am much more concerned with being fruitful by increasing the horizons in terms of which the problems treated here are handled than in solving problems. I seek, however, neither to encourage a cavalier attitude toward evidence nor to have my enthusiasm for—even faith in—some of the propositions presented here confused with a demonstration of their tenability.

I I

ORGANIZATION

This work has four parts preceded by this introduction and followed by a summary. The introduction states the general point of view and content of the work in the first section and introduces the basic distinctions employed throughout the work in a third section. In the course of making these distinctions, some of the aspects and organizations common to societies, some of the elements of variation among societies, the general problem of modernization, and the general problem of stability are touched on briefly.

Part I is entitled *The Structure of Relatively Modernized and Relatively Nonmodernized Societies.* Its two chapters constitute the main comparative analysis of relatively modernized and relatively nonmodernized societies. Relatively modernized societies are discussed first because most of us are more familiar with them. In the next chapter the structure of relatively nonmodern-

[2] The presentation here of material as hypotheses about the facts is not a function of a preference for hypotheses rather than the collection of data. Throughout this work the discussion proceeds on very general levels. Even relatively noncontroversial hypotheses referring to all societies or all relatively modernized societies or all relatively nonmodernized societies cannot be said to be well confirmed by any reliable collections of data extant. I hope that all the hypotheses about the facts made here meet the first scientific requirement of such statements, namely that they be "conceivably falsifiable"—that they are neither nonempirical mystical propositions nor tautological propositions. I hope that all are fruitful in that either proof or disproof of them will teach us much more than we already know.

I see no harm in, and no alternative to, this perseverance in the absence of highly reliable confirmation as long as I have made the speculative nature of what is advanced sufficiently explicit.

ized societies is described increasingly by contrast with that of the former. In the course of the description the comparative analysis of the two emerges.

Part II is entitled *Aspects of Social Structure*. These seven chapters deal with aspects common to all societies and some of the main variations among them. The first deals with a special tool of analysis, applicable to any social relationship involving two or more individuals, and is the most technically sociologistic chapter in this work. In the following six chapters the whole question of aspects of societies is introduced at some length, and five aspects common to all societies and underlying all variations among societies are discussed.

Part III is entitled *The Organizational Contexts of Societies*. It deals with the types of organizations that constitute the most strategic subsystems of any society. As in the treatment of the aspects of societies in Part II, the common elements and main lines of variation dominate these chapters. There are five of these chapters: (1) Kinship and Family Organizations, (2) Governments and Associated Organizations, (3) Predominantly Economically Oriented Organizations, (4) Armed Force Organizations, and (5) Other Organizational Contexts: Churches, Schools, Predominantly Recreationally Oriented Organizations, etc.

In Part IV, *The Common Elements, Variations and Problem Foci*, Chapter 1 summarizes the common elements and the major lines of variation among societies from the points of view of any relationship, any aspect of society, and the organizations characteristic of any society. This chapter is especially concerned that, however dramatic the variations, one cannot be unaware of the common elements that underlie them.

Chapter 2 of Part IV concerns itself with the problem foci of this work, i.e., the problems of modernization and stability in international affairs. The analysis presented casts serious reflections on the relevance of the terms in which much of international debate is carried out. Ethically and sentimentally I could not agree more with those who speak of "respect for national sovereignty" and deny any intention to "interfere with governments or the people of other nations," but intellectually I believe this to be dangerously self-deceptive nonsense. The process of modernization being what it is and the world being what it is today, the choice between interference and noninterference in the affairs of others is not what it easily appeared to be in the eighteenth century—or even in the nineteenth or early twentieth century. The relatively high levels of self-sufficiency conceivable for the members of societies in those days gave these clichés meanings impossible for them today. As the interdependence of the people of the world increases inexorably, the question is not whether the citizens of one nation *will* interfere with those of another but whether they will interfere with one another in accord with certain ethical principles more or less generally acceptable—whether decency, honesty, dignity, creativity, humor, and health can be maintained at the inevitable levels of mutual interference. Interfere they will, and increasingly every day, unless the process of modernization is not only stopped but reversed.

The problem of stability is discussed primarily in terms of its implications for the possible outbreak of war between any two of the relatively modernized or very highly modernized societies. The stability or instability of these societies has many other implications, but for the sphere of international affairs this is the central one. Many of the often iterated major sources of international difficulties such as "the invincible rise of x-nationalism," the military threat of the "have-not" nations, the threatening development of societies involving huge populations in the midst of the modernizing process, etc.—all these problems would be relatively simple were it not for their implications for touching off a war among the members of two or more of the most highly modernized nations. The members of the nations most highly modernized in regard to their weaponry are plagued by instabilities which find ready outlets in the exercise of age-old prides and prejudices as well as new ones. The most final of such outlets conceivable for the present would be a wearisomely old-fashioned war with catastrophically new-fashioned weapons.

The concluding summary returns to some general considerations.

I I I

THE BASIC DISTINCTIONS

A. RELATIVELY MODERNIZED AND RELATIVELY NONMODERNIZED SOCIETIES

The distinction between relatively modernized and relatively nonmodernized societies is the most important of the general distinctions used throughout this work.[3] This classification of societies is

[3] It is used instead of the distinction between relatively industrialized and relatively nonindustrialized societies. For many the term *industrial* literally means factory-ized. For this analysis the concept of the factory is not literally the heart and soul of the concept industrial; agriculture may be as highly industrialized as the production of automobiles [e.g., much of modern farming in the United States, for example, is as highly mechanized or industrialized as almost any factory production]; recreation no less than communications may be industrialized; even universities and the process of learning in general may be highly industrialized, and so forth. The term *modernized* is more readily taken as a broader term.

relevant to virtually all questions of distinctions among societies, and it is especially relevant to all distinctions used in analyses of international affairs. I use a definition of *modernization* that focuses on the sources of power and the nature of the tools used by the members of a given society. Although these are elements usually referred to as technological or economic, the approach is neither a special form of technological determinism nor of economic determinism. Simple technological or economic determinism, like all other monisms, falls in the category of theories that are either true but meaningless or meaningful but false. The definitions used here, if used carefully and properly in the sense appropriate to scientific work, do not even lead one into technological or economic biases. I define modernization in these terms because it is convenient to do so, because the continuum of classifications so set up is relatively easy to understand, because measurement in terms of the concept so defined is not difficult to imagine, and above all because its use so defined is fruitful for the formulation of hypotheses.

I seek a *definition* of the concept modernization, not a full or realistic *description* of the thing to which the concept refers. This definition, like any definition proper to a scientific field, is intended as a parsimonious tool for the identification of the class of phenomena referred to. In scientific contexts definitions are not intended to approximate detailed descriptions.[4] The elements used in a definition are not necessarily conceived to be the most important elements of the phenomena they are used to identify. They may be so conceived, but above all they are the elements that most easily and precisely enable one to make the sorts of distinctions useful for the scientific analysis intended. What are the most important elements will vary with whatever criteria one wishes to employ for the term important. In most of the discussions to follow, other elements will be far more "important" than those used in the definition.[5]

The causal significance of the defining elements is closely connected with the question of importance. I do not view the

[4] I have tried to use a parsimonious definition, confining interest to two elements, sources of power and tools, of which the latter might even be dropped. I have above all tried to avoid a definition that approaches a realistic and complete description of the thing defined. I do so for the simplest of reasons: (1) there is no end to the attempt to be descriptive, and (2) the more descriptive the definition, the more of the analysis true by definition, i.e. tautological.

[5] From certain points of view the most important thing about snakes is that an enormous number of human beings are afraid of them. There is hardly any usage of the term *snake* that would be served by defining it as something most people are afraid of.

defining elements as causing the other elements or aspects of the phenomena concerned. For example, all highly modernized societies are open class systems in some sense, but the development of such systems is by no means necessarily caused by the sources of power or kinds of tools used to define modernization. In specific cases it can often be argued that some of the defining elements were, in fact, caused to develop by some of the other elements characteristic of the systems so identified. Indeed, if monistic arguments are avoided, this is always a theoretical possibility.

In scientific analysis, elements different from those used in the definition but also characteristic of the phenomena so identified, should not follow tautologically from the definition. This is not to say the defining elements are irrelevant. It may be possible, given the setting in which such phenomena are found, to draw highly relevant deductions from the presence of a given unit as defined. It might, for example, be possible to maintain that the defining elements could not be present unless certain others were also, and hence to predict on the basis of the *known* presence of the defining elements that those other features would also be present.[6]

Finally, the definition of modernization used here is arbitrary in two senses. First, there are an infinite number of other possibilities for defining this concept in such a way as to have exactly the same referent. Second, for different purposes, one might wish to define the concept as having a totally different referent. Anyone who feels strongly that the term modernization *must mean* something other than its explicit definition here should feel free to substitute any other term or symbol provided he does so consistently.

My definition of modernization hinges on the uses of inanimate sources of power and the use of tools to multiply the effect of effort. I conceive each of these two elements as the basis of a continuum. A society will be considered more or less modernized to the extent that its members use inanimate sources of power and/or use tools to multiply the effects of their efforts. Neither of these elements is either totally absent from or exclusively present in any society.

I define *inanimate sources of power* residually as any sources of power that are not produced from human or other animal

---

[6] If such predictions do not follow tautologically from the definition, they may prove to be untenable. Even if they are, something will be learned. In the example given, a prediction could only be incorrect if: (1) the hypothesis about the mutual relevance of the predicted elements and the defining elements is in general incorrect, (2) observable data have been overlooked, (3) the unit and/or its setting are not the sort they were thought to be, or (4) some combination of the above three.

energy. I define a tool as any physical device that is ordinarily separable from the body of an individual who applies it and that is used to accomplish what he could not accomplish *at all* or could not accomplish so well without it.

It is important to much of this work that the most general differences among societies with regard to inanimate sources of power are those of degree, not kind. There is no society whose members use no inanimate sources of power, nor is there one whose members use only inanimate sources of power. If gravity is an element in gathering fruit, if sails are used to focus winds to propel a boat, if rivers are used to float logs, if fire is used to crack stones or to clear land—if anything of this sort is used to carry out any endeavor—to some extent inanimate sources of power are being utilized. The use of animate sources of energy may seem insignificant in social contexts at the other end of the scale. I do not know what fraction of the total power consumed in the United States is, in fact, produced by animals other than man or by humans directly, but it must be a small fraction in terms of units of measurement such as horsepower and watts. From other points of view, however small that fraction may be, it is of exceedingly great importance. Automation notwithstanding, most of the decision-making [and that in some way literally involves a consumption of power] is still done by human beings. There are many other contexts in which outputs of energy from animate sources are of the greatest significance. Academics like to think of teaching and research as examples.

I shall not attempt to give any precise directions for measuring different points along this continuum. I conceive the continuum to be established in terms of the ratio of inanimate to animate sources of power. As far as sources of power are concerned, the larger this fraction [or the positive number which represents this ratio], the greater the amount of modernization, and the smaller the fraction the less the modernization. Exactly how to measure this ratio and exactly how to determine where on this continuum a given society would fall are not matters about which I have any good ideas. It is sufficient for present purposes to assert that in principle it ought not be inordinately difficult to get relatively precise measures of this sort.

Throughout this work I rely upon no greater level of precision about this continuum than that relatively easily agreed upon in common sense terms. For example, despite some large dramatic uses of inanimate sources of power by the members of traditional Chinese society in the form of irrigation works, sails of various sorts, canals, etc., few would dispute the statement that the ratio of inanimate to animate sources of power was considerably lower for traditional Chinese than for modern inhabitants of the United States. Not all of the comparisons made will be as gross as this one, but in principle they do not present any greater problems than this one does.

Correspondingly, in the case of tools, there are no societies whose members employ no tools. It is also inconceivable to me that there ever be a society whose members never exert effort save through tools, whose tools operate without any exercise of effort by the members, or whose tools in some sense multiply effort as much as is physically possible. The use of a digging stick, however primitive, is the use of a tool. The digging stick is no less a tool than the most powerful and efficient modern power shovel. Both extend or multiply the effort expended upon them, though the two are used to extend and multiply effort in different degrees and ways. Here again, we have a continuum the opposite ends of which are not opposites, do not in fact exist, or perhaps are not even conceivable. Again, I have not set up any precise method of measuring the particular society. Here, I must be even more imprecise than in the case of power. I suspect that this particular continuum should in some way be based on the number and variety of tools relative to the size of the population involved and on some measure of the extent to which the use of these tools multiplies effort.

For reasons which will become obvious in discussions later, I feel that in some way this measure should reflect one special distinction among tools. It matters enormously whether given tools are such that relatively slight differences in skill in their use are significant for output. Here again, I rely on no greater precision about tools than afforded by common sense. Throughout this work, however, I shall deal only with gross comparisons. For all the lack of nicety of measurement, again, no one will disagree that in terms of such a continuum modern United States society must be judged much more highly modernized than traditional Chinese society and that traditional Chinese society must be judged much more modernized than that of the Australian Bushmen.

However cavalier I may be about the details of measurement of the continua of sources of power and use of tools, the question of one cutting-off point as far as the continua are concerned is absolutely vital. The distinction between relatively nonmodernized and relatively modernized societies is the central focus of this work. For several reasons I have deliberately set up these continua so that no one can say that there is any society completely devoid of any and all elements of modernization. First, to fail to do so is to beg an important question. That question is whether the distinction intended between relatively modernized and relatively nonmodernized societies is a binary or all-or-nothing distinction, a simple difference of degree, or a difference of kind based on different combinations of common elements as well as on differences of degree and unique elements. Although it is fruitful to consider relatively modernized societies different in kind from relatively nonmodernized ones from several points of view, it is radically misleading to imply—even inadvertently— that all, or most, of the elements crucial to the former are completely lacking in the latter. Therefore, the definition should be set up in such a way as to facilitate the recognition of common elements as well as variations.

Second, although I do not think the use of different sources of power and kinds of tools cause all or even most of the other characteristics of relatively modernized societies, given the setting of such societies and the characteristics of societies in general, such elements are interdependent enough with the others to be used as the defining elements for more reasons than the possibility of relatively simple and precise measurement.

Third, I wish these definitions to be fruitful in consideration of the process of modernization without, of course, making the analysis of that process follow tautologically from the definitions themselves. I believe that there is something peculiar, something "new under the sun," about the structures of relatively modernized societies. This new factor hinges on the fact that the structures of modernization, once they have reached certain levels of development, constitute a sort of universal social solvent. Given contact between members of relatively modernized societies and relatively nonmodernized societies, it is always possible—even easy—for some of the latter to find interest in *and* to understand some of the structures or devices of the former. By no means all of this, but part of this, is a function of the fact that no mentally competent member of any society is completely unable to understand the use of tools and inanimate sources of power. The significance of a modern milling machine may be difficult for members of a relatively nonmodernized society to grasp, but the significance of a sharper, more easily maintained cutting edge is not. The same also holds for some applications of inanimate sources of power. If it did not, the peculiarly solvent effect of the introduction of the structures of relatively modernized societies—even the introduction itself—might be quite otherwise. For one thing, the possibility of communications as between members of the two types of society, especially given difficult language barriers, would be radically different. This whole question is a critical one throughout this work.

It is important that the elements of both power and tools be considered as constituting some sorts of continua, unless there are untenable implications of doing so, but if they are to be continua, the cutting-off point used to distinguish between the relatively nonmodernized and the relatively modernized societies is essential to the analysis. If it is easier to imagine the elimination of the remaining or a considerable amount of the remaining animate sources of power, save for purposes of decision and control, than to imagine a replacement of the existing inanimate sources of power by animate ones without basic change in the structure of the society, the society is a relatively modernized one in terms of the power continuum. If not, not. If the levels of performance required for the stability of the society are out of the question without the tools used or if a return to more primitive ones and increased labor would involve catastrophic changes in the social structure, the society is a relatively modernized one in terms of the tools continuum. If not, not.[7]

The cutting-off point in terms of the combination of these two continua, is a more delicate question than the question of the continua themselves. The hypotheses developed here rest on such gross distinctions that the problem of the cutting-off point is not serious. It is not difficult to get agreement that the United States, the Soviet Union, England, France, present day Japan, and perhaps a number of other societies are well past the cutting-off point toward the relatively modernized end of the scale, whereas the societies of Burma, India, Ceylon, some of Latin America, and many others are well past the cutting-off point on this scale in the other direction. The location of this cutting-off point is, however, of first-order importance in questions such as: "When did Japan become a relatively modernized society?" or "At what rate is Communist China becoming a relatively modernized society?" Because of my difficulties in locating this cutting-off point more precisely, I shall try to stick to illustrations that are reasonably distant from the cutting-off point.

[7] I have not faced up to the theoretical possibility of the cutting-off point of the tools continuum being radically different from that of the power continuum. I have not set up these definitions to rule out the possibility of a society relatively modernized in terms of the tools continuum and relatively nonmodernized in terms of the power continuum or vice versa. The two continua are sufficiently interdependent that such divergencies are unlikely if not impossible.

B. INDIGENOUS DEVELOPERS OF MODERNIZATION AND LATE-COMERS TO THE PROCESS

By indigenous developers I mean the members of those societies who, acting in terms of their existing society, developed these structures mainly on their own and relatively gradually over a long period of time. Even during the eighteenth century there were international contacts and relationships, and in this sense the members of none of the societies referred to really did anything on a completely indigenous basis. Nevertheless, there is a sense in which societies such as those of England, the United States, and France can be considered the societies of the indigenous developers of modernization. Other societies are the societies of late-comers. German society was, of course, a relatively early late-comer society; the Russians were somewhat later late-comers; the Japanese still later; the members of the societies of the Middle East still later, and so forth. The late-comers who are of greatest importance from many points of view are those who did not get substantially into the process until it was already relatively highly developed elsewhere in the world.

Since the problem of modernization is one of the major problem foci of international affairs, treatment of the process of modernization as though it were pretty much the same process for all people regardless of the stage of development of the process elsewhere is one of the fundamental naïvetés of much present-day thinking. Variations among the societies of late-comers are also important. The problems associated with the process of modernization are not simply a function of the distinction between the "have's" and "have not's" of modernization. Many problems hinge on whether the "have's" have or have had, what they have, or had, as a result of indigenous development as opposed to relatively rapid importation of structures, goods and capital from relatively modernized contexts.

C. CENTRALIZATION AND DECENTRALIZATION

This distinction focuses on questions of coordination and control. As used here, it is closely related to the distinction between relatively modernized and relatively nonmodernized societies. By centralization and decentralization I mean nothing more precise than the layman has in mind when he uses these terms. I define centralization in terms of the organization of the action of the members of a social system about one or more foci. Complete centralization of a society consists of having a single member make and carry out all decisions and determine all coordination;

any departure from this constitutes some element of decentralization. Rule by members of a committee is not so centralized as rule by a single individual, etc. As will become clear, complete centralization and complete authoritarianism would be identical. Apart from this extremity or approaches to it, centralization and authoritarianism do not necessarily vary identically. In some cases they may even vary inversely. No society ever reaches the point at which the action of its members is completely centralized or completely decentralized. A completely decentralized organization would lack all structures of organization or coordination.

Despite the identities at the extremes, it is essential that the distinction between centralization and decentralization not be confused with that between authoritarian and nonauthoritarian. So concerned have men been down through history with questions of tyranny, and so relevant has centralization been to tyranny, that there has been a tendency to see nothing but centralization where other critical elements existed and to exaggerate the extent of centralization in tyrannous situations. Before the development of relatively modernized societies, no overwhelmingly centralized society could exist stably for any considerable period. Prior to these developments all stable societies save those of relatively small scale, no matter how despotic, were quite specific combinations of centralization and far-reaching decentralization. I do not mean to maintain that there were no cases prior to relatively modernized societies of overwhelmingly centralized large-scale societies or aggregations of societies. I do mean that these were short-lived, and that the "short-livedness" was related to the attempt to achieve levels of centralization beyond the technical means available. Think of the attempts at world conquest. Only with the radical increases of modernization in the last century did the possibility of combining stability and overwhelming emphasis on centralization appear. Not only did it appear, but, as will be explained, the further the process of modernization goes, the greater is the degree of centralization that must be achieved if stability is to exist. Correspondingly, with the increase of modernization characteristic of the world today, decentralized elements must play an increasingly smaller role in social organization if the societies concerned are to be stable.

The impossibility of stable overwhelming centralization prior to modernization is most simply a function of the state of development of communications in general and logistics in particular. The increasing importance of centralization as the level of modernization increases hinges mainly on the increasing levels of interdependency of the various parts of any relatively modernized society, of the members of any such society, and of the members of all of the societies of the world.

D. AUTHORITARIAN AND NONAUTHORITARIAN

Different from but closely related to the distinction between centralization and decentralization is that between relatively authoritarian and nonauthoritarian societies, organizations, etc. I shall make less of the distinction than is usually made in comparative treatments of political systems. My use of the distinction hinges on the extent to which an individual is, may be, and/or can be ordered about or forced about by representatives of the government or the state or of whatever system is involved. It also considers the relative lack of any recourse enabling him to challenge such control. As a human being, my main concern with this distinction is an ethical one; in the present work my major concern with this distinction has nothing whatever to do with ethics per se. Many of the technical problems of social engineering, the problems of correcting mistakes, and many other problems are functions of differences in these respects. These considerations, rather than anything having to do with the dignity of individuals or the like, are of concern here.

E. LARGE-SCALE AND SMALL-SCALE SOCIETIES

Scale here is reckoned in terms of the numbers of people involved and the extent of the areas inhabited by them. Large-scale societies are those that involve large numbers of people, say at least a million or more for purposes of example, and large geographical areas, say at least a few thousand square miles, also for purposes of example. The treatment of social phenomena in this work hinges almost entirely on hypotheses about societies that are large-scale in this sense. Occasionally reference will be made to small-scale societies for purposes of perspective, but whatever the significance of small-scale societies may be for us ethically, they do not in the practical world of international affairs loom large in the minds of most men.

F. RENOVATING AND REVOLUTIONIZING
SOCIAL CHANGE

Change is a central focus of this work. One of the most fundamental distinctions with regard to social change is that between renovating social change and revolutionizing social change. For some societies social change generally takes the form of radical alterations in the general social structure of the society. This sort of change has been characteristic of most societies in world history. There have been rare cases of societies that over a long period have been characterized by structures of renovating change; the changes have taken the form of restoration of a previously existing state of affairs rather than a starkly new departure in social structure. Perhaps the most dramatic case of this kind of a society is traditional Chinese society, which was characterized by structures of renovating social change for a period of nearly two thousand years. It is difficult to find a comparable case elsewhere, but there are many cases where, over much shorter periods, changes were renovating rather than revolutionizing.

Here incidentally, I should like to warn against a dangerous cliché; by the term *revolution* I refer to the radical nature of a change not necessarily to the violence of the means by which it is achieved. Many have implicitly assumed that unless there is active fighting in the street no revolutionary changes occur.[8] This unnecessary impoverishment of the language carries with it a literally awful impoverishment of perception.

One of the special features of relatively modernized societies is a peculiar set of structures of revolutionary change. The members of a relatively modernized society, unlike the members of any other societies, have the problem of socializing children for an unknown future. In relatively modernized contexts revolutionary social changes may be confidently, even if fearfully, predicted at the rate of at least one set every three decades or less. Characteristically the childhood of each man's children will be more different from his childhood than his was from his father's. This means at least a general social revolution per generation for the relatively modernized. Moreover, such rapid change may obtain without what is ordinarily referred to as a political [i.e., governmental] revolution of any far-reaching sort. If this is so, we live in a spectacularly peculiar period of history.

G. SOCIAL ASPECTS AND SOCIAL ORGANIZATIONS

This distinction is not ordinarily made when members of relatively modernized societies discuss social phenomena, but it is

[8] I know of no area in which revolutionary change, in the sense intended here, has been taking place at a more rapid rate than in Japan since World War II. Nevertheless, in 1960 I heard a famous and exceedingly sensitive Japanese novelist take the position that, what with the general possession of arms in the hands of a large number of soldiers immediately following the surrender, he and many others expected a revolution to take place, but that nothing had happened and nothing had happened since. The implication was clear in his words that no really important changes had taken place since.

precisely the same distinction which laymen and scientists alike take for granted and apply with skill when they distinguish between properties of an object [e.g., shape, color, weight, etc.] and objects [or parts of objects] themselves [e.g., chairs, organisms, stones, etc.]. This distinction has already cropped up above in remarks about different aspects of societies, social systems, or organizations on the one hand and the societies, social systems, or organizations themselves on the other.[9]

Organizations are much easier to define than the aspects referred to here. By organizations I refer simply to the membership units characteristic of societies. A society as a whole is itself a membership unit. Governments and families are such units. Churches, political parties, and schools are other examples. The nature and content of the social structures that constitute these units are subject to the widest variation, especially in the kind of societies with which most of us are familiar. The chapters of Part III treat the organizations that, if not universal, are at least sufficiently widespread to merit our special attention.[10]

[9] I have treated this as a distinction between analytic structures and concrete structures in *The Structure of Society,* Princeton University Press, Princeton, 1952. The general system of analysis on which this work is based is derived from that work. Any technical terms not defined herein, and technical elaboration on many that are, can be found there.

[10] Certain elements of my usage need clarification. In the first place, all organizations discussed, unless specially indicated, will be social organizations [i.e., systems of action involving a plurality of actors whose behavior is not adequately explicable in terms of the heredity of the species concerned and the nonspecies environment—in this case, of human heredity and the nonhuman environment]. Hence, for brevity, the prefix social will be dropped. The term *organization* will be used synonymously with the term *social system* and used in preference to the term *social system* when referring to units ordinarily called organizations rather than social systems by laymen. A society as that term is used here is a strategically peculiar case of the general category of social systems or organizations. A society as the term is used here is a special sort of a social system in that all social systems other than a society are either subsystems of one society [e.g., Princeton University is a subsystem of United States society] or else the result of interrelationships among the members of two or more societies [e.g., the United Nations Organization]. Although a society is a specific kind of social system or organization, it is such a special one that the term *society* will always be used here to denote it explicitly. The terms *social system* and *organization* never include societies unless modified by the adjective any [e.g., *any* social system] or suffixed by the phrase, including societies [e.g., social systems, including societies].

The definition of the term *society* used here is a slight variant of that presented and discussed in Chapter 3 of *The Structure of Society.* A society is defined as a system of social action: (1) that involves a plurality of interacting individuals whose actions are in terms of the system concerned and who are recruited at least in part by their own sexual reproduction, (2) that constitutes a set of social structures such that action in terms of them is at least in theory capable of self-sufficiency for the main-

The aspect of societies are no less familiar in one sense than the organizations discussed, but the careful treatment of them in the fashion insisted on here is a source of great difficulty. The aspects most relevant here have to do with special foci of attention, such as the economic, the political, the religious, etc. In ordinary language these different aspects are frequently referred to as though they were different things. For example, one refers to *the* economic factors and *the* political factors. Usually *the economic* is defined as having to do with allocations of goods and services, or by some rough equivalent; and *the political* is defined as having to do with the allocation of power and responsibility, or by some rough equivalent. Given such definitions, there are no such *things* as *purely economic* actions or factors or *purely political ones*. In ordinary discussions of social phenomena as well as in most technical discussions we fall unselfconsciously into such expressions as, "I shall now discuss the economic, political, and social factors involved." As a minimum such statements imply that *the economic* is nonpolitical and nonsocial; *the political* is noneconomic and nonsocial; and *the social* is noneconomic and nonpolitical. But such implications are nonsensical and seriously misleading. There is no such thing as an act that involves an allocation of goods and services but no allocation of power and responsibility. There is no allocation of power and responsibility that does not involve some allocation of goods and services. Neither economic nor political aspects are nonsocial. Both are special cases of the social unless one intends to imply that the economic and political aspects are explicable in terms of human heredity and the nonhuman environment or to set up a differently restricted definition of the term social.

The terms *economic* and *social* as used here, and as used generally, do not refer to different things. They refer to different ways of looking at the same thing. As social scientists, what we observe is action and its results; that is, we observe individuals or sets of individuals doing certain things and/or what we believe to be the results of such action. There is no social action that does not involve some allocation of goods and services; there is no social action that does not involve some allocation of power and responsibility; and I might add, there are no actions that do not

tenance of the plurality of individuals involved, and (3) that is capable of existing long enough for the production of stable adult members of the system of action from the infants of the members. One will not be misled seriously if he considers societies to refer roughly to the systems of action ordinarily called nations, countries, or societies, though for some technical questions and some of the "new" nations such identification could be misleading.

involve educational aspects, religious aspects, etc., depending on how those are defined. From this point of view the term social is a more general term than terms like economic, political, etc. The latter refer to different ways of looking at what we describe as social behavior or social action. Social behavior in its turn is only analytically separated from nonsocial behavior. While an individual thanks a friend, buys an automobile, orders a subordinate, etc., he is "held down" by gravity, his body operates homeostatically, etc. One may view a human being from the point of view of physics, from the point of view of biology, or from the point of view of the social sciences. In so doing one does not refer to different things but so different ways of looking at the same thing.

This distinction is an especially difficult one if applied in the social field. But every individual who reads this work is in a sophisticated sense quite used to making exactly this sort of distinction in a wide variety of fields. We discuss ordinary physical objects such as a chair in terms of what I would call here, by analogy, its parts or subsystems or organizations. We refer to its legs, its seat, its back, its arms, etc. If one pulls these apart, he does a certain violence to the chair, of course. In some chairs, especially modern ones, the dividing line among these parts is not easy to discover. Nevertheless, even when the back of a chair and its seat are formed of one continuous sheet of plastic, one is still able to refer to that portion of the sheet of plastic which is serving as its back as distinguished from that portion of the sheet of plastic which serves as its seat. The dividing line may be more or less arbitrary, but it does no great violence to our thinking to conceive of them as separable—of say, putting the seat in one room and the back in another. The screws or dowels that hold the chair together are also subsystems or parts of the chair. From many points of view it is exceedingly important to be able to consider a chair in terms of concretely distinct subsystems or units. We can, and frequently do, also consider a chair in terms of a different set of concepts. We speak of its form, of its shape, of its color, of its weight, of the density of its materials, of its temperature, etc. These concepts do not refer to different parts of the chair. They refer to different aspects or properties of the chair, that is, to different ways of looking at the chair. It is nonsense to speak of physically separating the shape of a chair from its mass.[11] They are separable only analytically, not con-

[11] We have little or no difficulty in maintaining the distinction between the paint of a chair, which is part of the chair in the sense intended here, and the color of the chair, which is a property of the paint, which is part of

cretely; one cannot conceive of putting the mass of a chair in one room and its shape in another.

In analyzing social phenomena—in analyzing any phenomena for that matter—for some purposes it is useful to refer to concrete distinctions [i.e., distinctions of units or subsystems or parts of things], for other purposes to these aspects or properties, and for most purposes to some combination of the two. It is quite necessary, however, to avoid confusing aspects with parts or subsystems. Confusion usually takes the form of referring to one of these aspects as though it were a unit or a thing or as though that aspect exhausted all the relevant aspects of the unit. Such confusion is a fallacy which has acquired a special sort of fame. It has two particularly apt names. Professor Alfred North Whitehead dubbed it the fallacy of misplaced concreteness. Professor Morris R. Cohen called it the fallacy of reification. The most classic case of this fallacy in social-science history is, of course, the vulgar concept of economic man. The sophisticated among the early economists realized that their conception of economic man was a special sort of abstraction, but many of their followers did not. Quite apart from the aesthetics of science, such fallacies generally lead to oversights, especially of interdependencies critical for understanding the phenomena under examination.

The fallacy of reification is hardly less characteristic of the work of professional social scientists than of lay conversation, and the prevalence of this confusion is not difficult to understand. A particular kind of widespread, highly developed specialization of organizations is one of the unusual features of relatively modernized societies.[12] This is specialization of interests in one of the types of aspects discussed here. Most of the members of a modern business firm are supposedly overwhelmingly preoccupied with the economic aspects of the action in terms of the organization. The members of a government are supposedly primarily oriented to the political aspects of their organization and of the action in terms of it. Universities are presumably organizations whose members are preoccupied with educational aspects. We are familiar with endless examples of this sort of specialization, and the simple need for economy of words could account for referring to these organizations as economic organizations, political organiza-

---

the chair, if one likes. One way of changing the color of the chair may be to remove its paint. But color [or its lack] is an aspect that the chair always has if it can be seen. Color is a property that usually can be easily identified but cannot be conceived as separable physically from the other aspects of the chair. Color must be a property of something that has properties or aspects other than color.

[12] See below, pp. 38–46.

tions, educational organizations, etc. For most purposes it would be pedantic beyond belief to refer to such organizations as predominantly economically oriented organizations, predominantly politically oriented organizations, predominantly educationally oriented organizations, etc., but that is just what I do throughout. The economy of expression relinquished here is costly even in analyzing the most highly modernized of societies, but however preoccupied the members of a business firm may be with economic aspects, the political aspects of the operations in terms of such an organization are by no means negligible. Questions of control, chains of command, etc., are vital.[13] The United States government is almost always referred to as a political organization, but it happens to be *the organization* in terms of which the largest allocations of goods and services in the entire world take place [roughly 100 billion dollars a year], unless the Soviet government holds that position. No business leader, or as far as I know, no organized set of businessmen begins to have nearly the economic impact of operations carried out by members of the United States government routinely.

We do not think of the family as an economic organization, and in such vital matters as national income accounting in relatively modernized societies, we do not ordinarily take into account, save possibly by inference from the amounts of power consumed domestically, etc., the kinds of vital services which take place in a family context: such services as child care, laundry, cleaning, and the preparation of food. Though highly relevant in other respects, these probably constitute only a small fraction of the total national income characteristic of a highly modernized society. Nevertheless, our tendency to regard economically productive activity as overwhelmingly and properly carried out in terms of specialized organizations such as business firms and factories may cause us to overlook vital elements of economic allocation in terms of such nonspecialized organizations as families.[14]

As soon as we step outside the circle of relatively modernized societies however, and most of the societies in the world are still relatively nonmodernized, the problem is magnified. In these

---

[13] Indeed, most modern novels about life in an environment of such organizations stress political aspects and other aspects far more heavily than the economic aspects themselves. Novelists of this genre are usually exceedingly naïve about the economic aspects, and perhaps about the others as well.

[14] Exceptions are beginning to crop up. Professor Fritz Machlup attempts to measure some contributions in the form of child care. See F. Machlup, *The Production and Distribution of Knowledge in the United States,* Princeton University Press, Princeton, 1962, pp. 52–56 and 103–106.

contexts [15] organizations specialized in terms of economic, political, or other aspects, are much rarer. Analyzing these societies in
terms we have come to take for granted as laymen in relatively
modernized contexts leads to one of two [or some combination of
the two] sorts of difficulties: (1) we tend to assume that organizations which seem analogous to highly specialized ones in relatively modernized societies have comparable levels of specialization, or (2) important implications of action in terms of relatively
nonspecialized organizations tend to be overlooked because, as
members of relatively modernized societies, we habitually overlook them. In the latter respect, it is one thing to ignore in
national income accounting the goods and services produced on a
family basis by members of United States society; it is quite
another thing to overlook them in the case of traditional China.
The overwhelming proportion of all economic allocation, education, etc., that takes place in terms of relatively nonmodernized
societies takes place in terms of family units—at all periods of
history, everywhere.

For these reasons I shall pursue the distinction with great rigor.
Even for the sake of economy in communication I am not
prepared to shorten phrases like predominantly economically
oriented to economic. I shall persist in that level of jargonizing
because the very clumsiness and awkwardness of the phrases will
call continuous attention to the distinction insisted upon here. I
am stubborn about this because virtually all social science literature slurs the distinction of aspects and things.

Parts II and III of this work are concerned with these aspects
and organizations. Five aspects are distinguished: (1) role differentiation, (2) solidarity, (3) economic allocation, (4) political
allocation, and (5) integration and expression. Briefly, role
differentiation refers to the aspect of "who does what when."
Solidarity refers to the aspect of "who sticks with whom" under
varying circumstances, in what way, and how strongly. Economic
allocation refers to the allocation of goods and services. Political
allocation refers to the allocation of power and responsibility. The
categories integration and expression are catch-all categories. I
find them unsatisfactory, but I have not been able to improve
upon them; they cover such aspects as those having to do with
education, religion, recreation, artistic expression, emotional
reactions, etc.

The major types of organizations discussed are the following:
(1) kinship and family organizations [especially the family],

[15] See below, pp. 93–95.

(2) governments and associated organizations, (3) predominantly economically oriented organizations, (4) the armed forces, (5) churches, schools, predominantly recreationally oriented organizations, and miscellaneous organizations. These five aspects are relevant to any and all societies; [16] and these five types of organizations are each highly relevant to problems of modernization and as setting factors for international affairs.

H. IDEAL AND ACTUAL STRUCTURES

The distinction between ideal and actual structures is used on virtually every subsequent page of this work. Unless specific notice to the contrary is given, the term *ideal* is used with only one meaning. It is defined as what some set of individuals regards as right, good, proper, preferable, etc. When a structure is called an ideal structure, it is to be presumed that on challenge the caller is prepared to identify the individuals from whose points of view it is an ideal structure. Thus if I say, "Bullying is a violation of American ideal structures," I am alleging that, in general, if one questions members of American society, they will tell him [or he may find out in some other fashion] and that they sincerely believe bullying is bad. This allegation [or hypothesis about the facts] may or may not be tenable, but it is at least conceivably testable.

The term *actual* is defined as that which an objective omniscient scientific observer would observe, whether the people observed were aware of it or not. An actual structure refers to any structure in terms of which behavior in fact takes place. Thus, ideally speaking, Americans are against bullying. Actually speaking, there is, of course, a considerable amount of bullying indulged in by Americans.

The distinction between ideal and actual structures is one of the most vital and useful tools of analysis of any society, any time, anywhere. In one form or another men have been aware of it since time began for them. In this sense modern social scientists cannot be said to have discovered it. It is, however, so obvious and such a humble distinction that many social scientists either neglect it or overlook its importance. A large set of theoretical propositions based on this distinction can be stated. These propositions constitute some of the most general, the least questioned and the most useful—as far as developing other propositions and understanding phenomena are concerned—of any

[16] Discussion of their derivation may be found in *The Structure of Society*.

propositions in social science. Some of the most important of these follow briefly because I use them again and again in one way or another throughout this work:

1. There is not [and in all probability there never has been] a society whose members never distinguish between ideal and actual structures.

2. For no society [and for no subsystem within a society or resulting from the interrelationships of the members of two or more societies] do the ideal and actual structures of the members coincide exactly. In individual cases they may coincide. For example, there are individuals who hold that bullying is a bad thing and who, in fact, never bully anyone. Actually, however, there is no organization whose members live up to all of the ideal structures that as members of the organization they actually hold, let alone those they merely profess.

3. To some extent the members of every society not only distinguish between ideal and actual structures, but they are also aware that these do not always coincide. They may use different terms for the distinction. They may be more or less concerned with the lack of coincidence of ideal and actual structures. They are, however, never completely indifferent to the distinction or the lack of coincidence.

4. Some of the sources of stress and strain characteristic of any social system inhere in the fact that the ideal and actual structures of the members of the system do not coincide exactly. Not only are the members of societies aware that their ideal and actual structures do not always coincide but they are also upset by some of these inconsistencies.

5. To some extent, and not paradoxically relative to the preceding proposition, the possibilities of integration characteristic of any society inhere in the fact that the ideal and actual structures of the members do not coincide perfectly. Not only do people get upset because their ideal and actual structures are at variance, but also some of their possibilities of adjusting as well as they do result from the fact that their ideal and actual structures differ. For example, in traditional Chinese society the ideal structures for family size were quite different from the actual structures. Another one of the ideal structures was that of equal inheritance of family property among all the sons. The latter could not have been lived up to as well as it was—indeed, it would have necessarily been abandoned very early in Chinese history—had it not been that

relatively rarely did more than one son survive to maturity. Even with the small actual average size of the membership of traditional Chinese families, subdivision of the land was carried well past the point of diminishing returns even for the members of traditional Chinese society. People could not adjust to interaction with other members of their society as well as they do if they actually lived up to the letter of all of their ideal structures if only because some of the ideal structures are always inconsistent with others.

6. That the ideal and actual structures of a society do not coincide cannot be accounted for solely in terms of hypocrisy of the members of the society. Cynics may hold that people who do not in fact do what they say should be done are simply insincere, but that is the sort of naïveté which gives cynicism a bad name. Hypocrisy is rarely scarce. It may be defined as a discrepancy between *actual* ideal structures and *professed* ideal structures. But, by no means all, or even the vast majority, of discrepancies between ideal and actual structures fall into this category. Some hypocrisy is highly vulnerable to social techniques such as exposure and ridicule. The general failure of coincidence between ideal and actual structures could never be remedied by application of such techniques. It is one of the irreducible facts of human social existence. No dissemination of knowledge about it threatens the truth of this generalization.

7. The ideal and actual structures of a given society cannot coincide for at least two sorts of reasons. The first has to do with the cognitive capacities of human beings. Assuming that consciousness is a characteristic of human behavior, the amount of knowledge that each individual member of a society would have to "carry about with him" all the time, were the ideal and actual structures of a society to coincide exactly, would overload any known cognitive storage capacity of the human brain. Each individual would have to know exactly everything that was expected of him, ideally speaking, in every conceivable circumstance at every conceivable point in time, and he would have to act in accordance with that knowledge. The second line of reasoning is somewhat different. Any system for which the ideal and actual structures coincided exactly would be exceedingly brittle. So interdependent are so many social structures that, given such a perfect system, any change in the setting or environment that resulted in any sort of failure of the ideal and actual structures to coincide would require

complete revision of the entire set of ideal and actual structures. It is not wild to theorize that no such system could exist
stably for any considerable length of time.[17]

These distinctions and the theories based on them are applied
throughout this work. From time to time subsidiary theories in
these terms will also be suggested. For example, differences in
ideal structures as between the leaders of a given society and the
general membership of the society have radically different implications in some types of societies than in others. One of the main
utilities of this distinction is that if one keeps it constantly in
mind, many things that otherwise seem paradoxical are no longer
so. Many critical observations which should be made, but frequently are not, will be made if the distinction is kept in mind.
Since some 200 years before the Christian era, the traditional
Chinese family unit has been described as having a large number
of members. The membership of the average unit has usually
been described as consisting of individuals of many generations,
many sons and their wives, etc., all living together. Never, however, did more than a small minority of the total Chinese population realize such a state. It is the actual family style approximated
by the traditional Chinese gentry. Peasants rarely achieved it.
Somewhere between 80 and 90 per cent of all Chinese in traditional Chinese history were peasants who rarely lived, family-
wise, as traditional Chinese were supposed to live. Nevertheless,
one of the most significant structural features of traditional
China is the fact that the ideal structures which the gentry both
held and to some extent approximated in actuality were also the
ideal structures for the vast majority of all Chinese regardless of
whether they were actually able to live up to them or not. Or take
another example, many societies have been described as polygamous by social scientists, travelers, etc. Until recently most of
these were usually described by asserting or at least implying that
the average male [or even the great majority of them] had several
wives. Actually that has probably never been the case. It is true
there are many structures permitting polygamy of one sort or
another [i.e., polygyny or polyandry]. Some members of such
societies do have multiple wives or multiple husbands. Rarely if
ever, however, has the segment of the population that actually
had multiple spouses amounted to more than a relatively small
proportion, usually a special elite group in the case of polygyny, of

[17] Elaboration of sets of theoretical propositions in terms of these two
concepts is only just begun by these seven propositions.

the total membership of the society. For it to be otherwise, it would have to be an unusual society indeed, since in all known cases the ratio of male children to female children at birth is slightly in excess of one to one. Even if somewhat more males than females die off in childhood, at marriageable age the ratio of females to males is nothing like two to one unless there is systematic killing of male children. For all males of marriageable age to have two or more wives at the marriageable ages of males and females, there would have to be a ratio of roughly two females for every male or more. Alternatively, there might be structures in terms of which the older men all had several wives and the younger men none, that the younger men *always* marry widows of the older men as their first wives, etc. Structures of this sort are unusual. What have usually been described as polygamous societies are not, in fact, polygamous for the average individual. They are rather societies in terms of which, ideally speaking, polygamy is permissible or even desirable. One of the most important facts to realize about polygamous societies is that the average individual of marriageable age is not able to achieve polygamy even if it is an ideal structure for him [or her]. Achieved polygamy is usually characteristic of elite status.[18]

This sort of discrepancy is bound to come to light if one asks habitually whether an apparently descriptive statement about a social situation refers to the ideal or actual structures. Moreover, when one asks an individual to describe some part or aspect of his own society, the answer is more likely to be in terms of the ideal structures than in terms of the actual structures—especially if there are considerable discrepancies between the ideal and actual structures.[19] Ordinarily descriptive written materials are also more likely to stress ideal than actual structures. Especially in situations with which one is unfamiliar, it is well for any person to keep this distinction in mind.

[18] It has been recently shown [see P. Kunstadter, R. Buhler, F. F. Stephan, and C. F. Westoff, "Demographic Variability and Preferential Marriage Patterns," *American Journal of Physical Anthropology*, vol. 21, no. 4, pp. 511–519] that the probability is exceedingly small that the membership of any society can survive while adhering strictly to a cross-cousin marriage structure. Careful attention to the ideal—actual distinction will probably entail alterations in the whole field of kinship analysis. See Part III, Ch. 1 [especially pp. 426–430, below].

[19] As recently as the 1940's Chinese who knew perfectly well that they and most other Chinese did not live in terms of a large Chinese gentry type family, when asked what the Chinese family was like described the large gentry type. They did not do it to mislead, though it usually had that effect. In general material on China used in this work is taken from my book, *The Family Revolution in Modern China,* Harvard University Press, 1949 [Reprinted by Octagon Books Inc., N.Y., 1963].

I

THE PROBLEMS OF MODERNIZATION
AND THE PROBLEMS OF STABILITY

Finally in this introduction, return to the distinction involved in the two central problem foci: the problem of modernization of the relatively nonmodernized and the problem of stability of the relatively modernized. The main concern of this work is the analysis of modernization and the structure of societies as setting factors for international affairs. I do not wish to become embroiled in the evaluation of different goals of public policy. I am not concerned with what any of us might like or dislike in international affairs or in our future history. I am interested in extremely general statements which may be useful because (1) they are tenable, and (2) they are highly relevant to international affairs. I think the most general forms of all of the problems in international affairs may be classified under the two main headings used here. All of the present relatively nonmodernized societies will change in the direction of greater modernization. They will change in that direction regardless of whether their members wish it or whether the members of some other society or societies wish to force such change upon them.[20] In fact, some combination of the two is likely to be the case.

Most of these movements in the direction of greater modernization will be accompanied by far-reaching instabilities of the widest variety. The most important thing as far as policy implications are concerned, however, will not be the stability of the process but the nature of the process in general. If we understand this process, we will know more about what the members of such societies wish, what sorts of things upset them, and what they are likely to do. We may not like greater modernization, we may love it, we may be neutral about it, but it is nevertheless going to be terribly important to each of us. The fact that greater modernization is going on all over the world will be a much more important variable in explaining the actions of people than terms such as nationalism, freedom, human dignity, greed, lust for power, or pride. In the world in which we live, increasingly no member of any society, whether relatively modernized or not, will have for long the privilege of standing aloof from the problems of modernization. Modernization is a general process; it touches us all.

The problem of the members of relatively modernized societies, especially of the most highly modernized ones, is the prob-

[20] See below, pp. 125–129.

lem of living with the form of society they have already achieved. Relatively modernized societies are exceedingly recent phenomena. The most superficial examination of recent history reveals a constantly ascending spiral of bloodier and bloodier wars in which the leadership is taken by members of the most highly modernized societies. They did not invent wars, but they have certainly maintained a rate of technological advance in weaponry that has never been achieved before. The technical means literally to wipe out world-wide civilization was not within the reach of the members of any society prior to our time. Now our best scientists tell us it is well within the reach of the members of at least two societies.

As far as the relatively nonmodernized societies are concerned, the question of whether they are stable is not nearly as relevant to problems of international affairs as the problem of how their members will proceed in the process of modernization itself. Their societies are going to be unstable in the most profound sense in any case. For international affairs, the most extreme form of the problem is whether behavior in terms of highly modernized societies impels the members of one of them to modern wars with those of another. Do these societies contain within themselves sources of instability such that modern global wars are likely to result? Regardless of whether other societies have, or had, such sources,[21] do these? I hope our societies do not, but they probably do. If we intend to try to do anything about this, given the past record, we ought to look carefully into these matters to seek a way out. Even though we cannot eliminate problems of instability in general of these societies, if we can lower radically the probabilities of instabilities likely to result in modern global wars involving the members of two or more of the most highly modernized societies, the prognosis of a long future in which we can turn our attention to other problems of international affairs, even to other problems of living, is considerably enhanced.

[21] After all, the members of no other societies have had such weapons. Of one thing we are cynically certain! No weapons are "so terrible they will outlaw war"—however much we wish it.

PART I

THE STRUCTURE OF RELATIVELY MODERNIZED AND RELATIVELY NONMODERNIZED SOCIETIES

THE STRUCTURE OF RELATIVELY

MODERNIZED SOCIETIES

I
DEFINITION OF MODERNIZATION

The degree of modernization has been defined above as having to do with inanimate sources of power and tools [see pp. 9–15]. The greater the ratio of inanimate to animate sources of power and the greater the multiplication of effort as the effect of applications of tools, the greater is the degree of modernization. Among the members of relatively modernized societies uses of inanimate sources of power not only predominate, but they predominate in such a way that it is almost impossible to envisage any considerable departure in the direction of the uses of animate sources of power without the most far-reaching changes of the entire system. The multiplication of effort by applications of tools is high, and the rate is probably increasing exponentially. The application of tools is constantly being pushed into new spheres.

Relatively modernized societies constitute phenomena quite new in social history. The origins of some of their aspects are ancient, perhaps, but then by definition the origins of anything can be traced indefinitely far back into history. However long their pedigrees, the specific combination of elements characteristic of relatively modernized societies do not begin to emerge with any clarity prior to the early part of the nineteenth century. High degrees of modernization are no more than roughly fifty years old at present. Indeed, some of the most striking aspects of some of the most highly modernized societies are probably not a great deal more than a quarter of a century old. The fact that a given trait exemplified by a relatively modernized society and crucial to it existed in, say, Renaissance society or early Greek society does not make it useful to consider either of the latter as modernized or relatively modernized as the terms are used here.

Although this type of society is quite new in social history, no people in history have completely lacked the elements used here to define the degree of modernization. It is partly because of the presence of some such elements as these that no society has members completely unable to comprehend or sense advantages in some applications of power from inanimate sources and tools.

As modernization is studied in greater detail, the question of the exact location of a dividing line between relatively modernized and relatively nonmodernized societies will become more important. The present state of the field and the objective of this work are sufficiently rough so that we may beg or loosely answer this question. No one is likely to contest use of the society of the Australian aborgines as an example toward one extreme of the continuum and modern United States society as an example toward the opposite end. Americans have not gone as far as it is possible to go in these directions. Indeed, they are going further every day. United States society, however is the most extreme example of modernization insofar as these defining elements are used. Among Australian Bushmen the use of inanimate sources of power is negligible quantitatively. Most of the power they use is human power. The tools they use are important to them and multiply their effort, but not a great deal. In the United States power from animate sources has become negligible quantitatively. It is certainly a small fraction of the amount of power from inanimate sources.[1] It is considerably easier to contemplate increasing applications of power from inanimate sources in the remaining fields in which power from animate sources is used than to contemplate the reverse. Any considerable attempt to return to animate sources of power in United States society could be carried through only after a massive reduction in the population and a radical change in all social systems in terms of which the members of that society operate. The same sort of catastrophic consequences would accompany comparatively small regressions in the work ratio furnished by tools in the United States. This would not be equally the case among Australian Bushmen, though in some cases one might argue that any decrease in the efficiency of their tools might plunge them below the subsistence level altogether. Despite this difficulty the contrast is on the whole sufficiently clear to be usable.

I intend none of the arguments put forward to rest on the exact location of the dividing line between relatively nonmodernized and relatively modernized societies. In principle it is unfortunate in technical works to define by example, but for present purposes I shall attempt no further refinement of this dividing line than

[1] Again, however negligible quantitatively this power from animate sources may be, it is not necessarily negligible from the point of view of direction and control. The increase of automation is making some changes even in this field, but this revolution has only just begun.

some examples of societies which fall well on one side or the other of it. Most of the western European nations are relatively modernized today. There are of course conspicuous differences in the level of their modernization. England, France, and at least West Germany represent high levels of modernization. The same is probably true of Italy, Belgium and Switzerland. Spain and Portugal are still relatively nonmodernized, though perhaps at the upper end of that scale. The same might be said of the Eastern European countries, excepting such a case as Czechoslovakia, of course. The Scandinavian countries represent interesting combinations of some highly modernized fields and some relatively nonmodernized ones, but as wholes I would place them well up in the scale of relatively modernized societies. Canada, Australia, and New Zealand would fall on the relatively modernized side of the dividing line. The Soviet Union would fall well on the relatively modernized side. Nothing in Asia would fall on the relatively modernized side of the line save for Japan which would fall far on the relatively modernized side of the line. Communist China would certainly not fall on the relatively modernized side of this line unless we are to take the pronouncements of her present leaders as the gospel of accomplishment. India's position is on the relatively nonmodernized side of the line, further toward the other side in some respects than Communist China at present, though one would doubt whether that can long continue to be the case. No Middle Eastern societies save those of Israel and Turkey would be on the relatively modernized side of the dividing line. Israel for peculiar reasons is probably well over that dividing line, and Turkey may be. No African country save South Africa and isolated portions of Algeria could qualify as being on the relatively modernized side of the line. The Latin American societies raise some of the most difficult cases of judgment. The urban segments of several of these societies are certainly relatively modernized, but the societies as a whole probably fall on the relatively nonmodernized side of the line. Some of these estimates are questionable, but I shall not knowingly make use of any save safe examples.[2]

Finally, the elements discussed here are presented solely as defining elements. One should expect no more from them; I do not. They are not viewed as a complete description of the phenomena which they define. They are not to be given any special causal significance in understanding this set of phenomena. The

[2] This is a good opportunity to emphasize once again that all of the apparently definite statements of fact used here are hypotheses about the facts.

two main elements used for purposes of definition here are regarded as good elements to use for definitions for four reasons. First, there is no alleged case of these phenomena not characterized by these two conditions. Second, no society that I do not wish to consider as a relatively modernized case has these two characteristics as far as I know. Third, of various alternative elements of definition I know of few that do not pose even greater problems of measurement than these. Measurement of these elements, moreover, depends not on the concepts of social science but rather on the concepts of the natural sciences and their engineering applications. Since these are much more highly developed disciplines than any of the social sciences, I would prefer to use their relatively better developed, relatively more precise, forms of measurement rather than those available from my own field. Fourth, although these defining elements should not be confused with causal elements, they are highly relevant to the phenomena I wish to discuss.

I I
STRUCTURAL FEATURES OF
ANY RELATIVELY MODERNIZED SOCIETY

A. ASPECTS

1. SPECIALIZATION OF UNITS

In the Introduction [pp. 19–26] organizations were distinguished from their aspects. These are the units which will be spoken of here as more or less specialized. There are at least two forms which such specialization may take. The action of the members of these units may be specialized with regard to some concrete activity, and they may also be specialized with regard to one or more of the aspects of action discussed above. Historically there are many examples of specialization in the former sense accompanied by little or no specialization in the latter sense. In these cases the specialization is in some important senses incidental to the organization whose members are specialists in the activities concerned. Throughout history craftsmen and even whole village populations have been specialized with regard to the output of certain particular types of products, for example, dolls or some special form of cloth, etc. However, the organizations in terms of which those activities are carried out—usually a family unit in the case of the craftsmen and, by definition, a village unit in the case of the village example—are not usually specialized with regard to a specific aspect of the behavior of its members such as the economic aspect or the political aspect. The units are viewed by the members who belong to them as general living units. Neither the family nor the village is more predominantly economically oriented than other families or villages. The villages, if anything, are predominantly politically oriented organizations, but even that may be questionable.

The contrast may be somewhat easier to grasp in terms of economic aspects. The economic aspects of a family-type organization are *never* irrelevant to its general character, and often they are strategic for an understanding of many other characteristics of the family. Nevertheless, the family members as family members are also much concerned with child bearing and child rearing, recreation, solidarity, etc. Orientation of family members to economic aspects of their behavior in family terms cannot be said to predominate in the sense that activities in terms of a modern business firm can be said to be predominantly economically oriented. Even the latter, of course, cannot be held to be exclusively economically oriented, which is one of the major reasons for avoiding reference even to such specialized organizations as economic organizations.

The kind of specialization of organizations that is strategic here is specialization in terms of one or more of the aspects of the action. Examples of specialization of this sort are to be found in relatively nonmodernized societies. *Governments* are a frequent example of this sort. Sometimes there are specialized predominantly economically oriented organizations in relatively nonmodernized societies. Some of the merchant firms in such societies as those of the Hanseatic League, the Venetian city-states, etc., are examples. In general, however, in relatively nonmodernized societies organizations specialized in this sense are comparatively rare and, above all, are relatively restricted in number and variety when they do appear. In relatively modernized societies without exception one encounters the large-scale possibility of organizations whose members are predominantly concerned with a single aspect of behavior or even a special form of that single aspect. In modern United States society, our most extreme case, we have an unending variety of units of this sort. We have units overwhelmingly specialized with regard to economic aspects, political aspects, education, religion, etc. If we look at the predominantly educationally oriented units, for example, we see the most bewildering variety of special cases of that type of unit.[3]

[3] Schools [see pp. 342–344 and 624–634] are just such units. In the category of schools there are elementary schools which have to do with the broadest, most elementary forms of literacy, secondary schools, col-

It is difficult to make out a case to the effect that any of these specialized units is universal in social history. The only type of membership unit that is apparently universal in social history is some sort of family unit. Yet, in no known society has the family unit ever been specialized in this sense. In some instances the extent of activities covered under the heading of family concerns is a great deal broader than in others, but even in a society like our own in which the focus of family orientation by contrast with the sphere dominated by it in other societies is restricted, the family is not such a specialized unit. The most general highly specialized unit in social history is undoubtedly a government. As defined here a government is always to some extent predominantly politically oriented. Every known society of any considerable scale in world history has a government as one of its subsystems. Even if governments are not characteristic of all possible societies, they are characteristic of all societies of major interest in this work.

Even specialized units are by no means devoid of other aspects than the one emphasized [see pp. 23–25]. There are certainly critical economic aspects of any government. Indeed, from many points of view the aspects not emphasized by the members of these units may be more important than the one which is, if only because they tend to be overlooked. The mistake of referring to these units as though they had no other aspects is a function of the fact that members of relatively modernized societies have come to take them so very much for granted. Our society is such, never mind how it got that way, that if certain political aspects of ideally predominantly economically oriented units or certain economic aspects of ideally predominantly politically oriented units come to the fore, we are virtually bereft of any explanation except one of social evil.

In the context of United States society, for example, reference to the government as though its members were primarily concerned with economic aspects or reference to the members of a business firm as though they were primarily concerned with polit-

----

leges, etc. Colleges are much more specialized in terms of subject matter. We have colleges of dentistry, medicine, law, etc. Indeed, we have developed schools specialized along almost any substantive line one may think of. We take this sort of elaboration so much for granted that we tend to overlook the fact that the vast majority of all education in world history has taken place not in terms of such doubly specialized units but rather in terms of units that were not educationally specialized at all. The vast majority of all education in world history has, in fact, been carried out in terms of family units. Only in quite recent times in terms of relatively modernized societies has this ceased to be the case for any save a relatively small minority of the population.

ical aspects is almost always done in a context of derogatory social criticism. This holds true even though the United States government has a larger budget, and a more strategic one for the budget of other organizations, than any single so-called *big business* or organized set of business firms. For the members of various business firms, allocation of power and responsibility in terms of their firms is often considered the most important one affecting them. In the context of United States society derogatory criticism focused on the economic aspects of the activity carried out in terms of the government tends to take one of two forms. Either the activity is dubbed illegitimate because it involves graft and corruption, that is, it involves an improper allocation of goods and services by members of the government to people who have no right to them, or on the other hand, it involves a drift toward socialism, that is, the activity is seen as entailing a deliberate attempt on the part of some members of the government to change the structures of the government in order to produce a greater involvement in economic allocation than the critics deem proper.

Correspondingly, if a member of our society criticizes a business firm for the involvement of its members in supposedly specialized politically oriented activities, that criticism too tends to take one of two forms. Again, it is either graft and corruption, that is, representatives of the business firm are trying "to buy political influence" for their own ends and thereby "corrupt the government," or they are trying to take over the government. Ideally speaking, in our society the right of businessmen, as representatives of their businesses, to be involved in politics at all is questionable. If they try to influence the government in this role, they are presumed to be trying to do it for the profit of the business firm to which they belong. They are trying to get a special bill favoring their business or some special advantage of another sort. This is simply graft and corruption seen from the opposite point of view. It is not a matter of chance that the question of the ethical defensibility of lobbying has always been a touchy one for us. Instead of socialism, the criticism takes the form of fascism or paternalism, if one feels that members of a business firm are trying to take over the government or the functions of government not just for personal profit but for the sake of control itself.

These attitudes toward government and business are a function of the fact that United States society is what is generally referred to as a capitalistic society or at least one in which it is regarded as quite legitimate for predominantly economically oriented units that are not directly owned or controlled on a governmental basis to exist. In a relatively modernized socialist context there would presumably be no basis for criticizing members of the government on this score. If such a state had been carried to the extent frequently referred to as an ideal by socialist thinkers, any private involvement in predominantly economically oriented activities would, by definition, be illegitimate.

Modern man in the context of relatively modernized societies moves increasingly in terms of just such specialized units. Apart from friendship units and family or other kinship units, he moves in terms of little else. He purchases and sells, he votes, he worships, he creates, he learns, he is transported, he recreates, and he thinks, all in terms of such units. Prior to his evolution, the overwhelming majority of all men in social history spent their average days and nights without reference to any such units whatsoever.

Perhaps the most obvious implication of such specialization in general is that the more highly specialized the units are in a given society, the lower is the need to generalize all skills in that society and the greater is the need to generalize some basic skills. Specialization here is discussed primarily in terms of specialization of interest with regard to a particular aspect of behavior, but specialization in the more ordinary sense always accompanies this sort of specialization. Thus, in regard to education, we not only have predominantly educationally oriented units, but we also have exceedingly detailed distinctions among those. In discussing the skills that are important for the members of a society, it is useful to distinguish between *basic skills* and *intermediate skills*. *Basic skills* are those that virtually any adult member of the society must acquire at one time or another in his life cycle, if he is to operate effectively in terms of the society of which he is a member. For a society like ours literacy is such a basic skill. Virtually every member of any society must be able to count. He must know how to use the language characteristic of his society and so forth and so on. *Intermediate skills* are those skills in which only a segment of the membership of the society need be proficient in order to operate. For example, only a small proportion of the members of our society need know how to run milling machines, how to use a computer, how to use a cyclotron in research, etc. These intermediate skills may be of the greatest significance, but they need not be possessed by more than a limited portion of the membership of the society. As the proliferation of highly specialized units mounts, there are great economies in the kind of skills that can be generated because it is possible to train only a small specific segment of the membership of the society in these special skills without worrying about whether the remainder of the members even understand them.[4]

Proliferation of these highly specialized units cuts down on the need for most skills to be basic skills [i.e., for the skills of most members to be interchangeable]. Granted, there is no society for which all of the skills of all of the members are basic skills, but it is characteristic of most of the relatively nonmodernized societies that the ratio of basic skills to intermediate skills is high. It is certainly high by contrast with that ratio among the members of any relatively modernized society.

Although the need to generalize the vast proportion of all skills diminishes, the importance of generalizing some of the skills certainly does not. One of the special features of the relatively modernized societies is the fact that perhaps a larger absolute number of basic skills must be generalized. For example, in relation to language, the average member of any society has to be able to speak and understand the language of other members. In addition to this command over the spoken language, virtually all of the members of relatively modernized societies must become literate during childhood. Even the enormous proliferation of technological devices which play to aural capacities or simple visual rather than literate ones does not make it possible to oper- ate in terms of a relatively modernized society with high levels of illiteracy.

Closely related to the lower need to generalize most of the skills of the members of the society concerned is the question of "economies of scale" and the like. In relatively modernized contexts it is possible to do highly specialized and limited things on a very large scale. There is not space or need to discuss the technical aspects of economies of scale that are so highly devel- oped in the works of professional economists. The implications for the interrelationships among the members of different units

[4] It is not necessary to do exhaustive reading in sociology to be aware of this. The layman may not be accustomed to being asked to marshall his knowledge of this but he certainly has it. Every layman is thoroughly aware of the fact that the ordinary housewife must know the difference be- tween right and left and up and down and how to recognize a policeman. It is absolutely unnecessary that a housewife under ordinary circum- stances be able at a glance to distinguish between a major and a lieuten- ant colonel of the United States Army. Most housewives cannot do this and couldn't care less. It is, however, absolutely necessary that virtually every member of the Armed Forces be able to do this at a glance because too many things depend on the conception of the line of command in his life, including, perhaps, his life itself. There is of course a special category of housewives who need this information at their ready disposal. They are army wives.

in the society, and among the units in terms of which the members of the society have different parts are the important ones for this work. As the level of specialization of these units increases, as the emphasis on intermediate skills and economies of scale mount higher, the individual member of the society plays parts in terms of an increasing number of different units. These parts are referred to technically as roles. The term *role* is defined as any socially differentiated position in terms of which an individual may and/or does act. The increased differentiation of the individual's roles in terms of different organizations increases the problem of coordination in two forms. First, there is the coordination of the various roles of the individual by the individual. Second, there is the more general problem of coordination. How are all the various roles of the various individuals coordinated? It is also important to look at the problem of coordination the other way around. This problem in any social context is simultaneously a problem of the separation of various roles. The question of separation arises a great deal more often and is a great deal more important in relatively modernized contexts, if only because so many more roles are distinguished and ideally speaking are kept separate by the members of such societies. The separation of roles is, however, a problem common to all societies.[5]

In terms of a relatively modernized society, how does a person keep his role as a citizen separate from his role as a member of a university? These are roles supposedly kept separate in many respects. As a citizen I am legitimately interested in who wins an election for the presidency. As a member of a university faculty I might use means at my disposal for imposing my beliefs on, say, the graduate students of my department. It is quite illegitimate, ideally speaking, to take advantage of these facilities.

I emphasize this "separation implication" of the general term coordination because its general connotations stress bringing things together. Coordination of roles is just as much a question of keeping certain roles insulated from one another. This insulation is never perfect, but it is always increasingly important in relatively modernized societies. There is an especially important illustration of this point in the context of family problems and the general process of modernization. One of the reasons why the process of modernization is so highly disruptive of the general structure of relatively nonmodernized societies is that the vast

---

[5] Here again is one of those similarities among societies that makes it possible for men from diverse social settings to understand one another's problems.

majority of members of the relatively nonmodernized societies orient more of their behavior to family considerations than to all other considerations taken together, and that ceases to be the case as modernization is achieved.[6]

The increase in specialization of the organizations in a society impinge on the action that is ordinarily carried out in family terms in different ways. In terms of our own society and in terms of highly modernized or relatively modernized societies in general, the question of these interrelationships is ticklish and tough. We go to great extremes in our assumptions and views about these matters. Ideally speaking, we maintain that what goes on in terms of a man's family should not interfere with what he does in terms of his occupational roles. We assume that if a man has a responsible executive position, he does not permit his executive

[6] I shall return to this whole general question at great length. The present illustration, however, requires some amplification lest it be misinterpreted. I mean that the actions of the vast majority of members are overwhelmingly family oriented in that, day in and day out, they make their decisions in terms of the implications of their behavior for the persistence of their family organizations. This does not mean, however, that family structures always occupy the same position in general social structure in all of the relatively nonmodernized societies. This is not the case. For example, in premodern Japan the average individual in fact oriented most of his behavior to family considerations, but in many contexts, if there was a question of family interests versus that of his overlord, he put the interest of his overlord first. In traditional China to behave in such a fashion would have been considered bestial. In terms of no relatively modernized society is anything like so great a proportion of even the average person's action oriented directly to family considerations.

This distinction between relatively modernized and relatively nonmodernized societies says a great deal about the place that family structure has in the general social structure of these two different types of societies. It is not, however, equivalent to the implication that "the family is more important" in relatively nonmodernized societies than in relatively modernized societies. At least this is not the case unless one defines more important as meaning that more of the individual's activities are oriented to family considerations. If one defines more important in this way, then the statement is correct, but it adds nothing to what has already been said about the proportion of an individual's actions that, ideally and/or actually, is family oriented.

There is another sense in which it is definitely not correct to say that the family is more important in relatively nonmodernized societies than in relatively modernized ones. The kind of family structure characteristic of relatively modernized societies is remarkably uniform. The place of family structures in the general social structure in such societies is also remarkably uniform. It is crucial for relatively modernized societies that the family structures of those societies take the particular form that it does, just as it is for societies like that of traditional China and premodern Japan that the family took the specific forms it did. To say that the family is relatively less important in relatively modernized societies and imply that elimination or change of the family units would have fewer implications for a relatively modernized society than for a relatively nonmodernized society is clearly mistaken.

decisions to be influenced by family considerations. We also know perfectly well that in actuality his executive decisions are affected by family considerations. It is still neither irrelevant nor hypocritical to maintain that ideally speaking these two realms of behavior are separated from one another.

One of the reasons this coordination and, if one will, separation of roles has special implications for family organizations lies in the fact that every member of every society under ordinary circumstances always has family roles in addition to whatever other roles he may have in other organizations. An individual may have a role in the government of his society and not have a role in any of its universities. He may have a role in a given business firm and not in the entertainment industry. Regardless of what other organizations he belongs to, however, ordinarily he has a role in some family organization of his society at all stages of his life. This is true of all societies, whether they are relatively modernized or not. Therefore, as problems of coordination of these interrelationships of a nonfamily sort increase, they always impinge on family structures to some degree. They also impinge in a more direct sense. A considerable amount of this increase in specialization of units is the result of conducting in other organizational contexts activities that formerly were conducted in terms of the family itself. It is not a matter of chance that (1) the impact of modernization is always felt in the realm of kinship and the family, that (2) it is commonly felt at the beginning of the process, and that (3) these changes are uniform in direction.

2. SELF-SUFFICIENCY OF THE UNITS

Another characteristic of the organizations of relatively modernized societies has to do with their degree of self-sufficiency. No specialized units in any society approach self-sufficiency. In relatively nonmodernized societies there are many units that approach self-sufficiency quite closely. These are not only family units; they may be village units or provincial units too. They are usually family units, but the important thing is that such units exist at all, regardless of what their other characteristics may be. A unit is defined as approaching self-sufficiency insofar as the activities of its members in terms of it are capable of perpetuation of the unit, more or less indefinitely into the future, with little contact with persons outside the membership of the unit. Here, is another of those touchy differences of degree, but again I shall deal only with sufficiently gross differences of degree so that the exact location of the dividing line will not raise serious problems for the analysis.

In traditional Chinese society the family unit was characterized by high levels of self-sufficiency. Due to strict rules of family exogamy, the recruitment of wives was one respect in which family units were not self-sufficient. Family members, however, generally produced most of what they consumed and would have liked to consume most of what they produced. For most Chinese the interaction of family members with others did not extend often beyond the geographical boundaries that in part defined their particular village organization. If they did, they rarely extended beyond the limits of a small number of neighboring villages. Traditional Chinese society was complicated and varied, but as societies in general social history go, the level of self-sufficiency of family and village organizations was quite high. The level of self-sufficiency characteristic of the average traditional Chinese peasant family unit is never approximated in highly modernized contexts.

To illustrate the problem of self-sufficiency and relate the illustration once again to the family question I should like to start with the problem of recruitment. Every highly specialized organization depends on other organizations for the recruitment of its members. Although the members of such units may be and commonly are trained in the context of the units, there are also many critical respects in which the members are never trained in terms of such units themselves. In the last analysis, the members of all units in all known societies are ordinarily generated in terms of family units. In all social contexts there is always a question of how personnel gets from family contexts into nonfamily contexts. The formation of these nonfamily relationships is never a matter of indifference to the members of any society, but it is particularly important for the members of relatively nonmodernized societies.

Apart from nations considered as wholes, the units which ordinarily are the foci of attention in problems of international affairs [e.g., governments, armies, international organizations, etc.] are ordinarily units whose members do not generate their own new members by sexual reproduction of existing members as do the members of a family unit. They are also units which are not ordinarily joined by new members until those new members have reached adulthood. Usually most of the general training and education which the new members need in their roles in any specialized units has been gained by these new members in contexts other than the specialized unit.[7]

[7] The general relevance of some educationally oriented system to all of these highly specialized organizations poses one of the most spectacular

Regardless of the sort of specialization of the unit concerned, there are always problems of allocations of goods and services. How does one get the means for the activities to the persons who must utilize them; how does one motivate the actors to participate in the units concerned; etc.? If the unit concerned happens to be a government, despite the fact that it is presumably predominantly politically oriented, there is still the important question of paying the personnel so they do not have to do other things in order to make a living. Whether the society is capitalistic or socialistic, this basic problem is not altered. The activities that the personnel must engage in if the governing is effective will not leave this personnel with either the means or the energy to create their own food, shelter, clothing, etc., in terms of relatively self-sufficient family units. If they are to perform specialized governmental tasks, there must be some systematic way of conveying these goods and services to them.

As the level of modernization increases, the self-sufficiency of the various units diminishes. The self-sufficiency of the family units is always directly diminished, since any increase in specialized units must in the last analysis recruit personnel from some family context, no matter by what means. The relative immunity of family members from contact with members of other units, therefore, always declines. Family members depend more and more on the members of other units for an increasing variety of things. It may be income; it may be power; it may be education. Whatever it is, these interdependencies constantly increase.

With an increase of specialized units, self-sufficiency declines

---

problems for modernizing societies. In all of the modernizing societies public educational systems on a large scale must be introduced early in the process. The late-comers to modernization cannot develop their systems by bits and dabs or on a privately financed basis. The ultimate consumers of the education produced cannot be precisely enough located, especially in advance, to finance educational systems on this basis. Observers of modern United States society, which is probably characterized by the largest systems of privately financed higher education, have seen some rather interesting developments in this connection in recent years. As the possibility of continuing this financing largely out of personal contributions from the individual fortunes of members of the society has declined, members of private corporations have come increasingly to realize that, while they cannot in any precise sense assess the value of the services of individual private colleges and universities in providing trained personnel or as centers of research, it is nevertheless to the "interest" of such corporations to make unrestricted gifts to private universities so that those benefits will not be discontinued. Various schemes are being tried. Nevertheless, in no relatively modernized social context, whether dominated by people with the ideology of socialism or of capitalism, can the general education be privately financed or treated as a commodity such as automobiles, houses, etc.

in two senses. First, there is an increase in specialized units which do not even approach self-sufficiency ideally speaking. Second, the approach to self-sufficiency of the remaining relatively nonspecialized units also declines, as illustrated in the case of the family above. In all relatively modernized societies some relatively nonspecialized units always remain. These are never confined to family units alone, though family units are probably the most important category of units of this sort in any and all societies. It is important to realize that the self-sufficiency of the relatively nonspecialized units of such societies declines despite the fact that these units are not necessarily becoming more specialized. The ordinary family unit in relatively modernized societies is no more overwhelmingly oriented to one of these aspects as opposed to another than was the traditional Chinese family. The degree of specialization and the degree of self-sufficiency are not the same things, nor are they inevitably linked to one another in any simple fashion. The following generalizations, however, will hold: (1) Taking the society as a whole, as the level of specialization increases the level of self-sufficiency declines. (2) The more specialized a given organization is, the less self-sufficient it is. (3) As the level of specialization increases in the society, even those units which are not increasingly specialized become less self-sufficient. (4) In the long run, once the process of modernization is started, the levels of modernization and specialization always increase. (5) A further increase in the specialization of a relatively specialized organization or in that of other organizations in the society does not necessarily complicate the problems of its members. Insofar as it does not, it is because the very level of specialization of the organization concerned may enable its members to minimize the implications of their other roles for their actions in terms of the organization in question. (6) On the other hand, the increase of specialization in general always increases the problem of adjustment of the members of the relatively nonspecialized units insofar as the level of self-sufficiency of these units continually declines without the level of specialization of such units necessarily increasing.

Before leaving the closely interrelated questions of specialization and self-sufficiency of the units concerned, I should like to mention three other examples: predominantly recreationally oriented units, predominantly religiously oriented units, and again the family. In most of the relatively nonmodernized societies the distinction between work and play is not so starkly drawn as it is in terms of relatively modernized societies. In some of the more advanced of the latter it has become fashionable to speak of that portion of one's life spent in work as though it were something different from living. In some respects living is what one does when one is not working. Nevertheless, there probably has never been a society whose members failed to make any distinction at all between serious activities and play or recreation. In relatively modernized societies the existence of units highly specialized with regard to recreational aspects is one of the interesting developments. In most societies the units in terms of which recreation is carried out are not so highly specialized. A good part of the recreation is carried out in terms of family units, neighborhood units, etc. Insofar as predominantly recreationally oriented units develop, the self-sufficiency of the family units even with regard to the relaxation of their members declines.

With regard to churches, some of the developments have been even more interesting. A *church* may be defined for present purposes as a predominantly religiously oriented organization. There was a time, however, in the history of European societies in which the church was more nearly a relatively nonspecialized unit. It had its specialized orientations to religion, but it was also conceived to be a general organization in community life. In some cases, for example, the church and the local government were the same. There has been a tendency with the development of modernization in European society for the churches to become more and more specialized with regard to religious orientations as such, and participation of church members as church members in other areas of social action tends increasingly to be minimized. A layman's way of putting this was that church membership became primarily a Sunday affair. Curiously enough with the development of high modernization there is a reverse tendency cropping up in the predominantly religiously oriented organizations in the United States. The Community-House activities associated with the church or with the synagogue become as important a part of the behavior of the members of a given church as the more strictly religiously oriented activities themselves. In some cases these other activities may become even more important. There are even cases of churches or other predominantly religiously oriented units whose members build their Community Houses before they build an actual church or synagogue building. In these cases religious services and the like are carried out in the Community House. Until the members of the congregation can collect enough funds to build a separate church building, the main hall of the Community House is as much a dance floor as it is a center for worship. If one wishes to be paradoxical, it may be regarded as a reversal in the trend toward specialization of a specialized organization. The incorporation of recreational aspects of activities in the church setting in this sense makes some inroads on the self-sufficiency of other relatively nonspecialized units, but it increases that of the churches concerned.

Finally, with regard to the family again, in virtually every relatively nonmodernized society the overwhelming amount of training of all sorts of an average individual, as an infant, as a young child, as an older child, as a young adult, as a mature adult, and finally in old age, is inculcated on the average member of the society by members of his own family or kinship unit. As modernization increases, elements of these training functions are almost immediately taken over by members of nonfamily units. This is especially true of the training for performances in adult roles. Training of the young by older members of their family or kinship units for adult roles is probably one of the major methods of reinforcing the structure of control of family heads over family members in general, of parents over children, of the older over the young, etc. As soon as a substantial proportion of the members of the society perform specialized adult roles requiring special training outside the family context, this source of reinforcement of family control is radically undermined. One of the major elements of self-sufficiency which is therefore diminished is the degree of self-sufficiency in the control of members of the family unit. One of the major problems in the process of modernization in all social settings is the general problem of control. In virtually every one of the relatively nonmodernized societies the family unit is a major focus of social control. Undermining the stability of the family units is most likely to increase the general problem of social control. It is characteristic of all societies with governments that action in terms of the government can and does make some inroads on control in terms of family units. Ordinarily in relatively nonmodernized contexts, one of the most important forms of decentralization lies in the fact that these inroads are made as little as possible. In the process of modernization, leaders operating in terms of the government do not have the same degrees of freedom as far as noninterference with the structures of family control is concerned. In all cases of modernization operation in terms of the government not only interferes increasingly with the structures of family control, but alternatives to family control methods must be found if chaos is to be avoided. When such an alternative is not skillfully and thoroughly developed in terms of the government organization, disintegration of family control is not avoided, but general social chaos and hardship increase.

3. AN INCREASINGLY UNIVERSALISTIC ETHIC

In Part II, Chapter 1 below I shall deal quite extensively with the concepts of universalism and particularism. For present purposes [see section E of this chapter] I shall not define these terms beyond the following. A relationship or ethic will be considered relatively universalistic to the extent that it stresses "what a person does or can do that is relevant to the action or purpose under consideration." A relationship or ethic will be considered more or less particularistic to the extent that it emphasizes "who a person is" rather than what he can do or does that is relevant. These two concepts are not binary concepts. They refer to a scale of indefinite differences of degree. An ethic or relationship may be more or less nearly universalistic or more or less particularistic.

To return to the example of bullying used before, the condemnation of the use of superior force over a weaker opponent to coerce him into a particular line of activity, regardless of who does it or under what circumstances it is done, is an example of a highly universalistic ethic. If such behavior is regarded as bullying and condemned if it involves two individuals of the same class position but not if the coercer is a nobleman and the coerced is a peasant, then to that extent the ethic concerned is a highly particularistic one. Ideally speaking, the members of the societies considered to be modern democracies pride themselves on their emphasis on highly universalistic ethics. Members of these societies frequently invoke such mottoes as "All men are equal before the law." Voting criteria are supposed to be predominantly universalistically determined. Discrimination against people in voting on the basis of race, creed, or color is regarded as an intrusion of particularistic elements, though such terms are rarely used. At one time it was a practical impossibility to elect a member of the Catholic faith to the Presidency of the United States. It is a practical impossibility today to elect a true believer in Judaism or Islam to that position. The fact that a true believer of the Catholic faith *has* been elected to that position implies an increase in the level of universalism in certain respects.[8]

There are societies whose members, ideally speaking, place

---

[8] This is, of course, not without certain tinges of arguments about particularism, however, since many allege that a large number of people voted for the candidate in question *because* he was a member of that faith rather than on the basis of his sheer merit for the position. Insofar as individuals voted either for him or against him on such a basis there was an intrusion of particularistic elements.

little or no emphasis on either a predominantly universalistic ethic or predominantly universalistically defined relationships. There is no society for whose members questions of universalism are actually irrelevant. To some extent germane abilities always get to be a criterion in some fashion or other. In ethical matters the emphasis in relatively nonmodernized is heavily on predominantly particularistic ethics. This is not always the case, of course. Roman law contained many highly universalistic elements. The Ten Commandments are on the whole a highly universalistic ethic as is the ethical injunction, "Do unto others as you would have others do unto you." In relatively modernized contexts the emphasis on predominantly universalistic ethics is always heavy and increasing. Neither ideally nor actually does the emphasis on a universalistic ethic ever eliminate all particularistic emphases. For example, specific ethics of kinship remain, and kinship is always predominantly particularistic.

Increases in emphases on highly universalistic ethics abound whenever societies become increasingly modernized, regardless of whether their governments are authoritarian or nonauthoritarian. Many of the highly universalistic ethics to which we are most accustomed happen to be closely associated with nonauthoritarianism and concepts of democracy, but it is possible to set up highly universalistic criteria that are quite undemocratic.

Why is this emphasis important in a relatively modernized society? Quite apart from judgments of good or bad about these criteria, increasing problems of scale and coordination alone require an increasing emphasis on predominantly universalistic criteria if the society is to be stable. In handling questions on a predominantly particularistic basis it is always important to know in some detail exactly *who* a person is. Only in relatively small-scale sedentary environments can one count on being able to identify accurately in personal terms most, if not all, of the individuals with whom one must interact in the course of a day. As specialization increases and as self-sufficiency declines, the increased interdependence and interaction of members of different subsystems make it increasingly impossible to keep in mind who each individual is in all the contexts in which he must interact with others. In the heyday of small neighborhood stores, a merchant could know each and every one of his customers as an individual and to some extent treat each and every one of them differently. No modern department store in either a capitalistic or socialistic society could possibly exist on such a basis. The development of mass production and of mass consumption —the increase of interaction in general—make the cognitive problem posed by a highly particularistic ethic impossible, even if that problem is considered alone.

Although the emphasis on universalistic criteria can never be complete, it increases in the transition to and the maintenance of relatively modernized societies. It will be argued later that the scale and complexity of interaction in terms of relatively modernized societies must continue to increase if the societies are to be stable. Although the stability of such societies is problematical, interaction of the members has continued to increase in scale and complexity with consequent problems for particularism.

The problem of the preparation of youth for adult roles, the socialization of the new members of these societies, adds further impetus. Their preparation has to be carried out on highly generalized objective impersonal bases at least in part because of the lack of certain knowledge in advance as to what roles these individuals will have in the society and what their future lives will be like. In relatively nonmodernized contexts the future of the individual is more predictable.

As relatively modernized societies become more modernized predominantly particularistic ethics, though never eliminated, are increasingly restricted. Actually predominantly particularistic ethics remain much stronger than they do ideally. Supporters of particularistic identifications in terms of class, regions, race, creed, color, etc., are put in increasingly defensive positions. The largest basis of particularism which remains in such societies is nationalism. National pride, national identification, the ethic of patriotism, however admirable and however broadly defined, all involve a particularistic identification. At its most nearly universalistic, the ethic of patriotism remains particularistic even in the formulation, "My country, may she always be right, but right or wrong, my country." Nationalism is so broad a form of particularism that under many circumstances it does not complicate the problems of action in terms of a relatively modernized context. Most choices of personnel have to be made without crossing national boundaries. This is much less true today that it was fifty years ago. With continuing technological improvements, it will be much less true ten years from now than it is today.

As modernization has increased in the world, not only has the self-sufficiency of the various subsystems of the societies concerned declined, but the self-sufficiency of any given society or nation has also declined. That decline poses radical problems for the doctrine of national sovereignty. We inherit that doctrine from a period in which self-sufficiency was higher than it now can be. Nationalistic ethics are becoming an increasing problem, regardless of our likes or dislikes. Some decrease in particularism on a nationalistic basis is evident in the development of organizations such as the United Nations and the European Common Market. Welcome or not, the doctrines of national sovereignty are breaking down, whether on a relatively authoritarian basis [e.g., foreign conquest, occupation, and control] or on a voluntary basis.

Men in this world will not soon cease to think in nationalistic terms. That may never come, but a great deal of thinking in highly nationalistic terms is already suspect. Nationalism might conceivably be replaced in the future by continentalism, and continentalism in its turn, especially if we feel ourselves threatened by beings from another world, might be replaced by worldism. Nevertheless, one may generalize about relatively modernized societies as follows: (1) elements of particularistic ethics will always survive in them both ideally and actually, (2) the actual survivals will be greater than the ideal ones, and (3) the survivals tend to be either more narrowly confined [e.g., family oriented or nepotistic ethics] or diluted by being defined in terms of broader and broader identifications [e.g., the progression from localism to nationalism to continentalism, etc.].

4. COMBINATION OF CENTRALIZATION AND DECENTRALIZATION

All societies are combinations of centralized and decentralized structures of action. The most extreme form of centralization would be one in which a single individual made all decisions as to what each and every other member of the society would do at any and all times in any and all contexts. He would presumably be able both to make these decisions and to see that they were carried out. Complete decentralization would require every individual to decide what to do and when to do it without reference to anyone else. There would be no accepted methods whereby one individual could coerce or influence another. Neither such extreme could exist. No society could survive if decentralized to the extent of permitting infants to make all their own decisions. Such infants would not survive. On the other hand, the problem of cognition alone would make a completely centralized society impossible. A single mistake by the ruler would probably shatter everything. The system would have to be completely rationally planned and therefore incredibly brittle.

The degree of centralization always increases with modernization, if it has not already been high previously, and continues to increase with further modernization. Although the question of authoritarian versus nonauthoritarian practices is highly relevant, the increased level of centralization may be considered quite apart from the question of authoritarian versus nonauthoritarian structures. One of the special features of relatively modernized societies is that, for the first time in world history, it is possible to combine overwhelming centralization with the possibility of stability. None of the highly centralized systems in world history prior to the development of relatively modernized societies have been very stable, and most of the stable despotisms have not been nearly as centralized as they are sometimes described. Technological advances in communications and logistics make possible stable moves in the direction of ever increasing centralization that is not possible without them.

There is a range of variation of combinations of centralization and decentralization among relatively modernized societies despite the fact that it is possible to hold that all of them are characterized by increasing centralization. Most of us are concerned as to whether this increasing centralization is combined with increasing authoritarianism. The extremes of centralization and authoritarianism are inseparable. Apart from the extremes which cannot exist, as the level of centralization increases, the level of authoritarianism probably increases, and that probability, in turn, increases with the degree of centralization already achieved. There is an element of acceleration involved in this process.

Emphasis on authoritarian elements can, however, be carried far beyond the level required by the degree of centralization essential for a given state of modernization. United States society at present is far more highly modernized than is the society of the Soviet Union. It is also considerably less authoritarian as a society. Whether the United States society is more highly centralized than that of the Soviet Union or less so is an interesting question. Except for the element of governmental authority, United States society is considerably more centralized than the Soviet Union. At this point the comparison between the two societies may be argued along several different lines, but the net result of the argument will be to show that the degrees of centralization and authoritarianism can vary independently of one another *within restricted ranges* and, perhaps, even independently of the level of modernization actually achieved.[9]

[9] The possibilities here may be outlined as follows without actually making a choice among them. If the level of modernization of United States society is higher than that of the Soviet Union but the level of authoritarianism is lower, then to some extent the level of authoritarianism can

In the long run the level of modernization, the level of centralization, and the level of authoritarianism vary directly with one another if modernization is increasing. Over a broad range of such possible increases, however, it is certainly possible (1) for the rate of centralization to increase more rapidly than that of authoritarianism, (2) for the rate of authoritarianism in restricted areas to increase more rapidly than that of centralization in general, (3) for the rate of modernization to increase faster than centralization or authoritarianism, (4) for the rate of authoritarianism to increase faster than the rate of modernization or centralization, etc. Not all of these possibilities have the same implications for stability. If a society is to be stable once a relatively modernized stage has been achieved, unless the society was already highly authoritarian, modernization, centralization, and authoritarianism will probably increase. Furthermore, modernization by late-comers cannot be achieved without increasingly high levels of centralization and authoritarianism unless those were already at high levels when the transition began.

The problems of coordination and control steadily increase with the increasing specialization and interdependency characteristic of relatively modernized systems. Nonauthoritarianism comes to consist increasingly of protection of the rights of minorities or of dissenters in general to express themselves. The degree of freedom for the expression of either individualism by ideal or individualism by default [10] becomes increasingly small. Certainly there are variations among relatively modernized societies in the extent of such nonauthoritarianism [e.g., the relative freedom of expression of dissent in Great Britain or Japan today by contrast with Czechoslovakia or China].

The history of modernization exhibits another range of varia-

---

vary independently of the level of modernization. If the level of centralization of United States society is higher than that of the Soviet Union and the level of authoritarianism is lower, then to some extent the level of authoritarianism and the level of centralization at least do not always vary directly. If the level of centralization of United States society is lower than that of the Soviet Union but the level of modernization is higher, then, despite the fact that modernization and centralization may in general vary in the same direction, they do not necessarily vary directly over all ranges. From most points of view relevant here the level of modernization of the United States is higher than that of the Soviet Union; the level of centralization of the United States is higher than that of the Soviet Union; and the level of authoritarianism is lower than that of the Soviet Union. United States communications are more highly centralized than those of the Soviet Union if only because of the higher development and application of the technology of communications. Governmental control on the other hand is less centralized.

[10] For definitions of these concepts, see below, p. 228.

tion among relatively modernized societies. This is the political scientist's distinction between national and federal systems. It is significant only in the relatively early stages of modernization. The high element of actual decentralization connoted by the concept of federal systems decreases as the level of modernization increases, even though the ideal structures continue to receive allegiance. Increasingly members of the central government interfere with states rights, and only puristic "states righters" are prepared to make the sacrifices in other benefits that would have to be made to have it otherwise.

Stress on the possible variations of combinations of centralization and decentralization should not imply a general independence of centralization and modernization. As modernization increases, the trend is overwhelmingly and irreversibly towards more centralized structures in every case. The degree of centralization may be relaxed for a time, especially if the prior degree of centralization was higher than required by the level of modernization already achieved. One of the fundamental hypotheses of this work, however, is that in the long run modernization and centralization cannot vary inversely. Unless the process of modernization is stopped by a holocaust, the degree of centralization all over the world will continue to increase. A holocaust is quite feasible.

The minimal reasons for maintaining this hypothesis have to do with problems of coordination and control. There is a radical increase in the degree of interdependency at advanced levels of modernization. What the members do in terms of one unit of a society has increasing implications for what they and other members do in terms of other units. The implications of any slips continually increase. Thorstein Veblen in quixotically memorable phrases described this long ago. He referred sardonically to the increasingly delicate "interstitial adjustments" of the "closely concatenated processes" of societies. With increasing modernization the implications of what goes on in terms of one part of a society are increasingly manifested in terms of others. The implications of any breakdown in communications, whatever the source of the difficulty, increase radically. The increasing importance of "the traffic problem" in every increasingly modernized context is no more an accident than the ubiquity of modern forms of juvenile delinquency, regardless of the assertedly important ideological differences among societies.

The increase of centralization that accompanies increases of modernization need not be concentrated solely in terms of the government. The increasing centralization must always be concentrated in the government to some extent, however, and it must be concentrated in terms of the government to an increasing extent as both centralization in general and modernization increase. A given society may be so organized that all of its increases in centralization are increases in the centralization of its governmental system. Socialistic, communistic, fascistic, and similar societies—in the usual ideological definitions of those terms—are probably good examples of societies of this sort. This need not hold for all societies, however. In the United States context a considerable part of the increases of centralization are to be found in the increased centralization of a wide variety of nongovernmental organizations. Business firms, labor unions, universities, etc., all afford examples of increasing centralization. Relatively small organizations newly and strategically placed may radically increase the centralization of the system.

Many trends that appear to move toward decentralization from centralization turn out to increase centralization. Measurement may be difficult, but consider the movement of people into suburbs and even exurbs. Had they continued to live in our large cities, the density of population of those cities would be higher than it is now, but the decentralization of the surrounding rural areas would also be greater. The increase in centralization of activities in the suburban and exurban areas has far outrun the decrease or slowed rate of increase of centralization characteristic of the urban areas.

Increases in centralization outside the governmental context may exceed those in governmental terms. The two cannot vary at random, however. Increases of centralization in terms of organizations other than the governmental system increases the relevance of action in terms of those organizations for the actions of others who belong to the same or different societies. The more centralizing the effects of operations in terms of a given organization become for other members of, or organizations in, the society, the more acute are the problems of its relationship to the government. When representatives of the state do not, ideally speaking, control everything, it is not a matter of chance that action in terms of large-scale organizations is generally considered both easier and more important to control than action in terms of small-scale organizations. The increasing implications of any slips require an increasing interest of governmental representatives in all other systems whose centralization or centralizing effects increase. This in turn increases the level of centralization of the government.

Whether or not one likes increasing centralization, there is no denying it. The cases that appear to contradict this are those in which the levels of centralization exceed the level of centralization requisite for a given stage of modernization. Then cutbacks in the excess are quite conceivable. More decentralization than that is not likely to be long tolerated by the members of the society. It can only be carried out at the expense of what one might call *demodernization,* which cannot be stably maintained in the present day world, or in any probable future world.

Comparison of the relatively modernized and relatively non-modernized periods of any generally selected set of societies will show an increase in the levels of centralization. So will any comparison of different degrees of modernization of any society after becoming relatively modernized. No general social inventions give any hint of changing the direction of this tendency. There is no reason to believe that this tendency is a function of belief in any particular political ideology. There are ideologies that would make a virtue out of as much centralization as possible as well as ones that claim it a major vice. Advocates of neither set are responsible, and none of them show any ability to alter these phenomena.

Some decentralization will persist [e.g., on a family basis]. No society has yet existed without families, and this is not simply the result of a lack of social inventiveness. Although the family itself may remain a focus of decentralization, the growing centralization of the setting in which its members operate may actually increase the centralization of the family regardless of whether the ideal structures for the family concerned are highly authoritarian, highly centralized ones, or highly permissive, highly decentralized, ones. As more and more of the actions of family members are centralized in terms of other organizations, activities on a family basis will decrease. This decrease will increase the actual centralization of family units, whatever the wishes of their members. For example, the problems of transportation for general and special schooling result in a centralization of activities around the "family chauffeur" that is considerably greater than that around more authoritarian family heads in rural environments of fifty years ago.

5. RELATIONSHIP ASPECTS

The relationship aspects are taken up in some considerable detail below [pp. 133–174]. For the present I wish to comment briefly on four pairs of these terms, one of which has already been discussed above: (1) rationality and traditionalism, (2) universalism and particularism [pp. 52–55] (3) functional specificity and functional diffuseness, and (4) avoidance and intimacy. The first pair refers to the kind of knowledge [cognition] or thinking relevant to a given relationship. The second refers to the criteria for belonging to a given relationship. The third refers to the explicitness with which a relationship is defined and delimited. The fourth refers to the kind of emotional or affective involvement of the individuals concerned. Relevant differences of degree may be distinguished with regard to all four pairs. Thus one may speak of a greater or lesser emphasis on rationality or traditionalism, on universalism or particularism, on functional specificity or functional diffuseness, or on avoidance or intimacy.

As the level of modernization of a given society increases, the emphasis on rationality increases. That is to say, there is an increase in the emphasis on explaining one's reasons for doing a given thing in scientifically defensible terms as opposed to explaining on the basis of "we've always done it that way." The explanation that "we've always done it that way" or "that's the right way to do it for traditional reasons" is never eliminated, though in general the contexts in which such explanations are invoked diminish. In many contexts in which they are not eliminated such explanations tend to be offered with increasing defensiveness. An emphasis on traditionalism is not, of course, the equivalent of irrationality, i.e., of ignorance or error. In most sedentary agrarian contexts the methods used for tilling the soil are frequently explained or justified on what would here be called traditional grounds. Given the means available to the individuals involved, the traditional techniques probably are in fact rational ones. The great difference between emphases on rationality and traditionalism has not to do with whether a given activity is in fact rational or not. It has to do with an attitude, with whether people feel it should be rational or not. If traditionalism is emphasized, even though the actual practices are in fact rational, the implications of this emphasis are important. Problems of efficiency are not immediately posed, but if the means change and what was formerly done is no longer rational, traditionalists are likely to continue the old methods although they are now irrational. When available means are likely to be changing, this distinction means more.

One further reservation: no amount of devotion to the ideal of rationality guarantees rationality. As moderns we like to think of ourselves as exceedingly rational, but how rational we are is open to question.

A relationship is considered relatively more universalistic insofar as it emphasizes what a person can do that is relevant to the relationship, rather than who he is. An emphasis on the latter is an emphasis on particularism. A relationship is considered more or less functionally specific to the extent that everything the relationship is to cover is explicitly defined and explicitly delimited. Any departures from this are in the direction of functional diffuseness. Thus the ideal structures of a contractual relationship in United States society epitomize a predominantly functionally specific relationship [i.e., all rights and responsibilities of all parties are explicit]. The husband-wife relationship in practically any society is an excellent example of a predominantly functionally diffuse relationship. Some of the elements of predominantly functionally diffuse relationships may be [and usually are] precisely defined and even precisely delimited. Nevertheless insofar as unforeseen obligations may legitimately become relevant, the relationship contains important elements of functional diffuseness. Thus many obligations characteristic of the husband-wife relationship even in our society are relatively clearly defined and delimited, but there are also many obligations commonly covered by this relationship which are not.

Relationships characterized by avoidance rather than intimacy, are those whose members stress either emotional neutrality or emotional displays that minimize contacts and involvements, such as respect, by contrast with emotional displays that, whether positive or negative, get one deeply involved with others on a highly personal basis. Predominantly intimate relations may take the form of love, hate, etc.

Characteristically the structures of all [11] relatively modernized societies reflect an increasing emphasis on rationality, universalism, functional specificity, and emotional neutrality or avoidance. It is also characteristic of them that these emphases are much higher and more general throughout social structure than is the case for *any* relatively nonmodernized society.[12] Emphases

[11] Although this is characteristic of the structures of all relatively modernized societies, it is by no means characteristic of all of the structures of all relatively modernized societies. It is essential to stress differences of degree in the discussion of these paired concepts. As indicated below in this chapter and elsewhere in this work [e.g., pp. 64–65, 137–138, 141, 677–683] to speak of relatively modernized societies unqualifiedly as universalistic and of relatively nonmodernized ones as particularistic sinks a mite of insight in a sea of misunderstanding.

[12] The level of emphasis on emotional neutrality or avoidance may be high in relatively nonmodernized contexts. To the extent that this is the case, movement in the direction of greater modernization may for a time at least actually decrease the emphasis on avoidance. There are many respects in which modernization is likely to increase informality and hence to some extent the emphasis on intimacy. In the long run, however, there is always a sense in which the emphasis on emotional neutrality or avoidance increases as a society becomes a relatively modernized one—no

on traditionalism, particularism, functional diffuseness, and intimacy, however, are never entirely eliminated. For some organizations they may not be eliminated at all. Nevertheless, the direction of emphasis is *always* changed for the society as a whole unless the emphasis was previously in the direction of rationality, universalism, functional specificity, and avoidance. In relatively nonmodernized contexts overwhelming emphasis on rationality, universalism, and functional specificity are confined to restricted spheres. Indeed, ideally speaking, explicit emphases on rationality, universalism, and functional specificity are relatively rare and mild when present.

There are many reasons for this change in emphasis. One of the simplest ways to throw light on this is to develop some of the implications of the increasing use of increasingly efficient tools and of inanimate sources of power involved in the definition of modernization used here.[13] When one reaches relatively highly developed stages of the use of inanimate sources of power and complicated and efficient tools, rational calculation becomes much more strategic for many lines of action.[14] It becomes important in both the use and repair of the power and tools involved. Without an increased emphasis on rationality and on scientific thinking in general, it is unlikely that the increases in use of inanimate sources of power or of increasingly efficient tools can ever take place at all. The continual increases in variation and efficiency make even a relatively stable coincidence between

matter how high the emphasis before the transition. As the process continues, the number of individuals with whom the vast majority of individuals interact increases enormously, and an increasing number of these interactions are of such short duration as to preclude any considerable intimacy. In this sense in the context of relatively modernized societies, the vast majority of individuals participate in far more numerous and varied predominantly emotionally neutral or predominantly avoidant relationships than in any relatively nonmodernized social context.

[13] These are by no means the only arguments which could be used. They are not presented as causal arguments. Causal arguments involving them can be formulated, but all such arguments will also involve other strategic variables. Nevertheless, after a given stage of development of tools and inanimate sources of power is reached, they have interesting implications.

[14] One sees constant evidence of such conflicts in even the most highly modernized social contexts. The whole issue of featherbedding in labor relations contains important elements of this. What may have been quite rational from at least the point of view of specific interested parties may become quite irrational under changed conditions of technology. The same may be said of many practices staunchly defended on overwhelmingly traditional grounds by businessmen, civil servants, politicians, academics, doctors, lawyers, etc. Most of the individuals most deeply concerned in these matters are extremely sensitive about any implications that their behavior in these contexts is nonrational—let alone irrational.

traditional ways of doing things and rational methods unlikely.

Once these tools and sources of power are developed, the different implications of selecting people on the basis of what they can do as opposed to who they are become stark. As long as tools remain simple and easily mastered and combinations of tools and inanimate sources of power multiply effort only slightly, small differences in skill among the people who use them are insignificant. Some of the differences in skill of individuals available to dig with spades may be considerable, but at the end of a long day's work, they will not make much absolute difference in the amount of earth moved. Relatively small differences in skill, however, of operators of modern power shovels may make enormous differences in the absolute amount of work done at the end of a day. Not only that, small differences in skill may make a great deal of difference in terms of the repair costs, of other damage done, etc. Selection of personnel on the basis of who they are rather than what they can do means that one cannot take advantage of such differences either to maximize accomplishment or minimize damage.

If relationships are vaguely defined and delimited, it is difficult to emphasize and expect rational behavior. If one does not know what is likely to be involved in a relationship, it is exceedingly difficult to select people on the basis of what they can do that is relevant rather than on the basis of who they are. Furthermore, when levels of mass production and mass coordination are reached, if one cannot treat people on the basis of quite limited involvements, such large-scale relationships become impossible. If one has to deal with all consumers personally, regardless of whether one is a socialist or a capitalist, there cannot be mass production of food, clothing, automobiles, or anything else. Neither businessmen nor government officials can distribute the output of a highly modernized production of goods and services on the basis of functionally diffuse relationships with particularistically selected consumers.

Finally, with regard to avoidance or emotional neutrality, insofar as one becomes directly involved emotionally—especially if one becomes intimately involved—it is difficult to keep such relationships highly functionally specific. It is difficult to think of people with whom one is emotionally involved on the basis of what they can do that is relevant rather than on the basis of who they are; it is also difficult to deal with them rationally. Not only is love blind, but most of the intimate emotions certainly increase the problems of objectivity, and limited involvement.

No increase in modernization ever eliminates traditionalism, particularism, functional diffuseness, or intimate emotional involvement, and no relatively nonmodernized society is devoid of structures of rationality, universalism, functional specificity, and emotional neutrality or avoidance. Nevertheless, for most of the time most of the relationships of most of the members of relatively nonmodernized societies are carried out primarily on the basis of traditionalism, particularism, and functional diffuseness.[15] In terms of relatively modernized societies those emphases, ideally speaking at least, are increasingly restricted to the context of relatively nonspecialized organizations such as family units, friendships, etc. Even for relatively specialized organizations the trend toward emphasis on rationality, universalism, functional specificity, and avoidance is never complete. All save the most naïve are well aware of the discrepancies between ideal and actual structures. Given previous history, however, the surprising thing is not how far actual practice departs from ideal structures in these respects, but how little.

Perhaps one of the best illustrations of the meaning of this sort of shift of emphasis is the change in the attitude toward nepotism.[16] One of the hardest things for the members of relatively modernized societies to understand is the attitude of members of the relatively nonmodernized societies toward nepotism. There is no relatively modernized society for whose members an emphasis on nepotism is not a source of embarrassment in many social contexts.[17] Few members of few nonmodernized societies consider neoptism anything to be embarrassed about. They are more likely to consider a lack of nepotism as occasion for embarrassment. A great deal of nepotism continues to be characteristic of United States society, but those who practice it are likely to be on the defensive.[18]

[15] These relationships may be characterized by high levels of either avoidance or intimacy. A great deal of intimacy in the relations among some adults and children and infants and among children is, however, unavoidable.

[16] Nepotism, in this sense is particularism on a kinship or simulated kinship basis.

[17] Many parents are even embarrassed if their estimates of their children's intelligence can be shown to be highly biased by such considerations.

[18] They find it necessary to justify the special position in a business firm for the son of the owner on some such basis as: "The business is a family business." The continuation of family members in positions of responsibility is something our customers and suppliers expect and rely upon. In other words, they tend to give as nearly universalistic a justification as possible of the nepotism itself, despite the fact that nepotism is inherently particularistic. They insist that it is at least germane particularism, which it may very well be. For the concept of germane particularism, see below, pp. 142–143.

We Americans expect defensive reactions toward charges of nepotism. We think that, if we point out that members of a relatively nonmodernized society, are engaging in nepotistic practices, they will be moved to do something to correct the situation. Again and again in the past history of our relations with the Chinese we have been surprised and even hurt to find that accusations of nepotism did not automatically result in reform. The Chinese found us equally hard to understand. From their point of view not to give preference to relatives was bestial, although in general they thought us kindly. Our differing evaluations of universalistic criteria had important effects on our relations.

6. GENERALIZED MEDIA OF EXCHANGE AND MARKETS

A *medium of exchange* is defined here as any good or service that can be exchanged for two or more other goods and/or services. The more different items that a given article or service can be exchanged for, the more highly generalized it is as a medium of exchange. A *market* is defined as any organization in terms of which action is primarily oriented to facilitating the exchange of goods and/or services among its members with some choice left to them [i.e., with some degree(s) of freedom]. As defined, both are susceptible to exceedingly wide ranges of variations. A given society or nation may be characterized by many different media of exchange. Characteristically this is the case. The different media of exchange may vary widely with regard to their levels of generalization. For example, although they in fact use multiple media of exchange, the members of many societies and of *all* relatively modernized societies designate a single medium of exchange as the legal or official medium of exchange. The term *money* is generally used to describe this special medium of exchange. In all cases the structures of control, issuance, etc., of monies are to some extent governmental structures. Money is usually a highly generalized medium of exchange. It is ordinarily much more generalized than any other medium of exchange available.

The degree of generalization of a medium of exchange may vary within the following extremes: (1) The minimal level of generalization of a medium of exchange is the minimum for a given medium to be identified as a medium of exchange at all [i.e., two other goods and/or services]. (2) The opposite end of the scale is a completely generalized medium of exchange [i.e., a medium in terms of which any and all goods and/or services can be exchanged].[19] There are many variations between these extremes. The members of most feudal societies cannot ordinarily use money to buy and sell land with any great degree of freedom. Even in highly modernized contexts some land is not subject to purchase and sale, such as entailed estates in the case of Great Britain and many national monuments in the case of the United States. Although there has never been a society completely lacking some [or even several] media of exchange, there have certainly been many societies characterized by media of exchange of low levels of generalization and highly subject to *ad hoc* arrangements by the individuals using them.

The range of variation of markets is also great. It is entirely possible that there be a society with no market as such, that is to say there need be no organization set up primarily in order to facilitate exchanges of goods and/or services among the members. It is quite conceivable that the members of a society conduct all such exchanges in terms of organizations not primarily oriented to the facilitation of such exchanges. Markets, too, have varying levels of generalization. The greater the number and the variety of goods and/or services that may be exchanged in terms of it, the greater is the level of generalization of the market. The more restricted the variety and amounts are, the more specialized the market. Markets may vary in other important respects. They may, for example, be more or less highly centralized. They may be organizations with only private members, or they may be subsystems of a government. Their members may emphasize traditional bases for exchange, or they may emphasize rational bases for exchange. Their members may carry out their exchanges on predominantly universalistic or predominantly particularistic grounds, etc.

Both highly generalized media of exchange and highly developed markets can exist as elements of relatively nonmodernized societies. Both are absolutely essential, however if relatively modernized societies are to exist. For the former they are possibilities; for the latter they are requisites. All relatively modernized societies must be characterized by a highly generalized, official or legal monetary unit. This unit inevitably becomes a standard of measurement for questions considerably broader than the exchange of goods and/or services. Not the least of these other matters is

[19] For important reasons discussed below [see pp. 259–260] there can be no stable society characterized by a completely generalized medium of exchange. That is to say—views of cynics and humorists to the contrary, notwithstanding—no society can persist whose members can literally buy anything with money.

social prestige. This is not merely because of the preoccupation with material concerns of the members of such societies. It is also due to the extent to which material indicators are regarded as functions of other values rather than vice versa. Thus to a large extent, cynics not withstanding, the members in general of relatively modernized societies regard the receipt of high incomes to be a function of high merit rather than high merit to be a function of high income. It makes little difference whether one chooses to illustrate this principle from socialist or capitalist societies.[20] Members of all societies of any considerable scale have to some extent developed relatively highly generalized media of exchange and, in most cases, the use of money as well. Relatively modernized societies must be characterized by increasingly highly generalized media of exchange and monetary units of a well defined sort, if they are to persist. The problems of some sort of cost-accounting system alone, let alone problems of inventory and actual exchange, make the development of such media requisite.

All societies of any considerable scale also have markets. Here again relatively modernized societies must have highly generalized markets as well as markets that are highly specialized in terms of the goods and/or services exchanged. In both relatively modernized and relatively nonmodernized societies, there may be actual markets that do not exist ideally speaking,[21] but in the relatively modernized cases many markets must exist both ideally and actually. If one could conceive of a completely centralized, highly modernized society, the leader of which reacted in no way

[20] With relatively few general exceptions, throughout social history, high income and wealth have been generally considered—both ideally and actually—to be a function of merit. This has held true even when some roles of highest prestige were not necessarily correlated with the highest incomes or greatest wealth as in the case of the Brahmin caste in Indian history. Communists and Socialists readily grant their leaders greater incomes and command over wealth than the common man among them, and in general carefully grade material rewards for services to the people or state.

This question of money as a measure and an influence outside the narrowly confined consideration of goods and/or services is discussed below in various connections [e.g., pp. 257–262, 762–765]. The subject is one about which modern man in general and modern thinkers in particular are unbelieveably skittish. It is frequently tied to quite remarkable preoccupations with distinctions such as that between materialistic and spiritual [n.b., not usually called spiritualistic] outlooks. For the present one might ask the following question: Given a society whose members used a highly generalized monetary unit, what structures would such a society have to have were there to be no positive correlation [or no significant correlation of any sort] ideally speaking, between high merit and high income?

[21] E.g., white slave markets, black markets, etc.

to changes in taste of the other members of the society—if that leader had perfect and complete knowledge—it would be possible to conceive of a highly modernized society with no markets. All allocation would be decided upon by a single source and would be subject to no alterations. Short of such centralization and such perfect knowledge, markets will exist. These markets may vary radically with regard to the extent to which they are free markets. As modernization increases, however, the levels of generalization and specialization of markets increase and the freedom [i.e., absence of regulation in terms of another organization or other organizations—usually in terms of a government] of markets declines. In general, the higher the level of modernization, the higher is the degree of centralization of markets. Apart from this qualification, variations in political ideology do not affect this hypothesis.[22]

Generalized media of exchange and markets are presumably familiar to all readers of this work. Monetary units have varied from huge stone pieces, which certainly minimized problems of theft and maximized a sort of ease of display, to the paper monies which we take for granted. Markets vary from periodic or even *ad hoc* local organizations in terms of which one may exchange agrarian and domestic industry products to highly developed security markets, department stores, etc. As the level of generalization of the media of exchange and of markets increase, there is always an increase in the possibility of emphasizing rationality within the sphere of the allocation of goods and/or services. It is not a matter of chance that economics was the first among the social sciences in modern times to acquire many of the trappings of a genuine science.[23] From its early development to the present day, some assumptions about the rationality of behavior of individuals engaged in the allocations of goods and/or services have occupied a central position among the assumptions vital to the field. Modern developments in this field of social analysis occurred subsequent to the beginnings of a long-run secular trend toward increasing generalization of the media of exchange and of markets.[24] Within broad limits the increase of generalization of

[22] This hypothesis must be qualified by the implications of the possibility mentioned above [pp. 58 ff.] of the degree of centralization existing at the outset of the change exceeding the requisite degree for the given level of modernization achieved.

[23] I refer here, of course, to such things as the emphasis placed by economists on systems of highly general theory, models, data, explicit assumptions, measurements, etc.

[24] Prior to these developments one would hardly regard economics as more highly developed than political science given such names as Aristotle, Machiavelli, and Hobbes.

the media of exchange greatly simplifies calculations about one's interest in one kind of goods or service relative to another. Whatever the meanings of these prices [e.g., $14,000 for a house or $20 a day for wages] to different individuals for different purposes, they make certain common calculations possible for all individuals for any purpose.[25]

Interestingly enough the increase of both these elements to some extent minimizes the need for knowledge. With the increased generalization of the media of exchange, one need not know all of the characteristics of all the goods and/or services that one has to take into consideration for whatever purposes. For many purposes it suffices only to know the price of such goods and/or services, that is, the rate at which the items concerned will presumably be exchanged for a monetary unit. The existence of markets, given even minimal degrees of freedom, makes it possible for both producers and consumers to gain information from the interaction of one another rather than to rely on complete predictions with regard to everything. This again holds true regardless of whether the producers and consumers, as differentiated for these purposes, act in terms of structures of private ownership or not.

Finally, there is always a problem of the interrelationship between allocations of power and responsibility and allocations of goods and/or services. Thus the development of media of exchange and markets is always relevant to governments and vice versa. It is not a matter of chance that the most highly developed monies are virtually without exception carefully controlled by members or representatives of governments. This begins in early stages of the transition to relatively modernized societies, if not before. It certainly increases as the level of modernization increases. With increasing modernization both markets and media of exchange inevitably become more centralized, and their centralization proceeds increasingly in terms of a government, if the society is to be stable.

The close mutual relevance of monies, markets, and governments may be briefly illustrated by a special interrelationship,

[25] Further, had it not been for the leg up given by the analysis of economic allocation in terms of a model importantly based on assumptions of rational orientations—whatever its gross or fine faults—it would have been much more difficult for those interested in other aspects of social phenomena to make scientific headway. Vilfredo Pareto seems to have understood this more clearly than any other social thinker in history. See his volumes, *The Mind and Society,* Harcourt, Brace and Company, Inc., New York, 1935, especially vol. I.

that between merchants and government officials.[26] Whenever, ideally speaking, such relationships are illegitimate they will nevertheless continue to take place in fact, and there will be graft and corruption by virtue of the very attempt to eliminate such relationships. Classification of these relationships as illegitimate never eliminates them. Actual allocations of goods and/or services are always highly relevant for actual allocation of power and responsibility and vice versa. This has nothing to do with economic or materialistic determinism as such. Allocations of goods and/or services are not one whit more material than allocations of power and responsibility. Members of many societies have decreed such separations, but they have never been made to stick. Ironically, in this regard capitalistic societies have been a great deal more sophisticated than many others such as those of Imperial China and some modern socialist societies. Increasing centralization of all relatively modernized societies, quite apart from questions of ethics, makes recognition of the impossibility of such separations more important.

B. ORGANIZATIONAL CONTEXTS

1. BUREAUCRACY

In the heraldry of social forms the coat of arms of bureaucracy consists largely of a field strewn with epithets. There is no language in which the term *bureaucracy* exists unencrusted with derogatory connotations. In some cases it may have no connotations of any other sort. The term *bureaucracy* refers to an "organization's organization." Although there are many ways of organizing organizations, in modern times, bureaucracy has come to epitomize large-scale organizations. The term is usually defined descriptively following Max Weber. Parsons has summarized that description as follows: "Bureaucracy, as Weber uses the word, is a rather complicated phenomenon. It involves an organization devoted to what is from the point of view of the participants an impersonal end. It is based on a type of division of labor which involves specialization in terms of clearly differentiated functions, divided according to technical criteria, with a corresponding division of authority hierarchically organized, heading up to a central organ, and specialized technical qualifications on the part of the participants. The role of each participant is conceived as an office where he acts by virtue of the authority vested in the office and not of his personal influence. This involves a

[26] This matter is treated in more detail below [see pp. 333–336, 494–495, 543–548].

clear-cut distinction in many different respects between his acts and relationships in his official and his personal capacity. It in general involves separation of office and home, of business funds and property from personal property, above all of authority in official matters from personal influence outside the official sphere." [27]

Bureaucratic organizations are absolutely essential if relatively modernized societies are to exist. As the level of modernization increases, all epithets to the contrary notwithstanding, the level of bureaucratization increases. The two phenomena vary directly, though the function which interrelates them may be a complicated and largely unspecified one. Like centralization, to which it is closely related, the increase in bureaucratization has little to do with the varying ideological sentiments of members of relatively modernized societies. Both the Republicans and the Democrats of our society curse it, but the leaders of neither stem this tide. Nor will they; nor could they, save at a catastrophic cost. The Russians also use the term as an epithet, but they if anything have carried bureaucratization beyond the requirements of their level of modernization. Like centralization, bureaucratization is not confined to governmental organizations. Our business firms, our research laboratories, both profit and non-profit alike, our universities and our colleges, our grammar schools and most of the intervening schools, our churches and associated organizations—all of them [28] are bureaucratized; a substantial portion of our forms of recreation are bureaucratically organized. Apart from our families and our friendship units, most organizations to which we belong are either bureaucratically organized or are in the process of being organized bureaucratically. Since the productivity per bureaucrat cannot increase faster than the scope of activities bureaucratized under relatively modernized conditions, there can be no prospect of an absolute decrease in bureaucratization—and not a steady state either—nor, probably, of personnel involved either.

[27] See Talcott Parsons, *The Structure of Social Action*, McGraw-Hill Book Company, Inc., New York, 1937, p. 506. Descriptive definitions in addition to being unwieldly, make much of the ensuing discussion. "True by definition." If the focus is on the phenomenon defined itself, that is a drawback. That was not Weber's focus, nor is it the present one.

[28] Sometimes the bureaucratization of churches and associated organizations has peculiar obstacles to hurdle. From the point of view of devout members of certain sects, any form of religious authority as such over the individual other than his own conscience is beyond the pale. For a fascinating study of what can happen when this is the case see Paul Harrison, *Authority and Power in the Free Church Tradition*, Princeton University Press, Princeton, 1959.

For those who believe in democracy and the "sacredness and dignity of the human individual" the solution for the problem of bureaucracy is not to do away with all bureaucracies. That is a visionary, childish, or meretricious view. It is rather to organize bureaucracies such that impersonality, which is one of their special utilities in relatively modernized contexts, does not result in injustices or such that, if it does, those injustices can be corrected. Varying the proportions of private and public control over various organizations and many other proposed solutions to these problems have little or no relevance to the question. Private organizations in relatively modernized societies, apart from family and friendship units, are every bit as highly bureaucratized as governmental units which correspond to them in scale and specialization. The most efficient private organizations may well be more highly bureaucratized than comparable governmental subsystems. Except for the charge that individuals are being treated in a dehumanized fashion [i.e., impersonally], every accusation about the shortcomings of a bureaucracy—even from the point of view of the accuser—is not so much a charge that bureaucracy is bad but that the bureaucracy accused is a bad bureaucracy.

The minimal reasons for the increasing importance of bureaucratic organizations are closely related to the remarks made above about the importance of problems of coordination and control in the face of increasing specialization and lack of self-sufficiency. I can illustrate comparatively, how the bureaucrats of traditional China coped with large-scale administrative decisions and planning in terms of capital formation, of individuals to be handled, and of other organizations involved. The irrigation works of traditional China, constituted, and clearly still do, one of the engineering marvels of history. It took an extraordinary amount of technical talent to conceive and build them. Management of them required continuous operation, expansion, and improvement from time to time. In spite of these demands, traditional Chinese society with its bureaucratically organized government was highly stable for 2,000 years—a record probably never equalled unless ancient Egyptian society qualifies—despite outside conquests and all sorts of internal indigenous revolts which transferred power from one set of individuals to another. The Imperial Chinese Bureaucracy was certainly not irrelevant to that strange stability.

The bureaucrats of relatively modernized societies however, are faced by an additional order of problems which were not ordinarily acute for Chinese bureaucrats. The creation of large-scale irrigation works required high levels of ingenuity, but they were characterized by slow rates of obsolescence and decay. The irrigation layouts of some Chinese provinces are not obsolete even now. In relatively modernized situations the rates of both obsolescence and decay are extraordinarily high. The equivalent of canals gradually silting up cannot be permitted. Or rather, if it is permitted, the resulting chaos, discomfort, etc., reaches far and wide—fast. Thus the scale of organization characteristic of relatively modernized societies continues to increase; the importance of technical knowledge continues to increase; the emphasis on clear-cut responsibility, quickly determinable, continues to increase; clear-cut lines of action continue to increase in importance; etc.

Ever increasing automation and increased leisure time—both prominent features of the new social revolution taking place in terms of relatively highly modernized societies—will not change this trend. The increased leisure time and increased standard of living of American families has resulted in increasing bureaucratization of leisure facilities. At one time we walked or drove on bureaucratically produced highways until we got away from it all in nature. Now the preservation of nature herself is increasingly bureaucratized as must be the preparation of facilities for increasingly large numbers to enjoy her. Increasingly we drive off bureaucratically constructed highways into bureaucratically organized parking lots, camp sites, and the like.[29]

2. FAMILY SYSTEMS

The ideal type of family unit varies widely through history. As will be discussed below, [see pp. 426–430] actual family units have not varied nearly so widely as variations in ideal structures have lead most of us to believe. Nevertheless, both within and among societies the variations have been considerable. One of the special characteristics of relatively modernized societies is their quite unusual type of family unit. Whatever the previous ideal family structure was, during the transition toward relative modernization, the ideals always change toward what anthropologists and sociologists call a *multilineal conjugal family* unless they already took that form.

The term is justifiable jargon. Ideally speaking the members of such a family unit are a father, a mother, and nonadult children,

[29] It is one of the ironies of modern intellectual history that, although a sense of humor is generally lacking in the treatment of these matters, one of the most important generalizations in modern social science, *Parkinson's Law,* has on the whole been highly regarded only because it poked fun at everyone's favorite target—bureaucracy. We have, alas, had more fun with it than we have learned from it.

or in the absence of children, a husband and wife. The members reckon solidarity more or less equally in terms of both the paternal and maternal lines of descent. More accurately, they deemphasize both equally. Insofar as relationships continue among the members of the family unit and their grandparents, ideally speaking, one is not expected to prefer one's maternal grandparents to one's paternal ones or vice versa. Many people would regard such lack of distinction as barbarous. The one remaining clear-cut sign of greater accent on one line of descent is the continued use of the father or husband's surname as the family name.

When the children belonging to such a family mature and marry, they organize a new family unit. Ideally speaking they do not live with the parents of either the husband or the wife. The use of the term conjugal to describe the unit accents the primary importance, ideally speaking, of the relationship between husband and wife. The children upon maturation choose their own future mates, with little let from parents or others. This form of family system, though known outside the context of relatively modernized societies, is rare. Carried to the lengths with which we are familiar, and given its relation to other subsystems, it is unique in social history.

It is frequently noted that activities in terms of the family have been radically reduced in relatively modernized contexts. This does *not* mean that the family units are less important than formerly, unless family importance is defined by the restriction of such activities. It is not at all true, however, that under these conditions the activities still performed in terms of the family are not crucial for the existence of the society. It is not correct to infer that, once the reduction of activities has reached a certain point, family units become negligible or that one can continue to restrict the functions performed on a family basis indefinitely. It is also misleading to imply that this type of family is less critical for this type of society than other types of family are for other societies.[30]

The reduction of education in terms of the family is one of the most spectacular examples. In relatively modernized societies the family as an educational unit has had its wings cut back radically. Less and less training takes place in terms of such units. Virtually none of the technical education for adult roles takes place in family terms in relatively modernized societies. The decrease in family-based education reaches into younger and younger age categories with further increases of modernization.

[30] See above, footnote #6, p. 45.

Universal schooling is one of the obvious sources of this restriction. One of the signs of relatively high modernization is the increasing generalization of the prekindergarten or nursery school. The decrease of family educational functions is never complete. More of the crucial education of the vast majority of individuals takes place on a family basis than on the basis of any other organization for the members of this as of all other societies. The family remains the organization in terms of which, everyone ordinarily first learns to eat, to walk, to talk, to perform various other bodily functions, etc. With increasing modernization, more education takes place in nonfamily contexts, but so far there has been no society in terms of which education on a nonfamily basis has been generally extended to these fundamental initial bits of learning.

In most societies in world history the family units have ordinarily been important units in terms of which production and consumption are carried out. These units have been important not only in the relevance of the kinds of production and consumption carried out in terms of them but also in the sense of the proportion of that production and consumption to the total production and consumption carried out in terms of the society. In relatively modernized societies it is increasingly only the former sense in which the production and consumption carried out in family terms is of importance. Here there is some imbalance. Family units become a much greater focus of consumption from the point of view of the members of the units than of production. Little of the total gross national product [as currently measured] of the members of a relatively modernized society is in fact produced in terms of family units, although a large proportion of personal consumption is carried out in family terms. Even with regard to consumption, because of the large amounts consumed in other organizational contexts, the relative amount carried out in family terms goes down, although the absolute amount increases enormously if one contrasts the per family consumption characteristic of relatively modernized societies with that of relatively nonmodernized ones. Certain forms of production continue in family terms. Although these are critical, they are frequently ignored. A considerable amount of food preparation, laundry, child care, etc. continue in family terms, as do their consumption counterparts. But the conception general among the members of relatively nonmodernized societies of family units as the ordinary units in terms of which most production and consumption is carried out is gone forever.

Perhaps, it it not gone forever. With certain levels of productivity and forms of income distribution which characterize high modernization as opposed to relative modernization, there may actually be developing a new form of recreational family which may modify this state of affairs. It is a new possibility on the social horizon. As the work week shortens, the possibility of the third great social revolution developed and exported in American history grows.[31] This is the *leisure revolution*. It is one of the most peculiar social revolutions in all world history.

This third revolution might also be called the altruistic revolution as well as the leisure revolution. Its leaders will turn out to be the most altruistic revolutionary leaders in world history. This social revolution is carried out by people who have the highest per capita standard of living in world history in terms of real income with an extremely even distribution of that income. For the first time in world history the *problem* facing the members of a society has become, not how one keeps people well adjusted while they work, regardless of whether they distinguish work from leisure, but rather, how one keeps people well adjusted while they are not at work. Once the work week has become forty hours, even if one discounts eight hours a day for sleep and three hours a day for meals, here remain more hours for leisure than for work. Most of the members of most societies in world history either do not distinguish sharply between work and leisure activities, or if they do, consider the overwhelming proportion of their time as spent working. The United States work week is already reduced to forty hours, and there are strong pressures about for a further reduction of it—with no loss in real income to the persons concerned, of course.

The leaders of the other revolutions produced and exported by members of United States society have had a major personal stake in the products of the revolution. In this sense they were at least as much self-interested as altruistic. They regarded themselves as benefitting from the fruits of those revolutions. Jefferson and Franklin were avidly interested in what they regarded as political liberty. This was the fruit of their revolution. Henry Ford and others were interested in the fruits of the mass production revolution. The leaders of the leisure revolution are a different breed. They consist largely of professional and administrative elite. They are lawyers, doctors, scientists, executives, etc. They operate in terms of bureaucracies. They exercise great privileges. They undertake great responsibilities. They may or may not reap

---

[31] The first revolution developed and exported in American history was the "political" revolution of the eighteenth century. The second was the mass production revolution of the early twentieth century.

great material rewards. One thing is absolutely certain, however, they do not enjoy increased leisure. A leading figure among them who works less than sixty to eighty hours a week is rare. They will not enjoy the fruits of their revolution. In this sense they are the most altruistic revolutionary leaders in world history.

Given a leisure revolution, a recreational family may become more widespread. Individuals once again will participate on a family basis in all sorts of activities that have been dying out. Craft activities such as pottery making are a possibility as a leisure activity for the members of such a society. There is already a marked example of this sort of thing in the case of "do it yourself" work at home. I have heard many of my colleagues explain that they do it themselves because they cannot afford plumbers, carpenters, etc., but I do not believe them. With rare exception, given our skills, despite the high costs of plumbers, carpenters, etc., it would be cheaper to call a professional plumber than do it ourselves. Even if the individual is unusually skillful, at home he must be terribly "overcapitalized" in tools to work efficiently. Even granting that labor costs in "do it yourself" work are zero, the cost of inefficient uses of materials, overcapitalization in tools, personal injuries, etc., make the price of "do it yourself" work exorbitant. Such poor and expensive work would be one of the great luxuries of our day were it considered apart from its recreational value.[32]

Wives do well to be tolerant of husbands when they are at the height of this mood. House repairs may do more than professional baseball teams for close parent-child associations. We may actually get a return to all sorts of family activities previously thought abandoned. Craft production as a matter of recreation rather than as a matter of livelihood is a possibility. For the talented such production may even become an important source of family income, but this is likely to be self-defeating. If it becomes really lucrative, the family members will have to give it up on a family recreational basis and go into a family business.

There are many possibilities open for the future development of the family in relatively modernized societies. None of those

[32] Plumbing is an excellent example of all this. Even if the "do it yourselfer" is skillful at plumbing, he must be terribly overcapitalized with regard to tools. He uses his tools no more than once every two months, if he has bad plumbing. If he has good plumbing, he uses the tools once every six months, or maybe once every two years or so, whereas the professional plumber uses them day in and day out. They each need roughly the same tools, however, if they are to work efficiently. He makes many more mistakes than the ordinary plumber, hard as that may be to imagine. He usually injures himself in the course of his work. Modest to substantial medical costs are not a small factor in "do it yourself" work, etc.

lines of development point to an abandonment of the multilineal conjugal family unit as the ideal type of unit in society. Since this type of family, with the restricted activities in terms of it in relatively modernized societies, is quite rare in social history, and since in other societies the general structure of controls is intimately hooked up to the general family structures, the disruptive impact on other societies of this feature alone is far reaching.

I I I

TWO MAJOR PROBLEMS FOR THE MEMBERS
OF ANY RELATIVELY MODERNIZED SOCIETY

Two major problems confront the members of all relatively modernized societies, whether recognized or not. One of these is new, and the other is an ancient problem posed anew in acute form. The new one is the problem of *socialization for an unknown future*. The acute form of an ancient problem is the problem of coordination and control.

A. SOCIALIZATION FOR AN UNKNOWN FUTURE

This problem is one with which laymen are more familiar than social scientists. With rare exceptions the members of relatively modernized societies are all faced with it. Adults must train and educate the young, teach them how to behave, prepare them in a myriad ways for a future neither adult nor young envisages. Such a problem has been rare in world history prior to modernization, even for elite or bizarre individuals. It has never pertained to the general population of a society. Think of what it means as a problem of knowledge alone. How does one train people so that they can act in terms of a system which the trainers expect to be radically different, in unknown ways, from the system they currently know? It is in this sense that the layman has been more sophisticated about this than the social scientists as a group. As laymen, most of us expect our children to live in a radically different world from the one in which we grew up and have lived in so far. We constantly tell them so. We are correct in doing so, for the probability is great that they will have to live in a very different world, indeed. As social scientists, we may or may not build this into our work.

The ordinary expectation for the members of all relatively nonmodernized societies has been that their children would live in roughly the same kind of world as the parents. The discrepancy began to be dramatic in our time. I grew up in Galveston, Texas, a member of a family long of that place. My father and others often told me what Galveston was like when he was a boy. Galveston traffic was then horse-drawn. When he spoke to me of this, I used to think that it would be impossible that my children would find my way of life as a child as different from theirs as my father's was from mine. I thought there would never be such a gap again. My children are still small, and the gap is patently greater. As a small child I lived in a world with practically no airplanes, except a few military planes of questionable reliability. There was no television; radio was much a plaything and a wonder, but on the whole inconvenient; atomic energy had never been heard of. The levels of centralization and bureaucratization of United States society were quite different. My childhood was even more different from my children's childhood than my father's was from mine. The normal expectation now is that their children's childhood will be more different from theirs than theirs is from mine. One must also keep in mind the fact that the time span from childhood to childhood in these cases is a thirty year gap at most. This is what has become of what we still express as a goal, "I want my child to have a better future than mine." All this has come about so quickly that it is no surprise that we have not yet learned to understand it, that we have not yet analyzed it thoroughly, and that we have not learned to cope with it.

In this context it is easy to understand the importance of a predominantly universalistic ethic. If people are taught to act on the basis of what they can do that is relevant in many contexts rather than on the basis of who they are, the possibility of individuals adjusting to a new situation is increased. It is inconceivable that there exists a situation in which achievement and objective criteria are totally irrelevant, though almost any special set of relatively personal identifications may become irrelevant overnight. There will always remain many particularistic criteria and many particularistic ethics. There will always be some clustering around the family, but as this problem increases the relevance of any such identification to other contexts becomes increasingly precarious.

Here again, then, a predominantly universalistic ethic and the emphasis upon it, without anyone planning it, is highly relevant to the general situation of relatively modernized societies. What other strategy could be devised to meet this situation? Consider the problem of knowledge posed. If one asks how one should train individuals to operate in terms of a certain corporation the immediate reply is "What kind of a corporation?" If one says, "I have no idea what kind of corporation," they will say, "How can I help you devise a training system for those people apart from devising one that will presumably fit any corporation at any time?" If one says,

"You are doing that every day of your life. You train your kids for an unknown system. You brag about it. You say that your kids aren't going to be brought up the way you were, that your kids aren't going to have the same kind of future you did, that they are going to be living in a different world." If one brings out the problem that way, people realize what it means, though it may upset them.

It is a peculiar problem. Within the memory of many living members of even our most modernized societies there existed a view of a society in which virtually every member of the society as far back as could be remembered could count on his children and his children's children growing up and living under conditions roughly similar to his own. Now virtually no one can. The one thing certain is that the future is going to be different and at a constantly accelerated pace. Whereas members of relatively nonmodernized societies teach their children roughly what their children need to know for their adult lives, we teach our children what we needed to know for our lives rather than what they will need to know for theirs.[33]

This is a problem of radical social change with a time span of twenty to thirty years. That is revolutionary enough in social history, but the pace will probably not continue to be so leisurely. There is also acceleration involved. In the discussion of stability below [pp. 770–790], the hypothesis that these relatively modernized societies must change constantly and probably at an increasing rate is suggested. It is enough to contemplate the possible meaning of one radical social revolution per generation. How is one to contemplate changes of such magnitude once or perhaps as much as twice per generation? What if the periodicity of such changes becomes ten years rather than twenty or thirty? Can it become five? I do not know the answer, but I am certain of two aspects of the problem: (1) the rate of change will continue to increase, but (2) there is some limit beyond which large sets of human beings cannot react effectively to heightened rates of

---

[33] The cognitive question alone is one of the major challenges to man. I do not begin to understand the causes of modern juvenile delinquency, although I am sure that its universal association with the modernization of societies is not a matter of chance. It is one of the most frequently analyzed, and to many one of the most vexatious, phenomena of our day. So far none of those analyses has been very satisfying intellectually or therapeutically. We have tended to overlook the cognitive element in juvenile delinquency. In addition to the relevance of rejection and questionable parental treatment, etc., one of the most relevant problems is posed in the question one frequently hears from young people whenever they do something of which others disapprove: "How was I to know?" When one is reared for an unknown future, there is no more important question.

change. Either these societies will approach such limits only asymptotically, or the prognosis is bleak.

B. COORDINATION AND CONTROL

The other problem is a much more ordinary and familiar one. It is the old problem of coordination and control. The members of every one of these relatively modernized societies are faced with this problem in an acute form. Again it has nothing to do with whether they are democratic, socialist, communist, or fascist societies. Severe problems of coordination and control exist and proliferate for any people who act in terms of the structures of increasing modernization. How do the myriad of highly specialized and differentiated activities get coordinated and regulated? How are activities kept from "getting out of hand"? For these societies the lower limit of practicable coordination and control lies in the implications of any breakdown. For example, the members of relatively modernized societies will not tolerate a modern depression. One cannot say that a depression will not take place, but one can with some confidence predict what will follow if a genuine depression does take place. There will be rapid and perhaps violent change in the personnel in control. There will be a revolutionary change in the power situation at least. It may not be by guns, but it will be radical, and it will be fast. No one knows exactly where the lower limit of necessary coordination and control is located, but it certainly has to do with the implications for the system as a whole of any breakdown. The more highly modernized the society becomes, the less such breakdowns are tolerable. The possibility that the members of any relatively modernized society will tolerate any breakdown that results in the continuation of the system but at much lower levels of productivity and the like is increasingly small. The action they take may make matters even worse from their point of view, but they will not be indifferent.

The upper limit of coordination and control is equally important. It is becoming more important all the time. Less coordination and control than the minimum is neither feasible for, nor popular among, the members of any of the relatively modernized societies. The most radical conservatives are continually being frustrated by this state of affairs. On the other hand, how far are we in some cases from approaching greater coordination and control than we can handle? Here again one runs into the twin problems of knowledge and brittleness. Quite apart from what people may or may not like in terms of coordination and control, there is the question of how much coordination and control there can be without overloading the cognitive capacities of the individuals who must plan and direct operations, or without the structures becoming so brittle that any small changes within the society, regardless of the source, will fracture the whole system. This is not to say that the attitudes people have toward coordination and control are irrelevant. The degree to which the members of a given society are habituated to centralization and/or authoritarian treatment is of great importance in scientific guesses about their reactions to increases of coordination and control. Nevertheless, even were such differences of degree of no importance whatsoever, there would still be an upper limit on the extent to which coordination and control can be carried. The lowest conceivable limit of coordination and control would be like the lowest conceivable limit of centralization—complete anarchy. The upper limit would be complete centralization. Neither limit can in fact be reached or maintained by the members of any relatively modernized society, or of any other kind of society for that matter. Well within those limits the members of every relatively modernized society face critical problems.

As indicated above again and again, those problems have little to do with the specific form that ideological differences frequently take in today's political arguments. From the point of view of the problems of coordination and control the terms *conservative* and *radical* take on new meanings. If we are to retain these terms and have them mean something in terms of the realities of the situation, it is necessary to distinguish two forms of radicalism: (1) the *fundamentalist* or *conservative* form of radicalism and the *reformist* or *radical* form of radicalism; *fundamentalist* or *conservative radicals* are radical to the extent that, usually by being naïvely antibureaucratic, their attempts to minimize the elements of coordination and control threaten to cut the effectiveness of coordination and control below the point necessary to prevent catastrophic breakdowns, and (2) the *reformist* or *radical radicals* threaten to carry the development of coordination control beyond the limits of available knowledge for adequate planning and execution and beyond tolerable limits of brittleness.[34]

Ideological wishful thinking is not helpful in these matters. I happen to like the implications of the clichés of democracy. They are my ideals, and the implications of these assertions for those

[34] Herein may lie the most tragic aspect of our poorly developed social sciences. They do not tell us nearly what we need to know for the levels of planning we already require.

ideals are dire. Nevertheless, these aspects of human society are as much a matter of human creation as are the ideals and structures of democracy. The range of variation possible for either democratic or authoritarian structures in relatively modernized societies lies within limits set by these considerations.

THE STRUCTURE OF RELATIVELY

NONMODERNIZED SOCIETIES

I
DEFINITION

A. RESIDUAL DEFINITION AND EXAMPLES

Relatively nonmodernized societies, although defined residually to relatively modernized societies, may be identified by the following characteristics: (1) their members depend overwhelmingly on animate sources of power, (2) the inanimate sources of power utilized [e.g., rivers for transport, wind, etc.] tend to be fixed in amount or to increase slowly, (3) the tools used multiply effort modestly, and (4) the tools used are sedentary. All societies in world history prior to the nineteenth century were relatively nonmodernized. Highly modernized societies did not exist until the twentieth century. Only a small minority of nineteenth-century societies became relatively modernized. In the twentieth century the vast majority of societies remain relatively nonmodernized, but the process of modernization has begun in all of those whose members are in contact with the members of relatively modernized societies.

B. OTHER CLASSIFICATIONS

The classifications of relatively nonmodernized societies sometimes seem nearly as numerous as the scholars who have treated of them. Most beg questions rather than answer them. Most overlook the fact that, despite the enormous variety of detailed social structures, all of the relatively nonmodernized societies have more in common with one another in more general respects than any one of them has with any relatively modernized society. Nevertheless, most of these distinctions have in fact gotten at some important differences among these societies. A few may be illustrated here.

1. LARGE-SCALE—SMALL-SCALE

The distinction between large-scale and small-scale societies has already been defined [see p. 18] in terms of the number of people and the amount of space covered. The distinction is not talked of a great deal, but it is significant. Up to a point, it enables us to distinguish between the types of society on which the professional anthropologists have made so much valuable material available and the sorts that most scholars and public officials in the sphere of international relations refer to as nations. It is a distinction, if one likes, between "small" societies whose members, let us say, are confined to one island or fairly small regions and societies of much greater complexity in terms of the areas covered and number of people interrelated. It has not yet proved fruitful to seek a general theory of social structure in terms of the scale of societies, but many structural problems do hinge on differences of scale. The utility of the distinction for present purposes is that the treatment here will hinge on relatively large-scale societies rather than small-scale ones.

2. LITERATE-NONLITERATE

One of the most frequently invoked distinctions is that between literate and nonliterate societies. This refers to the question of whether or not a written language is a feature of the society. Few large-scale societies relevant to international affairs are nonliterate. Most of the large-scale societies on which we have evidence, archaeological or otherwise, have some written forms of communication. The level of literacy characteristic of these societies varies enormously, but the proportion of literate to illiterate members prior to the development of relatively modernized societies has varied less than is generally assumed. Before the nineteenth century the upper limit of literacy of the population of a large-scale society probably never exceeded 30 per cent nor dipped below 5 per cent.

For discussions of relatively large-scale societies, the important distinction is among differing rates of literacy rather than between literacy and nonliteracy. The differences in literacy rates as between, say, the Hanseatic League societies and the Venetian city-states on the one hand and the medieval German principalities on the other are significant for many purposes. This is not, however, a distinction between literate and nonliterate societies but between societies which probably had radically different literacy rates. The implications of such comparisons for the kind and type of elite that can be maintained, etc., are sufficiently obvious examples of the utility of the distinction.

The implications of the invention of printing are not entirely clear. The assumption that with the invention of printing the literacy rate automatically increases until the general membership of the society is literate is not borne out by the Chinese or Western Europeans. With or without printing, the literacy rate in neither Europe nor China ever exceeded 30 per cent until parts of Western Europe and the United States [1] became relatively modernized.

3. PRIMITIVE-NONPRIMITIVE

Another popular distinction is that between primitive and nonprimitive societies. This classification raises terrible problems because the term *primitive* has come to have such pejorative connotations. I have never encountered a really precise and rigorous definition of this distinction. The distinctions between large-scale and small-scale societies, especially if combined with that of literate and nonliterate, will probably handle all distinctions of this sort that are not intended to be invidious.

The distinction does not mean much more than the distinction between simple and complex societies without rigorous specification of the bases for judging simplicity or complexity. It is probably true that societies described as primitive have simpler structures of allocation of goods and services than do societies described as nonprimitive. On the other hand the so-called primitive societies usually have kinship structures of a complexity far beyond those of the most highly modernized societies.

4. NOMADIC-SEDENTARY

Another classification of relatively nonmodernized societies is that of nomadic and sedentary societies. Nomadic societies are societies whose members herd and/or hunt or fish. The sedentary ones are the agrarian societies. This distinction enables one to make a useful generalization: *all stable large-scale societies are sedentary as opposed to nomadic.* There are many cases of relatively small-scale nomadic societies persisting stably for long periods of time. All of the major instances in history of large-scale nomadic societies, however, have been quite unstable, es-

---

[1] This matter continues to be a source of fascination to many as the basis of policy proposals. For example, there are those who maintain that the literacy rate was kept low in China as part of a more or less deliberate plot on the part of the wicked Chinese bureaucrats who maintained their elite status largely by preservation of an exceedingly complicated and difficult method of writing. Chinese writing is certainly complicated and difficult. This line of argument reckons, however, without the fact that in the West relatively simple phonetic alphabetic writing has existed for something like four thousand years. Despite our debt to the Phoenicians for this, it is doubtful that our rate of literacy surpassed that of Imperial China until the nineteenth century. Arguments, therefore, that the difficulty of the writing is the primary or central villain of the piece are conclusively naïve. In qualification of these remarks, I must add that recently I have been told that the inhabitants of Iceland have been nearly universally literate for several centuries. If this is true, the case of Iceland is significant as the only known case of nearly universal literacy among the members of a relatively nonmodernized society.

pecially if their members took control over the members of large-scale sedentary societies. One of the best known examples of such societies is that of Genghis Khan. It is interesting to note that only those parts of his empire that were never converted to Mongol patterns of nomadism or from them remained stable.[2]

There is a close relationship between the management of large-scale societies and agriculture, especially if the large-scale societies are relatively nonmodernized. The proportion of the population engaged in sedentary agrarian pursuits never becomes a minority until very advanced stages of modernization. It is difficult to maintain the levels of productivity in food production required for a large-scale society solely on a nomadic basis.[3] The problems of food productivity per acre increase exponentially with population increase. There are also problems of the minimum level of communications necessary to hold members of a nomadic society together. The problems of communication seem paradoxical. They are maximized for those very societies whose members use the fastest means of communication available given their level of technology; frequently the members of nomadic societies have very fast horses or camels. One of the more obvious problems, which also increases exponentially with population increases, is that of keeping the members of one tribe or subsystem from drifting willy-nilly into the current grazing or hunting area of another. The problems of communications of sedentary agrarians are minimized by the high level of self-sufficiency which can be maintained and the very minimization of the problems of movement.

[2] The most dramatic case of this is the fate of the Mongols who dominated the traditional Chinese. For a bit, the fate of Chinese society was touch and go. A considerable school in the Mongol camp felt that the Mongols should wipe out, not decimate, the Chinese living in the areas of China they chose to take. They felt that the land should be turned over to grazing, that the Mongols should live there only as Mongols always had lived elsewhere. But a Chin Tartar, Yeh-lü Ch'u-ts'ai talked Ögödei out of this policy. Yeh-lü Ch'u-ts'ai was a fast tongue. He convinced Ögödei that there was more to be gotten from the Chinese as taxpayers than from the area as grazing land. Ögödei went along with this, and although the Mongols themselves resisted Sinification better than had others, they had to use buffer bureaucrats and abandon many of their own structures while they ruled China. Neither the customs nor the laws of the Mongols were adapted to the large-scale governance of a highly sedentary society. The most the Mongols could do was alter the domination of the Chinese bureaucrats in limited spheres of influence, wipe them out, become Chinese, or rule so inefficiently as to foredoom their dominance. Insofar as Mongol distinctness was maintained in China, it was at the price of the last of these possibilities.

[3] Most nomadic societies of any scale involve structures of raiding sedentary agrarians.

5. WESTERN-NONWESTERN

This classification and its associated clichés have entered most discussions of these matters and have obscured virtually every discussion they have entered. It is a distinction that is important from certain points of view. Some of the religions of the soi-disant Western societies are quite distinctive. Some of the forms of government are distinctive, and many other features of Western societies are distinctive quite apart from the fact that they are of course the features best known and understood by Westerners. It is also extremely interesting that scholars spoke little of this distinction until modernization came to be a major focus of interest. At just this point, the distinction between Western and nonwestern societies tended to beg rather than answer the important questions addressed.

It is childish to poke fun at this distinction by pointing out that what constitutes Western is to some extent a function of where one stands on the globe. The distinction means more than can be handled by that line of attack. The interest is in aspects or elements held to be inherent in Western societies as such by contrast with, let us say, Near Eastern or Far Eastern societies. This school of thought has its own prophets, best exemplified by the philosopher, F. S. C. Northrup. He is, however, only an especially articulate spokesman for a very popular point of view. The distinction aimed at is that between relatively modernized and relatively nonmodernized societies. The terms *Western* and *Nonwestern* have been plausible because of one indisputable fact. That is the fact that all of the earliest, indigenously developed, relatively modernized societies were clearly special cases of Western or European, or European-derived societies. What the usage ignores is that societies, whether Western or not, have more in common with one another structurally speaking if they are relatively nonmodernized than any one of them has with any relatively modernized society, whether Western or not. The social structure of Tokugawa Japan has more in common with that of eighteenth-century United States society than with that of modern Japan. Modern American social structure has more in common with that of modern Japan than either has with either that of eighteenth-century United States or Tokugawa Japan.

The distinction between Western and Nonwestern societies also contains elements of sheerest nonsense. Part of this nonsense has to do with the mysterious Orient. The mystery of the Orient is nothing but an elaborate unconscious euphemism for an unusually difficult language barrier. Scholars who speak and read these languages well do not on the whole find the societies concerned mysterious in this romantic sense, nor do they find many of the differences asserted to inhere in the Western-Nonwestern distinction. What is no less important, they do not find the equally mysterious assumed similarities alleged to characterize the so-called Nonwestern societies. Apart from partisans of the particular school attacked here, I know of no scholars who do not find the range of variation as among Indian, Chinese, and Japanese societies prior to modernization at least as great as the variation between any one of them and any Western society prior to modernization. Western society in this dichotomy does not refer to *any* and all Western societies. After all both Merovingian and Carolingian France as well as Spain and Portugal would have to be included along with the United States, West Germany, and England of today. The emphasis on science, the levels of specialization, the lack of self-sufficiency, the materialistic orientations, the concern with predominantly universalistic ethics, objective recruitment, bureaucracy, etc.,—these taken together are not characteristic of Western societies in general, but only of those Western societies which became relatively modernized. Furthermore the alleged impact of Western structures on Nonwestern societies vanishes strangely save for cases of the impact of relatively modernized Western social structures on relatively non-modernized societies at whatever point of the compass.[4]

Distinctions like the Western-Nonwestern one are unsatisfactory for two other reasons. First, many of the allegations are simply incorrect. For example, the contention that Nonwestern

---

[4] History affords a perfect comparative case. From the time of Marco Polo on members of traditional Chinese society and of Western societies had contacts that fluctuated in intensity but were continuous. The leaders of Tokugawa Japan, for reasons which need not detain us here, cut off, save for the merest trickle, all contacts with Westerners in 1638. This contact was not renewed until modernization had made considerable headway in the West. Then, as all know, Japanese society was reinvaded by Western influence following Perry's expedition in 1853. This peculiar Japanese experience enables us to distinguish between *Western influence in general* and *relatively modernized Western influence in particular* on the members of a relatively nonmodernized society. For China, where the contact was continuous, it is not possible to separate these influences with any such precision. In neither Chinese nor Japanese society do the so-called disintegrative effects of contact with the members of Western society manifest themselves until those structures referred to as relatively modernized ones have developed. It is not *any* Western structures that disintegrate others. It is the introduction of relatively modernized structures that does so. Those structures happen to have developed first in a restricted set of Western societies. No other interpretation of the Western-Nonwestern distinction will enable one to handle the contrasting cases of Chinese and Japanese societies.

societies are uniformly oriented to compromise as a way of set-tling disputes whereas the members of Western societies are uni-formly oriented to litigation and resort to the courts, is simply fallacious. The Hindus have been among the most litigious of people, and the Chinese have never been adverse to use of the courts provided they felt that the courts were either fair or favora-ble to them. Conversely, there is no more favored maxim among Western lawyers of the most highly modernized societies than that the mark, par excellence, of the really good lawyer is that he keeps his clients out of court. Correspondingly, the idea that Nonwestern peoples are more spiritually oriented than Western peoples is either unclear because what is meant is not defined with any precision or is flatly incorrect. The idea that the Western mind somehow places greater emphasis on rationality than the Nonwestern one is patently contradictable in many spheres. Prior to the development of relatively high levels of modernization, the members of large-scale societies never exceeded the traditional Chinese in their emphasis on and interest in rationality, despite their great interest in and emphasis on tradition. It is all too easy for Western philosophers to forget that for many centuries in the West the light of science was barely kept alive by the efforts of a much contemned minority. The idea that Nonwesterners look at phenomena as they really are whereas Westerners see those same phenomena only through the biased or arbitrary glasses of the special concepts of science is childishly naive from the point of view of any epistemologist.

Second, the fallaciousness of the propositions asserted in terms of this distinction is by no means the worst problem connected with it. That honor is reserved for the fact that use of the distinc-tion seems to explain a great deal but in fact usually begs the question. References to the Oriental mind form one of the best illustrations of this in the whole field of social writing. There cer-tainly are important differences in the attitudes of the members of different societies. Some attitudes toward time, for example, vary considerably among the members of different societies. We may be told that the Chinese attitude toward time is different from that of members of United States society, and that this is a typical result of the Oriental mind. In the absence of a clear-cut and precise definition or description of the Oriental mind that is to some degree independent of this observation about the attitude toward time—and I have never known an adept of such usage to have such a definition or description—nothing has been contri-buted to our understanding. We have in effect been told that "their attitude toward time is different because it is different." An explanation of the difference in attitudes toward time as a function of particular physical, psychic, or even of social characteristics of Orientals as distinct from Americans would constitute a major theoretical break-through in biology, psychology, or the social sciences. No scientific improvement in any field has so far been shown to flow from any such observations. It is unenlightened to feel enlightened by them.

Proponents of the Western-Nonwestern distinction have one strong point in their favor. Relatively modernized societies did first develop in the West. They have not developed independently anywhere else.[5] The spread of structures of relatively modernized societies has so far proceeded overwhelmingly from those areas in which they first developed. Now, of course, there is an increasing spread of them from late-comers to the process, e.g., the Japanese. It is surely not a matter of chance that those structures first developed in the West, but beyond that social science is not now in a position to go definitively. Max Weber maintained that the strategic necessary but not sufficient variable in this development was the Protestant Ethic. Some would contest that, and some would agree with it. If one agrees, there arise the further questions of why the Protestant Ethic or its equivalent developed in the West and only in the West, why, if it developed elsewhere, it did not have the corresponding effect, etc. Use of the distinction is never confined to this context, nor has it illuminated this question. It has been an appealing distinction, but its use has done more harm than good.[6]

6. MISCELLANEOUS

A myriad of other classifications has been applied to relatively nonmodernized societies. Those interested in kinship have sometimes distinguished between matrilineal and patrilineal societies. A favorite in some circles has been the distinction between folk and urban societies. There have been taxonomies based on the

[5] It is by no means certain, of course, that relative modernization could not have developed anywhere else. Arguments can be presented that, had the Japanese continued unmolested, they might have developed relative modernization independently. It is difficult, however, to see how this possibility could be conclusively proved.

[6] There have been side effects—of this and other unjustifiable jargon—which one may not wish to disturb. They fall largely within the sphere of adjustment immortalized in another context by a ditty once popular among junior naval officers:

> "The officers ride in a whaleboat,
> The captain he rides in a gig
> It don't go a —— bit faster,
> But it makes the old —— feel big."

distinctions between status and contract, mechanical and organic societies, gemeinschaft and gesellschaft, etc. All of these distinctions are too specialized if used rigorously, too badly defined to be used, or too erroneous in their implications if used, to be of service here. As insisted here, although the variation of relatively nonmodernized societies is enormous and fascinating, all have more in common with one another in more generally relevant respects than any one of them has with any relatively modernized society. I shall not take up all the features that relatively nonmodernized societies have in common. Paralleling the discussion of relatively modernized societies, only a set of common structural features especially relevant for the problems of modernization as a setting for international affairs is presented here.

I I
STRUCTURAL FEATURES OF
ANY RELATIVELY NONMODERNIZED SOCIETY

A. ASPECTS

1. SPECIALIZATION OF UNITS

Relatively few of the membership units of relatively nonmodernized societies are specialized in terms of one aspect of action such as the economic, the political, etc. Despite this dearth of specialization some form of government, however loosely organized, always exists for any large-scale society. Relatively nonmodernized societies are by no means bereft of specialization in other respects. Highly specialized craft work, for example, is a frequent product of the members of such societies. Most of the organizations in these societies, however, are not specialized as a modern business firm is. Even highly specialized craft work is usually carried out on a family or other nonspecialized basis. The craft work characteristic of these societies—though it may appear bizarre and incredibly refined—is relatively unspecialized by contrast with the level of "product differentiation specialization" characteristic of any relatively modernized society.[7]

All large-scale relatively nonmodernized societies are characterized by at least one specialized unit, a government, but there is greater variation in the form of government displayed among relatively nonmodernized societies than among relatively mod-

[7] Never underestimate the specialization in this sense of a lapidary or of a craftsman who carves sixteen lacework ivory balls, one within the other, from a solid piece without splitting any of the outer balls! Never underestimate, either, the spectacular specialization reflected in any dictionary of occupational distinctions for any relatively modernized society —or even the job classifications for any large-scale factory operation.

ernized ones. It would be difficult, on general theoretical grounds, to maintain that there *must be* specialized units other than governments even in large-scale relatively nonmodernized societies. Nevertheless, ideally, and/or actually, there always are some forms of predominantly economically oriented organizations. Merchant firms are, perhaps, the best example of this. Although merchant firms are often a family enterprise, just as craft shops are usually family enterprises, when a merchant enterprise reaches any considerable scale of operations, the separation between the merchant firm and the family is greater than is common for crafts. The relevance of specialized abilities on a scale barring recruitment solely on family terms is a feature of these cases.[8]

Other specializations of units in relatively nonmodernized societies vary enormously. Organizations specialized on the basis of religion, education, entertainment, etc., are common. The degree of specialization of these units varies widely. Sometimes [e.g., traditional China or Tokugawa Japan] the specialization and differentiation of such units are highly developed, but the degree of specialization never approaches that taken for granted by the members of any relatively modernized society. The vast majority of members of a relatively nonmodernized society rarely, if ever, actually interact with others in terms of such specialized units, let alone actually belong to such units. No active member of any relatively modernized society can avoid continuous multiple involvements of this sort.

Not only are the degree of specialization lower and the extent of members involved more restricted in every way, but also relatively nonmodernized societies are not characterized by the continuous and striking increase in the specialization of organizations taken for granted in relatively modernized contexts. Increases of specialization of subsystems of relatively nonmodernized societies are usually slow, sporadic, and modest. Furthermore, a general reversal of the trend to greater specialization is never characteristic of a relatively modernized society. Such a reversal is by no

---

[8] Closely allied and highly relevant to these phenomena is the fate of particular craftsmen whose works catch on in major population centers. Long prior to modernization of any considerable extent it is difficult to keep the operations of the most popular doll maker of a center like Kyoto on the basis of a relatively nonspecialized unit. Such operations tend to get out of hand from the point of view of the members of the units in terms of which they originate. "Getting out of hand" frequently consists of increases in specialization of the unit in terms of which these activities are carried out. In the example used here the master craftsman is also increasingly forced into the actual roles of a merchant executive specializing in his craft product.

means out of the question in a relatively nonmodernized context. There is some reason to believe that something of a reversal of this sort took place in Europe following the fall of the Roman Empire.

The sedentary nature of the level of specialization and the reversibility of a trend toward greater specialization are important characteristics of relatively nonmodernized societies. Even more important for present purposes, however, is the restricted involvement of vast portions of the population of such societies in specialized organizations or in interrelations with the members of specialized organizations. Even hermits do not approach self-sufficiency in relatively modernized contexts. When they must interact with others, they inevitably interact with some who act in terms of highly specialized units. One of the major implications of this difference is that the members of relatively nonmodernized societies must make a major readjustment not only to an increased number of roles as modernization increases but also to an increased compartmentalization of roles. The facile making and breaking of contacts that we take for granted may seem to most of them bewildering, callous, and insincere.

It is important, however, to realize that some specialized units do exist in relatively nonmodernized societies. Just as with inanimate sources of power and tools, the presence of some such units makes possible a level of communication between the members of relatively nonmodernized and relatively modernized societies which would be much harder to understand in the complete absence of such common features. With relatively few exceptions, such as the problem of socialization for an unknown future, the major distinctions between relatively nonmodernized and relatively modernized societies rests on different incidences, emphases, and combinations of factors and aspects rather than on their presence in one case and complete lack in the other.

2. SELF-SUFFICIENCY OF THE UNITS

High levels of self-sufficiency are approached by the organizations in terms of which most, often the vast majority, of the members of a relatively nonmodernized society act most of the time. This approach to self-sufficiency is particularly true of kinship and/or neighborhood units. The majority of the members expect that they, in concert with other family members, the members of larger kinship units, or the members of some sort of neighborhood unit, will produce most of what they consume, consume most of what they produce, and have little or no contact with anyone outside those units. In general they both expect and prefer this. They never attain such an ideal exactly, but they often approximate it. If cut off by a calamity of nature or some other factor from the contacts they ordinarily do have with members of other units, they are usually able to operate in terms of their preferred units with considerable stability.

There are some fairly notable exceptions, or at least qualifications, in social history. These are best exemplified by the Venetian city-states and the Hanseatic League societies. These are examples of the few great trading societies of history. A real question may be raised as to whether the social systems usually referred to as those societies in fact constituted a set of separate societies. They probably did not, but that is a technical question which need not detain the discussion here. In any case they are examples of fairly large-scale social systems with subsystems characterized by much lower levels of self-sufficiency than is common for most of the members most of the time in relatively nonmodernized contexts.

There are many implications of the high levels of ideal and actual self-sufficiency of the organizations in relatively nonmodernized societies. Relatively high levels of self-sufficiency make it exceedingly difficult to centralize such a society. The greater the level of self-sufficiency, the greater the requirement for virtually man by man supervision if one wishes to centralize in ways which are not congenial to the members. Increases in centralization involve lowering the degree of self-sufficiency. The economy in supervisory manpower, alone, that lowered self-sufficiency permits recommends it. Rulers must, however, pay a price for this stratagem. Alterations in the level of self-sufficiency have far-reaching implications for the social system as a whole. The rulers of the most stable of the relatively nonmodernized societies have not in general tried to centralize the government or other organizations of their societies to a point inconsistent with high levels of self-sufficiency.

The vulnerability of organizations and the self-sufficiency of the organizations vary inversely, but there is also a sense in which the vulnerability varies directly with the degree of self-sufficiency. This vulnerability usually shows itself in what the members of such units or observers of such phenomena are likely to consider as unconnected changes. The best example of this is training or [education] conducted outside a family context. Ordinarily the training an individual gets during his entire life as a member of a relatively nonmodernized society is carried out in family terms or simulated family terms. In the craft shop, for example, when apprentices are not actual members of the family they often acquire a sort of assimilated family rank. To train someone outside of a family context for a job which he may hold outside of a family context may seem on the surface to have few implications for the general stability of the family. Training, however, is intimately connected to the general structures of respect and control of the family. It may never have occurred to other members of the family that training could take place outside the family context. Realization that it can opens up new possibilities of action to all of the family members. To some extent it diminishes the prestige of family members of the older generation. Now the young see that some of the roles that older more respected members of the family have fulfilled can be fulfilled by others on a nonfamily basis. If families were stable despite considerable amounts of internal stress and strain among the members, the most casual opening up of such alternatives may have explosive effects. Introduction of structures of modernization has in fact had explosive effects on the social structure of relatively nonmodernized societies. The family context is commonly one in which these effects are felt earliest. One of the commonest outside influences first introduced is some training by outsiders of individuals for adult roles. Not only does the individual learn that he can prepare himself for adult roles and hence continued existence, even if he defies his family elders and runs away, but he may also be more impressed by and respectful of the new training afforded by the outsider than of the old. As his respect for his family elders declines, so does their ability to control his behavior, or even their ability to keep him a member of the family. Thus general controls are undermined, and the ability of families to persist in the face of stresses and strains generated quite apart from modernization may disintegrate explosively.

3. PREDOMINANTLY PARTICULARISTIC ETHICS

Members of relatively nonmodernized societies emphasize predominantly particularistic ethics overwhelmingly. They never approach, ideally or actually, the emphasis on predominantly universalistic criteria characteristic of relatively modernized societies. When they emphasize predominantly universalistic criteria, they do so for restricted contexts, and the emphasis is more likely to be actual than ideal. The importance of predominantly particularistic ethics in these contexts is closely connected to the enormous focus of attention on kinship in general and the family in particular. The vast majority of the members of all relatively nonmodernized societies make family considerations the major

determinant of all their decisions.[9] Even though other considerations are important and may occasionally even take precedence
over these, for the ordinary man in all history prior to the nineteenth century the most important question was, "How will this
affect my family?" Kinship is inherently particularistic; it is
specifically a sphere in which the individual is identified, above
all, on the basis of who he is. Kinship identification is determined
at least in part on the basis of an actual or fictitious biological
relatedness, on the basis of some particular sexual relationship
with a person, usually of the opposite sex,[10] or on some combination of the two. Initial kinship identification is always as
someone's child and not a function of anything the individual has
done which is germane nor of any of his special objective
qualifications or achievements. Kinship identification is never
entirely biological. There is the general, if not universal, practice
of adoption, and there is also the fact that, although it is usually
easy to determine who the mother of a child in fact is, the
question of paternity is by no means so simple.[11]

Traditional Chinese society is probably the most extreme case
of a large-scale society whose members oriented most of their
action, ideally and actually, to kinship considerations. Ideally
speaking members of that society always expected, and were
expected by others to take family considerations into account.
Moreover, those considerations ideally took precedence over all
others.[12] One of the major responsibilities of the Chinese Emperor

[9] See also pp. 120–122 and 377–435.

[10] It is necessary to be ponderously careful in these matters. Societies
vary enormously with regard to the attitude of their members toward
homosexual relationships. There are societies in terms of which it is quite
legitimate for homosexual partners to be "married." This structure is not a
great rarity in social history. Even when this procedure is perfectly acceptable, such relationships never constitute more than a small minority of the
sexual relationships which are considered legitimate.

[11] Malinowski alleged that the physiological process of conception is not
understood even in a crude sense in all societies. He gives an example of
one society whose members saw no connection between sexual intercourse
and the birth of children [see B. Malinowski: *The Sexual Life of Savages*,
Halcyon House, New York, 1929, pp. 179–186]. Some are uncertain
whether the people concerned were teasing Malinowski or Malinowski was
teasing his readers. Nevertheless, even in that setting an infant was always
connected in a kinship sense to some particular marital pair.

[12] It was even conceivable that one be forgiven for an attempt to assassinate the Emperor or one of his representatives if it were shown that one
did so in order to avenge a genuine wrong done to one's father or some
other ancestor. Practically no other excuse could justify such behavior.
Obversely, if a person did attempt to assassinate the Emperor or one of the
Emperor's officials, he was likely to pay for it with his life, and his relatives
might be wiped out too, specifically in order to prevent the possibility of
vendettas.

was to prevent the development of a situation in which family oriented actions could conflict with one another or with governmentally oriented action. Such conflicts constituted prima-facie evidence that the Emperor did not have "Will of Heaven," which was the sole legitimation of his position.

Tokugawa Japanese society presents an important variation. The ordinary member of that society was expected in most instances to be as family or kinship oriented as his Chinese counterpart. If, however, a conflict between loyalty to his overlord and loyalty to his family arose, loyalty to the overlord came first, no matter the cost. Ordinarily such questions would not arise unless one was of the samurai class or better.[13]

Kinship-oriented particularism is almost certainly the most universal form of particularism. There are, however, many other frequent forms in relatively nonmodernized societies. Particularism based on neighborhood or class identification are examples.[14] The list of possible bases for predominantly particularistic ethics is indefinite. The important thing to remember is that it is quite possible for the members of relatively nonmodernized societies to place no discernible ideal emphasis on universalism at all.

There will be some actual emphasis on predominantly universalistic criteria even if there is none ideally, because there is no society [and there can be no society] whose members pay no attention whatsoever to what a person does or can do that is relevant. The often cited emphases on universalism in relatively nonmodernized social contexts have probably been exaggerated. One of the most notable cases of this is the democratic practices of the Greek city-states. Even Athens at her height was a democ-

[13] In this connection I should like to digress for a moment and point to a device which may be useful for quick insight. It is always interesting to ask, "To what extent are the words appropriate to action in terms of one type of unit 'exported' to cover relationships carried out in terms of other units?" For example, traditional Chinese applied kinship terms to practically any relationship construed important to the individual but not in fact a kinship relationship. One referred to a close friend as a brother, usually by the term for elder brother, and to a teacher as an older brother of one's father; etc. Export of kinship terms to nonkinship spheres indicated the importance of the latter. Nothing could indicate a greater importance for them without violating the ethical structures of that society than this simulation of kinship.

Contrast this with our practice. It is frequently said of a given father and son that their relationship is more than that of a father and son; they are real friends; they are real companions, or they are real pals. We rarely export terms from the kinship sphere save in a derogatory sense such as in the sardonic phrase, "oh brother."

[14] To some extent class identification is always closely related to kinship because one's initial class placement is via one's kinship position.

racy only for her citizens who by no means coincided with her total population. Citizenship was predominantly particularistically defined. The degree of universalistic emphasis of Roman law may also require qualification.

There are certain obvious implications of heavy emphases on particularistic criteria. Either there must be easily and ubiquitously observable signs indicating who a person is to all other persons with whom he comes in contact, or the ordinary individual must be so restricted by himself or others that he rarely comes in contact with anyone ignorant of who he is. For most of the people most of the time the latter has probably held true. Even when signs were easily observable, the individuals concerned were not ordinarily highly mobile either socially or spatially.[15] This has obvious implications for these societies once the mobility of these people increases radically spatially and/or socially, in the process of modernization.

4. COMBINATION OF CENTRALIZATION AND DECENTRALIZATION

However despotic their rulers, relatively nonmodernized societies are never stable without major provisions for decentralization. The major structure of decentralization in the last analysis is always the actual if not ideal autonomy of the nearly self-sufficient units within the sphere of their self-sufficiency. Within this sphere the members are almost always left entirely to their own devices. Interference with individual members may be spectacular, but general behavior is centralized only slightly in terms of the government or any other large-scale unit. Traditional Chinese society had many highly centralized features, but only rarely did the Chinese Imperial bureaucrats reach down directly from the Emperor, as it were, to specific family members. Almost always the day-to-day elements of centralization were achieved by virtue of the essentially autonomous cooperation of the members of the relatively self-sufficient units. Thus, in traditional China troops were not ordinarily sent to collect the grain for taxes. The peasants made initial deliveries. Imperial troops were not ordinarily sent to punish villagers. Culprits were surrendered to the District Magistrate or kept in line at home. The most spectacular

---

[15] In Tosa Han [fief] in Tokugawa Japan members of the Eta, an outcast class organization, were required to wear a particular kind of hairdress so that others could avoid contamination. After dusk they were not supposed to stir abroad lest that hairdress be unnoticed. Even so, the Eta of Tosa probably did not move around a great deal even within Tosa Han.

cases of centralization had to do with the collection of taxes and the levying of *corvées* for purposes of public construction. The former affected most of the population but in specifically limited respects, and the latter affected a limited portion of the population in limited respects.[16]

In many of the cases, and certainly in the case of traditional China, the members of the government in a pinch were quite capable of moving troops into any village or town and thereby of controlling its members directly. It is also true that that society never could have been run on the basis of anything approaching such actual direct control. There were never that many men under arms. They were never that well organized. Transportation was never highly enough developed to shift available manpower about at the rate necessary for such centralization. The logistic difficulties made it quite out of the question. At the highest point of its development there were never enough members of the Chinese bureaucracy—certainly one of the administrative marvels of all history—to administer any such large-scale activity.[17]

Tokugawa Japan was probably the most highly centralized feudal system in world history. It was certainly the most stable feudal system in world history, persisting in its main outlines for a period of two and a half centuries. Despite genuine power available to the Shogun, most operations involved a great deal of autonomy of the members of a han [i.e. a fief]. Within the han there was important decentralization to the village level and within the village to the family level. The Shogun was in an excellent position to bring pressure to bear if he chose to do so, and from time to time he certainly did. Ordinarily, he did not do so, and for two hundred of those two hundred and fifty years few members of the hans got out of line in any manner seriously threatening to the position of the Shogun.

[16] I mention the case of traditional China in particular because this case is the main basis for the important work of Professor A. Wittfogel. Professor Wittfogel has increased our understanding of the centralized elements of traditional Chinese society in particular and of centralization in relatively nonmodernized societies in general. He has done this at the expense of some neglect of the importance of the elements of decentralization throughout Chinese history. He probably would not or could not have made the contribution for which we are indebted to him had he not overstated and oversimplified the case. Now that we are in receipt of his findings, considerably more limited scholarship can qualify those findings importantly [see A. Wittfogel: *Oriental Despotism*, Yale University Press, New Haven, 1957].

[17] The total membership of that bureaucracy including many who were not scholars probably never exceeded half a million men by the most generous estimate. Most scholars would select a much lower figure.

There certainly were cases of high centralization prior to the development of relatively modernized societies, but none of these were stable for any extended period of time. The best examples were the famous cases of large-scale conquest, but the rapidity with which these organizations broke up and decentralized is well known. Vestiges of these empires often persisted for centuries, but the centralized features which strike us so forcibly rarely survived for long the death of the leader who initiated them. The vestigial systems that persisted for centuries were always highly decentralized.

The sedentary nature of the relatively nonmodernized societies lessens the importance of centralization and also makes it in a sense inefficient. Most of these societies, if large-scale, have been sedentary in the fullest sense of the word. They not only have low rates of change, but their members are largely agrarian, i.e., they are sedentary in a locational sense.[18] The members of any highly centralized organization must gather and keep records of the activities involved. There is little point in gathering and keeping records of who is planting what and what the land distribution is, and so forth on a large scale if those matters are going to remain stable year in and year out. For most of these societies inheritance structures are highly stable. The nature of techniques and crops does not vary markedly from one year to the next. Local records suffice to avoid or settle disputes. The relative lack of change makes questions of centralization considerably less relevant than would be the case with less sedentary equally large-scale societies. It also makes such centralization uneconomic. Everyone knows that the peasants in a given area are planting rice in a given year and intend to plant it next year, and the year after that. Everyone knows that they are going to harvest with the same tools, at roughly the same time of year, with roughly the same amount of labor, and so forth and so on. Under such circumstances centralization is inefficient in a special sense. At the same time that high levels of centralization are unnecessary for most purposes, the amount of attention required for centralization is comparatively great because of the close approach to self-sufficiency of many of the organizations. Centralization may be quite important for a leader's dream of power, but as long as the general situation is

[18] Even the nomadic societies are sedentary as far as change is concerned, but they are rarely societies of any considerable scale, and it is the relatively nonmodernized societies of some considerable scale which are of greatest importance here. Nevertheless, the remarks here should apply equally well to nomadic societies if they are relatively nonmodernized.

highly sedentary, increases in centralization will not alter markedly the kinds of organization which can exist stably. Such increases are more likely to be disruptive than otherwise.

The state of technology of communications is vital for the question of centralization. In relatively nonmodernized contexts, it is too poor to support large-scale overwhelming centralization. There have been structures of efficient and rapid communication for limited purposes. Even the most spectacular examples, however, were not sufficiently developed to permit either the efficiency or the scale of communication necessary if decentralization were to be virtually eliminated or radically reduced. Neither the necessary flow of information nor that of people and goods could be handled. Bad logistics have laid low more power megalomaniacs than have ever been brought to book by heroic resistance.[19]

Among relatively nonmodernized societies the range of variation of combinations of elements of decentralization and centralization is considerably greater than the corresponding range of variation in relatively modernized societies. Here again there is an hypothesis which runs through virtually everything I have asserted so far. For all of their important differences, all relatively modernized societies are in fact becoming more and more alike all the time and the range of possible variation among them decreases all the time. The limits of stable centralization for relatively nonmodernized cases are important, but their members can carry centralization much further and remain stable than the members of relatively modernized societies can carry decentralization and remain stable. Accounts of high levels of centralization in relatively nonmodernized societies are usually overdone. Accounts of decentralization in the relatively modernized cases may not be overdone to the same degree but the allegations of the amount of decentralization possible and practicable are usually sentimental, nostalgic, and romantic. One of the wists of highly

---

[19] In traditional China, centuries before the Romance of our Great West, there was a pony express capable of transporting such items as True Relics of the Buddha and important Buddhist Sutras in a matter of days from India to the capital of China, across thousands of miles, many of them over exceedingly difficult terrain. Apart from the set of Roman roads probably no means of communication in world history prior to the development of relatively high levels of modernization exceeded in sophistication and complexity those developed in traditional China. Nevertheless, neither those of China nor Rome were capable of the level of transportation of either information or people which would have been necessary for the kind of day-to-day centralization which members of the United States take for granted—or anything remotely approximating it.

modernized people is that somehow increases in modernization will make possible substantial increases in decentralization.[20]

In relatively nonmodernized societies the range of combinations of centralized and decentralized elements goes all the way from the loosest sort of tribal or interkinship organization to societies in which, for all of their elements of decentralization large-scale bureaucracies exist and for which large-scale communications and public works are erected and maintained. Textbooks in anthropology, history, political science, and sociology treat these variations in a degree of detail which makes it unnecessary here. There is, however, one form of the combination of centralization and decentralization, *feudalism*, which deserves some special comment because the term is used for both analysis and propaganda. Propaganda-wise the tendency is to refer to practically any society that is relatively nonmodern as feudal. This is plausible primarily because the well-studied feudal societies were relatively nonmodernized and shared many characteristics with all other relatively nonmodernized societies. For example, the large-scale relatively nonmodernized societies are all characterized by a particular bimodal [or radically asymmetrical (see below, pp. 65–279) distribution of income. That is to say a small number of their members are wealthy people, and the vast majority of the members live on the bare margin of subsistence. All such societies are characterized by great differences in authority among their members. All have highly particularistic ethics and so forth. Feudal societies have all of these characteristics in common with other relatively nonmodernized societies, but they also have a set of special characteristics with far-reaching implications for the problems of modernization of late-comers. These implications are different, indeed, from the implications of the structures of nonfeudal societies, even though those nonfeudal societies also have the common characteristics mentioned above. I object to the use of the term

---

[20] In the late 1930's there was in this country a really delightful group who called themselves "Decentralists," I believe. They had read and misunderstood Veblen. They felt that life was dominated by huge bureaucratic organizations, and that the situation was getting worse. They developed ways and devices for getting us out of this terrible spiral. One of these was to get people back to grinding their own flour and making their own bread. These processes had gotten into the hands of the corporate colossi, and we were now not only more centralized but we got poorer bread as a result of it. They suggested that we buy wheat, grind it ourselves, make our own bread and at one and the same time interfere with the heinous trend and improve our diet. In order to facilitate this they had persuaded representatives of one of the corporate colossi to manufacture for them and their converts a little dandy gem wheat grinder for the home. If people would just buy these grinders, plug them in and . . .

feudal as an epithet for purposes of propaganda not merely because it injects a pejorative note into analyses about which it is difficult to be objective at best. I object much more because it is a debasement of the languages. Such usage [21] makes it more difficult to understand certain important social differences.

If one means by the term *feudal* the kind of society which existed in medieval Europe in many areas, a quite specific combination of centralization and decentralization is involved. Feudal societies are societies in terms of which to a high degree positions of power and responsibility are ideally allocated along with control over land. Control over land in these cases means, of course, control over certain forms of income. The members of these societies emphasize loyalty to an overlord. A given individual judges his relations to other people in important part on the basis of how his overlord is related to them. Ordinarily his loyalty to his overlord takes precedence over his loyalty to his overlord's overlord. Succession to positions in the hierarchy is ordinarily determined by inheritance on the basis of kinship. Class distinctions are usually extremely rigid. Some feudal societies are, ideally speaking, characterized by completely closed classes. In those cases there is little possibility of actual mobility between different classes though some mobility within a given class is always countenanced.[22]

The main form of decentralization characteristic of feudal societies is the considerable autonomy permitted to a given overlord within the area under his control. Usually a King or an Emperor or a Shogun is considered to be the supreme overlord. Usually his control over his subordinates is quite limited. Tokugawa Japan, probably the most centralized feudal society in world history, and certainly the most stable, was exceptional in the strength of the control of the Shogun. This is not the place for an extended discussion of feudal social structure as such, but feudalism is a specific social form, radically different from most other arrangements in which there are great discrepancies of wealth, large amounts of authoritarianism, and so forth. Furthermore the differences between feudal societies and other societies with

[21] This special form of unjustifiable jargon may be called *culpable* jargon.

[22] The level of actual mobility in such cases is always higher than the level of ideal mobility. The actual mobility may be highly disruptive of the *status quo;* it may also have integrative effects. Both effects are usually via the "illegitimate" mobility of talent. This contrasts sharply with societies with high mobility structures ideally. In the latter the structures of actual mobility are likely to be less than the ideal structures call for—again with both disruptive and integrative implications for the *status quo.*

which they are often confused are strategic for the problems of late-comers to the process of modernization. After all, the most successful of all of the later late-comers to modernization have been the Japanese who made the transition to high modernization specifically from a feudal basis.

Traditional Chinese society is one of the best examples of a society frequently described as feudal in the misleading sense. In the strict sense, Chinese society has not been feudal for upward of 2000 years. The social structure of traditional China, in many respects [e.g., open classes both ideally and actually, a bureaucracy whose members were recruited on the basis of a civil service in the ordinary sense, etc.] was superficially much more like the social structure of relatively modernized societies than was that of Tokugawa Japan. Furthermore there is absolutely no comparison between the extent of available natural resources of the sort generally deemed relevant to modernization in the two cases. There is also no question but that the Japanese made the transition to modernization with much greater ease than did the Chinese and that they have carried the process to levels which the Chinese do not approach, even remotely. In this comparison at least, strong feudal structures constitute a better basis for rapid and efficient modernization of late-comers than do nonfeudal social structures. This holds true despite the fact that the nonfeudal social structures may have much more in common with the so-called democratic aspects of some relatively modernized societies.[23]

[23] Many assume that, since all relatively modernized societies have open-class structures, both ideally and actually, societies with open-class structures are a better bet for rapid and efficient modernization. This is not necessarily the case. A substantial portion of the errors in thinking about problems of modernization can be classified as failures to take into account one of the following propositions: (1) The requisites [i.e., the conditions necessary for maintaining a given system] for relatively modernized societies are not necessarily the same as the prerequisites [i.e., the conditions necessary for achieving a given system]. Thus it is by no means true that by finding out what characteristics are present in a relatively modernized society can one simply say "put these into effect" in society X and relative modernization will be achieved quickly and efficiently. It may not be possible to put the requisites into effect directly. (2) The prerequisites for late-comers to modernization are not necessarily the same as the prerequisites were for the indigenous developers of relatively high degrees of modernization. It does not necessarily follow that the history of England, the United States, France, etc., give us the best clues as to what late-comers have to do if they wish to modernize. (3) The prerequisites for one set of late-comers are not necessarily the same as for another. What worked in Japan, for example, will not necessarily work in Turkey. For an understanding of these differences the most important element is careful research into the basis from which change toward modernization takes

In analysis of centralization and decentralization I urge great care about the use of the term feudal. Ordinary usage, intentionally or unintentionally injects a note of evaluation which obscures analysis of the problems involved. Many are interested in analysis of these problems primarily because of an interest in evaluations. Knowledge of the role of feudal structures in modernization is important for policy decisions with regard to relatively nonmodernized societies. To use the term as an epithet for any structures regarded as unenlightened or wicked is to gloss over critical distinctions.

5. RELATIONSHIP ASPECTS

The particular set of relationship aspects emphasized by the members of all relatively nonmodernized societies is critical. All of them emphasize traditional rather than rational action. I must reemphasize something already mentioned in the discussion of the emphasis on rationality in relatively modernized social contexts. Traditional ways of doing things are not necessarily irrational or even nonrational. Many, if not most, of the traditional ways of doing things—particularly those which become the focus of great technical advance during modernization—coincide with the rational way of doing things, given the means available. For example, in the areas of both craftsmanship and agriculture, the traditional techniques, given the available means are often rational techniques. Traditional techniques of this sort are almost never silly or superficial. Even if traditional techniques coincide with rational ones, however, the fact that emphasis is placed on doing things *because* it is traditional to do them in the given way

---

place, that is research into the previous history of the society concerned. The structures of modernization which have developed elsewhere and will be introduced from outside the societies of the late-comers are relatively easy to describe and relatively constant in most strategic respects. The bases from which the changes take place, however, vary widely. It is knowledge of these variations as well as knowledge of relatively modernized patterns themselves which furnish the largest number of clues about the differences in prerequisites for one set of late-comers as opposed to another. (4) One of the special implications of the second proposition above is that social structures most like those of relatively modernized societies are not necessarily the best basis for transition to modernization.

Errors from these sources would not be so formidable were it not for the following propositions: (1) Some of the requisites for relatively modernized societies are the same as some of the prerequisites. (2) Some of the prerequisites for late-comers are the same as those for the indigenous developers, and (3) Some of the prerequisites for all late-comers are the same.

This whole matter is elaborated below, see pp. 737–740.

has different implications from an emphasis on doing things in a given fashion *because* there is a presumably rational explanation of doing them that way. If a farmer cultivates crops in a particular way because his forebears always have done it that way—even though that is rational given the means available—and the available means change, the traditionalist is likely to continue to employ the old means, even though they are no longer rational. Not only is his likelihood of changing quickly less, but if he does change, the implications for his conduct in other respects are greater, specifically because the switch involves an abandonment or defiance of the previously accepted traditional emphases. Perhaps the most outstanding feature of traditionalism is the emphasis on continuing to do something in a specific way because the perpetuation of doing it in that way is regarded as good, respectful, and right. To change a given traditional way of doing something, particularly under the kind of pressure usually involved in a more or less dramatic demonstration that another technique is vastly more efficient, is likely to call the emphasis on tradition in general into question. This is not to imply that traditions do not change. They change, and in many cases rapidly. Especially in relatively nonmodernized social contexts changes in tradition are usually not carried out self-consciously by the members. Even when the change is relatively rapid, the individuals involved are usually convinced that the new structures have been the traditions all along.[24] The continuous confrontation which the rapidly changing rational technology characteristic of relatively modernized societies affords any given set of accepted means makes unselfconscious alterations of tradition impossible, or at least, a great deal less likely. It is one of the ironies of history that the terms *conservative* and *old-fashioned* have on the whole been laudatory ones until relatively modernized societies developed. In terms of relatively modernized societies, apart from the area in which it is fashionable to be

[24] Professor Joseph R. Strayer whose special concern is medieval history is fond of pointing out that the general idea of the importance of tradition in medieval society is correct but that quite incorrect implications are often drawn from it. What is considered a tradition may be of very recent coinage. Particularly in the absence of high rates of literacy and carefully kept records, a request for a special exception to feudal dues granted only a year before may by the following year be regarded as a long-standing custom. He illustrates the process involved by a feature of universities which are strongholds of traditionalism even in relatively modernized societies. As an experienced departmental chairman he knows that a special request granted to a senior in any given year may be regarded as a "right" of hoary sacrosanct tradition by any freshman entering the university in any subsequent year.

quaint, usually a restricted area for a restricted elite, anything dubbed conservative or old-fashioned is on the defensive. One of the reasons that so many things seem to come apart at the seams at once during the process of modernization is that any self-conscious challenge to traditionalism in any area *may* bring into question traditions in *any other* area, and that it inevitably brings into question traditions in *some* other area.

In the discussion of relatively modernized societies, I indicated that it was not possible to have societies whose members place no emphasis whatsoever on traditional ways. It is possible to have societies so overwhelmingly traditionalistic that members place little or no emphasis, ideally speaking, on rationality. This would not be possible, of course, if the traditional ways of doing things did not coincide to some considerable degree with rational procedures.[25]

Once it was fashionable to distinguish between rational and prerational peoples. Taken literally such a distinction would imply that prerational people are quite incapable of understanding that injuries or at least pain could follow from a fall. They would be unable to understand the distinction between a sharp and a dull arrowhead or knife. No such people have ever existed as far as is known. Malinowski pointed out that no known primitive people confused bad workmanship with improperly performed magic. There are no people who do not think rationally in some context and who do not appreciate some rational thinking. He understood and appreciated, however, that the emphasis could still be overwhelmingly on tradition as long as what was traditional coincided relatively well with what was rational. In this sense, a complete emphasis on tradition is theoretically possible. It is exceedingly doubtful that the actual emphasis on tradition has ever been carried to such an extreme, and it certainly has not for any large-scale society.

For any large-scale society there are always spheres of action, usually the most clearly instrumental spheres of action, in which rationality is emphasized and recognized to some extent. The extent of that emphasis, however, need not be great, and it may be associated with spheres of behavior of relatively low ideal status. One of the best examples of this has to do with the activities of merchants [see also pp. 113–114 and 543–548].

[25] Ideally speaking, it is possible for the members of a society to approach an extreme pole of emphasis on traditionalism which cannot be approached by the members of any society with regard to rationality. No society, for example, has ever been characterized by completely rationally based kinship structures. Furthermore, such kinship structures are improbable and perhaps not even possible.

Merchants always understand rational operations to a marked degree and place heavy emphasis upon them. Ideally speaking, merchant members of relatively nonmodernized societies frequently have low prestige, which may continue to be low ideally, even though they may become powerful and important actually. Although relatively nonmodernized societies vary to some degree in the emphasis placed by members on rationality both ideally and actually, ideally speaking the emphasis on rationality never reaches the point at which arguments based on traditionalism are generally defensive arguments.[26]

The criteria for forming relationships tend in relatively non-modernized societies to be overwhelmingly particularistic. Before a relationship can be formed the parties must know who everybody is. There is the widest variation in different bases for determining who an individual is. Despite this variation, however, kinship is the major basis of particularistic identification for the overwhelming majority of the members of these societies.

As already pointed out, kinship is an ineradicable basis for particularistic distinctions in all societies, and most members of most societies have oriented most of their action to kinship considerations. Under these circumstances, it is not surprising that so much of particularism is defined in kinship terms. The form of particularism emphasized is often the special form of particularism distinguished below [see pp. 140–143] as germane particularism. The criteria for belonging to a relationship depend primarily on who an individual is, but that identification is highly relevant to the nature of the relationship itself. When most of the interrelationships are on the basis of some sort of kinship unit, it may be highly germane to select work crews largely on that basis.

As indicated above [see pp. 63–65], one of the great problems of placing emphasis on particularistic criteria lies in the possibility that predominantly particularistic selection of individuals will interfere with the extent to which an emphasis on rationality can be maintained. The person selected on the basis of who he is may not be the person best fitted to carry out the job. On the other hand, what is here called germane particularism is to a considerable degree easily combinable with rationality, particularly when

[26] The reverse tends overwhelmingly to be the case in relatively modernized social contexts and becomes the more so the more highly modernized they become. Traditional emphases are not eliminated either ideally or actually, but the burden of proof comes increasingly to rest on the defenders of tradition rather than on the proponents of rationality. This is no small element in the frenetic insistence of so many moderns on a completely rational, scientific, objective ethic.

the elements of rationality are present, not so much because of the direct emphasis on rationality as because the traditional ways happen to coincide with what is rational. Again given the position of family units in such societies, it is probably rational to make up various groups of individuals for particular purposes on a family basis.

It is important to keep in mind that the vast majority of all relatively nonmodernized societies have been societies in terms of which the average individual lived out his life in contact with a quite restricted number of individuals. The number of different organizations in which a given individual has roles is also highly restricted. Furthermore, the possibility of the average individual coming into contact with individuals from another organizational context of which he knows nothing is also relatively slight. Under these circumstances it is not difficult to envisage virtually all the relationships in which he enters being predominantly particularistically defined.

There are certainly examples of great emphasis on comparatively universalistic criteria in such social contexts, especially in matters having to do with generalized media of exchange, markets, and bureaucracies [see below, pp. 113–120]. They may in fact exist quite apart from the two categories just mentioned. Although in theory it is possible that there be a society whose members placed no ideal emphasis on universalistic criteria whatsoever, such a society obviously could not continue to exist if individuals selected on a predominantly particularistic basis were totally incapable of performing tasks vital to their survival. Societies may actually have gone out of existence because predominantly particularistic selection interfered with the minimal requirements of operations in terms of them. The most spectacular cases of this are likely to be the result of particularistically selected leaders of governments.

Another emphasis characteristic of the relationships in relatively nonmodernized societies is that on functional diffuseness. Relationships in these societies are rarely precisely defined and precisely delimited, i.e., predominantly functionally specific. Frequently in such societies there are important elements of careful definition. For example, in Chinese society the minimum obligations of a wife to her husband were quite clearly stated. The relationship was, however, by no means precisely delimited. As indicated above, the modern contract relationship is an extreme case of functional specificity. In this respect the use of the term *contract* for the feudal contract is misleading. The feudal contract was typically a predominantly functionally diffuse relationship. Although there was a considerable amount of detailed definition as to some of the obligations involved, the relationship was by no means precisely delimited.

The importance of kinship considerations is highly relevant to the emphasis on functional diffuseness. Kinship relationships are always overwhelmingly functionally diffuse. Any society in terms of which a very considerable proportion of all relationships are carried out on a kinship basis is a society characterized by an overwhelming emphasis on functionally diffuse relationships. Here again, unlike the case of relatively modernized societies, the emphasis on the opposite pole may be quite slight or even nonexistent. It is quite conceivable that there could be relatively nonmodernized societies with no ideal structures of emphasis on functional specificity whatsoever. It is not possible to have a relatively modernized society with no emphasis whatsoever on functionally diffuse relationships. One of the problems of functionally diffuse emphasis in relatively modernized contexts is that, if the relationship is predominantly functionally diffuse, it is difficult to confine it to predominantly universalistic selection or to predominantly rational cognition. In societies in terms of which neither rationality nor universalism is highly emphasized this particular order of problem is not likely to arise. These emphases in relatively nonmodernized contexts are not likely to cause trouble because they clash with the implications of other emphases on their opposite extremes. The clashes and conflict in relatively nonmodernized societies among relationship structures are likely to be conflicts between one set of predominantly traditionalistic emphases and another, between one set of predominantly particularistic emphases and another, or between one set of predominantly functionally diffuse emphases and another.

These interrelationships, whether in conflict with one another or not, may have some special effects. In relatively nonmodernized social contexts effects comparable to emphases on rationality, universalism, and functional specificity are sometimes obtained by a balance of traditional, particularistic, and functionally diffuse emphases. For example, in traditional Chinese contexts a given family member of a given Chinese village would, if given the opportunity, exploit other villagers to the benefit of his own family members. Often the members of one of the families were so much more powerful than the others that exactly this sort of exploitation resulted. On the other hand ordinarily there was a more nearly even balance of power among members of different family units. In village management of various sorts not only was one family-based particularism often played off against another, but neighborhood particularism was often played off against family particularism, and frequently the result was the same sort of selection which would have been obtained had selection been on a predominantly universalistic basis. This matter of obtaining predominantly rational, universalistic, and functionally specific results as a function of varying balances of emphases on tradition, particularism, and functional diffuseness is important for an understanding of problems of modernization. Some apparently inexplicable upsets at local levels have probably been a function of the fact that initial moves in the direction of emphases on rationality, universalism, and functional specificity have actually lowered the extent to which those qualities have been achieved. This has been the result of the fact that the efforts to achieve the new structures have wiped out delicate balances of the old, which gave such results, without replacing them efficiently with the new.

6. GENERALIZED MEDIA OF EXCHANGE AND MARKETS

Highly generalized media of exchange and markets do not necessarily exist in all relatively nonmodernized societies. It is unlikely that any of these societies be totally devoid of generalized media of exchange. Nevertheless, the level of generalization of any media of exchange which do exist can be exceedingly low, and certainly there can be societies of this sort without markets. Both highly generalized media of exchange and markets, however, do exist in all known cases of societies of any considerable scale. Both the degree of generalization of the medium or media of exchange and the development of markets may be highly restricted by contrast with the extent of either of these in relatively modernized societies. To the extent that generalized media of exchange and markets exist, an element of rationality is exceedingly likely to be injected into the society even though tradition is emphasized. As indicated again and again, there is always some rationality, regardless of whether it is ideally called for or not. There is in the first place the kind of rationality that happens to coincide with the traditional forms preferred for traditional reasons. In the second place, there is the sort of rationality which comes from sources other than ideal sources. The likelihood of some rational orientation wherever there are highly developed media of exchange and highly developed markets, contributes to the peculiar role of merchants in these relatively nonmodernized societies. The role of merchants is likely to be a marginal or outcast role ideally speaking in relatively nonmodernized societies specifically because of ambivalent attitudes toward rationally oriented experts in exchange. Actually speaking merchants frequently become powerful and even prestigious, and there are even cases such as the Hanseatic League societies and the Venetian city states in which both ideally and actually the merchant is a man of great prestige, but these tend to be exceptions in world history.

There is a more detailed discussion of the basis of these assertions below [see pp. 543–548]. For the present, suffice it to illustrate the situation by the general point that anything which injects an element of rationality into a situation which ordinarily emphasizes traditionality tends to create special problems of integrating the activities concerned with the general ideal structures. One of the most flagrant examples of this is one on which sociologists dote. It is the problem of the relationship between prostitution and ideal family structures. One of the great differences between them is the setting within which sexual relationships take place. Specifically sexual relations in a family context are sexual relationships taken out of a market, taken out of a generalized medium of exchange setting. Prostitution is a sexual relationship taken in specifically that kind of setting.[27] Sex in the family context and in the context of prostitution as referred to here both involve women. In even the most highly mechanized societies no satisfactory substitute has been found, as a popular musical maintains, "There is nothing like a dame." Since exactly the same sort of personnel can be involved in either or both relationships, there are likely to be conflicts between sex carried out on a family basis and on the basis of generalized media of exchange in markets. Most of the attacks on prostitution as a social evil dwell on real or hypothetical examples in which the practice of prostitution somehow undermines a given family situation. One of the more dramatic examples always invoked to exemplify the evils of this practice is the tale of an otherwise upright family man who in resorting to prostitution finds he is expected to carry out the relationship with a member of his own family—usually in the most telling case with his daughter. This

[27] In the revolt against the restricted position of women in the nineteenth century one of the focal war cries was based on the allegation that in fact family practice was a great deal more like prostitution than the upholders of morality cared to admit. Lady Cicely Hamilton in a famous book, *Marriage as a Trade* [Moffat, Yard & Co., New York, 1909], pointed out that insofar as women accepted limitations on their freedom in return for support by their husbands, etc., or insofar as their husbands justified such subservience on that basis, the implication clearly was that marriage was only a special form of prostitution. Many of the early feminists delighted in the shock value of this point of view.

not only emphasizes the subversiveness of the practice for family stability, but also contains a high-minded emphasis on "just deserts."

It is not necessary to depend upon the prostitution—family case for illustration of this point. There is exactly the same sort of conflict implicit in the hiring of labor on a generalized-media-of-exchange-market basis. When labor is carried out in a family or neighborhood context, work as well as sexual services are ordinarily carried out without a cash nexus involved. Most of the members of most of the societies of the world carry out most of what we would consider labor and the like on just such a predominantly particularistic basis. To inject considerations of a cash nexus into those relationships can be every bit as upsetting and have every bit as far-reaching implications as to inject such considerations into areas ordinarily concerned with sexual relationships. In relatively modernized contexts so many of these other activities have long since been drawn into the generalized-media-of-exchange-market context that the example of prostitution is one of the few vivid examples left. As far as relatively nonmodernized societies are concerned, any highly developed markets or highly generalized media of exchange are always accompanied by a conflict of ideal and actual structures, by special forms of insulation of this sphere of activity from others carried out on other bases, or by highly developed cases of both. The fact that the role of merchants, ideally speaking, is frequently denigrated is one of the most frequent ways of insulating their activities from the general practices in other contexts.

B. ORGANIZATIONAL CONTEXTS

1. BUREAUCRACY

The presence of bureaucratic systems is not universal among relatively nonmodernized societies. This is one of the characteristic differences between relatively modernized and relatively nonmodernized societies. Bureaucratic systems are requisites for the former. Although they are not requisites for the latter, there are certainly some outstanding examples of them. Following the work of Max Weber, scholars tend to point to relatively few bureaucracies in relatively nonmodernized contexts, the outstanding examples being the Catholic church, those of the early Egyptian dynasties, traditional Chinese society, Roman society, etc. Instances of bureaucracies are far more frequent than this, although they are not as frequent ideally as they are actually.

This may be why so many have been overlooked.[28] Some elements of bureaucratic organization probably appear in all cases of large-scale relatively nonmodernized societies, and there is always the problem of combating the effects of particularism in a predominantly particularistic setting. When quite high levels of skill are necessary for large-scale purposes of administration, how is personnel to be recruited when, ideally speaking, ostensibly, recruitment is only on a particularistic basis? There are many fascinating variations of methods in terms of which members of these societies accomplish this purpose. Some of them are undoubtedly used self-consciously; others probably are not. The most striking method is the one seen so clearly by Max Weber. The members of these societies sometimes hit upon the device of a bureaucratic system as described by Weber, both ideally and actually. All such systems have a major problem built in. This is the problem of insulating the predominantly universalistically defined bureaucratic system from the enveloping sea of predominantly particularistic relationships.

The second method does not involve what Weber would have considered a bureaucratic system, ideally speaking. It achieves comparable results by special handling of a predominantly particularistically recruited system. The bureaucracies of Tokugawa Japan were excellent examples of this. A third device is that of selecting for bureaucratic personnel individuals who are outsiders from the point of view of the general membership of the

[28] One of the most important reasons for raising the question of the distinction between ideal and actual structures is the fact that the former are frequently taken for the latter. The reverse confusion is less likely. The reason is in one sense simple—in another complex. When a member of a given society describes his own society, whether as an informant or not, he is very likely to state its ideal structures. Ordinarily he does not do this with any intent to deceive [see above, pp. 28–30].

The fact that most individuals tend to describe ideal rather than actual structures in their own society, although they may disagree as to what the actual ideal structures are, is simple enough to observe. Why this is so general and why social analysts have been so systematically insensitive to this unintentional distortion is a much more difficult matter. Some of the reasons may be stated as follows: (1) The members of all societies learn to take most of their ideal structures very much for granted and are familiar with them. (2) The ideal structures characteristic of a given society are important empirical features of any society. In this sense it is not a distortion to describe the society in terms of them. It is only a distortion to infer that the description in these terms exhausts the relevant material on the level of generalization under discussion. (3) The ideal structures on any given level of consideration are always far simpler, better known, and better understood by the members of a society than are its actual structures. Conscious or unconscious chauvinism has probably never accounted for more than a tiny fraction of the presentation or acceptance of ideal structures as actual ones.

society and setting up methods for keeping them outsiders. The Janizariat of Turkey and the general use of eunuchs are good examples of this device. Finally, on a relatively small scale some of the effects of a bureaucratic system may be achieved by the balancing of various particularistic interests of the sort already mentioned above [pp. 112–113]. The first three of these devices are the most important in relatively nonmodernized societies, if bureaucratic systems of any large scale are involved and, I shall describe them briefly.

The traditional Chinese bureaucracy was a bureaucracy in Weber's sense both ideally and actually. Recruitment for the bureaucracy was conducted via a set of civil service examinations. When the members acted properly, those examinations were very carefully guarded. This led not only to highly universalistic selection, but also to some of the most elaborate methods of cheating on examinations seen in world history. The examinations were rather like the old British Civil Service examinations. The candidates were examined on a general classical background. Technical know-how directly applicable to the job was learned on the job. Occasionally certain categories of individuals were excluded from participating in the examinations, but on the whole the examinations were open to anyone who could achieve a sufficient level of education to enter. Once one succeeded in the examinations, he could become a member of the bureaucracy. Some levels of success in the examinations carried with them automatic appointments at high levels. No attempt was made to teach members of the bureaucracy that they should not put their family interests ahead of their bureaucratic duties. Considerable attempts were made to so insulate the bureaucrats that nepotistic inclinations could not interfere with operations in terms of the system. For example, an official was not permitted to serve in the province which was his family seat. Needless to say, in the course of a dynasty these attempts at insulation always broke down. The various forms of breakdown were as subtle, sophisticated, and fascinating as the forms of cheating developed.

The bureaucracies of Tokugawa Japan were organized along fief lines. The Tokugawa Shoguns had their bureaucracy and each of the daimyo [i.e., major feudal lords] had his own bureaucracy. Ideally speaking most of the positions were inherited ones. To this extent these systems were not bureaucracies as envisaged by Weber, but Weber, too, was so preoccupied with ideal structures that he tended to ignore actual ones. Ideally speaking the supreme obligation of a bureaucrat was not to his family but to his overlord [i.e., to his bureaucratic duty]. So fully were these ideal structures actualized that, if a son was not well fitted for a particular inherited bureaucratic position, his father might well disinherit that particular son and adopt a boy or man of suitable promise or accomplishment. Apparently the level of adoption among the samurai [i.e., the feudal bureaucrats] was considerably greater than one would have expected on the basis of normal replacement of sons for simple purposes of succession. This was explicitly not a civil service by examination, but rather a "civil service by adoption." As such it avoided a problem which the traditional Chinese were never able to lick. Given the ethics of the samurai, the greatest possible devotion to one's family name was a devotion that required even the destruction of one's family if that would serve one's overlord. Therefore, a civil service by adoption tied up the selection on the basis of relevant skills, loyalty to the bureaucracy, and loyalty to one's family in a package that minimized many of the conflicts which always resulted in graft and corruption in the Chinese case. There is some reason to be skeptical about the alleged graft and corruption of the samurai during the Tokugawa regime. One marked characteristic of the end of that regime was the high level of poverty of many of the samurai. If they were corrupt, they were the most inefficiently corrupt group of public servants in world history. The members of the Chinese bureaucracy were far more efficiently corrupt.

There was another interesting civil service device in operation in Tokugawa Japan which might be called "civil service by usury." It is probably a frequent form of civil service recruitment. Merchants in Tokugawa Japan were specifically ineligible to hold office in the bureaucracies of the various fiefs. For reasons too complicated to go into here, they were in some special respects protected by the Tokugawa Shoguns and expected to sap the financial power of the various overlords of the rest of Japan. Before the regime was greatly advanced, a considerable proportion of the daimyo were deeply in debt to the merchants. They constantly sought extensions of their loans and new loans. On such occasions, merchants sometimes pointed out that, on the basis of existing operations, they could neither extend the present loans nor make new ones, but that, if certain changes were made in the way in which fief affairs were handled, perhaps something else could be done, etc. Insofar as their suggestions were heeded, there existed a "civil service by usury." Administrators of fief affairs thus utilized the plans of some of the ablest talents available in Japan during that period. No matter how great their administrative contributions,[29] these merchants were not ordinarily, if

[29] This leaves to one side all questions of exploitation of peasants, etc.

ever, given actual samurai rank and made members of the ideal bureaucracies of the various fiefs.

The device of the Janizariat is quite well known. These men were usually slaves or captives or both. They were frequently, if not always, of a different religion than the members of the host system in terms of which they operated. They were charged with administrative offices, and to the important among them high privileges were accorded. They could not, however, have legitimate descendents. Therefore, the question of succession of their heirs to office was ostensibly ruled out. The turning over of administrative affairs to eunuchs is, of course, an obvious method of cutting down on the possible interference of some nepotistic considerations in succession to administrative posts. Both of these cases, I might add, imply quite clearly that the major source of particularistic interference with objective standards of administration of the bureaucracies concerned is likely to be kinship-oriented particularism.

The fourth instance referred to above may not be properly referred to as an actual bureaucratic system. It is at least an approximation of the results often sought by uses of bureaucracies, however. Particularly at local levels in all relatively nonmodernized societies the balancing of predominantly particularistic factors is probably the major device whereby effects equivalent to bureaucratic ones were achieved. These balances are not ordinarily devices in the sense of having been carefully thought out. Probably in most cases they are not explicitly thought out at all. Nevertheless, they do exist. Thomas C. Smith quotes Professor Ariga Kinzaemon as indicating that the role of headman in Japanese villages, ideally speaking, rotated among a number of qualified family heads, but that if one of the several lineages in a village was much stronger than the rest the role of headman might come to rotate in some such sequence as 1,2,1,3,1,4,1,2, . . . rather than rotating in the order 1,2,3,4,1,2,3, . . .[30] Such balances of particularistic interests are not without analogies in relatively modernized societies. Many of the soi-disant virtues of pluralism and "countervailing forces" inhere in just such balances.

Virtually all of the bureaucracies of relatively nonmodernized societies have structures which stress on-the-job learning by the bureaucrats. Like the Chinese systems, most had to have members with considerable talent for devising and carrying out major programs, but by contrast with relatively modernized societies,

[30] See Thomas M. Smith, *The Agrarian Origins of Modern Japan*, Stanford University Press, Stanford, 1959, p. 58.

the factors overseen by the bureaucrats were not characterized by high rates of obsolescence or rapid rates of deterioration in the absence of constant detailed supervision. The day-to-day pressure on these bureaucrats never approached the pressures characteristic of relatively modernized societies with their high levels of specialization and interdependency.

2. FAMILY SYSTEMS

Relatively nonmodernized societies have the widest possible variation in family types. Their variations include the multilineal conjugal family which is characteristic of relatively modernized societies. All of the variations commonly described in standard anthropological and sociological texts are to be found among them. Indeed it is only these societies which exemplify those variations.

Two of the best known are the *patrilineal extended family* which was the ideal family in traditional China and the *famille souche* or *stem family* which was the ideal family in Tokugawa Japan. Ideally speaking, the members of the former consist of the following relatives: father, mother, sons and their wives, the sons of sons and their wives, and all of the nonadult children of the youngest married couples who belong to the unit. Daughters "marry out" of the family; wives "marry in." Such family structures call for the maximum proliferation in terms of numbers of generations represented, numbers of marital units present, number of siblings of a given sex present at any one point in time, etc. *Famille souche* units are similar save for the fact that not only do all daughters marry out, if they are patrilineal families, but also all sons save one, usually the eldest son, marry out. The sons who marry out set up branch families. Ideally speaking, families of these two types contain a large number of members. Actually, despite variations of these ideals, the average number of members of the average family has been exceedingly uniform throughout history. In brief [31] this is to be accounted for by the high death rates and the limitations of adoption characteristic of the vast majority of societies with family structures stressing the desirability of numerous family members. Regardless of what the ideals may be in a given relatively nonmodernized society, few grandparents, for example, long survive the birth of their grandchildren.

In all relatively nonmodernized societies the family unit is overwhelmingly the main unit in terms of which the socialization of individuals takes place. For most individuals in all history [and

[31] For amplification see below, pp. 428–430.

prehistory, if one may conjecture there] prior to the development of relatively modernized societies training and education has been in terms of some family organization. This continues to be true of all early socialization even in relatively modernized contexts today, but for the relatively nonmodernized man this is also true of virtually all other forms of socialization as well. When training and education of the latter take place in specialized contexts such as schools, only a very small minority of the population participates in them. As already indicated above, one of the major contrasts between relatively nonmodernized and relatively modernized societies is the extent to which the portion of socialization outside a family context continually rises in the latter context.

Not only is virtually all of the socialization in all of the relatively nonmodernized societies carried out in family terms, but also most of the behavior of most of the members of all such societies is oriented to family considerations. This does not mean that in case of conflict between family and other orientations that the family orientations always take precedence. They may, and Chinese society has already been cited as a dramatic example of this. Even when this is not the case, family orientations are more important than any others for ordinary daily operations. When, ideally speaking, family orientations do not take precedence over nonfamily orientations, conflicts between family and other orientations do not ordinarily arise. In the Tokugawa period of Japan such conflicts did arise from time to time for the samurai. When they did, the samurai was expected to sacrifice his family interests with vim and vigor. Such sacrifice was the expression par excellence of the true samurai spirit. It would be hard, however, throughout the two hundred sixty-five years of the Tokugawa regime to estimate the extent of the frustration of samurai anxious to show their mettle but denied the opportunity of such a dramatic conflict. The number of cases in which such conflict actually occurred must have been relatively small. One may even suspect that this is one of the reasons why the famous tale of the Forty-Seven Ronin became so popular in Japan. The Forty-Seven Ronin did have just such an opportunity to show what virtuosi of feudal loyalty they were. Each one of them destroyed his family, but interestingly enough, because of his tremendous loyalty to his overlord he ensured the perpetual fame and prestige of his family. The lack of opportunity for such conflicts, when they are possible, is the basis of an important distinction between relatively nonmodernized societies and relatively modernized ones. As modernization increases, the possibility and probability of conflicts between family and other orientations increase enormously. A considerable part of the discussion of various age periods such as adolescence in relatively modernized contexts moves almost exclusively in terms of conflicts between family and other orientations.

Family relationships are always predominantly particularistic relationships. Since the vast majority of orientations for the average member of relatively nonmodernized societies are family orientations, if problems of particularism arise, they are usually questions of family-based particularism. Even in relatively modernized contexts family considerations are a major source, if not the most important source, of particularistic considerations [and ignorance with its implications for capricious particularism (see pp. 141–143) is undoubtedly next], but in relatively nonmodernized societies, without exception, they constitute the overwhelmingly important source of particularism. The only close competitor is likely to be neighborhood loyalty or in some cases a particularistically defined loyalty to one's overlord or to some hierarchy of that sort.

Correspondingly, the family is the main focus of solidarity. Therefore, anything that threatens family solidarity threatens general stability. The family is the main focus of organization, and at least for day-to-day matters it is the main organization in terms of which control is exercised. If there is a structure of control that takes precedence over the family as in Tokugawa Japan, family control may be disintegrated without disintegrating the general control structures of the society. Usually, as in the case of China, this is not possible. To undermine the stability of family control is to undermine, at least initially, the prevailing structures of control of the entire society.

I I I
MAJOR PROBLEMS FOR THE MEMBERS OF
ALL RELATIVELY NONMODERNIZED SOCIETIES
IN THE MODERN WORLD SETTING

A. PROBLEMS OF STABILITY WITHOUT REFERENCE
TO MODERNIZATION

First, one must not forget that the members of all of these societies have some problems of stability that are not functions of their involvement in the process of modernization. There have never been any societies totally devoid of problems of stability. There have been spectacular cases of stability in social history such as that of traditional China, but that stability over two thousand years held only for some of the more general structures of that society. There were many detailed changes, of course, which took place during that long period. It is useful to note that all societies, however stable, have problems of stability even in the absence of outside influences.[32]

[32] Because of the general state of sociology and related fields I must digress here somewhat technically. It has become fashionable to *define* social systems as being in equilibrium. This creates a whole range of special problems. In the first place, it implies that systems of social action that are not in equilibrium are in some respects not social. Secondly, equilibrium is sometimes defined as including both itself and its residual category. In that case the equilibrium clause in the definition does no harm except by implication. If the term equilibrium means itself and everything else, then to define a social system as being in equilibrium is to say that a social system is a system which is either in equilibrium or not. This may sound as if it gets the analysis somewhere, but of course it does not. Every system of any sort is either in equilibrium or not. In the third place, if one defines the term so that it says something, one gets into the nasty predicament of having to maintain in essence that systems which were social systems must be explicable in nonsocial terms—usually the factors of the heredity of the species involved and the nonspecies environment—if the systems get out of equilibrium. No one wishes to go to such extremes, but that is in fact where many of us have gone.

One may, of course, define terms any way one wishes in science, if one is prepared to stick by the implications of the terms so defined. If those implications are absurd or lead to nonscientific elements, or are fruitless for the formulation of theories, one must try again, if one wishes to continue the game. If one defines social systems or societies as stable or equilibrium systems or as homeostatic systems, there are a whole host of problems which cannot be treated with these concepts. Those who use this device are led by it either to beg questions which they presumably address or are led to treat those questions in terms of concepts which in fact are quite different from the ones they have defined. It is not actually a difficult problem to solve. There is no need to define these systems as being *in fact* stable or in fact in equilibrium. One may distinguish those which are relatively stable or highly stable and those which are not, those which are in equilibrium for a given period of time, those which are in partial equilibrium states, etc. Even when one uses a stable case in order to derive certain properties of the general class, it is not necessary to assume that all instances of the special class will in fact be characterized by stability. Almost every automobile maker issues a statement as to how many pounds of air *should* inflate the tires on his make of automobile for proper functioning. A random sample of the automobiles in fact on the road would indicate considerable variance from this figure. This does not mean that it was foolish of him to present the figure in the first place, nor does it mean that the figure has no implications whatsoever for automobiles on which the tires are markedly over- or under-inflated. This may seem to be a petty quarrel among the acolytes of a fortunately restricted and bizarre sect. It is more than that, particularly when the problem of modernization of relatively nonmodernized societies is under study. In this case there is no question that there is going to be instability on both general and specific levels of concern. To define the units one intends to use in such analysis as stable units is to guarantee that one either begs the questions or in fact uses definitions other than the ones presented. It is a difficulty exceedingly easy to avoid. Any careful reading of the history of science or even a casual inspection of the roles of models in the natural sciences would be sufficient to prevent any social scientist from falling into this trap.

If one does not define societies as actually stable, whether or not any particular instance of a society is in fact stable at a given point of time is an empirical question. On the completely descriptive level any society, or any other phenomenon for that matter, is constantly changing in some respect, if only that of age. The actual degree of stability allegeable about a given society is to some extent a function of the level of generalization on which one wishes to consider the society. Thus in the period of traditional Chinese society's long stability the structure of equal inheritance for all sons remained highly stable as did the structure of requiring marriage outside the paternal lines of descent. On the other hand, some of the details of the treatment of different sons and the details of marital arrangements varied. On any given level of generalization with which one is concerned, if the unit is neither stable nor unstable by definition, its stability or lack of stability is something to be accounted for. Throughout history it appears that the maintenance of stability is not easy even in the absence of outside influences. Even if the members have yearned for stability, most societies have not been stable long. Scientific propositions about social stability are not highly developed, alas.

The nature of the problems of stability that exist quite apart from the process of modernization varies at least as widely as the ideal and actual social structures of these societies vary on whatever level of generalization one wishes to consider them. I have indicated above certain of these problems in connection with both traditional China and Tokugawa Japan. In traditional Chinese society virtually the whole structure of social control was a function of family solidarity. If the family got out of kilter, the whole society got out of kilter. In Tokugawa Japan on the other hand the relationship between family interests and the interest of one's overlord existed in a strong and flexible balance.[33] Quite apart from China and Japan, there always exists the problem of socialization of what one social scientist has referred to as the periodic barbarian invasion of every society—i.e., children. Any disturbance that interferes with these socialization processes threatens the general stability of the society.

The stability of any given relatively nonmodernized society may also be threatened by the activities of members of other societies. Most relatively nonmodernized societies have not ex-

---

[33] One of the strengths of the Tokugawa Shoguns lay precisely in the fact that they did not do what many people have accused them of trying to do. They did not try to get overwhelming centralization of everything. It would have cost them their rule had they tried to do so.

isted in total isolation. War is an extreme case of such interaction, but some of its implications for the stability of the societies whose members participate are both too numerous and too frequently commented on to require further mention here. Even in the absence of an extreme form of social action like war, acquaintance with structures of a strange and foreign nature, interaction with members of another society, etc., may pose problems of stability in terms of relatively nonmodernized societies. I do not intend to treat of these problems in any detail here. That is a special study in and of itself. I mention them because it is naïve to think that relatively nonmodernized people were not plagued with problems of stability before structures from relatively modernized societies were introduced. In trying to understand problems of modernization it is misleading to fail to separate out those problems that were functions of action in terms of the social structures as they were before contact and those problems that are functions of the contact of the existing structures with outside, relatively modernized influences.

B. PROBLEMS OF STABILITY AFTER CONTACT WITH THE STRUCTURES OF RELATIVELY MODERNIZED SOCIETIES

There is always a motive among the members of relatively nonmodernized societies for taking up some structures of modernization, with or without duress from outsiders. The problems of modernization of late-comers have almost uniformly been discussed in the context of imperialism. It so happens that all of the initial cases were in fact carried out under the spur of this particular sort of interference, but emphasis on this form of interference has grossly obscured the problems involved. Like most people today, I happen to detest imperialism as it has existed and have no desire to deny its evils. I do wish, however, to point out that the morals of imperialists are essentially irrelevant to the problems faced by members of relatively nonmodernized societies in contact with modernization. If there is contact, some set of members of that society will always attempt to take up some of those structures even if those structures are not forced upon them. They will do it for the following reasons: (1) There is no society whose members are in general unaware of material factors. (2) There is no society whose members fail to distinguish between being relatively better off and relatively worse off materially. (3) There is no society whose members in general do not prefer to be better off rather than worse off materially. (4) Peoples do vary widely, both within a given social context and from one context to another, with regard to the prices they are prepared to pay in order to be relatively better off materially and—even more importantly—in their *horizons* of such possibilities. Failure to envisage possibilities of improvement probably explain more of many alleged spiritual qualities than spiritual criteria which make people explicitly unwilling to pay prices for material improvement. One reason why increased use of money, as well as travel, is broadening is that the increased comparisons which result always extend the horizons of the possible. (5) Aesthetics, morals, and everything else to the contrary notwithstanding, the one respect in which the relatively modernized societies are always superior to the relatively nonmodernized societies, and by a considerable margin to boot, is the inordinate material productivity of their members following their ways. Once contact is made, therefore, there is always motivation for some of the members of a relatively nonmodernized society to try to take over some of the elements of the relatively modernized societies regardless of whether the initial contacts and the ensuing relations are imposed or voluntary. Unless the members of the relatively nonmodernized society are prevented from doing so by force, such attempts will always be made. Attempts to prevent them by force, short of extermination, have never been successful. (6) Furthermore, the elements common to all societies and the appreciation of some form of tools and inanimate sources of power by the members of any society guarantee that members of relatively nonmodernized societies will never be completely unable to comprehend at least some of the elements of greater material productivity with which they come in contact. In the desire to try these new methods the sources of instability inherent in the society concerned may be highly relevant. It may well be those members of a society who are most frustrated by the ordinary prevailing state of affairs who are most motivated to try the new, but someone would try something in any case.

Once the contacts are established, there will be some transfer of the relatively modernized structures to the relatively nonmodernized society.[34] When such transfers are made, they are inevitably subversive of the *status quo* of the relatively nonmodernized society, and usually explosively so. After these contacts, in addition to gradual erosion of some existing structures, many struc-

[34] Transfer of structures in the opposite direction need not concern the discussion now. Apart from occasional influences, the transfers are largely one-way.

tures with long pedigrees of stability begin to change with great rapidity.[35]

One of the most frequently cited problems bearing on social change is the so-called population explosion. I refer to the increase in the rate of population growth occasioned by the sudden drop in death rates that accompanies the introduction of modern medical technology, given much less resilient rates of fertility. Dramatic drops in the death rate can be effected quickly and cheaply. It is one of those material things which all relatively nonmodernized peoples seem to prefer and understand, at least in part. The birth rate never drops as rapidly as applications of modern medical technology can lower the death rate. Birth rates tend to be high and stable [e.g., averaging well over forty births per one thousand members of the population]. With sudden drops in the death rate—a large part of it in the lowered rates of infant mortality—the rate of natural increase for the members of such a society may easily jump from say five per thousand to twenty per thousand or more. The consequent rapid increase in population alone, especially since a good part of the increased population, initially at least, is in the least productive age brackets, poses all sorts of problems of order.[36]

Some of the problems posed by the population explosion are so obvious that for some they dominate the whole question of modernization. I would not want to detract one whit from the importance of this source of explosive implications, but it is by no means the only one. Even if we found a way to control the birth rate tomorrow by methods inoffensive to the people concerned, those methods would not preserve the general structures of relatively nonmodernized societies in their previous forms. There is still

[35] There is a tendency in considering questions of social change to imply that certain social factors are inherently slow changing as opposed to fast changing. This is not the case for at least two reasons: (1) The development of charismatic leadership can convert any social factor into a fast-changing one, though perhaps at catastrophic costs, and (2) social changes which knock out a key block in the retention of previously existing stresses and strains can be followed by spectacularly rapid alterations in general structures. Both of these sources of rapid change are quite familiar to students of the process of modernization. The second of these is, perhaps, far more likely than the first. In addition there may be all sorts of variations or approaches to both of these conditions which approach them in their implications for rapidity of change.

[36] Given a natural rate of increase of 2 per cent [i.e., 20/1000] a population will double in size in thirty-five years unless other factors intervene. Given a natural rate of increase of 3 per cent—a rate by no means out of the question—a population would double in only twenty-three years. It is not necessary to be a social scientist, a misanthrope, or a pessimist to see problems in such rates of growth.

ample reason to believe that the structures of every one of those societies would be revolutionized on extremely general levels and always in the direction of the structures of the highly modernized societies. In the modern world the problem par excellence for the members of every relatively nonmodernized society is modernization itself.

The various sources of explosive subversion of the structures of relatively nonmodernized societies will be explored throughout this work in summary below [see pp. 741–776]. I have tried to give here sufficient reasons why members of relatively nonmodernized societies cannot expect to avoid these problems. Once the contacts are made, attempts will be made to use some structures of the relatively modernized societies. Once those attempts are made, the existing structures will begin to disintegrate, some explosively. The structures of the relatively modernized societies do constitute for the first time in social history a sort of general social solvent for all other social types. This difficult aspect of the problem lies in the fact that although changes in the direction of modernization will always begin and although the subversion of the *status quo* will always reach a point of no return, successful achievement of the structures of modernization is by no means guaranteed. Indeed, conspicuously successful cases of latecomers have been few and far between.

The general subversive nature of the importation of the structures of modernization is discussed in some detail below [see pp. 741–776]. The argument there rests on four generalizations and distinguishes several basic sources of erosion. Here I shall only list the four generalizations and mention the major sources of erosion common to all of the relatively nonmodernized societies. The generalizations are as follows: (1) The structures of relatively modernized societies always will invade relatively nonmodernized societies if there is contact between the members of the two types of societies—regardless of whether force is employed to introduce them or they are taken up voluntarily. (2) The structures of relatively modernized societies can never be imported entirely piecemeal. Whether introduced by force or voluntary means, more is introduced than is bargained for or understood. (3) The structures of the relatively nonmodernized societies never coincide with those of the relatively modernized societies and are always incompatible with them to some extent. (4) Finally, with rare exceptions, the major sources of control in the relatively nonmodernized society are always eroded. Again this is independent of the intent of the members of either type of society.

Some of the most obvious sources of erosion are already implicit in what has been said in this and the preceding chapter. They are as follows: (1) The degree of specialization of organizations, (2) the decrease in self-sufficiency of the indigenous organizations, (3) changes in the emphases in relationships, (4) changes in family structures, (5) changes in literacy and the critical approach, (6) changes in the demographic situation,[37] and (7) increase in the generalization of the media of exchange and increase in the presence and specialization of markets. The history of no relatively nonmodernized society furnishes evidence which either disproves these generalizations or indicates that these sources of erosion are insignificant. The Japanese case furnishes us with one of the few instances of thoroughgoing latecomers who have coped with these problems with any high degree of success in terms of achieving a relatively modernized state, and that high degree of success was certainly related to their involvement in World War II. For the members of relatively nonmodernized societies in the modern world—whether they or we realize it, like it, or not—the major problem is how they will cope with modernization. All previous questions of instability, stability, social evil, etc., come to be important principally for their relevance in this context, whatever their consequences may have been before.

[37] Not only is the population explosion an increase in surviving infants, it also poses the problem of what to do with the aged. The number of surviving aged to be taken care of is also certain to increase radically.

PART II

ASPECTS OF SOCIAL STRUCTURE

ASPECTS OF ANY RELATIONSHIP

I
INTRODUCTION: DEFINITION AND EXPLANATION

This chapter gives explicit attention to a bit of analytic apparatus. I have developed it in greater detail elsewhere,[1] and I shall not try to reproduce it in full here. This will be the only chapter in this work devoted primarily to an analytic tool.

I define a *relationship* as any set of social structures that define the action, ideally and/or actually in terms of which two or more individual actors interact. I define a *social structure* as any pattern [i.e., as any observable uniformity] in terms of which social action takes place. I define *social* as the adjective descriptive of any phenomenon that is not adequately explicable [for the purpose in hand] in terms of the heredity of the species of actors involved and the nonspecies' environment. Since we are only interested in human societies here, *social action* refers to any action of human beings that is not adequately explicable in terms of human heredity and the nonhuman environment. Thus any structures of behavior that adequately describe, for whatever purposes, the interaction between two or more human beings also describes their social relationship, provided of course the structures are not adequately explicable in terms of human heredity and the nonhuman environment. The structures of interaction of two friends constitute a relationship; the interaction of individual faculty members of a university is in terms of various relationship structures; the operations of the members *qua* members of any large-scale enterprise, be it a business or governmental enterprise or whatever, involve a complicated set of relationships; etc. All relationships are social systems or membership units or concrete structures or organizations. The number of members may be as small as two or indefinitely large. The most restricted possible relationship is the most restricted possible social system,[2] and all social systems consist of one or more relationships, involving two or more members.

Since all social systems can be conceived of as sets of relationship structures, the analysis of them may be used as a tool for the

[1] *The Structure of Society*, Chap. 6.
[2] The most restricted possible social system would consist of structures interrelating only two members for a single act.

location of the more important social systems or organizations in terms of which social analysts must treat societies. The analysis of relationship structures is one of the tools with which we can combat the biases of ethnocentrism. There are certain social systems which we expect to find even if we study an unfamiliar society. We do not particularly expect to find these because there is anything "natural" about them, though this is frequently asserted. We expect to find them because we are familiar with them in our own experience and because most of the other societies with which we are familiar have also contained such organizations. Organizations such as families, governments, neighborhood units of various sorts, churches, business firms, friendship units, etc.— these are all organizations with which we are familiar. We are rather more surprised when we fail to find them elsewhere than when we do. Indeed, our initial approach to other societies is frequently to look for units of this sort. But there are also many types of units in many societies with which we are not at all familiar. It is quite impossible to approach any society without any conception of what you might find there. The idea that one deals with this sort of problem by approaching other peoples with a blank mind is a particularly virulent type of nonsense because it confuses inexplicitness with objectivity. To approach the analysis of any society [or of any other subject for that matter] with a completely blank mind would be like attempting to get to one's feet on a frictionless surface. In the latter case one would stay prone; in the former case one's mind would stay blank. Perhaps, if the members of that society were kindly, the person with a blank mind might be reared from scratch as though he were an infant and become thereby a member of their society but not an analyst of it.

In the absence of concepts of the specific types of units that are in fact present, one could always locate such units in a given society by observing the way in which individuals interrelate with one another and discovering which of these cluster in such fashion that one might refer to the people engaged as members of some common unit. This would be time consuming, but it would, in the long run, locate the organizations. Since we do not have blank minds and since there are some organizations common to all societies, we are never faced with the really costly problem of trying to locate all organizations by starting from scratch solely in terms of relationship structures. The analysis of any relationships is, however, useful as a tool when our preconceptions do not turn out to have a close fit with what we observe.

Another application of relationship structures is more important for present purposes. It leads to generalizations that cut across other distinctions and show common elements among them. For example, in the United States today, however different business firms and government may be, members of both organizations emphasize rationality, universalism, functional specificity, and avoidance. One can not only use these aspects of relationships to locate common features in different organizations of the sort just described; one can also use them to locate common features prominent in the conduct of different aspects of behavior. Again in the United States, outside of the family context the economic and political aspects of our behavior are, ideally speaking, carried out in terms of relationships which emphasize rationality, universalism, functional specificity, and avoidance. One may also use the same concepts to isolate variations across such lines. In the examples just given, although in business and governmental contexts we emphasize the same four aspects, and, I might add, relationships in both are hierarchically arranged, we usually expect business relationships to be predominantly individualistic whereas we expect government relationships to be predominantly responsible.[3] Thus in terms of all of the most general aspects of relationships developed here our business firms and government [and its subsystems] are identical, ideally speaking, except with regard to what will be called the "goal orientation" aspects [see below, pp. 147–149]. By no means all of the distinctions between business firms and government are explicable in terms of this one difference, but many are, and other differences are understandable in terms of differences in more specific forms of the aspects in which they are identical on more general levels. Though rationality is stressed by both businessmen and members of the government, the rationality concerns quite different matters, and so forth.

I I
ASPECTS OF ANY RELATIONSHIP

A. INTRODUCTION

The treatment here of aspects of any relationship is a development and adaptation of concepts that I have taken from the early work of Talcott Parsons. He, in turn, developed them partially on the basis of the work done by F. Töennies. The development here is not the form conceived by Töennies or favored by Parsons cur-

---

[3] The terms *individualistic* and *responsible* as used in this connection will be explained below.

rently. Nevertheless, Töennies indirectly and Parsons directly are the sources from which these developments came.[4]

In selecting subcategories of relationship structures two considerations are paramount. First, the distinctions should be ones that are relevant for *any* relationship. Second, the subsidiary categories or aspects should be ones in terms of which some variability is possible. If a given subcategory has only a unique value, it is only useful as a constant in hypotheses about all relationships and can only be a variable in distinctions between relationship and nonrelationship structures.

For present purposes we need aspects of relationships with subcategories capable of binary distinctions at least. Rather than binary distinctions, I have chosen polar distinctions which permit considerable variation in degree of approximation to one extreme form or another of a given aspect. These distinctions could be converted into binary ones, but only at the expense of leaving out the vast majority of cases I wish to treat since they are not at one extreme or the other.

It is also essential that the distinctions are not such that virtually all of the cases fall in one subcategory as opposed to the other or close to one pole of the distinction as opposed to the other. For example, one of the aspects chosen here is the *cognitive aspect*. One could distinguish among cognitive aspects of different relationships on the basis of whether or not explicit biological knowledge were involved. If one did, only a small number of all the relationships one would wish to analyze would be ones involving such knowledge. To think of relationships as

[4] In my book cited above I have discussed the distinctions between the scheme as presented there and that of Parsons. The differences are considerably greater today than they were then. In Parsons' work these aspects of relationships have developed into the famous "patterned variables." I have continued to use a form based on his earlier versions. The earlier versions [e.g., T. Parsons, "The Professions and Social Structure," *Social Forces*, vol. XVII, no. 4, May, 1939, reprinted, pp. 185–199, in T. Parsons: *Essays in Sociological Theory: Pure and Applied*, The Free Press, Glencoe, 1949], as qualified and amplified here are considerably less subject to confusion than the "patterned variables." There is another more technical reason for not using the present Parsonian version. Parsons insists that the distinctions drawn are binary distinctions. Thus a relationship is either *particularistic* or *universalistic*. Empirically this is simply not the case. The concepts so defined must always be used in a manner other than their definitions would lead one to expect. In fact the uses of the distinctions by Parsons in his own works and in that of his followers are almost always differences of degree rather than of kind. To insist that differences of degree are in fact differences of kind and to try to handle consequent overstatements by *ad hoc* qualifications to the effect that of course other elements are involved to some degree is to beg the very question one intends to answer.

biologically cognitive or nonbiologically cognitive would be useful only for extremely limited questions. We need some set of distinctions of greater general utility if the tool is to be generally applicable for the comparative analysis of any set of relationship structures.

Six aspects of any relationship have been distinguished here. They are (1) the cognitive aspect, (2) the membership criteria aspect, (3) the substantive definition aspect, (4) the affective aspect, (5) the goal orientation aspect, and (6) the stratification aspect. For each of these aspects a polar distinction is offered. Those are respectively (1) rational-traditional, (2) universalistic-particularistic, (3) functionally specific-functionally diffuse, (4) avoidant-intimate, (5) individualistic-responsible, and (6) hierarchical-nonhierarchical. These categories are defined and discussed below [pp. 138–152].

B. PROBLEMS ABOUT THESE CONCEPTS

There are considerable theoretical shortcomings about these concepts. First, I have no satisfactory theoretical explanation of why six and only six aspects are distinguished. Second, I have no satisfactory explanation of why this set of six rather than another set of six is presented. The only answer I have to such questions is that it can be shown that these six and their subcategories are in fact useful in formulating hypotheses. One may use them and get at a great number of distinctions, and those distinctions turn out to be generally relevant for social analysis and particularly relevant for the analysis of the problems of relatively modernized and relatively nonmodernized societies which are of interest in this work.

Third, I have insisted that these distinctions not be used as binary distinctions. Technically, however, in all six of the cases about which I have been able to be fairly precise, I have defined one extreme of the scale residually relative to the other. Thus perfect rationality is different in kind from any element of traditionality; perfect universalism is different in kind from any particularism; etc. Perfect instances of these extremes may not exist at all, and most of the cases of interest to us are not pure cases of the extremes. Actual classification of relationships in terms of any of these aspects is always to some degree a function of the observer's judgment, and that, to some extent, is always arbitrary. Moreover, for theoretical reasons discussed shortly, no relationship can ever be completely and purely universalistic, and it is unlikely that any relationship be completely and perfectly rational. Therefore, the differences dealt with here are differences of degree.

Moreover, it is quite useful in social analysis to distinguish whether ideal and/or actual emphases approach one extreme more closely than the other. Thus it is often useful to observe that employment structures characteristic of relatively modernized societies reflect overwhelming emphasis on universalism by contrast with those of other societies that reflect overwhelming emphasis on particularism. This is a relevant distinction despite the fact that there are *some* emphases on particularism, whether ideal or not, characteristic of even those relationships which reflect the most complete ideal structures of universalism in the most highly modernized society, and so forth. In general, to emphasize the nearly universal combinations of these elements a given relationship will be described as predominantly universalistic, rational, traditional, etc., if there is any possibility of confusion about whether the distinction intended is one of degree or kind.

C. USES OF THESE CONCEPTS

For the present two general uses of these concepts are asserted. First, as already mentioned, they can be used for the comparative analysis of any relationships. Implicit in this assertion, of course, is the assertion that they can be used to analyze any single relationship. Second, applications of the relationship aspects afford good reason to believe that different clusterings of certain of these relationship aspects are prominent features of societies. For example, if a relationship reflects heavy emphasis on rationality, it is likely also to be characterized by emphasis on universalism, functional specificity, and avoidance. This does not follow tautologically from the definition of the concepts involved. In the discussion of relatively modernized and relatively nonmodernized societies above, references have already been made to these relationship aspects. After detailed definition and illustration of these various aspects, their use for both comparative analysis and the formation of hypotheses about these clustering effects is discussed at some length.

D. RELATIONSHIP ASPECTS

1. COGNITIVE ASPECTS

Every relationship between two or more people involves some sort of knowledge, some sort of thinking, some sort of mental process, and that is defined here as its cognitive aspect. Subcategories of the cognitive aspects of any relationship are distinguished as follows: *rational* cognition is the kind of knowledge that, were it subjected to a theoretically omniscient scientific observer, would be found to violate none of the canons of science, that is to say, it would be in complete accord with the best scientific reasoning. Conclusions reached in terms of *traditional* cognition may coincide with conclusions reached on a purely rational basis. Even though this may often be the case, *traditional* cognition is defined as knowledge that is justified from the point of view of the individual who accepts it by argument to the effect that a given way of doing things is the prevailing and accepted way, and the way that should be continued because one's predecessors always did it that way. This is the essence of tradition in the social sense. Even when the conclusions of tradition coincide with those of rationality, the implications for action are importantly different. Having claimed this, let me go a bit behind this distinction and indicate some of the factors on which it rests.

This is one of those distinctions which, whatever its relevance to other species, is especially relevant to the human species. At the present stage of our development in the social sciences, it is fruitful to distinguish between the point of view of an observer and the point of view of an actor. The term *actor* is self-explanatory in this context. The term *observer* as used here is defined as a theoretically omniscient and objective scientific observer, literally a know-it-all. In considering any given act one may distinguish between the *end* of the act and the means [i.e., the methods, including use of materials] employed for that end. Either ends or means may be either empirical [i.e., can be analyzed in terms of sensory perception] or nonempirical. One may also distinguish as to whether from the point of view of the actor or the observer the ends and the means used are empirical or not. Thus if the action consists of going into a particular store to buy a pair of pliers, the end may be described as the purchase of a pair of pliers, and the means may be described as the selection of the particular store. Both ends and means are quite empirical. If the means selected by the actor are in fact adequate to the end he seeks, such action may be described as rational action. Even if he happens to have selected the wrong sort of store, such action is at least rationally oriented, although it is in fact *irrational*. On the other hand a given actor may simply pray that a pair of pliers be deposited on his desk. The end is still empirical, but the means contain an important nonempirical element. The physical act of prayer is quite empirical, but at least from the point of view of the actor the act of prayer is viewed as having some particular effect on some deity (ies) of some sort. This is quite nonempirical. The observer cannot tell one that he will not get a pair of pliers by use of such methods. The most that he can say is that many people who have behaved in that fashion have not ended up with pliers. There is no need here to elaborate on the various categories of nonrational and arational action which can be distinguished.[5] Value judgments such as the value of tradition itself in the last analysis always involve questions to which no observer can give a purely scientific answer.

In any social context the ultimate justifications of action from the point of view of the actors are standards of value to which no purely scientific solutions are possible. In this sense, if the range of action studied is enlarged, sooner or later one always encounters nonrational elements. Nevertheless, over a broad range of action, the selection of means may, ideally and/or actually, proceed much more importantly in purely scientific terms than not. When it does, I shall consider the emphasis, at least ideally speaking, to be on rational rather than on traditional action. The view that action should be as scientifically justifiable as possible is as much an evaluation as the view that action should be based on tradition as much as possible. Though both are evaluations which can be neither proved nor disproved by science, they are evaluations that have different implications for the actions of those who hold them. Those different implications can be studied scientifically and justify the distinction used here.

2. MEMBERSHIP CRITERIA ASPECTS

Every relationship is a system of action involving two or more actors who may be described as its membership. One may, therefore, always inquire why [or how] actors come to be members of such units. The reasons constitute the membership criteria. Following Parsons' early work, I have differentiated those into the two main categories of universalistic and particularistic. This distinction involves two lines of variation. The first has to do with the question of germaneness. Are the criteria concerned directly relevant to the purposes or main activities to be carried out in terms of the relationship? The second has to do with social barring. Is anyone prevented from participating in this particular relationship because of any social classifications which need not have anything to do with his abilities and/or accomplishments? The concept of social barring as used here is closely allied to the term *ascription* as it is ordinarily used by anthropologists and sociologists. Since to some extent one's life chances are always affected by one's kinship position, if one broadens the sphere of action enough, sooner or later, some criteria involving social barring come into play in every situation.

[5] For further elaboration see, *The Structure of Society*, pp. 240–248.

A relationship is defined as universalistic if the membership criteria contain no element of social barring and if they are germane. A relationship is defined as particularistic insofar as the membership criteria contain either nongermane elements, social barring, or some combination of the two. There are, therefore, three types of particularism: (1) *germane particularism,* i.e., involving social barring but germane criteria, (2) *capricious particularism,* i.e., involving no social barring but nongermane criteria, and (3) *ultimate particularism,* i.e., involving both social barring and nongermaneness.[6] I shall return to the three subcategories of particularism shortly. For the moment some more central considerations with regard to the basic distinction between universalism and particularism must be discussed. Membership criteria that tend to minimize but do not entirely eliminate particularistic elements will be called *predominantly universalistic.* Those that tend to minimize or eliminate universalistic elements will be called *predominantly particularistic.* Relationships may of course be ideally and/or actually *predominantly* universalistic or particularistic. The reason for insisting on these qualifications is simple. It is not difficult to find examples of relationships that are purely particularistic, ideally at least. The relationship between mother and son in many societies is such a relationship. Social barring is certainly involved. Unless a specifically different structure such as a structure of adoption is interposed, one and only one woman at any given point of time is eligible to stand in the relation to mother to a given son, if we define the term *mother* as it is defined in our own society. The criterion that only lords may join the hunt in a given forest is equally particularistic. A purely universalistic relationship is much more difficult to discover. As already mentioned, to some extent one's kinship position always affects one's life chances later on. Thus, if one considers the influences broadly enough, sooner or later one runs into some particularistic element since kinship considerations are inherently particularistic. On the other hand, *within a given setting,* the criteria concerned may be highly universalistic or even completely so, ideally speaking. For example, there are no doubt some particularistic elements in the determination of who is or is not admitted to Harvard College, but within the category of those admitted to Harvard College, admission to the Phi Beta Kappa honor society depends overwhelmingly, if not entirely, on

---

[6] The treatment of the cognitive aspects of relationships is an abridgement of the treatment presented in *The Structure of Society.* The treatment of the membership criteria aspects is an enlargement on the treatment there.

qualifications that are germane to the selection for this relationship and that are criteria from which no Harvard undergraduate
is socially barred.

In distinguishing between predominantly universalistic and
particularistic classifications one must keep in mind the distinction between ideal and actual structures. In our own society, for
example, relationships are frequently more nearly universalistic,
ideally speaking, than they are in fact. Whenever one classifies a
relationship as more or less particularistic or more or less nearly
universalistic, he must be prepared to elaborate on the following
questions if an explanation is called for: (1) From whose point
of view is the relationship so classified? (2) Is the relationship
so classified ideally and/or actually speaking, and again from
whose point of view? (3) Within what setting is the relationship
so classified?

Germane particularism may be defined as particularism in
which social barring is present, but the social barring itself is
highly relevant to the purposes of the relationship. Such a situation obtains in selection for succession to the throne of England.
There the relationship may be considered one of sovereign to
subject. At any given point in time, ideally and actually speaking,
one and only one person is eligible to succeed. Eligibility for that
succession is determined on the basis of kinship. The members of
Parliament can, if they wish, set the whole structure aside, but if
the system continues as at present, ideally speaking every individual save one at any given point in time is socially barred from
succeeding to the throne. Since one of the main functions of that
sovereign, however, is to symbolize a line of tradition and a family
responsibility for the welfare of England, etc., the criteria involved are germane to the purpose of the selection. To the extent
that such a situation obtains, a relationship will be considered
more or less germanely particularistic. It is important to distinguish this kind of particularism because it combines more readily
with a heavy emphasis on rationality than do the other types of
particularism. Ordinarily, for example, there is an important
element of kinship-oriented particularism in succession to positions of importance in a large number of family firms. The general emphasis on universalistic criteria may be great. Sons or
sons-in-law of the directors of these enterprises may in fact be set
aside if they do not have sufficient levels of ability, but there can
be little doubt that in most cases the fact that they are sons or
sons-in-law does give them a distinct differential advantage over
other possible competitors. If the level of ability which they in
fact achieve is sufficiently high and if to some extent the confi-

dence of people who deal with them is importantly oriented to continuation of the family line, these predominantly particularistic criteria for succession may be easily combined with a heavy emphasis on rationality and on predominantly universalistic criteria elsewhere in the firm.

Capricious particularism is a quixotic possibility. Criteria that involve no social barring but that are irrelevant to the purpose for which selection is made may be insisted upon. In consideration of all these types one must pay close attention to the relationship involved since what would be nongermane criteria for one relationship might very well be germane ones for another. For example, the insistence that redheads and only redheads be hired to operate the pumps in a gasoline station would probably fall under the category of capricious particularism. No member of a society like our own is socially barred from being a redhead. There are no preferential mating structures that make redheadedness especially unlikely, there is no discrimination against redheaded infants at birth, etc. But redheadedness is not germane to one's ability to run a filling station. On the other hand for certain types of color film processes redheadedness might conceivably be highly germane. Thus, what would be an emphasis on capricious particularism in the one case might be a heavy emphasis on universalistic criteria in another.

If the criteria involve both social barring and nongermaneness, the relationship may be considered *ultimately particularistic*. Many forms of social discrimination fall into this category. Typical is the kind of discrimination based on so-called racial or religious distinctions. These certainly involve social barring, and in many settings they are not germane to the purposes of the relationship unless that relationship be extended to include the preservation of racial or religious distinctions as a basis of social barring. This sort of particularism, of course, raises the greatest difficulties when other emphases are on rationality, functional specificity, etc.

For most of the general purposes in this work the broad distinction between predominantly universalistic and purely or predominantly particularistic relationships will suffice, but for more detailed applications, the additional subcategories will prove useful.

3. SUBSTANTIVE DEFINITION ASPECTS

The substantive definition aspects of a relationship have to do with the precision or lack of precision of the definition and delimitation of the relationship. This is one way of describing what is involved in the relationship. The categories distinguished here are functionally specific and functionally diffuse. A *functionally specific* relationship is one in terms of which the activities, considerations, rights, obligations, or performances that are covered by the relationship are precisely defined and delimited. The modern business contract relationship is a typical example of a predominantly functionally specific relationship. In a modern contract relationship, ideally speaking, an attempt is made to state explicitly everything covered by the particular relationship. All questions among the members of such a relationship [*in verbis legitimis:* parties to the relationship] are supposed to be settled by specific reference to the contractual document itself. The burden of proof is on whoever wishes to claim some additional obligation under the contract. To show that the special request is not covered by the contract is sufficient defense. It is obvious, of course, that all contracts are not perfectly clear-cut documents, but ideally speaking at least that is one of the criteria of a good contract.

A *functionally diffuse* relationship is one that is more or less vaguely defined and delimited. The relationship between husband and wife is always predominantly functionally diffuse. Frequently many elements in a husband-wife relationship are carefully defined, but the relationship is always to some extent vaguely delimited. If a new situation raises a question of how husband and wife should behave toward one another, it is not customary to settle such matters by seeing whether or not the situation is covered in the fine print of the marriage contract, even if there is one. When the emphasis is on functional specificity, the burden of proof is on anyone who wishes to justify an additional obligation. When the emphasis is on functional diffuseness, the burden of proof is on anyone who wishes to evade an additional obligation under the relationship. Justification of such evasion is not ordinarily based on what was clearly understood at the outset of the relationship, but rather on citation of some more important obligation to which prior allegiance is recognized.[7]

It is important to distinguish degrees of functional specificity and of functional diffuseness. One can characterize relationships as placing greater or lesser emphasis on one or the other of the

[7] In this connection, one must be careful about the use of the term *contract*. The modern business contract used as the example par excellence of a predominantly functionally specific relationship is quite a different matter from a marriage contract or a feudal contract. These contracts contain many elements of precise definition, but characteristically the extent of the relationships is vaguely delimited, even deliberately so.

extremes. Detailed and precise measurement of variations along the scale may be exceedingly difficult, but for many rough purposes a common sense reference to differences in the degree of emphasis will serve well enough. In this distinction as the others, the distinction between ideal and actual structures is also of the greatest importance.

Some of the worst misunderstandings about relationships occur when a relationship is predominantly functionally specific from the point of view of one member and predominantly functionally diffuse from the point of view of another. Thus, again, one must be prepared to give some indication of the point of view from which he is describing a relationship.

Some of the implications involved in this distinction and the other two previously made should be fairly obvious by now. To the extent that a relationship is or becomes functionally diffuse, it is difficult to emphasize rationality and universalistic criteria. After all, if one does not know in advance what is likely to be involved in a relationship, how can one emphasize rationality in its conduct or make selections on a predominantly universalistic basis?

4. AFFECTIVE ASPECTS

I do not feel at home with the concept of affect. The concept of affective aspects is an attempt to get at the kind of emotion, the degree of formality and informality, the feeling, etc., involved in a given relationship. Relationships among the members of any given society or as among the members of different societies vary considerably in the kind of emotional or affective displays made, the intensity of such displays which is expected and permitted, etc. There is no question but that the members of certain relationships are expected to emphasize elements easily recognizable as emotional displays and in considerable intensity. For example, a mother and son of our society are expected to love each other and to show it. The ticklish question for present purposes is whether or not there are nonaffective relationships, that is to say, relationships in terms of which no affectivity of any significance whatsoever is involved. This is a particularly important question if one wishes to handle relationships in a highly modernized society. In such societies there are an enormous number of relationships that are of the most fleeting and casual sort. To determine, either ideally or actually, whether precisely *no* emotional involvement is intended is even in principle a difficult proposition. Furthermore such a concept implies perfect indifference to a relationship of which one is at least in some sense aware. Such indifference is almost certainly a feat of affective virtuosity, and rare. For these reasons that concept is not used. The distinction used here is that between *avoidance* and *intimacy*. Here again the distinction is intended to be a polar distinction. Perhaps no relationship is at either pole, but the gamut that can be run is wide. It varies from relationships that are quite important for the parties concerned, but in terms of which the members must avoid any direct contact with one another, including seeing or being seen by one another, to relationships in terms of which direct, informal, almost constant contact with overt displays of emotion are both expected and demanded by the participants and/or by other members of the society. The relationship between mother and infant in all societies is likely to be intimate in this latter sense. Relations between ruler and subject or sacred figure and true believers often approximate the former.

The relationship between husband and wife is a predominantly intimate one in the modern United States. It is also predominantly intimate in some contexts in traditional China, but in the latter case it is far less so than in the former. There are also many social contexts in traditional China in which the relationship is not supposed to be an intimate one at all. According to strict Confucian etiquette the husband and wife are expected to display genuine avoidance in many contexts. The term *avoidance* may be used to cover relationships that, ideally and/or actually, are supposed to be devoid of emotional involvement as well as those in terms of which the emotional involvement is supposed to be considerable though minimizing overt contacts, etc. The most highly avoidant affect is probably that generally referred to as respect. The opposite of respect is probably contempt, and it is not a matter of chance that there is a wise old saw in many languages which holds that "familiarity breeds contempt." With regard to this aspect of relationships, as with the others, the prefix predominantly will be used. A relationship will be termed predominantly avoidant if it is one in terms of which the members or others emphasize restraint and/or formality in the overt display of affect and/or subordinate the overt display of affect to other aspects of the relationship. A relationship will be termed predominantly intimate if it is one in terms of which the members or others emphasize lack of restraint and informality in the overt display of affect and/or subordinate other aspects of the relationship to the overt display of affect. These affects may be of many different sorts. As indicated above, respect is one of the easiest affects to reconcile with avoidance; love, as that term is frequently understood, is one of the easiest to reconcile with intimacy.

For all the problems involved in their use, the concepts of

avoidance and intimacy provide a highly generalized distinction among relationships in terms of their affective aspects. The distinction has been chosen because of its general relevance to the analysis of social structure. The line of theoretical speculation that justifies this particular choice may be briefly stated as follows. In all social contexts situations arise in which the unrestrained display of emotional responses would or could be highly disruptive. There are also situations in which overt emotional expression is to a high degree adaptive in its implications. Current work in the field of personality development would seem to indicate that rather lavish informal displays of affection for infants and children are critical for the development of stable adult personalities. The distinction used here is based largely on the distinction between types of regulation of affective expression and hence is germane to this sort of consideration. More specifically, in all societies the structures of allocation of power and responsibility are of central importance. Furthermore, there are always some situations in which a premium is placed upon the efficient and even rapid exercise of power. Even slightly uninhibited displays of emotion can be extremely disruptive in such situations. Hence it may be argued that in all such situations the institutionalization of predominantly avoidant rather than predominantly intimate relationships is of adaptive significance for the members of the organizations involved. One of the most obvious cases of such a relationship is that between superiors and subordinates in military organizations. That is by no means the only case. Similar factors are involved in the relationship between a traditional Chinese father and his son. Because of the manner in which the family structures of traditional China fits into the total social structure of Chinese society, the strength of the father-son relationship is far more important than in modern American society. In general, whenever the intimate type of affective expression is not a central element of the substantive definition of the relationship, or at least whenever it is subordinated to other aspects of such a definition of the relationship, a premium is placed upon avoidant affects. It is not enough to repress intimacy in such situations; formal modes of affective expression are also needed. Because of the ubiquitous relevance of such considerations as these, the particular polar dichotomy suggested here has been selected.

5. GOAL ORIENTATION ASPECTS

The goal orientation aspect of a relationship focuses attention on some of what might be called motivational aspects of the relationship. Insofar as the ends sought in terms of a relationship are manifest to one or all of the members of the relationship, what can be said about them which is generally useful in analysis? The concepts used here are *individualistic* and *responsible*. A given relationship is more or less *individualistic* to the degree that each of the members of the relationship may be expected to calculate how best to secure his own maximum advantage from action in terms of the relationship without regard to the goals sought by the other members of the relationship. A given relationship is more or less *responsible* to the degree that each of the members of the relationship is expected to safeguard, even at the expense of some of his own goals, the relevant goals of the other members of the relationship. Again these are polar terms. Pure cases of either extreme, if they exist, constitute only a small proportion of the relationships in any society. The use of the prefix predominantly is of service here as in the other categories. A relationship will be called *predominantly individualistic* if the emphasis is placed on each member of the relationship looking out for himself. A relationship will be called *predominantly responsible* if the emphasis is placed on one [or more] of the members of the relationship safeguarding the relevant goals of the others if he is [or they are] to achieve his [or their] own goals at all. This distinction has nothing whatsoever to do with egoism or altruism, nor with selfishness or the lack of it. A relationship may be so structured that even the most selfish person must make sure that the other members of the relationship realize their goals if he is to realize his. Correspondingly, one of the most altruistic of men in terms of another type of relationship may have to take the attitude that each other member must look out for himself. Ideally speaking, for example, the most selfish of doctors *has* to behave responsibly in this sense towards his patients. On the other hand, a business-man who intends to give all of his profits away to charity must nevertheless continue to be a driver of hard bargains if he is to compete successfully for profits.

Illustrations used here will be compared in greater detail below. A business relationship in the United States today is, ideally speaking, a predominantly individualistic one. Each member is expected to seek to maximize his own interests. The relationship is not devoid of responsible elements. Presumably negotiations are carried out in terms of a general framework of honesty. Straight misrepresentation is fraud, as is payment with a bad check. On the other hand, if the buyer is willing to pay twice as much as would be necessary if he knew the situation better, the seller is not necessarily expected to enlighten him or to price the property at the going-rate despite his customer's ignorance. Students of social change could no doubt trace an interesting development of the businessman-customer relationship in the United States. At no time was the maxim of *caveat emptor* completely without limit. Members of the judiciary stood ready to act on certain practices classified as illegitimate. Nevertheless, the change has certainly been marked, and deals that were commonplace in the heyday of "captains of industry" would be considered unethical today. Despite these changes, the good businessman is expected to be able to take care of himself and is not expected to look out for the interests of others. If his concern for the interest of others exceeds the expected levels of probity, and if that concern is to the detriment of his own interests, whatever may be the evaluation of him in other respects, he has shown himself to be a poor businessman, perhaps even something of a fool.

On the other hand, the doctor-patient relationship may be described as a predominantly responsible one. Ideally speaking, the doctor is expected to protect his patient's interests. The doctor is not only expected to avoid direct misrepresentation. The doctor is also expected to protect the patient from the patient's own ignorance. If the patient wishes an unnecessary operation, the doctor, whether to his own financial hurt or no, is expected to refuse to perform it. If the accepted scale of fees for patients of a given income group is five dollars a visit, it is not ethical for a doctor to charge such a patient ten dollars simply because the patient is ignorant of the situation. Again it must be insisted that this tells one nothing of the personal character of the doctor. A doctor who scrupulously observes such standards may be selfish in the extreme, and the businessman who follows the others may be the soul of generosity. The practice of medicine is, however, differently structured than the conduct of business. The achievement of success in terms of the one is in part dependent upon the observance of this type of responsibility, and in terms of the other it is in part dependent upon the observance of this type of individualism. Two men almost identical in their personal ambitions for money, power, and prestige will behave quite differently in these respects if one is a doctor and the other a businessman. There is in all this every indication that socially acceptable behavior may be independent of individual personality factors to a high degree.

6. STRATIFICATION ASPECTS

This aspect is considerably simpler than those discussed above. *Stratification* may be defined as the particular type of role differentiation that distinguishes between higher and lower standing in terms of one or more criteria. In some relationships one member of the relationship is expected to have a higher ranking than another. The relationship between a traditional Chinese father and his son is of this type. There are also relationships such that, regardless of the rank of the members in their other roles, as members of this particular relationship their ranking is either considered equal or any question of differences in rank is considered irrelevant.

A relationship of the former type will be called a *hierarchical* one. A hierarchical relationship is defined as one for which the relative rankings of the members are different and in terms of which action is distinguished with regard to this ranking. The latter type of relationship mentioned above will be called a nonhierarchical one. A nonhierarchical relationship is one in terms of which no differential rankings of the members in any respect are considered relevant to the relationship. When the relationship is one such that its members are specifically expected to treat one another without reference to differential rankings, it will be termed *egalitarian*. The term egalitarian is used to distinguish this type of relationship from those in which differences in rank are irrelevant but are so simply by lack of definition of the relationship in this respect, e.g., in which the members are neither equals nor unequals ideally speaking.

Varying degrees of hierarchical relationships are familiar enough to require little or no comment. The example of a traditional Chinese father and his son has been given, but other examples are even more obvious. The relationship between officers and enlisted men, professors and associate-professors, employer and employee, union leader and union member, etc., are definitely of this sort. Nonhierarchical and egalitarian relationships are somewhat harder to find. Probably only relationships of short duration and ones such that any specific case of the relationship is socially defined as unimportant are nonhierarchical relationships of a nonegalitarian sort. So pervasive are rank-order structures and so strategic, if not crucial, are they structurally speaking that strong, explicit structures are usually required to keep hierarchical considerations out of the picture. Furthermore, only in rather fleeting relationships, specific cases of which matter little, would it be possible to have no definite structuring of hierarchical elements because of the great relevance of such elements to any action in terms of the relationship. Relationships of the casual-meeting or crowd-contact sort would fall into this category. This is not to argue that such relationships in the aggregate are unimportant for the society in which they occur. No relatively modernized society could exist unless a tremendous amount of action in terms of it could be carried out on the basis of the casual-meeting type of relationship. On the other hand, in many relatively nonmodernized social contexts relationships of this sort are relatively infrequent, and any great expansion of such relationships would probably be a source of disorganization.

Egalitarian relationships, though considerably less frequent than the hierarchical ones, are quite familiar to most people. Friendship is generally a relationship of this order in relatively modernized societies. Friends are expected to treat one another as equals and to consider one another as such regardless of other factors.[8] Strong egalitarian elements often enter relationships that are in other respects hierarchical. In some respects the members of a university faculty are equals despite the fact that the hierarchy of professors, associate professors, assistant professors, and instructors is of great significance to us. The faculty situation tenses instantly if we feel that the hierarchical aspects are being pushed beyond their proper sphere. The emphasis on egalitarianism in the face of hierarchical distinctions is perhaps symbolized by the official university use of the term of address Professor for all three ranks of the professor category, and by the fact that faculty members among themselves frequently avoid such terms altogether and use the more neutral term Mister.

Particularly among those who believe or profess belief in democracy there are some misconceptions about hierarchical relationships. The overwhelming proportion of all relationships in all societies contain hierarchical elements both ideally and actually. In fact, it is difficult for most individuals to give examples, apart from friendship, of relationships that are ideally and/or actually egalitarian. Family relationships certainly aren't; bureaucratic relationships aren't; relationships within the government rarely are; universities aren't; business firms aren't, etc. For men to be "equal before the law" does not imply a lack of hierarchy "before the law." A judge may *order* the defendent or the plaintiff, etc. It is common for those interested in either social analysis or social welfare to confuse predominantly universalistic criteria for treat-

[8] During World War II the egalitarian character of friendship as opposed to the hierarchical character of the officer–enlisted-man relationship was a frequent theme of conflict in comic strips, in the movies, on the radio, etc. Bosom friends who met but could not eat together because of the military distinction appeared in all sorts of stories. Whether or not old friends in uniform, meeting in a nonmilitary context, could treat one another as equals became, as it were, a test of the strength of the friendship, etc.

ment with egalitarian relationships. Societies could not persist on an egalitarian basis, nor could any other social system of any considerable membership or importance from the point of view of its members and other members in the society. Relatively modernized societies could not exist at all if social structures combining predominantly universalistic emphases and hierarchical ones did not exist in great and varied panoply.[9]

For comparative purposes the distinctions concerned with the stratification aspects of relationships are often quite revealing. Military systems seem on the whole to have been strictly hierarchical if their members were successful. But other relationships show greater variations from one context to another. Take, for example, the husband-wife relationship. Although modern, urban, middle-class Americans do not regard the relationship, ideally speaking, as egalitarian, they at least favor as close an approach to egalitarianism in this relationship as men have ever achieved. In traditional China it was definitely a hierarchical relationship with the husband much more highly ranked than the wife. There are cases in which the relationship is hierarchical but with the wife ranked well above her husband in most respects. With factual knowledge of only these three differences with regard to one aspect of one type of relationship, one can make a considerable number of predictions about other differences that must exist in these social contexts.[10]

E. APPLICATIONS

1. INTRODUCTION

First, the concepts discussed above are such that some statements can be made about any relationship, in any society, at any time in terms of them. This means questions asked about these concepts are always capable of yielding some answers relevant for comparative purposes. Second, they have been devised to illuminate the part played by specific relationships in more general social systems. Finally, like most sets of scientific concepts, these are designed to make possible the greatest accumulation of defensible knowledge about a given type of phenomena with the least amount of effort and to have that knowledge of maximum general relevance to the development of further generalized

[9] See below, pp. 296–300 and 670–671.

[10] Predictions based on these three facts taken alone might be extremely risky, but they would tell something, and the more such facts one has, the less risky prediction becomes.

knowledge about the field concerned. More specifically, however, this set of concepts is useful because it provides a framework in terms of which one may analyze and describe any single relationship and compare the following: (1) different types of relationships in a single society, (2) similar types of relationships in different societies, and (3) different types of relationships in different societies. For the purposes of rapid sketching of examples the following table has been set up:

TABLE 1

	X	Y
1. Cognitive aspects	Rational	Traditional
2. Membership criteria aspects	Universalistic	Particularistic
3. Substantive definition aspects	Functionally specific	Functionally diffuse
4. Affective aspects	Avoidant	Intimate
5. Goal orientation aspects	Individualistic	Responsible
6. Stratification aspects	Hierarchical	Nonhierarchical

The symbol X_1 will be used for rational [i.e., predominantly rational], the symbol Y_1 for traditional [i.e., predominantly traditional], X_2 will be used for predominantly universalistic, etc. I devised the notation to make certain typical clustering effects which will be discussed below more readily obvious, but apart from this, it is arbitrary. One could mix the various polar types between the X and Y columns at random or change the order of the rows. To do so would make the discussion a bit more cumbersome, but it would not change the implications or the meaning of the discussion in any way. Using the notation as set up, a relationship that is described as $X_1, X_2, X_3, X_4, X_5, X_6$ is a relationship that is predominantly rational in its cognitive aspects, predominantly universalistic in its membership criteria aspects, predominantly functionally specific in its substantive definition aspects, predominantly avoidant in its affective aspects, predominantly individualistic in its goal orientation aspects, and predominantly hierarchical in its stratification aspects.

In order to illustrate the use of these concepts and this notation I shall compare: (1) the doctor-patient relationship and the businessman-customer relationship in modern United States society, (2) the businessman-customer relationship in modern United States society and in traditional China, and (3) the businessman-customer relationship in modern United States society and the gentry father-son relationship in traditional China.[11]

2. EXAMPLES

a. THE DOCTOR-PATIENT AND THE BUSINESSMAN-CUSTOMER RELATIONSHIPS IN MODERN UNITED STATES SOCIETY

The doctor-patient relationship may be described in the terms used here as X_1, X_2, X_3, X_4, Y_5, Y_6. Ideally speaking, the doctor is expected to employ rational techniques in his treatment of the patient. It is well understood that, given the limitations of knowledge and the fallibility of man, the doctor sometimes acts irrationally, but the range of irrational actions is limited, and attempts are made to limit them further. Many medical errors are considered inescapable and nonculpable, but others, for example, repeated failures to diagnose correctly common ailments appearing in common uncomplicated forms, are likely to result in pressures of some sort being brought to bear on the doctor. Some irrational actions are considered sufficiently egregious to be grounds for civil suits against the doctor, and some are even grounds for his loss of license to practice. The latter form of discipline is relatively rare, probably because of the reluctance of qualified personnel to testify. This reluctance is by no means wholly understandable in terms of a "guild" or "There but for the grace of God go I" feeling. It is, at least in part, understandable in terms of the reluctance to shake by such exposure the element of public confidence in medical men. This element of confidence is certainly vital to the current forms of medical practice. Whether it would be broken down or bolstered by more frequent exposures of this sort is as yet an undetermined point. The fact that overt sanctions are not so evident as might seem justified on the basis of expressed licensing standards, medical

[11] These relationships have been chosen to illustrate the three major comparative applications of this scheme of analysis. I do not wish at this point to get sidetracked into any discussion of the validity of the assertions made about any of the relationships. I have not knowingly misrepresented any of the structures, but my hypotheses about the facts may be false.

The material used on the doctor-patient relationship was first brought to my attention in lectures delivered at Harvard by Professor Talcott Parsons more years ago than either of us cares to remember. Much of the material also appears in his article already cited above [p. 136] as one of the original sources for the development of this particular taxonomy of relationship structures. Professor Parsons is, of course, not to be held responsible for the present form of this material or any of the uses made of it despite the indebtedness of this treatment to his work.

I have not bothered to illustrate the analysis of a single relationship separately because that analysis can be illustrated by the description of the first two relationships discussed below.

society membership criteria, etc., does not mean that sanctions of this sort are totally lacking.

Doctors may in fact act nonrationally, or traditionally as the term is used here, in their treatment of patients. The use of traditional techniques which are not necessarily rationally justified is either definitely condemned or is not considered proper to the relationship. The complete substitution by a doctor of nonempirical means for empirical ones in the treatment of a patient is never sanctioned. Nonempirical means of some sort, for example prayers in terms of one of the established religious systems of society, are acceptable as a means supplementary to the application of scientific knowledge, but such activities are definitely not a central part of the relationship. They may be tolerated, sometimes even approved, but they are not required. Nonempirical means of other sorts are strongly condemned and are considered applications of superstitions or magic, both of which are felt to have no place in this field and to be bad. Doctors frequently carry out practices because that is the way they have been done in the past, but the usual traditional arguments are not considered justifications in this field. The argument, "We have always done it that way, and it's a good way to do it because we've always done it that way," is not in general acceptable. The argument, "We have not yet got a better scientific way of doing this than the one we have been using for quite some time," is as far as medical ethics permit the doctor to go.[12]

The patient on his side is also expected to act rationally in the following respects. He is expected to choose his physician on the basis of predominantly universalistic criteria. This involves an element of rationality since there is rationality involved in the process of understanding what criteria are germane to the end sought and in the process of judgment as to whether the doctor chosen in fact measures up to such criteria. Another rational element enters from the patient's point of view in that he is expected to know within limits when it is and is not necessary to consult his doctor [i.e., initiate the relationship], and he is expected to follow his doctor's orders rationally. The emphasis on

[12] As is well known, this is an area in which there is great pressure on the professional man to act. In similar circumstances in many societies, magical practices are frequent. They are specifically denigrated in the medical sphere. It is not a matter of accident that medical faddism is so prominent a phenomenon. Many wise doctors have pointed out that the most difficult thing for a doctor to do when his knowledge is inadequate is literally to do nothing. Fortunately, perhaps, the constantly changing nature of medical faddism—in this respect it is almost exactly the opposite of magical practices—probably minimizes any harm done by uncritical pursuit of any particular medical fad.

his rationality, however, is much less well institutionalized [13] than for the doctor.

The doctor-patient relationship is, ideally speaking, a predominantly universalistic one. The patient is expected to choose his doctor on grounds of competence and availability. The doctor is expected, within quite broad limits, to accept patients on the basis of need for treatment. These ideal structures often fail to coincide with actual ones. Patients often choose or reject doctors on bases that are medically irrelevant. Such considerations may range from liking a doctor's looks to not liking his political or religious affiliations. Doctors, on the other hand, sometimes choose or reject their patients on the basis of the patient's ability to pay, social position, etc. Again, the structure seems to be better institutionalized for the doctors than for the patient in both conformity and sanction aspects. Although the ideal structures are often violated from both points of view, the remarkable feature of the situation is that they are not violated more often, given, among other relevant factors, on the one hand the medical ignorance of the patient and on the other hand the tremendous relevance of monetary income as a symbol of success in such societies.

Ideally speaking, the relationship is functionally specific. It is the doctor's obligation to do what he can medically for the patient, and all of his orders and access to the patient must be justifiable on the grounds of their relevance to the patient's health. The patient on his part is expected to follow the doctor's orders [and to pay his fees unless he is being treated on a charity basis]. The doctor with respect to fixing fees is expected to take into consideration the patient's ability to pay. Often functionally diffuse elements creep into the relationship, particularly in the case of the general practitioner or family doctor, who may be a close friend and advisor of the patient in matters otherwise as well as medical. The appearance of functionally diffuse elements in the relation-

[13] The term *institution* is defined as a normative pattern, conformity with which is generally to be expected, and failure to conform with which is generally met with the moral indignation of those individuals who belong to the same general social system and are aware of the failure—or by some other sanctions from that source. The term normative pattern refers simply to any pattern involving a standard of conduct. Thus, "men should have only one wife at a given point in time," "no one should bully anyone else," "patients should select their doctors on the basis of their medical qualifications," etc., are normative patterns. A normative pattern may be more or less well institutionalized with regard to the level of conformity expected in terms of it or the degree and kind of moral indignation and sanctions which greet a failure to live up to this ideal structure. There is an extended discussion of this concept in the *Structure of Society*, pp. 101–109. The details of that discussion need not detain us here. All institutions in this sense are social structures.

ship almost inevitably go hand in hand with predominantly intimate rather than predominantly avoidant structures. Again, the
lead in breakdowns in these respects is more likely to be taken by
the patient than by the doctor.

The relationship is ideally a predominantly avoidant one; the
more so the more it is strictly confined to medical matters. Departures on the doctor's part are only in theory justified if they
contribute to the patient's health. Departures on the patient's
part may range from the often unobjectionable combining of a
friendship relationship with that of doctor and patient, to excur-
sions into intimacy of a sort most strongly condemned. Both
doctor and patient may be strongly condemned for some of these
departures in the direction of intimacy, and the profession as a
whole, as well as the public, is well aware of this. Doctors are so
thoroughly aware of it that elaborate precautions and procedures
have been set up to eliminate such breakdowns.

The relationship is ideally predominantly responsible rather
than individualistic. The doctor rather than the patient is primarily concerned here since he has the more active role in the
relationship. The whole structure of prestige in the medical profession is so set up as to require even the most selfish of doctors to
place the interests of his patients, both actual and potential,
before any goals of his own that do not involve their medical
welfare. The selfish doctor dares not acquire a widespread reputation for demanding assurance of payment before treating an
emergency case or for ordering profitable but medically unnecessary operations and the like. Again, the experts in the field are
reluctant to testify openly in such cases, but the sanctions
brought to bear are none the less strong. The patient on his part is
expected to heed the doctor's advice and pay his fees, but the
question of individualism or responsibility is not quite so relevant
from the patient's point of view, since he has little possibility of
sacrificing the doctor's interest for his own. Both he and the
doctor in theory share the end of restoring the patient's health.
Other goals such as minimizing the doctor's fee, etc., are not
supposed to enter since the doctor's responsibility covers making
such fees reasonable.

Finally, the relationship is of a relatively nonhierarchical sort.
Of course, the roles are sharply differentiated, but as far as
general social standing the doctor may be of either higher or
lower rank than the patient. In theory at least, none of the action
takes place because one member of the relationship is a superior
of the other in any power sense. A doctor's orders are not orders in
the ordinary sense that implies an enforcement agency outside

the person ordered and the possibility of orders not to the subordinate's best interest. Ideally, the doctor's orders are given the patient only so that the patient may achieve his own goal, i.e., restoration or maintenance of health. The only hierarchical aspect involved, ideally speaking, is that of medical knowledge, but even this is by no means a hard and fast requirement since doctors are usually patients of doctors other than themselves, sometimes of less able ones. However the members of the society as a whole may rank doctors relative to patients, and in this there is certainly a hierarchical element, the treatment by the doctor of the patient, ideally speaking, is determined by medical criteria and not by criteria of any other relative social standing.[14]

The relationship between a businessman and his customer in the modern United States may be described as an X_1, X_2, X_3, X_4, X_5, and Y_6. Both the businessman and his customer are expected to deal rationally with one another. Not to do so is bad business, and in terms of this relationship both parties are expected to behave in a businesslike fashion. Irrational action on the part of either member is the mark of a fool. Traditional action or other departures from rationality in general, simply are not considered good business, and in some cases come in for harsh criticism. The emphasis on rationality in the businessman-customer relationship is by no means complete. Some important traditional elements are still maintained, but the trend is overwhelmingly in the opposite direction. The mark par excellence of maintenance of traditional emphases is likely to be the presence of a family firm, but these in the old fashioned sense are becoming increasingly rare in all highly modernized societies.

The criteria for membership in the relation are predominantly universalistic. Both parties are expected to pick fellow members on the basis best calculated to serve the empirical ends sought.

[14] There is not space here to go into the question of how these peculiar structures developed or what their implications may be. It is important, however, to keep in mind the fact that the doctor-patient relationship, as we take it for granted, is a peculiar and unusual relationship in world history. To an unusual degree one member has a great deal of knowledge relative to the other member's concern, and the other member usually has little knowledge. In that sense the doctor could potentially do the patient great harm, if he took advantage of his knowledge. It is also interesting to keep in mind that we permit the doctor a kind of access to our bodies that is literally permitted to no one else in the society. Such access is deemed vital to modern medical treatment, but such access made available to any one on a nonmedical basis would immediately raise questions of proper conduct in general and of proper sexual behavior in particular. It is not a matter of chance that members of modern societies feel so strongly about doctors or that so much attention is given to the way in which the doctor-patient relationship is exemplified.

The businessman seeks to make a profit; the customer seeks to get the best possible value for his money. To refuse to sell at a profit to second generation Scandinavian citizens because one does not like them is bad business, as is refusal to buy from them on this ground. There are many departures from these standards by both types of members, but such departures become increasingly less common as business becomes large scale. Representatives of large-scale firms such as some of the automobile manufacturers would find insuperable obstacles in trying to enforce such predominantly particularistic criteria. Individual customers find their effect in such matters negligible and such activities likely to fall into the category of "cutting off your nose to spite your face." The accepted criteria for businessmen in selecting customers is their ability to pay, and that of customers in selecting businessmen is the ability to deliver the best goods at the lowest price.

The relationship is generally kept as functionally specific as possible. Ideally speaking, it is perfectly so from both points of view. The contract relationship is the archetype of this quality. If a contract is vague, it is a bad contract, at least from the point of view of the person who may find added unanticipated obligations as a result of such vagueness. In only a fraction of such relationships are actual contracts drawn, but the usual structures of a one-price market makes such things quite clear. A customer buys a soft drink. His obligation is confined to the payment of the price; the dealer's obligation is to deliver the product as defined by quite specific standards. If there is an insect in the drink, the dealer is liable; if the payment is less than the stated price, the customer is liable. To leave the obligations of such a relationship vague is always potentially bad business from someone's point of view.

Ideally speaking, the relationship is a predominantly avoidant one. Often there are departures in the direction of intimacy, but these departures are more likely to characterize small firms with a restricted, relatively unchanging set of customers. On the whole, the attitude in this respect is that business is business and that emotional involvement with one's customers, insofar as it is permissible, becomes inadmissible if it interferes with the profit goals of enterprise. Roughly the same situation exists from the customer's point of view.

The relationship is a predominantly individualistic one. It is not, however, completely individualistic with a completely unhindered *caveat emptor* outlook. There are restrictions on both parties. Certain standards of honesty, for example, are not only expected but are enforceable at law. Yet, neither member is held responsible for protecting the other against his own ignorance as is the case with the doctor-patient relationship. Within a certain framework of mutual regard for each other's interests, the businessman and his customer operate on an "every man for himself" basis. Ideally, this is never true of the doctor's relation with his patient.

Finally, this relationship is, ideally, nonhierarchical and in some respects even egalitarian. The customer has neither higher nor lower rank than the businessman in general, and of course, one individual may at any time be playing both roles in different operations. Ideally the members of such relationships deal with one another as equals. Proof of deliberate tinkering with this equality may be the basis for setting aside such transactions legally. Much of the antimonopoly legislation rests on the legal philosophy that the parties to a valid contract should be equals from many points of view for the purposes of that transaction. Of course there are many departures from the ideal structures in this respect.

I shall now compare these two relationships briefly on three levels. First, I shall compare them on the most general level discussed here. In that comparison the basic difference between the doctor-patient and the businessman-customer relationship lies in the fact that the former is predominantly responsible and the latter is predominantly individualistic. On this level the two relationships are identical in all other five aspects. Now, there is considerable feeling that the doctor-patient relationship, ideally as well as actually, is different from that of the businessman and his customer. For purposes of comparative analysis of the two, it is best first to see how much of the differences between the two can be explained in terms of the difference between X_5 and Y_5. Some of the differences, which we feel so strongly should and do exist, hinge on this difference at this level.

If differences on the most general level are not sufficient to explain the differences we wish to understand, we must proceed to the second level of analysis. Both relationships institutionalize structures of predominantly rational action and predominantly universalistic criteria. The specific contents of the rationality and of the universalistic criteria are, however, quite different. In the one case rational action is oriented to the restoration and maintenance of health, and in the other it is oriented to the allocation of goods and/or services. In other words, both are predominantly rational but their members are interested in rationality about different matters. In theory at least, those differences between the two relationships which are not explicable in terms of differences between X's and Y's [i.e., differences on the most general level] may be explicable in terms of the differing contents of the similar X's or Y's [e.g., both of the relationships described here are predominantly rational, but about quite different matters]. If the second level differences are insufficient to explain the differences noted between two relationships being compared, then one of four possibilities remains: (1) differences on the first level of generalization have been overlooked, (2) differences on the second level of generalization have been overlooked, (3) the list of aspects of relationships needs reformulation and/or additions at least on lower levels of generalization, or (4) some combination of the three foregoing difficulties is present.

In the third of the foregoing possibilities lies the third level of comparison mentioned above. If two relationships are in fact different in their structures but also in fact identical on the two levels of procedure cited above, the difference must be in aspects of one or the other or both of the relationships not given in the original list of six aspects. Even if the relationships are not identical on the two levels previously cited, additional differences on this third level may still be present. Any failure to explain differences between relationships on the previous two levels should lead to exploration of this third level. Its exploration may also lead to further development by discovering an aspect(s) which is (are) empirically observable in *any* relationship and hence should be added to the original list of six aspects.[15]

It is possible to discuss the doctor-patient relationship at great length, and its contrast with that of the businessman-customer in modern United States society is revealing about both spheres and about the society in general, but most of the relevant differences between these two relationships are, in fact, to be subsumed under either the most general differences in the goal orientations aspects and lower level differences in the other aspects.

---

[15] Two colleagues, Miss Kazuko Tsurumi and Mr. Andrew Effrat, have suggested further developments of this scheme. Miss Tsurumi has suggested a *communications aspect* with a polar distinction between *secret* and *open* relationships. Mr. Effrat in an unpublished paper has suggested a *volitional aspect* with a distinction between voluntaristic and non-voluntaristic relationships plus some six mixed forms. Both suggestions are promising, but I have not explored them enough to use them here. One of the rough rules of thumb of theory, however, is that once one exceeds six or seven distinctions on any one level [and these two aspects would give us eight] some more general less complicated level should be sought.

b. THE BUSINESSMAN-CUSTOMER RELATIONSHIP IN MODERN UNITED STATES SOCIETY AND IN TRADITIONAL CHINA

The material on the businessman-customer relationship in modern United States society need not be repeated. In traditional China the relationship took one of two forms. If the relationship was the expected predominantly particularistic one, it took the form $Y_1, Y_2, Y_3, X_4, Y_5, X_6$. Ideally speaking, it was expected to be based on particularistic criteria such as friendship, family connections, and neighborhood considerations which were already present or established by a go-between. If predominantly particularistic connections of this sort did not exist the relationship was likely to take the form $X_1, X_2, X_3, X_4, X_5, X_6$.

This difference between the businessman-customer relationship in China when based on predominantly particularistic rather than on predominantly universalistic criteria of choice, explains many differences in accounts as to the reliability or honesty of the Chinese businessman. If he were dealing with a friend or relative or family members who had dealt with his family members for years, or a person from his own village or a person introduced by a go-between who possessed one or some combination of these connections with both businessman and customer, the businessman emphasized the preservation of the relationship. He operated in a predominantly traditional fashion. The relationship was by definition highly particularistic, but it was also predominantly functionally diffuse. Extra requests by the customer might well be granted. Although something like friendship might dominate the relationship and displays of affect in terms of it were by no means out of the question, it must be borne in mind that the members of that society generally placed a heavy emphasis on highly formalized predominantly avoidant relationships. Given the fact that, ideally speaking, the position of merchant was frequently a lowly one, the relationship might be prominently avoidant. Most importantly, it was a highly responsible relationship. The merchant was expected to protect his customer at all costs even to the extent of his own financial ruin in some extreme cases. The relationship might be hierarchical in different ways. If the merchant were dealing with a gentry customer, the relationship was certainly hierarchical with the customer of higher rank than the merchant, of course. In other cases it might be hierarchical in the opposite direction. The differences between ideal and actual structures were especially important. In the strictest ideal sense the merchants ranked below gentry, peasants, and artisans. Actually, of course, if they were at all well off, they certainly outranked the latter two as well as many of the gentry.

On the other hand, if the expected predominantly particularistic connections did not exist, the picture was almost exactly opposite. A ruthlessly *caveat emptor* situation existed and was carried as an ordinary matter to an extreme that United States businessmen have not tolerated for some decades. Indeed, if the businessman could get by with it, his attitude was not simply "every man for himself," but rather " 'It's every man for himself and God for us all,' said the elephant as he danced among the chickens." Under these circumstances both businessman and customer acted as rationally as possible in an attempt to maximize their material gains from the relationship. The relationship was as functionally specific as either party could make it to his own advantage, and it was an avoidant one. It was ruthlessly individualistic, and that within a framework in which force and fraud were only limited by what the parties concerned thought they could get by with. It would be hierarchical with each party attempting to utilize hierarchical factors to secure an advantage. Thus, insofar as possible, it becomes a relationship of the X_1, X_2, X_3, X_4, X_5, and X_6 type. It must be emphasized that it was not institutionally expected that the businessman-customer relationship would be of this second type, and the Chinese tried to avoid this type of relationship if they could possibly do so. Cases of it, however, were frequently observable. If one entered such a relationship without establishing proper predominantly particularistic grounds either directly or via a go-between and was badly treated in terms of it, one was considered a fool for having gotten oneself involved in such a situation in the first place.

In comparing the businessman-customer relationship in modern United States society and in traditional China, one should first consider the differences in the relationship in China. Here the distinctions are almost, if not completely, understandable in terms of differences on the most general level of relationship aspects. In comparing either of the Chinese structures with those of the United States, differences on both the most general level and the second level of generalization mentioned above are significant. These relationships have been set up in Table 2, below, along with several others for ease of comparison.

In this tabular form, it is immediately obvious that the differences between Type A and Type B in traditional China apparently lie on the most general level since the structures tend to opposite poles except with regard to the possibilities of variation in the affective and the stratification aspects. The differences between Type A and the United States type again lie apparently almost wholly on the first level of procedure, but the differences between

TABLE 2

RELATIONSHIP	RELATIONSHIP ASPECTS					
	1	2	3	4	5	6
(1) Doctor-patient	X	X	X	X	Y	Y(?)
(2) U.S. businessman-customer	X	X	X	X	X	Y
(3) Traditional Chinese businessman-customer Type A	Y	Y	Y	X	Y	X
(4) Type B	X	X	X	X	X	X
(5) U.S. husband-wife	Y	Y	Y	Y	Y	X
(6) Traditional Chinese husband-wife	Y	Y	Y	X(Y)	Y	X
(7) U.S. employer-employee	X	X	X	X	X	X
(8) Traditional Chinese employer-employee	Y	Y	Y	X	Y	X
(9) U.S. lawyer-client	X	X	X	X	Y	Y(?)
(10) U.S. architect-client	X	X	X	X	Y	Y(?)
(11) U.S. father-son	Y	Y	Y	Y	Y	X
(12) Traditional Chinese father-son	Y	Y	Y	X	Y	X
(13) Japanese Emperor-Crown Prince Old	Y	Y	Y	X	Y	X
(14) New	Y	Y	Y	Y	Y	X
(15) Engineer-client	X	X	X	X	Y	Y(?)
(16) Certified public accountant-client	X	X	X	X	Y	Y(?)

Type B and the United States type obviously must be sought in considerable part on the second level of generalization or on the third [i.e., in some additions to the list of relevant aspects]. Actually, in comparison of the United States type and Type B the differences lies largely in differences in the cognitive aspects and the goal orientation aspects, both of which on the first level emphasize rationality and individualism. Most of the differences may be subsumed under the goal orientation aspects. The much greater individualism possible in Type B behavior in China makes it possible for the cognitive aspects to be far more ruthlessly rational than would be countenanced in the modern United States case. Approved rationality in the latter case does not permit taking into consideration the possible rational implications of applications of force and fraud as in the Chinese Type B. The differences between Type A Chinese relationships and the United States type are the ones conventionally associated with discussions of the contrast between traditional Chinese ways of doing business and modern, "objective," etc., forms of businessman-customer relationships.

C. THE BUSINESSMAN-CUSTOMER RELATIONSHIP IN MODERN UNITED STATES SOCIETY AND THE FATHER-SON RELATIONSHIP IN TRADITIONAL CHINA The United States businessman-customer relationship has already been described above. It takes the form X_1, X_2, X_3, X_4, X_5, and Y_6. The father-son relationship in traditional China takes the form Y_1, Y_2, Y_3, X_4, Y_5, and X_6. On the most general level these different types of relationships in different societies have only one element, predominantly avoidant affective aspects [X_4], in common. On the most general level the relationships are almost wholly different from one another, but there are critical differences on lower levels as well. For example, the matters about which the members of the one emphasize rationality and those of the other emphasize tradition are quite different. Even in the one similarity on the most general level, there are differences on lower levels, since the types and degrees of avoidance are quite different. Whether this particular comparison is interesting may be doubtful. Some comparisons of radically different types of relationships in different types of societies are, however, of considerable importance.

d. OTHER EXAMPLES In Table 2 additional examples have been given For example, the employer-employee relationship in the United States is ideally expected to take the form X_1, X_2, X_3, X_4, X_5, and X_6. Insofar as one can speak about the employer-employee relationship in most of the relatively nonmodernized areas, those relationships, ideally speaking, take the form Y_1, Y_2, Y_3, X_4, Y_5, and X_6 as illustrated by the employer-employee relationship in traditional China. The husband-wife relationship in the United States ideally takes the form Y_1, Y_2, Y_3, Y_4, Y_5, and X_6.[16]

[16] That is to say, even in the United States there is still a vestigial expectation that the relationship be a hierarchical one with some male precedence. Some might argue that Y_6 should be substituted here, taking the position that this relationship should be an egalitarian one. Whatever *should be* the case, even in America, the relationship retains hierarchical elements [with male precedence] even ideally speaking. It may also be argued that the pressure is not toward egalitarianism but toward female precedence.

Since this set of concepts can be used to analyze *any* two or more different relationships, it follows that it can also be used to analyze the same type of relationship at different points in time. Thus it can be used to analyze questions of changes in a given relationship over any given span of time. For example, a dramatic change has recently been reported in the structures of the Royal Family in Japan. This appears in Table 2 as the example of the relationship between the Japanese Emperor [or the Crown Prince] and the Emperor's [or Crown Prince's son, i.e., the present or future Crown Prince] according to previous custom and present practice. In the old days that relationship took the form Y_1, Y_2, Y_3, X_4, Y_5, and X_6. According to the present reported decision of the Crown Prince to rear his own son within a more ordinary modern family setting in Japan, the relationship would now take the form Y_1, Y_2, Y_3, Y_4, Y_5, and X_6. There is every reason to believe that the relationship between the present Crown Prince and his son will be a predominantly intimate one at least by contrast with the overwhelmingly avoidant one previously characteristic of this relationship.[17]

For purposes of comparison, Table 2 also includes the husband-wife relationship in the United States and in traditional China, the lawyer-client relationship in the United States, the architect-client relationship in the United States, the engineer-client relationship in the United States, the certified public accountant-client relationship in the United States, the father-son relationship in the United States, and the father-son relationship in traditional China. Given the detailed illustrations above, these should be sufficiently clear to support subsequent allusions to them.

I I I
USE OF THE RELATIONSHIP ASPECTS
FOR THEORY FORMATION

A. GENERAL EXAMPLES

The examples given above illustrate comparative analysis of different types of relationships in terms of the concepts suggested here. Four sources of differences have been suggested. Differences arise from: (1) differences on the most general level [i.e., differences in X or Y classification], (2) differences on lower levels of generalization [i.e., the relationships whether similar or different on the most general level may be different in the kind

---

[17] Under previous custom the Imperial children were literally reared almost entirely by persons who were not their parents.

and/or degree of "X-ness" or "Y-ness"], (3) differences in aspects on the most general level of relationships or on lower levels for which no concepts have been provided [i.e., aspects of any relationship or of specific ones not included in the present list of six general aspects], or (4) some combination of the three foregoing differences. The diverse choice of relationships used for illustrations constitutes an attempt to indicate that *any* relationships, however different or similar, in the same or different societies can be compared usefully in these terms. Insofar as analysis of this sort is successful, one in effect forms theories [or gets useful insights, if one prefers], by locating differences in relationships that are relevant to the analysis, whatever the purpose of the analysis may be.

Inferences drawn from the comparison of the doctor-patient and businessman-customer relationships illustrate this. As modernization increases, if a considerable amount of decision about the allocation of goods and services is left in the hands of members of private enterprises, there is nevertheless observable a continual increase in the level of bureaucratization of those private enterprises. This increase has caused growing talk about the professionalization of the business role. The patterns of X's and Y's characteristic of the doctor-patient relationship are also characteristic of a substantial number of so-called professional man-client relationships. For example, the lawyer-client relationship is, ideally speaking of the same form, and so are those of architect and client, certified public accountant and client, and engineer and client. There are important differences among all of them on the second level of generalization, e.g., they are not expected to be rational about the same matters, but the one difference between all of them and the ordinary businessman-customer [including other businessmen] relationship is that they are predominantly responsible. Given the line of analysis suggested here and the history of the well-established professions, the inference is that, as the professionalization of the business role increases, the most general alteration in the relationship of businessmen with their customers [including other businessmen] will be an increase in emphasis on the responsibility of the more expert members of those relationships for the interest of all others involved in them.[18] Modern business history shows an increase in emphasis on responsibility by contrast with individualism. Probably noth-

[18] One can generalize as follows: All relationships characterized by high emphases on rationality will involve members who have a high probability of being cognitive equals or will be characterized by high emphases on responsibility or will be instable.

ing else is more characteristic of the discipline of the modern business school, and few themes appear more frequently in the pronouncements of leading business figures. Even so marked lapses such as those implicit in recent alleged violations of standard and generally accepted antimonopoly rules continue to crop up,[19] the ticklish question in modern business development is not *whether* such increases in emphasis on responsibility will take place, but only *how* they will take place.

In many spheres this development has gone quite far. Veblen made much of the concept of sabotage as deliberate interference with efficiency for the sake of profit. It was Veblen's irony that a word developed from a desperate labor practice of throwing a wooden shoe into machinery to confound businessmen should be applied to business practices. Today some of Veblen's irony has come full circle. For many business leaders, particularly those associated with communications, the use of "strategic withdrawals of efficiency" to gain profit are virtually out of the question. The range of choice open to labor leaders is often larger than the range of choice open to business leaders. Certainly there are emphases on individualism in the relationships between union leaders and their "customers," whether those customers be representatives of their own government or of private business firms which are at least the equal of any emphasis on individualism characteristic of other businesslike leaders in our society.

The prediction of increased emphasis on predominantly responsible goal orientations can be broadened. Not only will there be an increase in emphasis on responsibility in businessman-customer [including other businessmen] relationships, but the same will also be increasingly true of relationships involving any leaders strategically placed in terms of bureaucratic organizations of considerable relevance to the allocation of goods and/or services. Thus there will be an increasing emphasis on responsibility in the relationships between union leaders and the customers of labor and between governmental leaders whose policy decisions can seriously affect economic allocations and members of all other organizations whether those be local, state, or federal agencies on the one hand, or private enterprises or labor unions on the other. At present, the major differences of these relationships from professionalized relationships in the ordinary sense

[19] Even in these instances, however, the reaction of the accused parties, much of the general reaction of other businessmen, and certainly that of the general public is censorious of such behavior to a degree hard to imagine some decades ago. Sworn testimony in court established clearly that many, if not all, of those convicted of these lapses were violating explicitly professed standards of their organizations.

inhere overwhelmingly in the emphasis on individualism as opposed to responsibility. In every bureaucratic sphere of any importance in which the emphasis, either ideally or actually, on individualism continues at a high level that emphasis is shifting in the direction of an emphasis on responsibility. With all increases in modernization it will continue to do so, if the systems concerned are to be stable and probably even if they are not. From this one may draw a still further inference, a riskier one: With the increase of modernization and the attendant increase of bureaucratization, all roles in bureaucracies tend to become increasingly professionalized.

I shall give one further example of such theorizing. The major difference between the traditional Chinese father-son relationship and the United States father-son relationship, is that the latter is predominantly intimate and the former is predominantly avoidant. There has already been considerable discussion of family developments in relatively modernized societies as opposed to relatively nonmodernized ones above, and there will be more below [pp. 377–435]. Suffice it to say here that in all increasingly modernized social contexts there will be an increasing emphasis on intimacy in the father-son relationship, if that emphasis did not exist before. The attempt of the Chinese Communists to carry out their commune policies in greatest detail does not alter the tenability of this proposition. It is characteristic of all other societies as they change in the direction of modernization.

B. THE CLUSTERING EFFECT

Inspection of Table 2 discloses clusters of relationship aspects. If a relationship is predominantly X in any of the first three aspects it is predominantly X in the other two and correspondingly with the Y aspects. Furthermore, if there is any X in any one of the first three aspects there is an X in the fourth aspect as well.[20] What does such clustering mean? If an emphasis on rationality, universalism, functional specificity, and avoidance must go together *by definition,* and if an emphasis on tradition, particularism, and functional diffuseness must go together *by definition,* such clustering effects would add nothing to what we already know. But, they do not cluster by definition. Emphases on rationality, functional specificity, universalism, and avoidance are likely to cluster, and if they fail to, one can make further predictions from

[20] It does not follow that if there is an X in the fourth aspect that there are X's in the first three. Although one can generalize to the effect that if there is X_1 or X_2 or X_3, there is also X_4, one can not generalize to the effect that if there is Y_1 or Y_2 or Y_3, there is usually Y_4.

that variation. When rationality is involved, both ends and means must be empirical and to a high degree explicit. Functionally diffuse elements are likely to interfere with rational emphases and force inclusion of traditional or nonrational elements if only by adding vagueness to an otherwise explicit situation. Again rational factors are likely to be interfered with by particularistic selections, especially if the particularism is not germane particularism, since such selection will not maximize or safeguard the ability of the members of the relationship to carry out rational action in terms of the relationship. Intimacy, as opposed to avoidance, is more likely to involve departures in the direction of traditionality [or nonrationality], functional diffuseness, and particularism. It is difficult to confine activity to rational considerations or to specifically defined and delimited factors or to objective selections when a person is intimately involved with others. These four elements by no means always go together. For example, rather close approaches to universalism are sometimes maintained by picking wives for one's sons, whereas this relationship may be and commonly is, predominantly traditional, functionally diffuse, and intimate. Also there may be radical differences between the ideal structures and the actual structures of the relationships. The ideal structures of relationships that are predominantly X in the first four categories are extremely difficult to live up to. One of the major developments in social science in the twentieth century came from the developments of the Harvard Business School studies of just such questions. The famous studies by Roethlisberger and Dickson [21] stressed the importance of the entry of particularistic considerations even into settings that were ideally speaking predominantly universalistic.

In Part I, above, one of the major distinctions between relatively modernized and relatively nonmodernized societies was the different emphases in different spheres that the members of those societies placed on the X and Y forms of the relationship aspects. Throughout this work, there is a great deal of hypothesizing that the role of changing emphases on different clusters of the relationship aspects is of the first importance in the transition from relatively nonmodernized to relatively modernized societies. Many problems of the transitions can be understood in these terms. The exploration of just how these relationship aspects tend to cluster and under what conditions these and other clusterings take place, has only recently begun in social science. The two major clustering effects illustrated in Table 2 may be rather

[21] F. J. Roethlisberger and William J. Dickson, *Management and the Worker*, Harvard University Press, Cambridge, 1941.

confidently relied upon. For any relationship in which there is a switch in emphasis from a Y to an X category in any of the first three aspects, one should expect a shift from an emphasis on a Y category to an X category in the other two as well. There would also be a switch toward X_4 if the emphasis was previously on Y_4. If such a switch does not take place, or if one finds an emphasis on an X in any one of the first three aspects and not in the other of the first four, he can draw one of two possible inferences: (1) the relationship concerned will prove to be highly unstable, or (2) it will be fitted into and buttressed by other relationships in a peculiar fashion.[22]

There is another general avenue for theory formation in these terms. Certain emphases on relationship aspects are characteristic not only of different societies but more importantly of their various subsystems. This has many implications for general theories of social change. One of the major reasons that the structures of relatively modernized societies are in fact a sort of universal social solvent of the social structures of other societies is that for certain structures likely to be imitated intentionally or unintentionally, the members of relatively modernized societies emphasize X qualities in the first four aspects whereas members of most of the relatively nonmodernized societies emphasize Y qualities in at least the first three aspects. Moreover, the disintegrative impact of the importation of such structures is never confined to the minimal departures from emphasis on the Y categories necessary to establish firmly an emphasis on the X categories for altogether new relationships. The disintegration may go quite far even though the emphases on the X category are not at all firmly established. For example, contrary to many sentimental views, the stability of the traditional Chinese family did not inhere in the fact that it was a type of family devoid of stressful implications for its members. The stresses and strains on family members were of considerable intensity at different periods of their lives, but there were many reasons why relatively few people attempted to run away. One of those reasons certainly had to do with the fact that they had little or no place to go. Ordinary employment was in a family context on, of course, predominantly particularistic grounds. If one sought employment elsewhere, there was also a heavy emphasis on particularistic

[22] In changes in relationship aspects generally it makes a great deal of difference not only whether there is a switch from an X emphasis to a Y emphasis [or vice versa] or from one type of X emphasis to another [e.g. from an emphasis on rationality about health to one about wealth], but also the sequence of changes is important especially when clustering effects are relevant.

criteria. One of the main criteria was a person's filial character. A runaway defied family structures and was for that reason alone not to be trusted. The possibility of viable alternative employment on relatively objective grounds, if one defied one's family head and fled, hardly existed. Family rebels were likely to be forced into the byways of the society in terms of which life, though rarely solitary, was likely to be nasty, brutish, and short. With the coming of the structures of relatively modernized societies, for the first time in two thousand years, the possibility of viable alternative employment on relatively objective grounds began to crop up. The threat of the disaffected to run away unless treated better became an effective possibility.[23] The modification of the authority of the family head was far-reaching. This was one of the reasons why family structures, relatively stable for two thousand years, had already begun to change radically long before the Communist regime, despite the fact that the actual development of modernization in terms of large numbers of modern factories and the like was modest.

I V
FINAL CAUTION

Let me recapitulate and warn about the use of this tool. First, it is a set of categories in terms of which any relationship in any society can be analyzed. Second, it is a tool in terms of which any two or more relationships or any particular relationship at different points in time can be compared with one another. Third, it is a tool that provides a systematic procedure for seeking out some of the major differences and similarities relevant to any particular problem. Fourth, even elementary applications of the tool for purposes of illustration reveal that certain of these relationship aspects tend to cluster with one another. Fifth, certain types of clusters are characteristic of some social systems and not of others. Sixth, the fact that certain of these clusters are characteristic of some subsystems and not of others has considerable relevance for theories of social change in general and for those of change from relatively nonmodernized societies to relatively modernized societies in particular. Given the state of the social sciences, none of these claims is modest, but I would claim more and maintain that it is quite unlikely that either the problems of modernization of relatively nonmodernized peoples or the prob-

[23] In addition, the Chinese family was the only general structure of social insurance for the aged. If the son ran away and was able to establish himself elsewhere, he not only won his own freedom, he also left his father and mother, if they survived into old age, without anyone to take care of them.

lems of stability of highly modernized peoples can be studied at all without some form of these concepts being explicit or implicit in the analysis.

There are, however, two major cautions which anyone should observe in using this tool of analysis. First, as I have tried to indicate nontechnically, it is by no means a perfectly developed tool of analysis. There are serious problems of a theoretical nature in its present state of development—let alone its further refinement and development. As a set of scientific concepts, it leaves a great deal to be desired. Second, insofar as it is at all well developed, critical acumen is still necessary. In the treatment above I have stressed again and again that combinations of say universalistic and particularistic elements are more likely than pure cases of either, even if pure cases are possible. It is, therefore, always legitimate for anyone to inquire "Why has this particular relationship been classified as 'predominantly,' or even 'more,' X_1 than Y_1?" In answering such a question one must specify not only what the criteria for such judgments are but also the set of actors alleged to make these emphases. For example, if I claim that the relationships between employer and employee in the United States today are predominantly universalistic, I may justify it by saying that, ideally speaking, from the point of view of virtually everyone in the society, the feeling is that no one should be barred from employment on the basis of race, creed, or color and that the only legitimate criteria are the possession of skills relevant to the job for which selection is being made. Any of those empirical allegations is subject to either confirmation or disproof.

In addition to the justification of the classification of a structure as predominantly X rather than predominantly Y there is also another kind of comparison. One may wish to maintain that the emphasis in the United States doctor-patient relationship is predominantly X_1, whereas that in the traditional Chinese doctor-patient relationship is predominantly Y_1. If challenged, one must be prepared not only to substantiate the classifications in the sense discussed immediately above, but also to say in what respect, if any, one justifies differences in the comparison as between the American and the Chinese case. If the emphasis is predominantly X_1 in one case and a predominantly Y_1 in the other, such justifications are relatively simple. If both are predominantly X_1 relationships, the statement that one of them is more predominantly X_1 than the other may be difficult to demonstrate. Nevertheless, it is at least in principle possible to make such statements. For example, with regard to the employer-employee relationship in ordinary manufacturing concerns in the United States by contrast with those in Japan there are far more elements of functional diffuseness in the Japanese than in the American case. In many areas of Japanese production the acceptance of a job and the acceptance for a job imply a lasting obligation of employee to employer and vice versa. This is a less prominent feature of the Japanese labor market than once was the case, but it is often still the case. In this sense the relationship between employer and employee is less precisely delimited in the Japanese than in the United States case.[24]

This tool of analysis shares a common tragic defect with all tools of analysis. No matter how infatuated one may become with it, it is never a substitute for either hard work or good ideas. Within any given frame of creativity and hard work, however, its use does at least facilitate the development of implications.

[24] Once again I must emphasize that the statements of fact in this illustration may not be tenable, but at least in theory they are susceptible of confirmation or disproof.

ASPECTS OF ANY SOCIETY—INTRODUCTION

I

THE DISTINCTION BETWEEN ASPECTS OF SOCIAL SYSTEMS
AND SOCIAL SYSTEMS (OR ORGANIZATIONS).

A. DEFINITION OF TERMS

This distinction has been presented above [pp. 19–26] and need
not be elaborated in technical detail. Social systems are defined as
sets of structures [i.e., patterns] that define the character of
membership units in terms of which social actions take place,
that is, units such that any given individual may be classified as
included or excluded [or some combination of the two] as a
member of the unit. Terms used here such as society, nation,
business firm, government, family units, etc., all refer to such
systems or organizations. These units are referred to technically
as *concrete structures.* What are here referred to as *aspects* of
societies or of other social systems or of organizations are referred
to technically as *analytic structures.* They are defined as patterned ways of looking at action that are not even theoretically
capable of physical separation from other ways of viewing action.
If one seeks a physical analogy to this distinction, *concrete* structures or systems refer to units such as tables, chairs, etc.; the
analytic structures or aspects refer to such concepts as the mass,
the shape, the color, etc., of the tables, chairs, etc.

B. EXPLANATION OF THE DISTINCTION

The use of this distinction is above all justified by virtue of the
fact that it avoids certain confusions. No social analysis can
proceed far without some reference to membership units of some
sort, be they as simple as some two-person relationships or as
apparently complicated as large-scale societies. Sooner or later in
social analysis one always must make reference to membership
units in terms of which actions take place. More often than not it
is sooner rather than later since only a peculiarly sophisticated
discussant of social affairs can begin his discussion in so abstract
a fashion as to refer to no social systems whatsoever. One may be
as preoccupied with process or change as he likes, but he cannot
discuss it without referring to process or change in terms of

something. That something in the social field will be some sort of social system. It holds equally that, although one may break down any given social system into subsystems which make it up, sooner or later, either in making distinctions among subsystems or in talking about the subsystems so distinguished, one must refer to some of their different aspects. The two aspects most generally discussed in the realm of international affairs are the economic aspects and the political ones. If one defines the economic aspects as having to do with the allocation of goods and services and the political aspects as having to do with the allocation of power and responsibility, and most explicit definitions of these two terms come quite close to these definitions, these terms do not refer to acts *in toto* but rather to particular ways of looking at such acts. The exchange of a watch for fifty dollars is an empirical act. One may be interested in it primarily as an exchange of goods, but that way of looking at that particular act by no means exhausts its implications. For example, if one of the parties to the exchange is holding a gun and the other party hands over his watch in exchange for fifty dollars, the implications of the exchange are quite different, even though fifty dollars has been given for the watch in this case too. If the gun is used threateningly, one might infer that the watch is worth a great deal more to the original owner than fifty dollars and that he would not have made this exchange save under duress. There is no exchange of goods or services that takes place in the complete absence of some allocation of power and responsibility and vice versa. This example is given to demonstrate that what are generally referred to as economic and political factors are never different things and are always relevant to one another. These two aspects of behavior are by no means the only two with such high mutual relevance. For present purposes I shall discuss five of these aspects. The five discussed here form a special list of aspects of *any* society, selected for their relevance to all societies.[1]

Insofar as one must, for purposes of analysis, deal with two or more such aspects as these, one commits a serious scientific fallacy if he asserts or implies that he exhaust the implications of any actual behavior by analyzing it solely or primarily in terms of one of these aspects. Indeed one does so even if he is interested in only implications for one of these aspects. It is exactly this fallacy that has been referred to as the fallacy of reification or the fallacy

[1] The argument for that relevance, mentioned in the introduction of this work, is pursued in *The Structure of Society* at great length. It need not be discussed here where the concepts are used as tools and not as a central focus of interest.

of misplaced concreteness. It is involved in the confusion of economic man with man [i.e., actual man]. The statement that man is by no means identical with the assumptions of economic man is not to imply that the restrictive assumptions of the latter are of no relevance for scientific development. It no more implies that than the statement that "terrestrial objects do not generally fall in a perfect vacuum" implies that a vacuum assumption is of no relevance to terrestrial physics. Since it is impossible to analyze any social phenomena [or other phenomena for that matter] scientifically without reference to both sorts of distinction made here, it is especially important to make sure that the fallacy of reification is avoided.

I have already indicated [pp. 23–25] that one of the major reasons for confusion on the score is that most of the people who indulge in scientific social analysis are used to societies in terms of which the specialization of many organizations in terms of a single one of these aspects has been carried so far that relatively less violence is done to the analysis by referring to them as though they were purely economic or purely political systems. I refer to such organizations as predominantly economically oriented, predominantly politically oriented, etc., to avoid such confusions. Such specialized organizations are by no means totally absent in relatively nonmodernized societies, but they are relatively rare especially by contrast with the frequency with which they appear as subsystems of relatively modernized societies. If one falls into the habit of using such terms as economic, political, etc., solely with regard to such highly specialized organizations, he must face up to the fact that he will have to forego almost totally their application save in restricted spheres in relatively nonmodernized societies and abandon them even in some critically important spheres of relatively modernized societies. In the context of most of the relatively nonmodernized societies, for example, most of what in a loose way is characterized as economic behavior in relatively modernized societies would disappear into action in terms of family units. Only the most extreme economic determinists undertake to describe family systems as predominantly economically oriented throughout history. Though verbally clumsy, the distinction as presented here, enables one to handle any of the distinctions that one ordinarily wishes to refer to in relatively modernized societies, many distinctions which ordinarily are glossed over even in relatively modernized societies, and either specialized cases or general cases in relatively nonmodernized societies. It also enables one to avoid the fallacy of reification from this source.

The remainder of this chapter consists of a list of the five aspects used here with a definition of the concepts involved and a brief illustration of each category. Following that there is a brief addendum. The remaining five chapters of this part consist of a detailed discussion of each aspect with many of its subcategories. Since these categories refer to aspects that are necessary [or requisites] for any society, obviously much of the discussion in Part IV about common elements in all societies consists primarily of a restatement of some of the observations in the following five chapters.

I I
LIST OF ASPECTS

A. ROLE DIFFERENTIATION

Technically the term *role differentiation* refers to any socially distinguished position. For present purposes, suffice it to say that role differentiation is concerned with who does what when. There is no society, there never has been any society, and there never will be any society all of whose members always do the same thing all of the time. That is to say, there is no such thing as a society devoid of structures of role differentiation. The number of different positions distinguished by the members of different societies varies widely. For example, the members of some of the highly modernized societies distinguish several hundred thousand occupational roles alone, whereas the members of most of the relatively nonmodernized societies have never distinguished more than a fraction as many roles in the occupational sphere. In all societies which persist, there will be definite structures of role differentiation because: (1) there are differentiated activities which must be performed if the society is to persist; (2) these activities must be assigned to capable persons trained and motivated to carry them out; (3) not all individuals are capable at all times of performing all requisite activities, and some are even incapable of performing activities on which their own survival depends; and (4) even were all individuals equally capable at all times, it would not be possible for each and every individual to carry on simultaneously all the activities that must be done if the society is to persist.

The set of roles which characterize the society, however, does not define a membership unit in the sense that that term is used here. It merely defines an aspect of social action that is observable in all such action. It defines an aspect of any social unit, but it does not define all of the aspects of any unit. There are no units the members of which do exactly the same thing all the time.

Moreover, the question of who does what when never exhausts the various relevant aspects of an organization for any given level of social analysis. In addition to the fact that different members of a unit do different things, social systems for many purposes must also be viewed in terms of structures of the allocation of goods and services, power and responsibility, etc.

B. SOLIDARITY

The structures of *solidarity* in a society may be defined as those in terms of which relationships among the members of the society are allocated according to the *content, strength,* and *intensity* of the relationships. In a somewhat less precise but perhaps more communicable sense, solidarity is concerned with who sticks with whom under what circumstances. Solidarity, as the term is used here, will cover an aspect of behavior of infinite gradation between two poles. The negative pole will be taken to mean complete antagonism—war at sight as it were. The positive pole will be taken to mean complete agreement and complete and mutual affective accord. The only element of discontinuity of the variation between these poles is at the point of perfect neutrality. This point may be ruled out for most purposes since even in the most casual of relationships some affective element is likely to be involved. Precise neutrality is rare. The term *content* refers to the type of relationship that is supposed to exist and the members between or among whom it is to exist. The content of the solidarity aspect of the relationship involving mother and child consists of the fact that it is a mother and child who constitute the members of the relationship and of certain standards of behavior of the one toward the other. By the *strength* of the solidarity I mean the relative precedence or lack of precedence taken by this relationship over other relationships of this general sort and over other obligations and commitments in the larger social sphere in which the relationship may occur. Thus for example, in the mother-child illustration, if the mother gives the child an order and the father gives the child a different order, if, ideally speaking, the child is expected to obey the father rather than the mother, the strength of the child's solidarity with the father is greater, ideally speaking, than the strength of the child's solidarity with the mother, and so forth. The strength of a given relationship is not necessarily the same from the point of view of the various members of the relationship. For example, the relationship between a mother and child may be stronger from the child's point of view than from the mother's. A mother's order to a child may take precedence over anyone else's order to the child, whereas a request or order from the child to the mother may very well not take precedence over the orders of others to the mother.

The term *intensity* refers to the state of feeling, affect, or emotion involved in the relationship. Here again I would describe the range of variation in terms of the dichotomy set up in the previous chapter between avoidance and intimacy. The intensity of a relationship or the intensity aspects of a large-scale social system may vary not only with regard to the kind of emotion involved but also with regard to the degree of emotion involved. In connection with the general treatment of solidarity two things must be noted with regard to intensity. In the first place, the intensity of a solidarity, like the strength of a solidarity, is not necessarily identical from the points of view of all of the individuals involved in any given social system. Thus the intensity of the solidarity of a mother-child relationship, like its strength, may vary depending on whether it is described from the mother's or the child's point of view. There is a second kind of variation, as important if not more important. It is possible for the strength and intensity of solidarities to vary in opposite directions in some sense. It is possible to have relationships of relatively low strength but high intensity. For example a child's emotional involvement with his mother may be the most intense emotional involvement the child has. It is not necessarily his strongest solidarity. There are, presumably, limits on this type of variation. Insofar as the type and degree of emotion are relevant to the strength of the solidarity, neither the actual nor the ideal kind or degree of emotion can vary at random relative to the strength of the solidarity if the system is to remain stable.

In considering large-scale social systems one cannot confine the analysis of solidarity aspects to those among the members of given units, such as family units. One must also be concerned with those structures of solidarity which relate the members of one type of unit to members of another type of unit. For example, it is necessary to ferret out the solidarity structures in terms of which relations among the members of family units and governments or of family units and business firms, etc., are carried out. One may say of social systems in general and of societies in particular two things: (1) there must always be some regular structures of solidarities, and (2) in any society there are certain minimal relationships among which the solidarity aspects must be specifically defined and in some manner generally communicated to the members of the system(s) concerned.

C. ECONOMIC ALLOCATION

The structures of *economic allocation* have to do with the allocation of goods and/or services as iterated above. The members of
any society must have food and usually shelter and clothing as
well if there is to be any survival of members to continue the
society. Since the minimum requirements in terms of goods and
services are never found in nature as completely free goods,
problems of the distribution of goods and/or services among
alternative possibilities always arise in the social context, if only
because of the possible effect of jealousies which can arise no
matter how intrinsically homogeneous the articles or services
concerned. It is theoretically possible that the members of one or
more types of relatively rare social systems consume virtually
negligible amounts of goods and services without producing them
or others save in negligible quantities. It is not, however, conceivable that this be true for the members of all the subsystems of any
given society or even of a substantial portion of them. Some
members of any sort of large-scale organization might survive
solely by virtue of economic exploitation of others, but this can
never be true of any save a relatively small proportion of the
members of any society unless the society concerned is on the
road to extinction. It is, of course, not conceivable that the members of any social system produce without consuming, though it is
by no means necessary that the members of any particular unit
consume exactly the same goods and services they produce. The
relevance of goods and/or services as means for other purposes is
an obvious basis for the relevance of economic allocation for
other structures in any given society or social system. They are
not, however, in any deterministic sense more relevant to the
other structures than the other structures are to them. In the
discussion below, following a convention which has come to be
relatively well accepted in such discussions, the structures of
economic allocation will be subdivided into two categories: the
structures of production, and the structures of consumption.

D. POLITICAL ALLOCATION

This aspect, along with the preceding one, constitute the two
aspects most likely to be confused with concrete distinctions.
Political allocation, for the purposes of this work, is defined as the
distribution of power over and responsibility for the actions of the
various members of the social systems concerned, involving on
the one hand various forms of sanctions, of which sheer coercive

force is the extreme in one direction, and on the other accountability to the members and in terms of the systems concerned, or to
the members of other interdependent systems. The term *power* is
defined as the ability to exercise authority and control over the
actions of others. *Responsibility* is defined as the accountability of
an individual(s) to another individual(s) for his own acts and/or
the acts of others. The existence of well understood and not at all
well understood structures of allocation of authority and responsibility are well known. What is sometimes not quite so well
recognized is that such structures are quite well known to most
unsophisticated and inexperienced individuals as well as to so-
phisticates. Virtually all small children, even before they know
the words used here or the equivalents in their own language, are
already used to react in terms of structures of authority and
responsibility. The political aspect of behavior in terms of organizations is not at all confined to the governmental sphere but is
identifiable in every social context. Furthermore, it is by no
means confined to individuals who are classified as adults. One
of the most interesting features of modern political science is the
fact that quite recently a large number of its practitioners have
become acutely aware of the fact that the manner in which children are taught to react to structures of power and responsibility
is vital in understanding many of the features of their behavior
in what are more commonly considered by the layman and other
political scientists to be more strictly political contexts. If this
healthy recognition is not killed off by fatuously faddistic applications, it will prove to be a basis of lasting improvement of the
field of political analysis.[2]

Four other observations need be made about the structures of
political allocation in any society, or any other social system for
that matter: (1) whatever the intentions of the members of the
system may be, the allocations of power and responsibility are
never completely rational; (2) the allocations of power and responsibility are never completely random; (3) not only are they
not random, but also if the system in which the structures are
found is at all stable, the elements of capriciousness in the struc-

[2] It should perhaps be added parenthetically that while the reappearance
of this in recent years in what is specifically referred to as the "behavioral
approach to political science" is to be applauded, insight to this effect is by
no means new. It would be difficult, for example, to make out a case to the
effect that St. Thomas Aquinas was unaware of the relevance of these
phenomena. Here again our modern tendency to think uncritically in
terms of highly specialized predominantly politically oriented organizations
has obscured these matters. The Greats of political theory in the classic
sense were nowise unaware of the significance of "political culture" though
the term was not minted by them.

tures of power and responsibility are quite limited, and (4) the structures of allocation of power and responsibility can never be analyzed solely in terms of applications of force or threatened applications of force, i.e., even in the most authoritarian systems there are elements of influence that are neither ideally nor actually functions of applications of physical coercion or threats of such.

It should go without saying that the structures of political allocation both within nations and as between nations is one of the major orthodox foci of attention for students of international affairs. Indeed, its only close rival is the focus of attention on the structures of economic allocation. Given the interests of students of international affairs and of persons responsible for making decisions in these matters, such preoccupations have certainly not been amiss. They have, however, sometimes been carried to such extremes of exclusion of consideration of other aspects and such narrow concern with orthodox distinctions within consideration of these aspects as to be self-defeating.

E. INTEGRATION AND EXPRESSION

The structures of *integration* and *expression* remain, in this work essentially a catchall category—i.e., a residual category, despite an attempt here and below to be more explicit about these concepts. The concept of *integration* used here denotes a positive adaptation of a given individual to action in terms of a particular social system. That is to say, these are the structures which help explain the adjustment of the individual member's behavior in such a way that the maintenance of the system [never mind whether the system is judged to be good or bad for present purposes] is enhanced and so that the satisfactions of the individual as a member of the system are enhanced. The matter is not a simple one. No structures are perfectly integrative, though certainly some may be malintegrative enough so that if they continue the system concerned will break up. Thus specific structures spoken of as integrative often [or always] have some malintegrative aspects. Therefore, one is well advised to use terms such as predominantly integrative. This, of course, involves difficulties of measurement, but at least in theory it is possible to conceive of making such measurements. For example, the disciplinary procedures used in terms of family units by adult members relative to the children have critical integrative aspects for those social systems. In these days of widespread amateur psychoanalysis, the general public of most relatively modernized societies is more than minimally aware of the fact that these disciplinary procedures are by no means solely integrative in their effects. The fact remains, however, that as far as we know no little child born into this world alive is inherently endowed with reflexes that will enable him either to gain satisfaction or to interrelate at all smoothly with others without the intervention of some sort of tutelage, however unselfconscious it may be.

The concept of *expression* used here denotes the type and limits of reaction, symbolic or otherwise, on the part of individuals or sets of individuals to the various phenomena with which they come into contact. The structures of expression in a society or other social system consists of those which define the type and limits of reaction, symbolic or otherwise, on the part of individuals or sets of individuals to the various phenomena with which they come into contact. One of the most notable types of these structures have to do with affective reactions, i.e., emotional displays, displays of feeling, etc. In all social contexts some types of emotional expression are considered appropriate and others inappropriate. The circumstances may vary, but the situation is never totally undefined from the point of view of the members of the system, although it may be sufficiently ill-defined to pose major problems for them. For example, under conditions in which Frenchmen would consider weeping by men quite appropriate, members of United States society would consider such behavior effeminate. The Japanese repress overt expressions of emotion in situations in which such repression would be considered most unnatural for members of United States society, and display relatively uninhibited emotions under conditions which would be considered just as inappropriate by those Americans. As already indicated above precisely neutral emotions or the complete absence of emotions is probably on the whole rare, but even if such cases do occur, they like the others discussed here are structured ideally and/or actually. Those structures, moreover, do not constitute a set of actions concretely separable from other actions. They constitute rather a special way of looking at any concrete actions.

I I I
ADDENDUM

The five categories of aspects discussed above constitute a set of aspects that can be considered requisites of any society. That is to say, structured aspects of these sorts must be present, if a society is to persist. That is not to say that, if they are present, the society cannot be destroyed in other ways. It is also not to say that these structures *must* be present because they are requisites. Such an argument would be teleological. Nothing, as far as we know scientifically, predetermines that the units of which they are requisites must persist. The foundation of the discussion of those respects in which all societies are alike is this set of requisite aspects of any society. No society lacks not only structured forms of these aspects but actually institutionalized forms of them, using the term institutionalized as defined above [p. 156]. In addition, the major lines of variation of societies discussed will be variations in terms of specific or specialized elaborations of these aspects rather than of totally different ones. Even the discussion of organizations, i.e., of units such as families, governments, business firms, the armed forces, churches, schools, etc., will not be on so general a level as discussion of these aspects will be. The organizations mentioned are all ones which in fact appear in one form or another in all of the societies that are likely to be of greatest interest to students of international affairs, but only in the case of family structure [and one other (see pp. 222 and 290–291)] can we mount an argument to the effect that it not only does, but must, appear in any and all societies. Initially the discussion of all of the aspects treated below will be in terms of an elaboration of elements of these aspects insofar as they can be expected in any and all societies whether relatively non-modernized or modernized.

I would push this line of attack still further, however. Although these aspects of any society are not necessarily aspects of every subsystem of a society, they are probably requisites for any subsystem of interest here. In this work I use as an assumption the hypothesis that all social systems other than societies are either subsystems of some particular society or else the result of interrelationships of the members of two or more societies. Therefore, if one analyzes any social system, regardless of whether he knows in fact whether it is a society or not, in terms of these aspects common to any and all societies, he will find out as a minimum in what respects that system is like or unlike a society. More importantly, he will discover in what respects the members of such systems must have minimal interrelations with the members of other systems if the system concerned is to continue.[3]

Even in the elementary and incomplete sense in which they are applied here, it is easy to illustrate the utility of such considerations. For example, one of the bases of role differentiation in any society is age, and within that there is always some category of old age. In any given society, if care of the aged takes place in

---

[3] This is of course one of the main reasons that this system of analysis was originally developed in the volume cited above [p. 20].

terms of the family unit and if changes tend to minimize the possibility of handling the care of the aged on this basis [e.g., if the family unit changes to one in which the grandparents do not ordinarily continue to live with their children], some set of the following consequences must be expected: (1) the members of some other existing subsystem in the society will have to take over such care, (2) some new subsystem in terms of which such care can be secured will have to be developed; (3) the aged must be systematically eliminated before they can become helpless; or (4) the members of that particular society are in for a considerable amount of unrest, and the society is in for further change. This happens to be a major problem for the members of every relatively nonmodernized society changing in the direction of modernization. It is particularly noteworthy because at the very time that the family unit is less likely to continue as the major form of old-age insurance, the survival of the aged increases. Or take another example, any organization whose members are adults and only adults is an organization which must have as one of its elements both structures of recruitment of personnel and structures of disposal of members when they cease to be adults and become aged. If such arrangements cannot be made with the members of other systems, either that organization must go out of existence, or it must change radically enough so that children are produced by the interrelationships of its own members acting in terms of its own structures, and corresponding adjustments for the aged would have to be made. These would constitute radical changes indeed.

ROLE DIFFERENTIATION

I
BASIC ROLE DIFFERENTIATION

Basic roles for any social system are defined as those positions in terms of which all members act at some time during their membership in the system. The set of basic role differentiations in a society consists of all of the roles which every individual acquires sometime or other during his life cycle, and examples are familiar to everyone. All the members of every society are differentiated on the basis of age, sex, generation, etc., and also in certain respects with regard to economic and political aspects, etc. There is a common core of these for all societies, no matter how much societies may vary from one another. Later in this chapter [pp. 200–219] some of the most striking cases of this common core of basic role differentiations are taken up briefly. Since this work focuses on large-scale social organizations of the type generally referred to as societies or nations, the illustrations of basic role differentiation taken up will be those common to any society. This common core is one of the major respects in which all societies everywhere at all times are alike. Correspondingly variations in the details of these differentiations, when considered on more descriptive levels, constitute one of the major sources of variations among different societies. Although the illustrations of basic role differentiations used here exist in any society, any other specific type of social system will also have a set of basic role differentiations which may be unlike those of any other social organization. No matter how great the variation of the sets of basic role differentiations may be, one generalization about them can always be made: to some extent the basic role differentiations of any social organization will contain some of those basic for any society. This is one of the reasons why, no matter how specific one's policy orientations may be, it is useful to have a study of the general social structure of the society or nation with which one must deal. Without the more general knowledge, neither the special organization nor the implications of dealing with the members of the special organization in a particular way can be understood.

I I
INTERMEDIATE ROLE DIFFERENTIATION

Intermediate roles are defined here as any positions in terms of which some, but not all, of the members of a given system act at some point in time during their membership in the organization. In other words, it is a residual category of basic role differentiation. It is all role differentiation specialized by categories of members. Illustrations are just as easy in this case as in the other. A substantial portion of all roles we generally think of are intermediate role differentiations. The role of typist, for example, is just such a specialized role differentiation as are the roles of doctors, legislators, or professors in our society. In some societies the role of student is an intermediate role differentiation. This is not true of all societies if one uses the term *student* in the ordinary layman's sense to refer not simply to anyone who studies anything but to one who is in fact studying as a pupil in a school as such. In this sense for a society like the United States, in which there is a structure of universal compulsory education at the elementary and secondary school level, every individual is expected to have student roles during the early years of his life cycle. Therefore this role differentiation is a basic role differentiation in the United States. The role of student in this sense was not a basic role differentiation in traditional Chinese society despite the fact that in that society the role of student was an important intermediate role.

There are some intermediate role differentiations in every society, but societies differ widely in the number and kinds of intermediate role differentiations distinguished. It is also true that all societies have some intermediate as well as some basic role differentiations in common. Perhaps the most obvious of these has to do with sex. Some sex role differentiation is basic in the sense that all members of every society are so differentiated at some point in their life cycles. Male roles as contrasted with female roles are, perhaps, the most universal and general of all intermediate roles in social history. There are, however, much less obvious and general cases of intermediate role differentiations that a large number of societies certainly do have in common. Some sort of governmental officials are examples of intermediate role differentiations present in a substantial proportion of all societies, if not in all societies. Unlike the basic role differentiations, the intermediate role differentiations of social organizations other than societies do not necessarily contain the intermediate role differentiations of the society in general except, of course, in the trivially tautological sense that if the role is found in that particular organization it is also found in the society. The intermediate role differentiation of a given subsystem of a society might be unique in that society. This distinction is worth illustrating. Many social systems other than societies are characterized by role differentiation on the basis of age just as are societies in general. Sex is another frequent such distinction. In the field of intermediate role differentiations members of a given organization may use many distinctions which are quite common elsewhere in the society or even common in a large number of societies. The role of employee, for example, is such a role. There may, however, be specialized role differentiations which characterize a particular organization and only that particular one. Now this is, of course, true in a trivial sense if one is referring to a completely descriptive level of analysis. On this level every organization is characterized by some unique intermediate role differentiation. Even on quite general levels of great practical significance, however, one of the important differentiating characteristics of highly specialized organizations is the number and kinds of intermediate role differentiations unique to such organizations.

Relatively modernized societies are always characterized by many more intermediate role differentiations for any given level of consideration of social phenomena than are relatively nonmodernized societies. Here again it is important to give explicit meaning to the phrase many more. I cannot give it a precise meaning here, but like other distinctions of degree used in this work the relevant differences are usually so gross that the distinction is, relatively speaking, clear enough. For example, the members of almost all societies of any considerable scale, whether they be relatively modernized or not, distinguish some specialized occupational roles. These are examples of intermediate role differentiation. The difference between even a sophisticated relatively nonmodernized society such as that of traditional China and a highly modernized society such as the United States in this respect, without going into any greater descriptive detail in the one case than the other, is probably the difference between several hundred [or some few thousand] specialized occupational roles and several hundred thousand specialized occupational roles. The less highly modernized the society compared with traditional Chinese society, the less extreme is the comparison, of course.

It is also important to consider the great variation among relatively nonmodernized societies in these respects. Some relatively nonmodernized societies have a considerable number of intermediate role differentiations. The myriad special distinctions of roles in the Hindu caste taxonomy are an excellent example of how elaborate such detail can get in a relatively nonmodernized society. Depending on the taxonomy used, without going into too much descriptive detail, one may make at least several hundred distinctions on this basis alone in Hindu society. The extent to which the traditional Chinese carried role differentiation on the basis of farming was probably on the whole not great, but the extent to which they carried it on the basis of craftsmanship was almost certainly as great as the level of variation approached by the members of any relatively nonmodernized society. Moreover, in traditional Chinese society the differentiation of highly specialized roles in the general field of learning was also elaborate. There were not only the publicly differentiated roles of scholarship; there was an even vaster proliferation of differentiated private scholars.

In considering the problems of modernization, the extent of intermediate role differentiations in a given society is of considerable significance. If the proliferation of such role differentiations is relatively slight, it is trivial logically, but not practically, to observe that any element of the general social structure which depends for its stability on the restriction of such role differentiation will be threatened by the changes which will follow increases in modernization. If the proliferation is carried quite far, it does not necessarily follow, however, that there will be less disturbance. The extent of disturbance will depend on the appropriateness of the range of intermediate role differentiation for conversion to relatively modernized forms of role differentiation just as much as it depends on the fact of the existing proliferation itself.

I I I
ACHIEVED AND ASCRIBED ROLES

The distinction between achieved and ascribed roles is now one of ancient tradition as the field of social analysis goes. This distinction is close to, if not identical with, the distinction already used in another context under the heading of universalism and particularism. I use it in this form here simply because the reader will meet it in this form in many other contexts, and it costs little additional effort to mention these terms here.[1] *Achieved roles* refer to those positions that an individual has acquired on the

[1] Purists about consistency should simply substitute predominantly universalistic for achieved and predominantly particularistic for ascribed.

basis of his qualifications or accomplishments relevant to the actions carried out in terms of the position. *Ascribed roles* refer to those positions that an individual receives on the basis of qualifications that are not necessarily directly germane to the action in terms of the roles and that are attributed to him by virtue of his social classification in other roles. The role of Nobel Prize winner probably is as close to an approximation of a purely achieved role as one can come; the role of successor to the throne of England is an ascribed role. Kinship roles are always in some sense ascribed roles, though the basis of ascription is often germane to performance in terms of kinship roles. Roles attained through competitions and the like always contain some elements of achievement. There has never been a society without some examples of both achieved and ascribed roles, both ideally and actually, but the difference in emphasis placed on achieved as opposed to ascribed roles varies widely not only from one subsystem of a given society to another but from one type of society to another. The members of some societies, as one would expect from the discussion of the distinction between universalistic and particularistic membership criteria, emphasize achieved roles little, though probably never as little as some social-science accounts might lead one to infer. Highly sedentary societies with relatively little differentiation of skills and social structures overwhelmingly oriented to family considerations are probably ones whose members most minimize the emphasis on achieved roles. In even the simplest societies, however, some roles focusing on craftsmanship or presumed virtuosity in magic, hunting, fighting, or the like are frequently achieved roles.

Those societies whose members emphasize achieved roles are always ones whose members place a major emphasis on ascribed roles as well. As a minimum there is always an important emphasis on kinship considerations in some contexts, and roles in kinship structures are on the whole ascribed roles. Relatively modernized societies are characterized by members who place much greater emphasis on achieved roles than do the members of relatively nonmodernized societies for any given level of detail on which the societies can be compared.

Since no society totally lacks ascribed roles ideally and/or actually, and since the members always consider some ascribed roles important, there is no society whose members do not to some degree understand an emphasis by themselves or others on ascription no matter how much the members of that society may emphasize achieved roles. To use kinship as our major example again, there is no society whose members do not understand or are completely unaware of the practice of nepotism, regardless of whether it is approved or not. Indeed, one of the problems posed by considering nepotism an evil in certain contexts inheres in the fact that there are always contexts in that society in which nepotism is not only respected but preferred by the members. There are always contexts in the most highly modernized societies in which one is expected to put some of his relatives first. Thus, insofar as there are any contexts in which one is not expected to place any of his relatives first, those contexts require careful differentiation from the others.[2]

[2] Even in societies in terms of which other ascribed allegiances take precedence over family allegiance, the problem of the separation of action in terms of those roles from action in which family considerations are supposed to take precedence is always a special problem. Although there are no societies totally lacking in critically important ascribed roles, there are societies in terms of which an emphasis on achievement is relatively little understood or appreciated by the members. It is necessary to be careful how one states and understands this. There is no society whose members are unable to distinguish differences in achievement. There is no society whose members fail completely to distinguish between good and bad workmanship, for example. It may well be, however, that there are societies whose members place comparatively slight emphasis on different levels of achievement. As modernization increases in a given context, the preexisting emphasis on the ascription of roles or on particularism in selection, as indicated above, is always a source of problems because, in the process, it always becomes necessary to increase the emphasis on achievement or on predominantly universalistic selection of persons for roles. Furthermore, even after high levels of modernization are achieved there always remains the possibility of conflicts of interest of every member of such societies because of potential conflicts in the interdependencies of various social contexts in some of which he has ascribed roles and in others of which he has achieved roles.

With the continued increase of modernization in the context of societies already highly modernized, a rather interesting and new extreme question is raised for the social future. Are human beings able to adapt easily to great emphases on achievement? It is not a simple question. With relatively rare examples such as the nationalistic spirit of the Japanese, we in general regard the spirit of nationalism as a concomitant of relatively modernized societies. A nationalistic ethic is a predominantly particularistic one. Membership in a particular nation is usually a function of ascribed rather than achieved roles, though one may achieve citizenship in a nation to which one did not previously belong. Of all of the popular bases for ascription of roles, national identity is the largest and the least likely to interfere in the ordinary arena of emphasis on achieved roles. Thus in areas in which predominantly universalistic selection is emphasized, ordinarily one is not faced with a choice from among individuals belonging to two or more nations. Until quite recently at least in most of the nations in the world an employer who wished to employ only members of his own nation usually had only such members to select from in the first place. With modern communications what they are, the sense of identification which seems to inhere in heavy emphasis on ascribed, nationalistic roles may raise increasing problems for efficient and well-organized operation of an increasing number of activities.

I V
FOCI OF ROLE DIFFERENTIATION:
CONCENTRATED OR DIVERSIFIED

All societies have a common set of foci of roles plus variations around those foci. This again is but another exemplification of the fact that there are respects in which all societies are alike as well as of the fact that there are lines of variation along which societies differ at more specific levels. For most of history and before, however, all role differentiation has taken place in terms of a relatively small number of social systems. Again, kinship units in general and families in particular are the best examples of this. For most of the members of the vast majority of all societies to date, the family has been the overwhelming focus of role differentiation most of the time. Most societies have been relatively nonmodernized ones, and for all of them the family unit has been the overwhelming focus of role differentiation for most of the members most of the time. Although roles outside the family context may have taken precedence over family roles, most of the roles have actually been family roles. As already indicated above, even in the most highly modernized contexts the family continues to be a focus of a considerable amount of role differentiation.

In addition to the role differentiation on the basis of families, all societies are characterized by some differentiation on a nonfamily basis. Nonfamily role differentiation may be concentrated in a small number of alternative organizations. When the number of social systems in terms of which the ordinary individual acts is relatively small, the foci of role differentiation may be thought of as *concentrated foci*. For most of the members of most of the societies in world history the foci have been concentrated in this sense. When, however, a relatively large amount of the role differentiation in terms of which the ordinary individual acts falls not only outside the family context but also is in terms of a relatively varied and numerous set of alternative social systems, the foci may be termed *diversified foci*. The case par excellence of this is, of course, the relatively modernized society. The more highly modernized the society, the more diversified the foci of role differentiation by contrast with all other societies.

Corollarially, for the members of these societies there are always special problems of the separation of roles from one to another context. Whenever an individual has roles in two or more organizations the possibility of role conflicts arises. Those societies characterized by concentrated foci of role differentiation are also characterized by a well-understood hierarchy of precedences among the different roles. These characteristics make it relatively easy for the members of such societies to minimize the problems of role conflicts, though these problems are by no means eliminated. There is no society for which the conflict of the actions called for in terms of different roles is not a serious theme of such drama as its members create. The Japanese, for example, in days gone by not only held that death was lighter than a feather whilst obligation was heavier than a mountain, but the dramatic theme of themes for the Japanese was that of conflict between two or more loyalties.

When the proliferation of social systems in terms of which the average individual has roles increases radically, the problems of these adjustments also increase radically. One of the marked characteristics of relatively modernized societies is that so many of the relationships into which one enters emphasize either avoidant emotions or, insofar as possible, an approach to neutral ones. The rapid adjustment of different expressions of intimacy is difficult for anyone. When the foci of role differentiation become highly diversified, one of the major forms of diversification is in terms of the kind of specialization previously discussed [see pp. 38–46 and 93–115]—specifically in terms of predominantly economically oriented as opposed to predominantly politically oriented roles. This particular distinction of roles always poses additional special problems of adjustment because of the considerable relevance of allocations of goods and services for allocations of power and responsibility and vice versa.

V

THE MUTUAL REINFORCEMENT OF ROLES

The various bases on which roles are as a minimum differentiated in every society will be sketched in brief detail below. There are not only a large number of different bases on which roles are in fact differentiated by the members of every society, but in addition to those differentiations that are, as it were, requisites of any and all societies, the number of different bases on which roles may be differentiated in any specific society or subsystem of any given society is, of course, enormously greater, if not in principle infinite. This variation raises the problem of the possibility of the implications of one role differentiation, or one set of them, contradicting the implications of another. If a given social unit is to be stable, as a minimum the role differentiations must be such that in no radical sense do they contradict one another in their implications. In all societies, if there is stability, the various sets of role differentiation in fact reinforce one another, although there may be many cases of contradiction among the implications of role differentiations. For example, if one looks at a family role such as that of the family head and one looks at various bases of role differentiation in terms of which precedence within the family context is usually reckoned [e.g., such bases as age, sex, generation, etc.], without going into any questions of origin, ordinarily in stable families the family head is in fact the oldest member of the family, a representative of the oldest generation, male, etc.—assuming that this is a society for which there is precedence on the basis of relative age, of representing the oldest generation, and of being male. In such situations the expected reinforcement may get out of kilter in individual cases. For example, the family head may be younger than another family member whilst representing an older generation, or a woman of older generation may take over command. It is the possibility of such conflicts which sometimes enables us to distinguish which of these various bases of precedence matter most to the members of the society concerned.[3]

The mutual reinforcement of the various different forms of role differentiation is considerably easier to illustrate in terms of societies in which kinship is *the* major focus of orientation. The reason for this is not obscure. Since kinship is always *a* major focus of orientation for the members of every society, there is always a potential problem, if there are any role differentiations which lie outside the kinship structure, of the implications of those role differentiations for the ones carried out in terms of kinship. If the kinship focus is expected to take precedence, or in

[3] In traditional China, for example, precedence within the family context rested on generation, age, and sex in that order. Ordinarily the family head was the eldest male of the oldest generation represented. If the family head died and had a brother younger than the family head's son, that brother took over as family head, ideally speaking. Generational considerations were so important that they even enabled women to take over effective headship, though ideally speaking this was considered improper. Nevertheless, the Chinese matriarch, almost always the widowed wife of the family head, was a famous figure in traditional Chinese life and literature. Despite the fact that she was supposed to bow to her sons in her widowed state, their maleness rarely triumphed over the filial piety owed a person of the older generation if she chose to be strong-willed. Had life expectancy been what it is, given modern medical technology, this possible conflict of precedence in terms of role differentiation in the family might have changed the structure of Chinese society radically. As it was, relatively few women survived long enough to threaten male claims to the family headship [see Marion J. Levy, Jr., *The Family Revolution in Modern China*, Harvard University Press, Cambridge, 1949 (Reprinted by Octagon Books Inc., N.Y., 1963), pp. 129–132 and 140–41].

specific cases to yield way to loyalties to members of other units, it is relatively easy to visualize sets of role differentiation which reinforce one another. If, on the other hand, kinship considerations are not expected to take precedence, or do not have a specific relationship to the activities in terms of other units, two sets of problems inhere. First, there are the problems occasioned by the implications of the role differentiation in terms of other units for the stability of the kinship units. The second set consist of the reverse of the first. What are the implications of role differentiation in terms of the kinship units for the role differentiations carried out in terms of the other units? In the former case, for example, if a son can get a job away from the supervision of family members and without needing any family influence to get the job, the father's control over the boy is likely to be radically diminished. In the latter case, if the son pays close attention to his father, and if his father wishes him to exploit his nonfamily connected job for the benefit of family members, he is likely to do so at the expense of the stability of the organization in terms of which he holds his job.

The greater the degree of diversification of foci of role differentiation, the greater must be the attention paid to insulating one set of roles from another. This is one of the respects in which the relatively modernized societies are peculiar and exotic in terms of general social history. For some years social scientists have been extremely aware of the extent to which predominantly particularistic considerations actually become quite important in what are, ideally speaking, the most predominantly universalistically oriented settings.[4] Given the general nature of social history before the development of relatively modernized societies, the surprising thing is not how much this is the case, but how little it is the case. The vast majority of all societies have had relatively concentrated foci of role differentiation. Before relatively modernized societies developed, the systems in which diversified foci of role differentiation existed were, to a great extent, restricted to such systems as cities and towns. The persons involved in such systems on a day-to-day basis ordinarily constituted only a small fraction of the total membership of the societies concerned. In the relatively modernized societies almost exactly the reverse obtains. The members of such societies whose role differentiations are highly concentrated—except for infants and small children—constitute a small minority of the total membership. They also constitute a minority that diminishes every day.

⁴ The work of Roethlisberger and Dickson in this connection has already been mentioned above [see p. 170].

We are accustomed to thinking of actors in the theatrical sense as individuals with specially developed skills in switching with the greatest of ease from behavior appropriate to one set of roles to that appropriate to a radically different set of roles. In this sense the great emphasis of modern social scientists on the term actor in their analyses is especially apposite since, in fact, most of the social scientists concerned deal largely with the phenomena of relatively modernized societies. In this special sense these are actors' societies. During the course of an ordinary day the average actor in such societies not only plays several different roles in terms of a given organization. That is not unusual in social history, perhaps, though in relatively modernized contexts this too is carried to great extremes. He also plays an enormous number of different roles in terms of an enormous number of different organizations, and hardly gives thought to his passage from one to another. The daily behavior of such actors constitutes quite a performance. Probably no one fully understands how and why men can act in terms of such systems with as little friction from such sources as they in fact do. The ability to operate effectively in such a complex situation is certainly related to the emphasis in such spheres on rationality, universalism, functional specificity, and avoidance. Relationships in terms of which facile switches from role to role are made with the unconscious ease of monkeys swinging through the trees require such emphases.

In this whole problem of role reinforcement, family life is of special importance. The family is a peculiar social organization in all societies in world history. First, it is unique in that we are relatively sure some form always exists and always has existed in every society. There is another peculiarity about it. Later in this chapter role differentiation on the basis of age will be discussed and divided into two parts: (1) role differentiation on the basis of absolute age and (2) role differentiation on the basis of relative age. Absolute age role differentiation is concerned with distinctions like infancy, childhood, adulthood, old age, etc. All societies are characterized by such distinctions, and the average individual throughout all of his absolute age distinctions always has a role as a family member. The traditional Chinese had a way of putting this with regard to women. They said that as a daughter she was subordinate to her father, as the wife to her husband, and as a widow to her son. This covered her life cycle as far as subordination was concerned. Males and females of all societies ordinarily belong to some kinship unit all their lives. This means that for every individual member of every society there is a major problem of role reinforcement within the family context and between the family and any other organizational context. In addition, all nonfamily organizations may be put in one of two categories. First, there are those whose members are supposed to consider family matters in determining their behavior in terms of the organization. Action in terms of family role differentiation is expected to determine many of the things which go on in terms of the role differentiations of such organizations. If the role differentiations of the family units do not reinforce one another, the resulting instability has implications for the other organizations as well as for the families. Second, there are organizations for whose members, ideally speaking, family considerations are not supposed to matter in determining their behavior in terms of the organizations. Such organizations are not unknown in relatively nonmodernized societies, and they are extremely common in relatively modernized societies. Although, ideally speaking, the structures of role differentiation in the family are supposed to be irrelevant to action in terms of these organizations, actually such is not the case. Each of us who has lived in a relatively modernized social context knows perfectly well that although ideally speaking family matters are not supposed to affect our behavior at work, they do in fact affect it and importantly, whether we or anyone else likes it or not. Thus ideally and/or actually the problems of role reinforcement within the family are reflected in all other organizations in any society.

Highly diversified foci of role differentiation pose significant problems of role reinforcement quite apart from the family considerations mentioned above. For example, it is not only necessary that role differentiation problems in the family context impair operations in terms of these systems as little as possible; it is also important that the structures of role differentiation within these organizations reinforce one another. In such organizations something like a chain of command is always important. The limits within which the authority of the director of such an enterprise can be undermined are restricted. In an extreme form military organizations, in terms of which the problems of authority are always a critical focus of concern, illustrate this. Among military personnel, especially in the context of a society whose members are as antimilitaristic as members of United States society, there is no more often repeated refrain than the observation that one is "saluting the uniform, not the man." There could hardly be a pithier way of putting the point that it is the office which any subordinate of that office must respect regardless of the personal qualifications of the incumbent of it. Whole dramas and operas such as the *Caine Mutiny,* and *Billy Budd* have been written about the theme of the inviolable importance of the office even in the face of the most obviously justifiable challenges on the basis of excesses committed by the incumbent thereof. A considerable portion of the talk about morale problems in various organizational contexts is to be understood in terms of maintaining reliable reinforcement of the role differentiation characteristic of such systems. Few such organizations reach any considerable scale without some differentiation of what might be called line and staff personnel. The line personnel are especially endowed with responsibility, and the staff personnel are in some sense expected to be especially competent intellectually, perhaps more so than the line personnel themselves. Still the line personnel are supposed to command the staff personnel. All sorts of problems arise if staff personnel take over line functions. In general, however, these problems do arise in any social context in which mental ability is supposed to be one of the prime qualifications for positions of authority. The fact that in relatively modernized social contexts a special aura of benign [sometimes malignant] impracticality is associated with all personnel in the society whose talents and interests are highly specialized along intellectual lines is not independent of the problems of mutual reinforcement role differentiations.

The extent of mutual role reinforcement is always relevant to the problems of control in terms of any society or any social system. One of the best examples of this is one of the phenomena most closely associated with the explosively disintegrative effects of the structures of modernization when they are introduced into a relatively nonmodernized social context. As indicated above in other connections, the members of most of the relatively nonmodernized societies ordinarily learn most of their roles from an adult in some authority over them within their own family context. The older members of the family are not only the individuals from whom affection, food, shelter, clothing, etc., flow; they are also the usual source of all relevant learning and training. In the context of relatively modernized societies the grousing of parents about the lack of respect of the young for the old and especially of the younger members of the family for the elder members of the family is always a rising crescendo. With the age of schooling in the specialized sense beginning as early as the age of two or three, there is hardly a period of conscious memory in the life of a relatively modernized child that is not increasingly associated with outside experts as well as those who belong to his own family. For those schools to work, it is absolutely important that the child respect his teachers, but in some respects what parents or other older family members tell the child is bound in fact to conflict or is bound to be conceived by the child to conflict with what teachers tell him. In any case in one sphere after another having to do with knowledge and skills the child becomes at least as dependent on people outside the family membership as on family members. One of the grimmest reflections of this sort of thing is the standard joke associated with the United States college graduate.[5]

When elements of modernization are introduced into a relatively nonmodernized setting, one of the first changes is that a large number of the individuals are trained by persons outside of their family setting. Frequently they are not only nonfamily members but probably quite young individuals to boot. At one and the same time, the feeling of dependency on and respect for family members is to some extent challenged; so is respect for those older than one, and so forth. Furthermore under these circumstances one can challenge family control and still find an alternative place to work, at the same time that one also sees that it is not necessarily more respected members of the family from whom all blessings flow. The introduction of structures of modernization provide alternative foci for respect as well as alternative bases for employment. Members of relatively modernized societies take it so much for granted that this sort of training will take place on a nonfamily basis that it almost never occurs to them that this particular introduction into a relatively nonmodernized social context is from many points of view far more dramatic in its implications than the gigantic dam with which such training may be associated or the new factory whose strange machines are such an obvious symbol of the transition. As has already been indicated above and will be taken up again below, when one adds to this that, in general, the structures of control of such societies rest importantly on family structures of control, the general implications of the problems of role reinforcement for general problems of control in such societies come to sharp focus.

V I
TYPES OF ROLE DIFFERENTIATION

A. ROLE DIFFERENTIATION ON THE BASIS OF AGE

In every society there are always structures of role differentiation on the basis of age. These structures are always oriented to at

[5] This is the story of the young man who on his graduation from college, after seeing relatively little of his father during the four-year period, remarks to someone that it is astonishing how much his father has learned during that four-year period.

least two different considerations with regard to age. First, there are always structures of role differentiation on the basis of what may be referred to as *absolute age*. Second, there are always role differentiations on the basis of what may be referred to as *relative age*. Absolute age classifications refer to distinctions such that an individual is classified in one and only one particular category at any given point in time. Absolute age distinctions of this sort are known as the categories of infancy, childhood, adulthood, etc. They are not absolute age classifications in the sense that everyone always begins his participation in one of these categories at the same point of elapsed time in his life cycle. The point may differ from individual to individual, but they are absolutely classified in the sense of being classified in one and only one of these categories at a given point in time. For purposes of praise or derogation one may refer to him as participating in two or more at a given point in time. For example, one may say that he is a child who acts like an adult or that he is an adult who acts like a child, but clearly in either case one is not in fact classifying him as being in more than one category at a given point but rather as being a person who has characteristics appropriate to another absolute age distinction than the one to which he properly belongs.

As a minimum, absolute age distinctions in every society cover at least four differentiations: (1) infancy, (2) childhood, (3) adulthood, and (4) old age. In every case with which I am familiar more than these four are in fact distinguished, but these four periods of development are always covered in some fashion by such distinctions. In the modern United States as a minimum we distinguish the following: (1) infancy, (2) young childhood, (3) older childhood, (4) adolescence, (5) young adulthood, (6) middle-aged adulthood, and (7) old age. Another social analyst might wish to distinguish the categories differently, but all would distinguish some set of categories which would cover the four minimal ones for any society. The specific distinction of adolescence, while not unheard of in other societies, is always present in the context of relatively modernized societies. In societies like that of traditional China such a distinction was made with regard to the gentry but not with regard to others. Members of all societies have relatively specific expectations and reactions to the performances of individuals in terms of these different categories. Although there may be many variations in these classifications on the basis of membership in different subsystems of the society, absolute age categories covering the life history of the ordinary individual are parts of the basic role differentiation of every known society.

Relative age role differentiation is role differentiation on the basis of age oriented to some consideration of lapse of time from a given starting point. As a minimum in all societies to some extent this is reckoned in terms of elapsed time since birth or some point of origin taken as birth by the members of that particular society, not necessarily the exact moment of physiological birth. Some differentiation of roles on the basis of relative age is characteristic of all types of families so far reported in the world. In some cases role differentiation on the basis of relative age is carried quite far. In traditional China, for example, precedence among sons was reckoned on the basis of age, and many societies in world history have structures of primogeniture about property as well as titles. In such social contexts relative age is a matter of the greatest importance in determining one's future.[6]

Relative age reckoned from birth is by no means the only form of role differentiation on the basis of relative age. Role differentiation on the basis of elapsed time spent in terms of a given organization is another important form, and this is, of course, exactly what is ordinarily referred to by the term *seniority* in both relatively nonmodernized and relatively modernized social contexts. The members of some societies consider it to be like any other predominantly particularistic criterion, they consider seniority good in and of itself. In terms of relatively modernized societies seniority is usually justified on the basis of a predominantly universalistic or a pseudouniversalistic argument. Thus one bases arguments in favor of seniority on "greater experience," "greater contribution to the joint effort," etc., in such contexts. In fact, of course, seniority in relatively modernized contexts frequently becomes a highly particularistic consideration and may interfere quite seriously with standards of performance, etc. This is especially true in spheres of rapidly changing technology.

In some societies role differentiations on the basis of age cut through practically all other social distinctions. This is especially likely to be true to the extent that the members of the society are

---

[6] I shall return to his matter [pp. 400–403] of patterns of primogeniture. Such societies must always be characterized by a *cadet class*. These cadets consist, of course, of the younger sons. In the context of such societies, the younger sons as well as the eldest son of a given family must be prepared to succeed to the family headship or whatever else is determined on the basis of primogeniture should the eldest son fail to survive long enough to succeed. Not all of the individuals so educated can in fact succeed to positions for which they have been prepared. Thus, there is a built-in set of members prepared for a set of roles which in fact many of them cannot live up to. In addition these are likely to be a highly articulate and important set of individuals, and they are always a source of unrest in the social contexts concerned.

overwhelmingly family oriented. Such societies are relatively nonmodernized. Even in terms of relatively modernized societies or other societies whose members do not expect age considerations to cut uniformly across other social distinctions, they remain important. For example, one does not ordinarily think of role differentiation on the basis of age in modern armed-force systems, but there are at least three major considerations based on age characteristic of such systems. First, armies are supposed to involve only adults. An individual is not permitted to become a member of the armed forces before he reaches maturity in some sense, and when old age is reached the individuals concerned are expected to retire. Second, for the army system, seniority is certainly an important factor. Length of membership is relevant to pay and other considerations. Third, even in reckoning such factors as promotion and the like, certain qualities presumably must be demonstrated before a given age is reached. Thus there is a sort of absolute age distinction with regard to eligibility for promotion. After a certain amount of time as a captain, if one has reached a certain age, he must be promoted or retire from the service.

Societies vary widely in the emphasis placed by members on relative age. Sometimes it is roughly uniform in all spheres of social action throughout the entire life span of the individual. In deciding on his behavior toward others with whom he comes in contact one of the major considerations is whether they are relatively older than he both in lapsed time since their birth and in membership in the particular organization in terms of which they are interacting. There are, however, other societies for whose members relative age role differentiations are important at one period of an individual's life, and much less important at other periods. For example, in terms of modern United States society, relative age is a matter of great importance in early years, but particularly as a person comes into full possession of his faculties, as those are generally reckoned, considerations of relative age receive, ideally speaking [and to a high degree actually speaking as well], minimal emphasis. In the latter part of life the emphasis on relative age increases. The period of minimal emphasis coincides, of course, with that period of the individual's life during which there is a maximum emphasis on predominantly universalistic criteria in an enormous number of the contexts in which individuals interact with one another. Even when seniority considerations are present in those spheres of action, the emphasis on relative age is less than the emphasis on relative age in the family context. Furthermore, seniority is rarely defended forthrightly as good in and of itself. Those who favor it tend to defend it as a practice on predominantly universalistic grounds, however transparently irrelevant those grounds may in fact be. The family context remains even in this society the one sphere in which predominantly particularistic criteria do not excite defensive reactions generally.[7]

The major variations of emphasis on absolute and relative age cut heavily along lines of the distinction between relatively modernized and relatively nonmodernized societies, as do so many others in this work. In this particular case they are in addition closely connected to the relevance of family structure for the total social structure. Both of these considerations are even more prominent in the next basis of role differentiation found in all societies.

B. ROLE DIFFERENTIATION ON THE BASIS OF GENERATION

The term *generation* is generally used in the sense in which I have used the term *absolute age* above. Thus in ordinary language, one frequently speaks of teachers and students as belonging to different generations. What one means is that the teacher and the student ordinarily belong to different absolute age classifications and that the teacher is likely to be of the same absolute age classification as the student's parents or grandparents. The term *generation* came to be used in this sense because of the implications of its use in terms of kinship structure. It is to its original and precise meaning that I intend to return the use of the term here. Accurate reckoning of similarities or differences in generation will be a function of kinship reckoning throughout this work. Generational similarities or differences will be determined solely in terms of the relationship of the two or more individuals concerned to some one or more common

[7] Even this statement requires some qualification. Family structures in United States society probably go further than any in world history in the extent to which elements of universalistic emphasis intrude. The relevance of this as a special sort of family training in a society whose members emphasize predominantly universalistic criteria so highly outside the family context is obvious enough. Relative age distinctions in particular tend to be justified on increasingly universalistic grounds even within the family context. Fathers, for example, are less defensive if accused of preferring sons to daughters [or vice versa] than of preferring the eldest [or the youngest] to the other children. Insofar as privileges within the family context are correlated to relative age distinctions, those in turn tend to be justified on predominantly universalistic grounds ["Your older brother can cross the street by himself *because he is better able to look out for the cars!*"], etc. Although members of United States families may seem increasingly to emphasize differentiated aspects rather than the "whole man" [or child], even for us the home remains the "castle of the me" as in all known societies.

ancestor(s). Thus father and son belong to different generations; brothers belong to the same generation, etc.[8]

Role differentiation on this very specific basis is characteristic of all societies. In a quite obvious sense, role differentiation on the basis of generation is confined to family and kinship circles. In terms of no society do the children do exactly what their parents do. The representatives of different generations do not do the same things and are not expected to do the same things at the same time in terms of kinship and family structures.[9] Depending on the position of family structure in the general social structure, the importance of role differentiation on the basis of generation will vary enormously from one society to another. The more important the position of the family in the general social structure, of course, the greater is the relevance of role differentiation on the basis of generation to the general social structure of the society concerned. More specifically, the greater the relevance of family considerations, ideally and/or actually, for action in terms of any other social system in the society, the greater are the implications of role differentiation on the basis of generation for action in terms of that other subsystem.

Matters of care and attention to children are always importantly differentiated on the basis of generation. Even in those societies in terms of which older siblings participate prominently in the care of their younger siblings, the role of older siblings in child care is quite different in kind from the role of family mem-

[8] Depending on the permissiveness of the structures of kinship endogamy or exogamy, generational comparisons of this sort can become quite complex. For example, in terms of United States society it is not inconceivable that the great-grandparent of one individual be a grandparent of another whilst another relative be a grandparent of each. Under these circumstances—especially given the more or less equal emphasis on all lines of descent characteristic of the members of American society, the individuals concerned are in some respects representative of the same and in others of different generations. Granted second marriages and adoptions, it is even possible for an individual to become his "own grandpa" as one popular record once had it, though this is not biologically feasible [hear: "I Am My Own Grandpa," Dwight Latham-Moe Jaffe, Lonzo and Oscar with the Winston County Pea Pickers, R.C.A. Victor 20–2563A].

[9] Representatives of one generation are, however, always expected in general to repeat in some future family context the roles of corresponding representatives of older generations in terms of the units in which they were reared. Thus sons are expected to become fathers, nephews to become uncles, etc. This is not inevitably the case in all individual instances, of course, but it is nevertheless true in general of all societies that an intergenerational relationship is predictive of a future one with the representative of the younger now representative of the older generation in a manner that does not necessarily hold true of relationships involving individuals of different absolute age categories.

bers or other relatives of older generations. The generational distinction is always an important focus of the allocation of power and responsibility in kinship structures in general and families in particular. Insofar as those are highly relevant to the general structures of control of the society, role differentiation on the basis of generation is an important general focus of political allocation. Even in relatively modernized ones in which governmental structures are ideally and relatively easily separated and carefully insulated from family considerations, role differentiation on the basis of generation remains an exceedingly important factor in understanding the general structures of political allocation because it is largely by means of behavior in terms of intergenerational relationships that the average individual in the society learns his initial responses to patterns of authority and responsibility. Those may be offset by later experience, but they are never irrelevant to later developments.

There is one other consideration with regard to role differentiation on the basis of generation which is so strategic for this work that it requires special mention here. In all of the relatively nonmodernized social contexts the vast majority of all teaching and training is carried out on the basis of generational role differentiation within a family or pseudofamily context. This is so overwhelmingly the case in most relatively nonmodernized societies most of the time for most of the members that any introduction of any set of structures in terms of which the role differentiation of teacher and student does not coincide with role differentiations on the basis of generation—is specifically not supposed to involve kinship or family considerations—is bound to have far-reaching general implications for change.

C. ROLE DIFFERENTIATION ON THE BASIS OF SEX

Unlike the term *generation*, the layman's use of the term sex is quite precise enough for present purposes. Role differentiation on the basis of sex is a prominent feature of all societies. There is an enormous amount of variation in the type of role differentiation on the basis of sex, but as a popular musical of the twentieth century maintains, it is a distinction which seems to "come naturally." There are, of course, in all societies the minimally expected correlations of role differentiation on various bases with role differentiation on the basis of sex. Biological kinship and social kinship never coincide exactly, of course.[10] The biological aspects

[10] The fundamental distinction in here is best put by a popular record referred to above [p. 205]. That song sings of the sad state of affairs of a young man who has married an attractive widow. That widow has an at-

of kinship certainly never exhaust the social aspects, nor do they determine them uniquely, but they are never completely irrelevant either. Thus in all known societies women, not men, are mothers even though men may actually go through simulated birth pains as we know from the famous couvade. Not only do women bear the children, but of course they nurse them if they are nursed [and until high levels of modernization are reached, the vast majority are nursed]. There are always role differentiations on the basis of sex in courtship, though they need not necessarily coincide with ours. Sex role differentiations closely dependent on physiological sex differences never exhaust the role differentiations on the basis of sex characteristic of any society. However much the members of a society may consider sex role differentiation to be biologically explicable, much of it certainly is not at present or envisaged states of development of the science of biology.

There are two universally present types of role differentiation on the basis of sex that are especially relevant for the present work. First, sex is always to some extent a focus for political role differentiation. There are spheres in which the males are expected to take precedence and vice versa. The exact allocation of power and responsibility with regard to sex distinctions is enormous, but there is no society, and there never has been a society, in terms of which the sex of a member is completely irrelevant to that member's positions in matters of authority and responsibility. Many societies are radically patriarchal in their ideal structures at least. The traditional Chinese structure has already been cited above. Family units are always major foci of this sort of distinction because such units are universal in all known societies and also because the degree of orientation of the average members of most societies to family or kinship structures is, and has been, overwhelming. Political role differentiation on the basis of sex always extends beyond kinship and family spheres of behavior. Even among the members of the most highly modernized

---

tractive daughter of precociously mature development. That daughter then marries the hero's father. The song complicates the tale further by the discussion of infants born to each of these marital pairs, but those are elaborations which need not detain us. If a man is married to a woman whose daughter is married to that man's father, that man has become "the saddest thing you ever saw," i.e., his own grandpa. However facetious this song may be, in kinship terms it is thus conceivable that a man become his own grandfather because in the social sense of kinship it is true that the husband of one's grandmother is one's grandfather. It is only barely necessary to point out that no present advances in medical technology and none conceived in the future make it possible biologically for a man to be his own grandpa.

societies, ideally and/or actually, the biases against women being in positions of supreme or crucial authority remain impressive. In terms of relatively nonmodernized societies no matter how much descent in the female line is emphasized, crucial roles of authority in both the kinship context and elsewhere are inevitably roles held by males, ideally speaking. In this respect the situation is little different as between the most highly modernized and least modernized of societies. In the history of the most highly modernized societies no woman has yet attained the major executive role in a governmental system if a single such role is distinguished. The number of women who occupy roles of any considerable authority in either the government or other organizations is certainly quite restricted given the general distribution of members of that sex throughout the general population and the inevitable accent among the members of such societies on "the equality of the sexes." Most, if not all, of the women in the greatest positions of power in world history seem to have held such power in terms of societies whose members did not for a minute consider themselves oriented to either the "equality of the sexes" or "female superiority"—rather the reverse.

Second, to some extent role differentiation on the basis of sex is always a specific basis for occupational role differentiation. Here again the differences always go far beyond those more or less obviously associated with the bearing and nursing of children. In all societies work may be divided into three categories: "men's work," "women's work," and work which may be done by either men or women. How work is differentiated on these bases varies enormously, but so differentiated it always is. Moreover, there is always in operation a sort of Gresham's Law about occupational role differentiation on the basis of sex. If a given occupation is identified with individuals of one sex and individuals of the opposite sex begin to enter that occupation, there are three possibilities: (1) the new entrants are immediately driven out, (2) the occupation ceases to be identified as exclusively male or female work, or (3) the individuals of the sex which previously was identified with these positions are driven out of those positions. The analogy to Gresham's Law inheres in the fact that to some extent when such invasions are made the individuals of the sex originally identified with the position are always replaced. One of the more spectacular examples of this in United States history was the replacement of male teachers at the elementary and secondary school level by female teachers.[11] The implications of

[11] An interesting development in educational circles today is the increasing reappearance of males in teaching roles at the elementary

the recruitment of women as regular members of the armed forces of the United States following World War II, as far as I know, have never been examined systematically from this point of view.

Members of relatively modernized societies go to lengths to minimize the focus of attention on sex as a basis for the differentiation of many roles. This, like so many other factors mentioned throughout this work, is one of the peculiar features of relatively modernized societies. The reduction of emphasis on this distinction characteristic of such societies, and the preoccupation with this reduction as an ideal to be sought should not obscure for a moment the fact that the members of none of these societies have come even close to eliminating this distinction either ideally or actually. Sex role differentiation continues to be exceedingly prominent and important in the kinship sphere, in the structures of political allocation, in the structures of economic allocation, and in most other contexts. In some respects it has certainly become even more important than it was previously. For example, the radical separation of the "production of family income" from the "consumption of family income," the overwhelming identification of the former as the male's responsibility and the latter with female supervision has almost certainly left women in the most highly modernized of such societies with far greater powers of decision and administrative responsibility with regard to income expenditure than women have ever known before in world history. At the same time this has left the home even more completely identified as the woman's sphere of influence. The last implication of these developments has frequently been underestimated.

Since sex role differentiation cannot be eliminated from the family sphere and in fact is never completely eliminated from other spheres either, this role differentiation remains in all societies highly relevant to both allocations of power and responsibility and the problems of allocation of goods and services, as well as to other aspects of social life. Since (1) the probability is exceedingly high that there will be far greater emphasis on the subordination of women to men in general by the members of relatively nonmodernized than by those of relatively modernized societies, (2) that subordination is likely to be an important feature of the general structures of control, and (3) that subordination is likely to be an important focus of stress and strain in such societies, we

---

and secondary school levels. They come in, however, on a different basis from what they had when they at one time dominated teaching in this as in most other fields.

have here another set of reasons why the transition to increased modernization has explosive effects on the social structure of relatively nonmodernized societies even though the absolute amount of influence introduced is relatively slight.

D. ROLE DIFFERENTIATION ON THE BASIS OF ECONOMIC ALLOCATION

To some extent roles are always differentiated in all societies on the basis of who does what when with regard to the allocation of goods and/or services. Perhaps the simplest and most universal distinction of such roles is that drawn between the roles of *consumption* and *production.* Here it is necessary to observe a note of caution. No activity is inherently either consumption or production. Its classification depends on the point of view from which the activity is observed. What the members of General Motors "do" is from the point of view of the members of the United States Steel Corporation *consumption;* they are consuming steel plates among other things. From the point of view of automobile buyers what is going on is the *production* of automobiles. Nevertheless, the members of all societies draw some distinctions between consumption and production.

The most important consideration with regard to role differentiation on the basis of economic allocation has to do with the sort of social systems or organizations in terms of which role differentiation on the basis of economic allocation is carried out. The vast majority of all social experience has been with relatively concentrated foci of such role differentiation. The example par excellence has been the family unit. This has never been the only unit in any society, but it has been the major unit for most of the members of most of the relatively nonmodernized societies in world history, and it remains an important unit in all of the relatively modernized societies as well. In relatively modernized contexts an important distinction emerges systematically. What are *considered* to be production roles tend overwhelmingly to be concentrated in highly specialized organizations whose members are, for their productive activities, radically separated from and insulated against the organizational contexts in terms of which they regard themselves as carrying out their consumption roles. This is carried so far that production roles tend to be regarded as roles in terms of which action is conducted outside the family context, and family roles are considered to be *the* major roles of consumption. In many senses this is a naïve point of view even with regard to the most highly modernized societies. An enormous number of roles crucial in their productive aspects continue to be conducted in family terms. Most obvious among these are the roles having to do with food preparation, at least the early care and rearing of infants and children, the provision and regulation of sleep and relaxation, much of the production of cleanliness, etc. There are also, of course, major foci of attention to consumption which fall outside the family sphere.

One of the major results of this degree of specialization, and of this level of naïveté about it, has been a tendency to regard the spheres of production and consumption as spheres isolated from one another in a radical sense never before approximated in history despite the fact that people have never failed to distinguish between the two to some extent. Actually this has resulted in the implicit development from the point of view of the individuals concerned of at least two radically different kinds of production and consumption: family production and consumption and nonfamily production and consumption. Since that distinction is ideally and actually implicit in the point of view of the vast majority of members of all such societies, there has been a systematic underplaying of the aspects of production in the family context and of the aspects of consumption in the nonfamily context even by professional social scientists. Since these distinctions ordinarily are not carried to such lengths by the members of relatively nonmodernized societies, once again the contrast implicit in the introduction of structures of modernization is likely to be great.

E. ROLE DIFFERENTIATION ON THE BASIS OF POLITICAL ALLOCATION

Political allocation is defined here as the distribution of power over and responsibility for the actions of the members of the social systems concerned, involving on the one hand various forms of sanctions, of which sheer coercive force is the extreme in one direction, and on the other accountability to the members and in terms of the systems concerned, or to the members of other interdependent systems. *Power* is defined as the ability to exercise authority and control over the actions of others. *Responsibility* is defined as the accountability of an individual(s) to other individual(s) for his own acts and/or the acts of others. As in the case of production and consumption, the concepts of power and responsibility are in a sense the obverse of one another. If an individual, A, has power over another, B, then to that extent at least B is responsible to A. This does not mean, however, that the power in a given system is balanced by the responsibility in that system. For example, although A's power over B, is B's responsibility to A, A is not necessarily responsible to anyone for the power that he wields over B. In Chapter 6, below, in the fuller discussion of the structure of political allocation, the instability inherent in any cases of imbalance of this sort is discussed. For the time being it is only necessary to point out that the distinction between power and responsibility, though different ways of looking at the same thing, is nevertheless an important basis for distinguishing roles from the point of view of the members of any society.

This distinction in and of itself implies some distinction in the allocation of roles in terms of any society. An individual may be involved in roles so defined that he and others with whom he interacts have identical roles with regard to power and responsibility. Friendship as we understand it in our society is just such a relationship. Ideally speaking, if a friendship is what we consider a true one, the powers and responsibilities of the participants in the relationship are equal.[12] Even so, the power roles of a given individual are not the same as his responsibility roles. He acts in terms of his power over his friends and his responsibilities to them, but these aspects of his activities may and must be distinguished.

Apart from the minimum necessity of distinctions among roles with regard to the allocation of power and responsibility in the above sense, the convenient and familiar case of the implications of infancy may be cited again as a basis for further universally necessary distinctions. Infants cannot in their own persons either wield power or bear responsibility in any effective sense. At the same time they must be subjected to controls to prevent harm to themselves as well as to prevent activities which might become a menace to others. In a modified form the same remark may be made about young children in general, though at quite early ages children do begin to operate in terms of structures of power and responsibility.

In all social organizations of any sort role differentiation on the basis of political allocation always goes beyond either the minimal distinction between power and responsibility or the implications of infancy and early childhood cited here. There are always important differentiations of roles politically on the basis of age, generation, sex, economic allocation, etc. Perhaps the most familiar case of interrelationship among these aspects is that between

[12] Despite all the talk of egalitarianism in many social contexts, egalitarian types of relationships constitute a restricted set of social relationships. The vast majority of all social relationships are in some respects hierarchical ideally speaking. Relationships are sometimes nonhierarchical if casual and fleeting, but rarely egalitarian [see above, pp. 150–152].

economic and political allocation. So highly specialized are many roles in relatively modernized societies that we tend to think of them as primarily concerned with one or the other of the two, but no observer is so naïve as to be completely unaware of the implications of allocations of goods and/or services for the allocation of power and responsibility, if only because of the minimal relevance of goods and/or services as means in the wielding of power and responsibility. It is also true that no one is so naïve as to be completely unaware of the implications of the wielding of power and responsibility for the allocations of goods and/or services if only because of the relevance of either confiscation or chaotic conditions for relationships predominantly concerned with exchange. But these two are no more involved with one another than each of them is with all of the other aspects so far referred to. This, again, is why these are distinguished as *aspects* rather than as different things. Economic allocation is quite important in understanding political roles. It is relevant regardless of whether one feels that possession of considerable power should be closely coordinated with possession of great wealth or not.[13]

Great wealth, however, is certainly no more often a high correlative of power than is a particular differentiation on the basis of sex or age. For example, throughout social history within virtually every society and certainly across the history of all societies the correlation between being male and having high power is far more consistent than is the correlation between having great power and having great wealth. The correlation between certain roles of power and responsibility and age roles is also marked. Since absolute age categories always differ more broadly than the general dichotomous role differentiation on the basis of sex, the situation with regard to age is much more complicated. Neverthe-

[13] Quite sophisticated references to this sort of thing appear in the current humor of any given society. In recent United States history the success in attaining important leadership roles in the political arena of a number of individuals coming from family backgrounds of great wealth has been widely commented upon as indicating a basic change in the American attitude toward elected officials. In the United States today, it is obviously quite possible to succeed in a political career despite the fact that one has been born with a silver or even a golden spoon in his mouth. There have been periods in American history in which such origins would have been more of a liability for one seeking high elective office. American ideals in these matters call for predominantly universalistic standards. It is certainly an intrusion of particularistic factors if an individual has an advantage in an elective race because of great personal wealth. It is equally an intrusion of particularistic standards if he suffers specific disabilities as a result of being born into a family context of great wealth. In actuality wealth and power cannot be distributed randomly relative to one another, but whatever their distribution in actuality may be, attitudes about their proper relationship certainly do change.

less, it is almost banal to point out that, ideally speaking, important roles of political leadership are never identified with nonadults.[14] In general, political leadership is likely to be heavily concentrated in the age category that we call middle-aged adults. There are numerous reports of so-called gerontocracies in which the aged members of the society wield power. More often than not, however, both the powers and responsibilities of the aged members of such societies are delegated to subordinates, or there are relatively early retirement structures for the aged, even though, ideally speaking, they hold power and bear responsibility.

There is one particular reason for paying considerable attention to role differentiation on the basis of political allocation. As indicated above again and again, one of the very few specialized organizations found in practically every known society of any scale, whether relatively modernized or not, is a government. Thus, for all such societies—if that does not, indeed, mean all societies—there are always some individuals who hold political roles with far-reaching implications for other individual members of the society regardless of whether the other individuals belong to the government or not. Political roles are by no means confined to governmental and closely associated organizations such as political parties. Political roles are distinguished in some way in terms of any and all organizations. Ordinarily the political roles which are most significant to an individual at any given point in time are those of the organization(s) in terms of which he is acting at any given moment. Governmental roles are always a potential exception to this. The stronger [i.e., the more effectively centralized] the government, the greater the exception. This holds true regardless of whether the individual is more oriented to governmental considerations than to, say, family ones and regardless of whether or not he gives priority or precedence to governmental considerations by contrast with those having to do

[14] Some of the social structures in terms of which this is realized are interesting. Structures of regency are usually invoked when infants and small children legitimately inherit roles of political leadership. On the other hand individuals who might otherwise be classified as nonadults may be considered to be adults as soon as they take over certain roles of leadership. The second type of structure is more likely to be a source of instability, if it recurs frequently, than the first.

In general role differentiations on the basis of age, generation, and/or sex are more likely to underlie other bases of role differentiation than the reverse. Political role differentiation, for example, is more likely to be a dependent variable of sex role differentiation than vice versa. It is far more common in human history, both ideally and actually, to regard individuals as weak because they are women than to regard them as women because they are weak. See also pp. 659–660 below.

with any other organization. Since problems of control are strategic for the members of any organization, and since a government is always an organization specialized with regard to problems of control, action in terms of a government, however weak, always has potential implications ideally and/or actually for action in terms of all of the other organizations in a given society.

This last consideration leads to the final emphasis in this connection. Nothing could be more mistaken than to consider role differentiation on the basis of political allocation to be confined largely to role differentiation in terms of a governmental structure. Because of our preoccupation with highly specialized organizations, we have come to think roughly in these terms, but it is misleading to do so. Role differentiations on the basis of political allocation are characteristic of every organization in terms of which an individual operates. Furthermore, those role differentiations are always of the greatest importance in understanding action carried out in terms of any given organization. The structures of political allocation in such organizations may be loose, permissive, even egalitarian in rare cases, or rigid, authoritarian, and hierarchical, but they are never irrelevant.

In this connection again the problem of reconciliation or reinforcement of roles is raised. The greater the proliferation of organizations in terms of which the ordinary individual operates, the greater is the number of political roles that he must coordinate in some fashion.[15] In relatively nonmodernized social contexts the fact that the ordinary individual operates in terms of few organizations means that this particular problem is minimized. Fewer possibilities arise. In relatively modernized social contexts these problems are mitigated by the presence of specific structures more or less carefully inculcated on the members. For example, ideally speaking, operations in terms of one of these organizations are insulated from operations in terms of another by virtue of the fact that operation in terms of one is supposed to

[15] It has become popular for intellectual winds to blow over whether a given approach overemphasizes integration and underemphasizes conflict. These arguments frequently seem to blow themselves out with the conflict people devoting most of their attention to the relevance of conflict to integration and vice versa. Since such controversies usually tell us more of the values of the participants than of social phenomena, they are avoided here. If there is to be any social organization, there must be some mutual reinforcement of differentiated roles, and the more highly differentiated and specialized the roles of individuals are, the more complex is the problem of interdependence among such roles. Both of these statements hold true quite apart from this sort of revival in new guises of old dichotomous logomachies like heredity versus environment, the dialectic [usually presented with a tone of authority as an undefined argument quencher], statics versus dynamics, etc.

be irrelevant to operation in terms of the other. Actually speaking, this insulation is never complete. Only under the most brittle circumstances, with extraordinarily high levels of self-conscious rational knowledge and emotional self-control could it conceivably be complete for any single individual let alone the membership in general of the society.

F. ROLE DIFFERENTIATION ON THE BASIS OF RELIGION

The term *religion,* as used here, refers to aspects of action directly oriented to ultimate ends or goals, that is to ends or goals that are not conceived as means to other ends but that are conceived as desirable in and of themselves, as their own basis of justification, etc. This definition of religion does not coincide with many of the conventional ones. It would cover major aspects of most of the phenomena which in common parlance we consider religious. It would also cover major aspects of many phenomena not ordinarily classified in that category. For example, regardless of whether one likes them or not, by this definition Communism and Nazism as followed in many respects by their true believers are as much forms of religion as are Judaism, Catholicism, Taoism, Shintoism, etc. Organizations or social systems will be considered *predominantly religiously oriented* if the religious aspects of the structures of action take precedence over all other aspects.[16] Such organizations are not uncommon as subsystems of either relatively nonmodernized or relatively modernized societies. Role differentiation within such specialized organizations always has an important religious element, of course, but there is nevertheless a great deal of role differentiation on the basis of religion that is not confined to such specialized organizational contexts. Frequently the family head has special religious roles. In traditional China he was, as it were, the high priest of the family's ancestor cult. In all societies there must be some role differentiation on the basis of religion, though there need be no such differentiation in many specific organizations. Religious role differentiation is no less strategic for societies in general than the other forms mentioned above, but all of those are exceedingly likely, if not inevitably, to be found in any organization within a society as well. This is not the case of role differentiation on the basis of religion. It is quite possible to conceive of organizations in terms of which no action directly oriented to ultimate ends is expected of the actors involved. There is an important distinction between relatively modernized and relatively nonmodernized so-

[16] A given organization might be predominantly religiously oriented ideally and/or actually.

cieties in this respect. In terms of relatively modernized societies role differentiation on the basis of religion tends to take place overwhelmingly in terms of specialized predominantly religiously oriented organizations while role differentiation on the basis of religion in terms of other organizations becomes increasingly less emphasized. In terms of relatively nonmodernized societies role differentiation on the basis of religion, while often present in terms of some specialized religious organizations, is also very widely distributed among other organizations that are not necessarily specialized in any religious sense.

G. ROLE DIFFERENTIATION ON THE BASIS OF COGNITION

Cognition may be defined as knowledge or understanding of the situation or of phenomena in general. Unless one falls back solely upon an instinct theory of human behavior or into metaphysics, some concepts of learning and knowledge are necessary in the analysis of human action. The presence of some differentiation of roles on the basis of knowledge is not only obvious but also necessary in every society. Infants must be taught the various forms of knowledge necessary if they are to operate in terms of the society. This, of course, implies the minimal distinction between teacher and student. Hardly less obvious are the implications for role differentiation of different types of knowledge. The distinction between *basic* and *intermediate* which was used with regard to roles in general can be applied to cognition. *Basic cognition* is that which, under ordinary circumstances, every member of a given society or organization ideally and/or actually acquires and uses. *Intermediate cognition* refers to those forms and bits of knowledge which ideally and/or actually are acquired and used only by specialized personnel, not by every member of the society or organization concerned. The more specialized the distinctions among forms of intermediate cognition, the greater is the role differentiation on the basis of cognition. As far as basic cognition is concerned, roles are not necessarily differentiated apart from the teacher-student distinction, some distinctions among different levels of skill, and the distinction between "have's" and "have not's" [e.g., literacy is an element of basic cognition in our society, but preschool children are usually have not's in this respect. See further pp. 663–664.]. In addition, the more highly developed the distinctions with regard to intermediate cognition, the more important it becomes that roles in fact be differentiated along these lines.

There is another basis for cognitive role differentiation. One may distinguish at least two types of cognition which are of great importance in understanding human behavior generally. First there are the *technologies*, i.e., the knowledge that serves as the basis for rational action of whatever sort. Second, there are forms of cognition about value standards, the normative patterns of the society, including both the values involved in ultimate and intermediate ends. These are different bases for cognitive role differentiation. The different subcategories possible within each serve as still further bases for cognitive role differentiation. In relatively modernized social contexts the elaboration of the technologies is carried out to a degree of differentiation and on a scale unparalleled in previous history. In the nontechnological sphere of cognition it by no means necessarily holds true that the differentiation in relatively modernized social contexts will be carried further than in relatively nonmodernized ones. Except for forms of cognition which are specific outgrowths of the kind of knowledge associated with modern science and technology, there is probably no cognition having to do with normative standards or other matters in relatively modernized societies that does not find some sort of reflection, echo, or source in relatively nonmodernized social contexts.

Finally, differences in cognitive ability, whether physiologically innate, socially determined, or some combination of the two, always open the possibility for the distinction of the expert in cognition. Because of the importance of knowledge for action in terms of any society, the expert in cognition is always important in some respects. As societies become increasingly complex in their technologies or in their general social structure, the role of the expert, and consequently the distinction between the expert and the nonexpert becomes of greater importance for the stability [and simultaneously for the lack of stability, of course] of the system and for future operations in terms of it.

H. ROLE DIFFERENTIATION ON THE BASIS OF THE NONHUMAN ENVIRONMENT

In all societies, even in the most homogeneous contexts, roles are differentiated on the basis of climate, geography etc. Members of the society do not do the same things in the spring of the year as they do in the winter. There are certainly societies whose members live in areas unmarked by dramatic seasonal variations, but in even the most equable climes, there are some seasonal variations, and some roles are differentiated with regard to these. There is also no society whose members have lived in a territory so uniform that no roles are differentiated on a geographical basis. In relatively nonmodernized social contexts differentiation of roles on the basis of these factors in the nonhuman environment are likely to be of great importance. It is commonplace in anthropological field work that one is likely to overlook something important unless observations cover a full year's time. The importance of such distinctions is so obvious that it would be hardly worth emphasizing were it not for two factors. First, social scientists fought so long and so hard against naïve biological determinism that some came to analyze social phenomena as though the factors of the nonhuman environment have nothing whatever to do with the case, or can be taken as constants without examination. Second, social scientists are usually members of relatively modernized societies. In such societies there are marked differentiations of roles on the basis of factors in the nonhuman environment, but technological developments certainly enable the members of those societies to offset the implications of elements in the nonhuman environment for social action to the maximum known degree. To a certain extent this makes it possible for many to ignore variations in the nonhuman environment. From a slightly different point of view, however, these very developments may radically increase the implications for role differentiation oriented at least in part to the nonhuman environment. In those societies whose members live in areas with marked seasonal changes, for example, the more highly modernized they become, the greater is the development of specialized goods and/or services specifically oriented to coping with elements of seasonal variation. Thus increasingly there develop roles oriented at least in part to the seasonal variations. We have, for example, not only experts in the manufacture of tires, but also people who are expert in the manufacture of snow tires. With the increase of leisure time and the increasingly even distribution of high incomes, a seasonal set of resort specialists is growing. It is perfectly true that modern technology to some extent does make it possible for many individuals to ignore variations in the nonhuman environment, but it is essential to keep in mind that to overcome or, from an individual actor's point of view, to make it possible to ignore those factors is by no means the same thing as ignoring them *in toto*. From this point of view increases in modernization may actually lead to a substantial increase in the differentiation of roles oriented to factors in the nonhuman environment.

SOLIDARITY

I

DEFINITION AND INTRODUCTION

The structures of solidarity have been defined [p. 179], formally, as those in terms of which relationships among the members of a society or any other social system are allocated according to the *content, strength,* and *intensity* of the relationships. In a more laymanlike sense it has been defined as directing attention to the question of who sticks with whom, under what circumstances. The fact that the strength of the relationship need not be identical from the point of view of all the members of a relationship was pointed out. The same fact was pointed out about the intensity of the relationship. Finally the possibility of solidarities whose degrees and kinds of strength and intensity do not reinforce one another in any neat sense, or even vary in opposite directions was mentioned [pp. 179–180].

For any society to exist, there are some requisite structures of solidarity. The factors that make role differentiation a requisite of any society also require relationships of some sort in terms of which different roles can be coordinated, as it were, i.e., relationships in terms of which different individuals interact in terms of different roles. As a minimum, for example, the care and rearing of children require that some structures of solidarity exist if they are to survive. If infants are to be cared for, there must be solidarities of some sort as between infants and adults. Considerations of solidarity always involve considerably more difficult problems than these which make it easy to see that some structures of solidarity are necessary. There are not only those structures characteristic of the relations among the members of a given organization; there are also the solidarity aspects of the relationships among the members of that organization and the members of any other organizations in terms of which the members of the first organization also act. In studying United States society, for example, not only the solidarity structures among the members of an individual family organization but also those relating the family members to members of the government, business firms, etc., must be considered. This draws attention to the general relevance of structures of solidarity for the relative positions of different subsystems in a society.

I I

SOLIDARITY STRUCTURES AS A BASIS
FOR DISCOVERING ORGANIZATIONS
OR SOCIAL SYSTEMS

There is a fairly obvious relationship between the structures of solidarity as discussed here and the general analysis of relationship structures discussed above [pp. 133–174]. The content aspect of solidarity involves some of the matters considered as the aspects of membership criteria and substantive definition of any relationship. The strength consideration is closely related to the stratification aspects, and the consideration of intensity is closely related to the affective aspects of any relationship. There is, however, a difference in the point of view involved. In considering the aspects of any relationship interest was focused on tools of analysis which could be applied to any conceivable relationship in any society. In considering the structures of solidarity, interest is focused upon the fact that relationships are universal in any society, however difficult it may be to prove that specific relationships as they are specifically institutionalized are a requirement for any society. Chapter 1 of this Part concerned itself with aspects of any relationship; the present chapter is concerned with the structures which inhere in any society or any other organization by virtue of the fact that there will be relationships that constitute subsystems of that society or that organization. The requisite basis of the structures of solidarity rests in the most general sense on the fact that the various requirements for the members of any society cannot be produced unless the members of that society enter into relationships with one another. Over the minimal basis for alleging that structures of solidarity are requisites of any society, there are many other equally compelling and not a great deal less obvious reasons. This gives the social analyst an extremely helpful hand with a rather difficult problem. Although it is difficult to maintain that a particular kind of social system is a requirement of any society, despite the ubiquity of families and governments, it is not difficult to show that certain structures of role differentiation and solidarity must be present.[1]

---

[1] It cannot be emphasized too strongly that none of these discussions in terms of what is required if a society is to survive is intended to imply that any given society or that societies in general must survive. That would be teleology, pure and simple. From a scientific point of view, at least, the continued existence of no society, let alone the welfare of its members, is foreordained. Whether such arguments can be supported on theological or metaphysical grounds need not interrupt the argument here. There has been a great tendency in recent social science literature to

The reason it is exceedingly difficult to allege that even a ubiquitous social system such as a family is a requisite of any society lies in the extreme flexibility and adaptability of membership units of many sorts. What can be done in terms of such a unit is subject to enormous variation. How is one to prove that an alternative to such an organization could not be invented such that operation in terms of that alternative organization would have all of the results which are necessary for the existence of a society? [2] The extraordinary flexibility of social systems and

assume that all social systems are in some special sense homeostatic. Some authors have even used an equilibrium assumption as part of their definitions of social systems. This is a quite fruitless strategem of analysis in most instances. It tends by either assumption or definition to establish something which is frequently at variance with the facts; it is a needless restriction on the range of variation of social phenomena which can be handled, if one uses these assumptions or definitions as one has set them up. There certainly are some social systems such that the actions of members in terms of them will have equilibrium or homeostatic properties, and there are certainly some that lack such implications unless one wishes to decide this issue by definition or assumption. The fact that one uses a stability assumption of some sort to ask a question such as, "What would a given society have to have *if* it were to survive?", in no ways implies that any society to which the results of such analysis are applied will in fact be one that survives. If, for example, I am able to maintain that certain types of attention by adults to infants are necessary for a society to survive and if I observe a society in which such structures do not exist, I can immediately conclude one of three or some combination of those three things: (1) my argument that such a relationship had to exist for society to exist is an untenable argument, (2) the system I am examining is not the kind of system which has to have that sort of a structure to survive or it is a society which is in the process of going out of existence, or (3) I have misobserved, and if I go back and reexamine the data more carefully, I will in fact find data on such a relationship. It is always teleological to say that a given structure must exist because it is a requirement of such and such a unit, although it may be quite correct to say that if that structure is a requisite of the unit and if the unit exists, that structure will also be found to exist.

There are various reasons having to do with the elegancies of scientific method which dictate that one should be exceedingly careful about such problems. Those reasons need not concern us here. What is of concern is that carelessness in these matters can lead to serious misjudgment of social situations. The idea that the traditional Chinese family had to continue to exist in its old form because it was essential to traditional Chinese society is misleading unless one also points out that traditional Chinese society did not have to continue to exist or that some form of Chinese society might continue to exist in a changed form such that the traditional Chinese family be no longer a requirement of that society. Arguments in terms of the requirements of a given system or situation are exceedingly dangerous if they get translated somehow into arguments either that a given structure must continue to exist because it existed before or that the system of which that structure is a part cannot change in so radical a fashion as to eliminate the necessity of that structure for the new system.

[2] Actually I am convinced that such an argument can be maintained, but it is too technical and too tentative to be presented here. Even so,

the ingenuity which individuals of the human species have shown about them make this a difficult question to answer in the relatively neat sense in which structures of role differentiation, solidarity, economic allocation, political allocation, and integration and expression can be shown to be requisites.

This is more galling to students of social phenomena whose major interest is in public affairs specifically because they must make decisions and act in terms of organizations rather than in terms of aspects of those organizations—however useful those aspects may be for analysis. The analysis of requisite structures of solidarity gives leads on what the organizations present in any situation are likely to be both in general and specific cases. Since certain solidarity structures must exist if any society is to exist, and therefore certain types of relationships must exist, organizations which incorporate those relationships must exist. This does not tell us the exact form those organizations must take, but it does indicate certain types of individuals who must be in some way or another organized in close relationships with one another.

There is no need to treat this in great detail here. Illustrations should suffice. If one considers role differentiation on the basis of absolute age alone, there are certain minimal implications for solidarity structures in any society. There must be such structures as between infants and adults, adults and children, adults and the aged, and adults and other adults. It is, perhaps, conceivable that there not be structures interrelating infants and other infants, infants and children, infants and the aged, children and other children, children and the aged, and the aged and other aged. If the solidarities dubbed necessary are in fact necessary, it is unlikely that those can be organized apart from some units in which these relationships appear as a set. It is also exceedingly unlikely that some if not all of the solidarities mentioned as not obviously necessary be either absent or neatly separated from those dubbed necessary.

There must also be some organizations in terms of which individuals of different relative ages interact and there must be some involving role differentiations on the basis of generation, sex, economic allocation, political allocation, and so forth. The most obvious example of an organization in which all of these solidarities inhere is, of course, a family organization. Claims of the Chinese Communist leaders and of students of the kibbutzim

the family and some organization in terms of which members of two or more families are interrelated are the only organizations about which I can mount such arguments that would apply to any society.

· 223 ·

in Israel notwithstanding, no society has ever been reported by any observer and reliably found to be devoid of families.

To some extent therefore, whether it is done self-consciously or not, we in fact always do locate organizations in terms of some considerations of solidarity structures. One of the bases for discriminating membership as among different organizations can be answered in terms of the question of who sticks with whom under what circumstances. In addition to that, any given organization can be described in terms of the varying solidarities of different members which, taken as a set, characterize that particular organization. By studying the content, strength, and intensity of solidarity aspects of relationships one can always isolate the various organizations in terms of which people act in any given social setting even if one lacks other means of identifying them.

I I I
RANGE OF VARIATION AND ITS RELEVANCE

In consideration of the structures of solidarity in a given social system one of the easiest questions to raise has to do with the number of solidarities self-consciously differentiated by the members of the society or the organization being studied. Is the number differentiated, for example, small or large? Here again we have our old numerical difficulty, but we are not concerned with dividing lines such as whether two hundred is a large number and fifty a small number but rather with whether one is dealing in terms of let us say several hundreds of solidarities by contrast with several thousands or tens of thousands or more. In general, the number of solidarities knowingly and importantly differentiated by the members of relatively nonmodernized as opposed to relatively modernized societies is small. There may be considerable differences among relatively nonmodernized societies. By contrast with the traditional Chinese, the Australian Bushmen differentiate relatively few solidarities, but the members of both societies differentiate relatively few solidarities, especially from the point of view of the average member of those societies, by contrast with those differentiated by virtually any member of any relatively modernized society.

The family is always a focus of solidarity differentiations in any society. So far there has been in world history no known society in which the solidarities distinguished in family terms have not been exceedingly important in explaining the development of the individual as well as in explaining the general set of interrelationships which characterize the society. In some societies the family unit may be in a sense *the* major focus of solidarity structures. Certainly one of the most extreme cases is that of traditional China. Proper behavior in terms of that society literally required that the individual put family considerations before all others. In solidarity terms that meant, for example, that ideally speaking the solidarity of a Chinese with his family head was the strongest solidarity he knew in terms of the entire society. Actually many individual Chinese no doubt transgressed against this moral standard, but there is little reason to doubt that, ideally and actually, for the overwhelming majority of all traditional Chinese the strength of the solidarity of any family member with his family head was stronger than his solidarity with any other family member or anyone who was not a family member. Perhaps few societies are as extreme as this, but a fairly close approach to it is by no means uncommon. In the Tokugawa period the solidarity of a Japanese with his overlord was stronger than his solidarity with anyone else, and second to that in strength was his solidarity with his family head. Thus, unlike the case of traditional China, the family was by no means the major focus of solidarity ideally speaking for everyone. Actually, however, for the average Japanese most of the time his family solidarities were the strongest solidarities in terms of which he acted. The vast majority of the members of that society never faced a situation in which the strength of their solidarities with family members was challenged by the strength of their solidarities with members of the society outside the family circle.[3]

One may generalize about societies throughout world history as follows:

(1) The family unit is always an important focus of solidarity structures.

(2) In some of them, ideally speaking, it is clearly *the* major focus of all solidarities.

(3) In all of the relatively nonmodernized societies, even if the family is not *the* major focus ideally speaking, it is always *actually the* major focus for the vast majority of the members for the vast proportion of their time.

[3] The samurai of Japan were supposed to be the great virtuosi of sacrifice of self-interest and family interest to the interests of their lords. For two hundred and fifty years relatively few of them had the opportunity to make such sacrifices and so attain the highest pinnacle of virtue distinguished by the members of that society. For the Tokugawa Japanese the focus of literature that took the place of romantic love or success in some other societies was this romantic sacrifice. For members of the society below the rank of samurai it was romantic even to consider one's self eligible for such sacrifices. Indeed, it was almost the commission of the sin of *lèse majesté* to act as though such a one were eligible to make such sacrifices. See above, pp. 121–122.

(4) In relatively modernized societies the family continues to be an important focus of solidarity structures, but neither ideally nor actually is it ever *the* single major focus of solidarity for the majority of the members of the society for the largest proportion of their time.

(5) The members of relatively modernized societies always have a large number of solidarities the strength of which in specific areas is always stronger than the strength of the individual's family solidarities.

(6) In all societies and in all subsystems of societies save those very few which are explicitly egalitarian, there always exists a hierarchical arrangement of solidarities. Even friendships which are usually institutionalized as explicitly egalitarian are in actuality often characterized by a hierarchical arrangement of solidarities. Indeed, this is more likely to be the case than not, despite the explicit ideal to the contrary.

(7) Explicitly egalitarian systems can never be developed to any great length in terms of either numbers of individuals involved as members of a single system or in terms of geographical areas or areas of social action covered. As the scale of social organizations increase, hierarchical arrangements of solidarities become increasingly important. It is also true, however, that in most of the small-scale social organizations the arrangement of solidarities is hierarchical rather than egalitarian.

(8) The dimension in terms of which solidarities are hierarchically arranged is most likely to be the dimension of strength of the solidarities. This is not inevitable. It is certainly possible to have a hierarchy of solidarities based on intensity, for example.

(9) Hierarchical arrangements of solidarities vary enormously in many ways even though the dimension of strength is likely to be the most strategic basis for such hierarchies. One of the most important lines of variation has to do with the degree of clarity with which the hierarchy is defined, whether it is based primarily on the strength of the solidarities or not.

The last of these generalizations is one of the most fruitful. In the illustrations given above of traditional Chinese society, one of the striking features is the clarity with which, at least ideally speaking, the hierarchical arrangement of solidarities is defined. An individual's solidarity with his family head is expected to take precedence over his solidarity with literally any other member of the society. In cases in which conflicts arise, the major criterion for settling the order of precedence of different solidarities is in the last analysis how one's family head would order one to settle such a controversy. One can generalize about societies or subsystems of societies further in the following fashion: the smaller the number of social units in terms of which an individual distinguishes different solidarities [i.e., the more concentrated the foci of solidarity], the easier and more likely it is that there be a clearcut hierarchical arrangement of such solidarities. This generalization follows almost trivially from the problem of cognition involved in appreciating the hierarchical arrangement of solidarities.

One of the special problems associated with relatively modernized societies is that the problem of clarity about the hierarchical arrangement of solidarities is vastly complicated in all these social contexts. The complications are minimized to the extent that many of the solidarities have to do with predominantly universalistically and functionally specifically defined relationships. To the extent that this is the case, the problems of solidarity arrangements are kept as much within a single organizational context as possible. The real case of conflict is conflict between a solidarity within one such context and some other solidarity which also characterizes an individual. This usually involves the question as to whether the individual should leave one of the organizations or the other. The greatest likelihood of conflict in these cases is not so much conflict involving members of two or more of these predominantly universalistically defined organizations, but rather conflict involving the solidarities an individual may have in terms of such an organization and in terms of a predominantly particularistically defined organization such as a family unit. However much emphases on predominantly universalistic criteria and functional specificity may simplify the matter ideally speaking, such emphases do not guarantee actual clarity. Some of the problems inherent in this situation are reflected in the frequent iterations of feelings that the members of such societies lead highly fractionated rather than whole lives. Individuals complain in their novels and in their letters to the editor that they are torn among too many "competing claims."

The flexibility of the human individual is generally conceded to be enormous. The inhabitants of relatively modernized societies accept as a matter of course, for all their difficulties of adjustment, a complexity of solidarities that would bewilder virtually any member of a relatively nonmodernized society. Here again inheres another of the special problems of adjustment in the transition from a relatively nonmodernized society to a relatively modernized one. Consideration of an emphasis on *individualism* is especially pertinent. In every society and indeed in every sub-system of a society there is some basis on which the individual member makes and/or is expected to make decisions affecting his future and the future of others with whom he interacts. Insofar as the individual himself is supposed to be or is the major basis for those decisions, *individualism* exists. Insofar as the individual is *actually* the major basis for the decision, *actual individualism* exists. Insofar as others with whom he interacts and he himself feels that he is *supposed* to make decisions on this basis, *ideal individualism* exists. In some cases individualism exists both ideally and actually. Elsewhere, considering this question, I have differentiated between *individualism by ideal* and *individualism by default.*[4] *Individualism by ideal* is present when individualism exists both ideally and actually. Individualism by ideal and ideal individualism are by no means the same. The latter may exist without the former but not vice versa. *Individualism by default* refers to a form of actual individualism in situations in which ideal individualism is explicitly not present. It does not, however, refer to the case of an individual who is supposed to and could make decisions on a nonindividualistic basis, but in fact makes them on the basis of his own considerations in defiance of custom. I shall call that form of actual individualism *deviant individualism.* Individualism by default refers rather to actual individualism which exists because the individual concerned cannot make decisions on any basis other than an individualistic one, whether he wishes to or not.

Individualism by ideal is a relatively rare social invention. Most people most of the time in most social settings have not been expected to make decisions on the basis of their own considerations. The general attitude toward individualism by ideal by members of societies other than the rare ones in terms of which individualism by ideal is institutionalized in some spheres has been parodied in a motion picture [5] by the statement of a traditional Chinese father who says to his son growing up in the United States, "When you are old enough to think for yourself, I will let you know." Neither individualism by default nor deviant individualism is so rare. There are always some individuals in any society who by force of one set of circumstances or another are not in a position to make nonindividualistic decisions, whether

[4] See: "Some Aspects of 'Individualism' and the Problem of Modernization in China and Japan," *Economic Development in Cultural Change,* vol. X, no. 3, April, 1962, pp. 225–240. I have benefitted from discussions of individualism with my colleague in history, John William Ward.

[5] See *The Flower Drum Song.*

they wish to or not. Furthermore, there are always some individuals who do not follow the nonindividualistic ideal structures even when they can.

Whenever individualism is present, there are special problems for stability in terms of the structures of solidarity in the systems concerned. After all, ideally and/or actually, whenever a conflict as between solidarities arises, the issue of how to settle it is thrown open. In situations that ideally speaking are nonindividualistic, when such a conflict arises, the issue of *how* to settle it does not necessarily arise. In many such cases the only issues which arise are: what is the nature of the conflict and what are the rules which one is supposed to apply to settle the order of precedence of solidarities. There is no question but that ideally and/or actually an emphasis on individualism always calls into question the going structure of loyalties or makes it easier to do so. This in turn has far-reaching implications for the general structures of control of the social systems involved. The rare cases of societies in terms of which individualism by ideal has been highly developed are also the rare cases of societies whose members heavily emphasize social change as an ideal.

In this connection a special problem in terms of solidarities and individualism inheres in the continual increase in the degree of centralization and of bureaucratization characteristic of relatively modernized societies as they become more and more highly modernized. It becomes increasingly difficult for individual members of such societies not only to move with sufficient flexibility from one place to another, but also to alter their actions from one role to another with sufficient flexibility, unless they behave on something approaching an individualistic basis. If some technique is not found of making the individual the major referent of his behavior, the detailed attention to detailed orders from a central source must be multiplied unbelievably. On the other hand, to the extent that the individual is made the focus of decision in these matters, the possibility that he may not make the correct decision is, of course, increased. Individualism in general and individualistically decided solidarities in particular may turn out to be one of the peculiar structures without which a highly modernized society cannot survive and with which it may not be able to survive either. For the most highly modernized societies such problems are well on the way to requiring us to revise our most seriously held predictions about social life as it will be lived in the penultimate decade of our century.

In summation, about the structures of solidarity in any society the following remarks may be made. As a minimum there will always be structures of solidarity oriented to the minimal interrelationships which must exist if the minimal differentiation of roles in a society are to be successfully coordinated with one another—if that society is to exist. That is to say, there must be solidarities oriented to role differentiations on the basis of absolute and relative age, generation, sex, economic allocation, political allocation, religion, cognition, the nonhuman environment, and finally solidarity itself. As a minimum in every society which survives there must be actual organizations in terms of which these solidarities are conducted. The number and detailed description of these organizations are subject to enormous variation, but insofar as the set of them for a given society must cover all of these solidarities, the substantive structures of those organizations are by no means completely arbitrary. Although it is difficult to prove this in a detailed sense, one of the clear-cut implications of this argument is that one of those organizations is exceedingly likely to be [or inevitably is] a family organization of some sort. In the study of any society, if one has not covered all of these minimal solidarities, something is seriously lacking in the analysis. If one does not cover this possibility, he may be suddenly faced with a difficulty which is a function of the fact that action in terms of a solidarity that he did not anticipate has taken precedence over action in terms of a solidarity that he previously believed invulnerable or unthreatened. Although they have not been worked out here, corresponding hypotheses can be developed with regard to the minimum presence of solidarity structures in any particular organization with which it is necessary to deal. Whenever roles are differentiated and the activities in terms of those differentiated roles have to be coordinated and those roles involve different individuals, some more or less explicitly recognized structures of solidarity must be present, if action is to proceed effectively.

ECONOMIC ALLOCATION

I
DEFINITIONS

A. STRUCTURES OF ECONOMIC ALLOCATION

Structures of economic allocation are defined as those structures having to do with the distribution of goods and/or services making up the income of the members of the social systems concerned and of the goods and/or efforts making up their output among the various members of those systems, and among the members of those systems and other systems with whom they are in contact. Structures of economic allocation may be subdivided into structures of production and structures of consumption.

B. STRUCTURES OF PRODUCTION AND CONSUMPTION

1. INTRODUCTION

Structures of production include all of the structures in terms of which the members of a given social system create or modify the goods and/or services which accrue in the name of the system [i.e., accrue in some fashion however transitory to its members]. These goods and/or services may be taken from the members or some set of them in a variety of ways as quickly as they accrue. *Structures of consumption* include all of the structures in terms of which goods and/or services are allocated to and utilized by the various members of the social systems concerned for the purposes recognized by the members of those systems. As already indicated above [pp. 210–211] production and consumption exemplify a special sort of distinction. What is production from one point of view is consumption from another. Nevertheless, it makes a considerable amount of difference whether a particular activity is looked at from the point of view of production or from the point of view of consumption. There are always some organizations in every society in terms of which distinctions between production and consumption are considered unimportant if made at all. These are, of course, never predominantly economically oriented organizations. They are either differently specialized or relatively nonspecialized organizations. The best example of this is again a family unit. In every society families are actually units in terms of which important forms of production and consumption take place. The activities of the members in terms of a given family are frequently not [or hardly ever] differentiated on the basis of production and consumption as such either by the members of that family or others of the society. It may nevertheless be of the greatest utility for an individual in attempting to analyze family units to make this differentiation. In relatively nonmodernized societies the families are units which combine most of the production and consumption of most of the members. The vast majority of the members of any relatively modernized society consider the family overwhelmingly as a unit in terms of which consumption rather than production takes place. But even from the point of view of those most accustomed to differentiate in these specialized terms, the actual activities carried out in family terms are rarely differentiated into those of production and consumption as such. What goes on in the family context is spoken of as consumption from the point of view of nonfamily activities of the members and the society as a whole. Within the family context it would be unusual to differentiate activities into those of production, e.g., preparation of food, cleaning of the household, rearing of children, etc., and those of consumption, e.g., eating of food, watching the television set, enjoying a good night's sleep, etc. In relatively nonmodernized societies the family context encompasses activities which would be sharply differentiated by the members of a more modernized society as predominantly production-oriented activities or as predominantly consumption-oriented activities [if considered from an economic point of view (on the asymmetry of the concepts of production and consumption see below, pp. 247–248, 504–513, and 522–523], but those actually involved consider their activities as family activities and not as specialized predominantly economically oriented activities in any sense.

The fact that such specialized differentiations are not commonly made in any sharp form by the members of a given society makes a great deal of difference to anyone who seeks to analyze and understand these phenomena. For example, in terms especially relevant to the problems of modernization, the tendency of any observer more used to the practices of members of a relatively modernized society to view family activities as legitimately primarily a special focus of consumption, if considered from the economic point of view, is likely to be viewed by members of a relatively nonmodernized society as either unfeeling, unknowing, or even as an interference with appropriately family-oriented activities. To pursue an occupational role outside the family context is to have a whole new world open up for most of the members of such societies. To do so is also likely to undermine a whole set of characteristic reinforcements for the stability of family structures and hence usually of more general structures as well.

2. STRUCTURES OF PRODUCTION

In analysis of the structures of production, one of the terms most frequently encountered is the division of labor. The term *division of labor* is defined here as role differentiation on the basis of production. It is important to realize that the members of a given society or of a given organization within a society may not make these differentiations in any sharp fashion. I have already indicated above that such differentiations are much more likely in relatively modernized societies and are most likely in terms of the highly specialized social systems that characterize such societies. Even in those settings, these differentiations are not made neatly within relatively nonspecialized organizations such as family units. Some distinctions among forms of production are minimally required in any society and are necessary in analyzing the division of labor in any society. These may be divided into three categories: (1) the production of raw materials [i.e., materials or objects which exist in a nonhuman environment and are either directly dissipated upon their acquisition or are dissipated in the creation of other goods or services], (2) manufactured goods [i.e., all goods which are modified by human activities for human purposes from a raw material state], and (3) the actual allocation of goods and/or services itself [i.e., the production of management, delivery services, salesmanship activities, gift bestowals, regardless of whether these activities are germane primarily to production for further production or to delivery for consumption].

Even in the simplest of societies, to some extent, structures of all three types of production exist, though they are by no means neatly differentiated one from another in a highly specialized form. The members of relatively modernized societies, of course, differentiate these in considerable detail in neatly specialized forms.

a. RAW MATERIALS The production of raw materials may take many forms. Certain minimal raw materials are necessary for survival itself, e.g., for food, clothing, and shelter. Raw materials may be subdivided into animate and inanimate products. Animate products may in turn be divided into those of a botanical character and those of a zoological character. Raw materials for products over and above the minimum necessary for survival may be similarly subdivided.

Structures of production of botanical raw materials are confined to structures of simple collection and structures of collection based to some degree on processes of cultivation. Collection in the absence of cultivation may vary all the way from structures such as gathering nuts and berries to structures involving the use of complex machinery in a planned deforestation for the purposes of timber production or a highly modernized fishing fleet. No society of any considerable scale can exist if the members resort solely to collection activities in order to secure a supply of organic materials. Insofar as the members of any society do depend on such collection activities, the range of variation of such a society will be to that degree more narrowly explicable in terms of human heredity and the nonhuman environment than would otherwise be the case. The addition of mechanical aids for collection increases flexibility to some extent, but it is safe to say that no considerable development of such mechanical aids can itself develop unless some structures other than simple structures of collection exist in the society or in other societies with which the members of the society concerned are in contact. When such mechanical aids exist, the requirements of their production and their maintenance introduce inflexibilities of another sort, usually those involving an increase in the interdependency of the subsystems within the societies concerned.

Although structures of simple collection cannot be completely ignored because of their role in the economic aspects of a society, the most cavalier reading of social history impresses one with the importance of structures of cultivation in all relatively stable societies of any considerable scale, and of clearly developed organizations in terms of which cultivation of whatever sort is carried out. Indeed, relatively few societies of any sort seem to survive in the absence of such a development. There are examples, however. Certain Eskimo peoples exist [or have existed] for whom concentration is perhaps overwhelmingly on animal rather than botanical sources of raw materials. On the whole, some structures of cultivation of plants are, if not ubiquitous, at least present in the overwhelming proportion of all known societies. The term *agrarian* will be used here to apply to those structured aspects and subsystems of any society which are concerned with the cultivation of plant materials.

Agrarian elements in a society always limit nomadism. Some of the members of such a society must be tied to specific areas during planting and harvesting seasons. The implications go well beyond this, however, since constant care and attention between planting and harvesting activities are necessary in most cases if there is to be any considerable harvest at all. The limits on nomadism are not the only implications of the presence of agrarian elements in a society. Some concepts of rights and obligations in locational factors [i.e., property rights in the land] and some conceptions of their distribution among the members of such societies are an inevitable concomitant. Conflicts over these, as well as other matters, must be held within certain limits; certain minimal responsibilities for cultivation must be allocated; and there must be specific structures of distribution for the products of such production, as there must be for any forms of production.

A large number of aspects of agrarian production have far-reaching implications for general social structures. The different plants themselves, the different characteristics of different soils, climates, and seasons, the different types of work units—all have widespread implications which cannot be ignored. The differences between relatively modernized and relatively nonmodernized structures of agrarian production are especially significant for present purposes. As pointed out before, the term *modernized* permits of indefinite degrees of variation despite the fact that the distinction between the terms *relatively modernized* and *relatively nonmodernized* identify social states characterized by other distinctions that differ far beyond the elements of tools and power in their definitions. It is useful to differentiate societies with respect to the degree and kind of modernization or lack of it. The range of variation possible for relatively nonmodernized societies is widely different from that possible for relatively modernized ones. In many respects the range of variation possible and actual in relatively nonmodernized agrarian systems is much greater than in relatively modernized ones. Furthermore, the higher the level of modernization, the greater is the isomorphism of the systems concerned. Members of relatively nonmodernized societies, for example, may organize such production in terms of an almost indefinite number of different types of differently [though usually predominantly particularistically] recruited units. Members of relatively modernized societies must increasingly emphasize more predominantly universalistically recruited units. The degree of self-sufficiency of the organizations is much higher in the relatively nonmodernized cases. Variations in the scale and variety of products, degree of specialization, etc., are much higher in the relatively modernized cases. The relative ease of comparability, especially as the level of modernization increases, increases the importance of the recognition of these factors for purposes of comparative analysis.

I have focused overwhelmingly on botanical raw materials above rather than on animal raw materials. With regard to animal raw materials, again the distinction between simple collection and cultivation [i.e., animal husbandry in this case] is drawn. Here the possibilities of combining both simple collection and animal husbandry with nomadism are considerable. In both cases the details of the nonhuman environment, the size of the membership of the society, and the type of animals involved place definite limits on the degree to which nomadism can be avoided and the degree to which it can be practiced if the society is to persist.

The greater mobility of animal as opposed to plant stocks means, of course, that animal husbandry does not have the same implications for sedentary structures as agrarian production. Structures relative to the use of space are also considerably different. The clear demarcation of hunting and fishing preserves as well as grazing possibilities is both more difficult and less practicable than is the clear demarcation of plots of land for cultivation of plant stocks. Extremely small, highly parcellated land holdings of the type characteristic of many agrarian-based societies are quite out of the question in animal-husbandry-based societies. The implications of greater spatial mobility of the membership of such societies for the organization of different social systems are considerable as are the requirements of locomotion and the like.

Sedentary animal husbandry also has different implications for social structures than does sedentary agrarian production. Given land capable of both agrarian cultivation and animal husbandry, other factors being equal and quite apart from the differences in mobility of plants and animals, the amount of land necessary to support human life via animal husbandry is much greater. For all of the inefficiencies of agriculture it is more productive per acre in terms of food and other raw materials than is animal husbandry, assuming land adaptable to either purpose. Given land adaptable in physiological terms for either purpose, animal husbandry can be more profitable than agriculture in terms of food production only under certain conditions. There must be a comparative advantage for animal husbandry between the area concerned and other areas with which its users are in contact, i.e., it must be possible for exchange to take place among the inhabitants of these areas such that persons involved in animal husbandry can more than equal their possibilities of agrarian food production through the exchange of the products of animal husbandry for agrarian products. Even apart from differences in productivity, animal husbandry would still require different social structures. The types of knowledge required vary widely, and different organizations are both feasible and necessary. The differences involved are well illustrated in history when members of societies characterized by agrarian production and animal husbandry and/or different types of animal husbandry have come into contact with one another. Conflict among the members has been a frequent feature. Conflicts between cattlemen and sheepmen, cattlemen and farmers, etc., in the history of the United States were not only notorious for the violence and bitterness involved, but also clearly reflected different ways of life. In England the enclosure movement and in China the contacts between the Chinese and the Mongols contained important elements of this sort. Throughout history cases of change from cultivation to animal husbandry or from one type of cultivation or animal husbandry to another have had far-reaching social implications. It is not necessary to be an economic determinist to learn the lesson that they really did have to teach us, namely that the structures of production are never without some implications for other types of structures in any society.

As in the case of agrarian production, animal husbandry too can be carried out on a relatively modernized or relatively non-modernized basis. In animal husbandry, too, the implications of the difference are far-reaching. Modernization in animal husbandry increases the practicable scale of production units and in fact places minimal requirements on the scale. The productivity of labor is tremendously increased, though the absolute productivity of all of the other factors involved need not necessarily be increased, at least not to the same degree that the productivity of labor is increased.

Modernization in this field requires the integration of raw material production with some manufacturing. The further modernization is carried, the greater becomes the interdependence in these respects and the lower the degrees of self-sufficiency possible for the organizations in terms of which animal husbandry is conducted. In a highly modernized society, for example, an obscure grievance precipitating a strike of power workers could create a major crisis within a matter of hours in the dairy production of the area concerned. Prior to the invention and spread of automatic milking machines, such interdependency was unknown. Increases in modernization both increase and decrease flexibility. As far as self-sufficiency is concerned the decrease is the more noticeable. Flexibility with regard to product differentiation, elaboration, etc., is increased. The possibilities of disposing of a product are increased, but the necessity of such disposal outside the membership of the organization in terms of which production takes place is also increased. It is always the essence of modernization that the use of machinery and power so multiplies the effort of the people engaged in production that the members of the unit in terms of which production takes place can never hope to consume directly all or even most of the products they produce. It is quite out of the question to set up a modern dairy production organization solely to supply the dairy needs of the individuals involved in the unit itself.

Apart from growing crystals and the like, the possibilities of self-propagation under control are out of the question with regard to inanimate products. One is confined to collection techniques, though these may vary widely. There is a difference between the ways in which the production of animate and inanimate raw materials may or must fit into a society. It is conceivable, perhaps, that puristic vegetarians use little or no animal or inanimate raw materials. A society whose members are similarly focused on animal products is also at least conceivable. Similar concentration upon inanimate raw materials is, however, quite out of the question because of the relative unavailability of inanimate raw materials as foodstuffs. Therefore, inanimate raw material production must, to some extent, be integrated with some structures of production of animate raw materials. In all the societies of concern here some inanimate raw materials are always involved, but the difference in degree of preoccupation possible on a raw material level as between animate and inanimate materials is nevertheless significant. Hunting, fishing, agrarian, or animal husbandry structures can conceivably well nigh, if not completely, exhaust the raw material production of the members of a society. This cannot even conceivably be the case with regard to inanimate raw material production such as mining and the like. In the production of inanimate raw materials distinctions among the degrees and types of modernization must also be explored.

b. MANUFACTURED GOODS As the term *manufactured goods* is used here, some element of manufacture enters the raw material picture whenever the production of raw materials passes the most rudimentary collection procedures. In both cultivation and animal husbandry, for example, almost at once some modification in selection of stocks takes place. Such elements enter the picture to a marked degree with increases in the level of modernization. Elements of manufacture in the production of raw materials must, therefore, be carefully distinguished. Structures of production of manufactured goods obviously cannot stand alone in any society or in any subsystem of any society. No matter how specialized organizations become, in relation to any manufactured goods, two other types of questions relevant to economic aspects inevitably arise. First, there is the question of the materials which are modified. What are they? How are they produced? How do they get to the manufacturers, etc.? Second, there is the question of the process of modification itself. What further goods and/or services are required for this process? Where do they come from? How do they get to the manufacturers, etc.? It may be conceivable for there to be a society in which virtually all of the structures of production are confined to raw materials and the services of allocation without any manufacturing, but if there is any manufacturing at all, there must be both structures of production of raw materials and structures of allocation as well.

Manufacturing, as conceived here, covers quite rudimentary modifications—rudimentary enough to make structures of manufacture an inevitable component in any society of any scale. Cooked food, sharpened tools, as well as modern blast furnaces are all examples of manufactured goods as that term is used here. Virtually all raw materials used by the members of any society of any scale undergo some modification by human activity prior to consumption. It is important to distinguish between raw materials and manufactured goods, nevertheless, since to some extent raw materials may be directly consumed without a modification beyond the gathering thereof. Such structures can never exhaust the structures of production in a society because of the helplessness of some of the members of the society, but they may be present for many. As soon as the question of modification arises, however, questions of the source and character of the things modified and the things used to modify them arise. The problem of sources of goods for modification plus modification itself always makes any altered or manufactured good different in kind as far as its social significance is concerned from any raw material.

As in the case of raw materials for present purposes the most important distinction with regard to manufactured goods is whether or not they are manufactured on a relatively modernized or a relatively nonmodernized basis. Here again relatively nonmodernized manufacture is subject to a wider range of variation in many respects than is relatively modernized manufacture. This is particularly true with regard to the types of organizations in terms of which such production may be carried out. The emphases, associated with high levels of modernization, on rationality, universalism, and functional specificity, for example, limit the possibilities of relationships in terms of which manufacturing can be carried out quite sharply. The organizations in terms of which manufacturing is conducted by the members of relatively nonmodernized societies are likely to be predominantly particularistic—indeed, they are usually family units. They are by no means inevitably so, however. In relatively nonmodernized societies the units in terms of which manufacturing takes place are also ordinarily the units in terms of which most of the consumption of the goods manufactured also takes place. In relatively modernized contexts, however, only restricted manufacturing can be carried out in terms of the same units in terms of which consumption of these items takes place.

c. ALLOCATION The production of *allocation* is more likely to be ignored than the production of either raw materials or manufactured goods. Two categories of allocation are distinguished here: (1) allocation in the *managerial sense,* i.e., the planning and supervision of the productive processes themselves, and (2) the *distributive sense,* i.e., the distribution of the goods and/or services produced to the persons or sets of people who will consume them. Both forms of allocation must take place if any society is to survive. Goods and services can neither be produced nor dissipated at random if a society is to survive. Allocation in both senses is always carefully structured in every known society.

What is production from one point of view is, simultaneously, consumption from another point of view, but the consumption of a given article is by no means necessarily simultaneous with its production. There is one sense, however, in which the production of allocation differs from the production of either raw materials or manufactured goods. The processes of allocation are at one and the same time produced and consumed. Both types of allocative processes share this characteristic. A given act involving allocation may be only one step in a further chain of allocation, but as it is effected it is consumed. The organization of a hunting party is done when it is done. Its members may stand idle for months, though organized, but they are in essence consuming their organizational characteristics all the time. Goods delivered to a wholesaler's warehouse may sit there forever, but the production and consumption of their delivery are simultaneous. An additional peculiarity of the managerial form of allocation is the possibility of its being consumed indefinitely. However indestructible the goods may be, they have some span of life as a particular type of goods. Some types of services are indefinite in these respects. The planning of a given activity is one of these. One of the interesting distinctions as far as allocation is concerned between relatively modernized and relatively nonmodernized societies is precisely the fact that in the context of relatively modernized societies the managerial sense of allocation is usually quite short lived. In the context of relatively nonmodernized societies the managerial sense of allocation may have a very long life indeed.

There is one important distinction between managerial and distributive allocation. The former is not separable from the production to which it is relevant whereas the latter is. Managerial allocation of some sort inheres in every process of production and is consumed simultaneously with the process of production. The distribution of the fruits of such production may be handled in terms of separate organizations altogether. No activity can exist without some direction whether centralized or decentralized. From the point of view of the general members of a society there must also be actual distributive mechanisms, but these need not be operated directly in terms of the units in terms of which the goods and/or services to be distributed are in fact produced. The members of one organization may build automobiles, and the members of another quite distinct one, either private or state, may drive them away.

Finally, the general relevance of the allocation of goods and services for the structures of political allocation must be noted briefly. Managerial allocation is inseparable from the allocation of power and responsibility in the productive processes. The actual distribution of goods and/or services is no less inextricably involved with questions of power and responsibility, but it is involved in a different way. Without some command over the allocation of goods and services, neither power nor responsibility holders would be alive to carry out their roles, but the matter goes far beyond this. The relevance of the allocation of goods and services as an instrument of coercion, persuasion, and influence in general, cannot be overlooked. One need not go to the unjustifiable extreme of holding that "man lives by bread alone" for such factors to be relevant. It is only necessary to realize that "no man lives by nonmaterial factors alone." As indicated [pp. 125–126] there is a limit to the degree of other worldliness possible for the members of any society which persists, even though some minimum of this may also be inescapable. No study which ignores the implications of the allocation of goods and services for the allocation of power and responsibility, and vice versa, can handle the problems which inhere in the general field of public and international affairs.

3. STRUCTURES OF CONSUMPTION

Much of what has been said immediately above would apply also to the consumption aspects if only because of the fact that what is production from one point of view is consumption from another. Nevertheless, implications of viewing economic allocation in terms of both of these concepts are quite different. It is primarily from the point of view of consumption that we learn how one set of activities implements another in terms of a given society. It matters, for example, whether the factors consumed are raw materials, manufactured goods, or allocation services. It matters whether or not they are produced under relatively modernized or relatively nonmodernized conditions. Just as revealing, however, are the implications of how command over consumption implements the allocation of power and responsibility, how much and what sorts of consumption are allocated to what sorts of educational activities, etc. Distinctions among the things produced have direct implications for how they may be produced because of the empirical nature of the processes involved. What is consumed also has relevance for how it may be consumed. Since goods produced by either relatively modernized or relatively nonmodernized processes can sometimes serve the same consumption purposes, the *purposes* of consumption become in a sense the more directly relevant part of the analysis. Three questions must be considered in the analysis of any organizations in terms of which consumption is to be studied: (1) what is the source and type of income of the members of the organization qua members, (2) how and by whom is the distribution of the income controlled, and (3) to whom and for what purposes is income allocated? These questions enter any consideration of the structures of consumption. Many of the factors touched on above have implications for the possible range of variation in these respects. The helplessness of infants, for example, at one and the same time precludes their services as managers and requires that the roles of others be so differentiated as to make consumption possible for infants.

In general, if one looks at economic allocation from the point of view of production, one stresses the manner in which given things get done. If one looks at economic allocation from the point of view of consumption, he tends to stress the implications of what gets done for subsequent events. The analysis of action from the point of view of production stresses the implications of action in terms of various organizations and general structured aspects of social systems for economic allocation; the analysis of action from the point of view of consumption stresses the implications of economic allocation for action in terms of various organizations and general structured aspects of social systems.

I I
SELF-SUFFICIENCY VERSUS INTERDEPENDENCE OF SOCIAL SYSTEMS

One of the most important distinctions among different sorts of social systems has to do with the extent to which action in terms of a given system combines most of the production and consumption of the members of the system, that is the extent to which its structures cover most of the economic aspects of the member's behavior. Obviously no social systems can be highly self-sufficient unless they are organizations of this sort. Because of general preoccupation with economic aspects of behavior as well as because of the relative ease of perception and measurement of goods and services, observation of the relative self-sufficiency of a given system with regard to the production of and consumption of goods and services by its members is, in fact, probably the quickest key to the question of whether or not it is highly self-sufficient in more general respects as well. Such a key should not be used uncritically. While economic self-sufficiency is a *sine qua non* of more general self-sufficiency, it is certainly not the only matter to be considered in making such a judgment. Despite the enormous mutual relevance of economic and political allocation, an organization may be highly self-sufficient economically without being highly self-sufficient politically.

A given social system will be considered economically self-sufficient to the degree and in the respects that its membership can and does both produce and consume all the goods and/or services necessary to and resulting from the operations of the members in terms of the unit. In this sense, no unit of any society is completely self-sufficient economically, though the society may be. To the extent that complete self-sufficiency is impossible, there are minimal requirements for relations among the members of any given unit and the members of some other unit(s). This is obviously true from the point of view of production aspects of economic allocation. The members of an organization in terms of which shoes but no food are produced must have contact, directly or indirectly, with some members of organizations in terms of which food is produced. This is no less true from the point of view of consumption aspects of economic allocation. The members of a unit who cannot and do not consume all that they produce must have interrelationships with members of other organizations who can fill this function of consumption or they must accumulate unconsumed products endlessly. The only alternative is to cut back production with the structural changes that would thereby be involved. The implications of the self-sufficiency of the units are, in general, all implications for the involvement of the members of the units concerned with the members of other units in the society, and specifically in this case, the implications are the implications of the economic aspects of the units concerned for other aspects of these and other units. Self-sufficiency may vary widely if not infinitely in degree and type. This is true of both consumption and production. Some specific formulation of the degree and type of self-sufficiency of the units concerned from both the point of view of production and consumption is necessary in the analysis of any society. From the point of view of production, self-sufficiency of a unit varies in two main respects: (1) to what extent do operations in terms of the unit produce all the necessary factors for the production carried out in terms of it, and (2) to what extent do the operations in terms of the unit produce the factors necessary for the consumption of the members of the unit apart from that involved in the production itself? The first question is always involved in considering any organization. The second is only involved directly in those organizations in terms of which both the production and the consumption of the members are combined ideally speaking. Examples may illuminate this distinction. The typical factory unit of relatively modernized societies is oriented consumptionwise to those materials necessary for the production carried out in terms of it. Raw materials, labor, machines, power, etc., are involved. Insofar as it has any self-sufficiency, its self-sufficiency is to be reckoned in those terms. The consumption activities of its members, apart from the factors mentioned above, are expected to be carried out in terms of quite different units. Some of these different units are always family units, but there may be many other types of units as well. The lack of self-sufficiency in production of these other units is not directly germane to the factory unit's self-sufficiency unless this lack of self-sufficiency interferes with the ability of the members of the factory to operate in terms of the structures of the factory. Thus housing for workers is not ordinarily a concern of the members of the factory units as such. On the other hand, if a decision is made to locate a plant in a place such that housing is inaccessible for workers, some provision of housing itself or of transportation for workers from available housing is directly germane to the self-sufficiency of the factory organization from the point of view of production.

On the other hand, in a society like that of traditional China, quite a different picture obtains. In that society the basic unit in terms of which production was generally carried out was the peasant family unit. Unlike the factory illustration above, that unit was also, ideally speaking, the unit in terms of which most of the consumption as well as most of the production of most of the members was carried out. In the case of the traditional Chinese family both types of consideration relative to self-sufficiency were germane all of the time. The traditional Chinese family unit lacked economic self-sufficiency not only if its members could not produce the tools, seeds, etc., necessary for agrarian production, but also if they did not produce the food, clothing, shelter, and services necessary for all of their consumption. Ideally speaking most of the members of that society were expected to carry out both types of production in terms of the same unit. They also expected to consume those goods and services in terms of the same unit. These peasant families were never completely self-sufficient. To some degree the peasants were involved in some interdependencies because of the import of goods from nonfamily sources—goods such as iron for tools, salt, etc. Had this been the sum total of the involvement of the members, interdependencies with the members of other units could have been kept at an absolute minimum by exchanging goods and/or services produced in the family context for the ones just mentioned. Actually interdependency was forced further because of exports in the form of taxes, rents, and interest on loans. Taxes were virtually unavoidable, and in many parts of China at many different periods of history the rates of tenancy rose quite high.[1]

The degree of economic interdependence of units of the second

---

[1] There was another interesting interference with the self-sufficiency of the peasant Chinese family, as China was, ideally speaking, an open-class society. Its class structure got badly clogged, and perhaps relatively few people did rise in proportion to the total population, but to rise was always a goal to be striven for. In a genuine sense, for members of a family to rise in the social scale in China, they had to get involved in increased interdependency with the members of other units. As a minimum they had to find some way to export and exchange goods and/or services produced in terms of their family for other goods and/or services or for money which could be used to buy additional land or still other goods and/or services for exchange.

type is less than in the case of units of the factory type, if operations in terms of the units take place according to expectations. This distinction is not only significant, however, when the operations take place according to expectations. They are equally relevant when this doesn't happen. Cases like that of the factory unit, for example, require carefully structured forms of economic interdependence of far-reaching proportions. Cases like that of the traditional Chinese peasant family do not, and commonly such societies lack a comparable development of carefully structured forms of economic interdependence. A given economic failure in the context of highly developed factories is likely to result in spreading the problems of the failure along the lines of this expected interdependence. Failure to dispose of factory products brings unemployment of factory workers; their unemployment lowers their ability to purchase foodstuffs, etc.; this in turn affects operations in terms of other units of production; and depending on the degree of interdependence, the effects of such an economic dislocation spread widely and rapidly among the members of the society concerned and among those of other societies economically interdependent with them. In the case of the Chinese peasant family such spreads are far more restricted. Only conditions such as drought, floods, and insect scourges which wipe out simultaneously the production of the members of large numbers of families bring widespread economic depression. When such depressions occur and spread, they are not generally understandable in terms of the units and the interstitial adjustments of their members. Furthermore, the problems of relief in such situations are further complicated by the fact that ordinarily in those systems the very units dislocated are the standard relief units. Organization of relief in the case of highly self-sufficient units generally requires the erection of structures of economic interdependency of a type not previously in existence.

Finally, a special observation is necessary with regard to the close interrelationship of the structures of economic and political allocation. The higher the level of self-sufficiency of an organization from the economic point of view, the greater is the problem of exercising centralized control over the members of the organization. To the extent that such units are highly self-sufficient in goods and services, control of the flow of goods and/or services is unavailable as a means of enforcing conformity on or requiring other performances from the members concerned. Given the general relevance of the allocation of goods and/or services for other aspects of behavior, one of the first things which must be done if one wishes to increase centralized control in societies with subsystems that are highly self-sufficient economically is to break down the degree of economic self-sufficiency of those systems. On the other hand, the less economically self-sufficient the subsystems of a society are, the greater are the implications for the existing structures of control of any breakdown in the allocations of goods and services in terms of the society. Highly self-sufficient peasant units are more difficult for members of a central government to control, but highly interdependent factory units pose much greater problems for the continued stability of a government if governmental control is inefficient or irrational from the economic point of view.

I I I
SPECIALIZATION OF THE SUBSYSTEMS

Specialization of the subsystems of a society from the economic point of view is subject to very wide variation, but limits are possible. For every society major elements of consumption always take place in a family context. There are no known exceptions to this. They are, of course, many societies whose members do not make the distinction between consumption and production as glibly as members of our society have been trained to do. Nevertheless, in both relatively modernized and relatively nonmodernized societies the family units are always a focus of consumption from the point of view of the members of the society in general and the members of the various families in particular. As indicated above, the members of relatively modernized societies frequently speak as though family units were the only units in terms of which consumption takes place save for individual exceptions of more or less unapproved hedonism. There is always some element of production in a family context too in all known societies, but the production element is more likely to be overlooked in critical respects. This is characteristic of relatively modernized societies. No one can look at the family organizations of relatively nonmodernized societies without being struck by the fact that a vast proportion of the production aspects of behavior are conducted in family terms. There may be examples of relatively nonmodernized societies in terms of which only a small proportion of the general production-oriented activities are carried out in family terms, but if such cases exist, they are rare. In relatively modernized societies, however, the development of specialized predominantly economically oriented organizations has gone quite far. The vast majority of these are not only specialized with regard to their economic aspects, but within the range of their economic aspects they are specialized from the point of view of their production aspects. In these societies there are not only predominantly economically oriented organizations, but almost certainly all of those are predominantly production-oriented as well. In considering such societies one hardly thinks of the family as a unit in terms of which production takes place, despite the fact that a considerable proportion of child care, the preparation of food, and other forms of production are still, even in the most modernized societies, carried out in family contexts. In both relatively modernized and relatively nonmodernized societies there are examples of specialized predominantly economically oriented organizations that are specially oriented to production. In no known social context, however, have organizations been specialized as predominantly consumption-oriented, predominantly economically oriented organizations. Such organizations may have existed as special forms of hedonistic expression, but they have probably never been generally approved or sanctioned by the members of the societies in which they have existed. From the point of view of the people who work in terms of them the most specialized recreationally oriented organizations such as night clubs, for example, are predominantly production-oriented rather than consumption-oriented if considered from the economic point of view. Even in societies in terms of which the members feel that most of the consumption is carried out in family terms, the family is never generally considered to be overwhelmingly oriented to consumption rather than to noneconomic aspects of behavior. Even in the most modernized societies family units are not considered to be more oriented to consumption than to solidarity, education, child rearing, etc. I mention this because there is an element of asymmetry here with regard to the concepts of production and consumption as they are actually embodied in social practice.[2]

The specialization of social systems is, of course, closely interrelated with the question of the self-sufficiency. Family units can never be specialized units in this sense, and organizations that are specialized in this sense can never approach the level of self-sufficiency that can be approached by family units. Members of organizations other than family units, whether specialized in these respects or not, must always have interrelationships with members of family units and other nonfamily units. The members of family units, if those units are self-sufficient enough, need

[2] This asymmetry is disturbing and/or interesting theoretically given the fact that what is production from one point of view is always consumption from another. Its possible significance is discussed in greater detail below, pp. 504–513.

not have relationships with members of other family units save for the minimal exchange of personnel necessary to comply with whatever form of incest taboo applies in the particular society concerned. As iterated before, the greater the specialization of a given organization, the lower is its self-sufficiency. The reverse is not necessarily the case, however. Relatively unspecialized units may be highly interdependent ones.

I V
FORMS OF PRODUCTION

From the point of view of observations strategic for the analysis of societies in general and for the analysis of relatively modernized as opposed to relatively nonmodernized societies in particular, volumes could easily be written on the forms of production alone. Some of what has to be said as a minimum has already been said above in the initial elaboration of the distinction between production and consumption itself. Here I shall only reiterate a few special considerations that are likely to be overlooked. A great many of the most essential observations about forms of production are fortunately treated at great length in the general literature of economics, and in the special literatures of industrial sociology, business school publications, and the field usually referred to as human organization and human relations.

First, no matter how varied societies may be, there are always some forms of production common to all societies. One of the best examples of this is infant and child care. The common details of this form of production are by no means as abstract as the observation that some form of production of food is common to all societies. It is possible to go into considerable detail as to what the minima of child care are for the members of any society. They not only involve food, shelter, clothing, and the services necessary for some level of cleanliness, but also, very importantly indeed, education and training, including virtually all of the training in those skills that form the foundation on which all other skills and learning rest in later life. This matter will be gone into in greater detail below [pp. 377–435]. For the moment, suffice it to say that these skills involve speaking, eating, sleeping, locomotion, perception in general, modes of thought, and initial adjustments to role differentiation, solidarity, economic allocation, political allocation, and integration and expression. Not only are these forms of production common to all societies, but a considerable portion of such production always takes place for the overwhelming majority of all of the members in terms of family units. Leaving to one side the so far inadequately examined claims of such devices as the Chinese communes and the kibbutzim of Israel, the members of the family organizations characteristic of the modern United States probably go further than any other family members in world history in the export of child and infant care to social contexts other than family ones. Even in the modern United States, however, the observations above hold.

The common core of forms of production always extends beyond infant and child care, but family units are an exceedingly good place to seek out most of the minimal common forms of production for all societies. The reasons for this should already be obvious from much of what has been said above. Prior to the development of relatively modernized societies, the family unit was more likely to be the unit in terms of which economic allocation took place for most of the members of any given society, most of the time, than any other organization. Neighborhood units of some sort and/or government units of some sort would be second to family units in these respects. It is one of the ironies associated with the most highly modernized societies that at the very time the level of specialization and the increase of material productivity characteristic of the most highly modernized of societies makes possible the most radical export of various forms of production from the family context, the increased time available for time spent in a family context as opposed to a specialized occupational context—the time made available by the leisure revolution referred to above—may actually increase the amount of time spent in a family context in activities of interest from the point of view of their implications for various forms of production. Insofar as this is the case, the members of the families concerned are more likely to view such forms of production as predominantly recreationally rather than as predominantly economically oriented.

Apart from generalizations about the importance of food getting and the like, two other forms of production are especially significant for understanding societies both from general points of view and more specifically from the point of view of the problems of modernization and stability. First, no matter how decentralized the organization of a given society may be, there must be some production of communication among the members. Insofar as one can measure these matters, the proportion of the output of the members of a society spent, as it were, on communications is a figure of great significance. When that proportion is low, the degree of self-sufficiency of the units *must* be high if the society is a stable one. In both general and specific cases many implications for problems of control and the like follow from these hypotheses.[3] Second, the members of any given society must, if the society is to be stable, engage in actions which may be viewed as producing governmental services. As a minimum every society must have some subsystem whose member(s) have especially general responsibilities for the maintenance of order, decision-making, etc. In societies of extremely small scale such services may be quite restricted, but no matter how decentralized any society of any considerable scale may be, these services can never be negligible from the point of view of the general structures of production in the society. To some extent both the minimal forms of productivity necessary for communications and government must be carried out in terms of an organization(s) other than ordinary family units.

If the members of a society are to survive, either the members themselves or other members with whom they are in contact must be capable of producing food. It is characteristic of all relatively nonmodernized societies of any scale that the overwhelming proportion of the members for the overwhelming proportion of their time are involved in the production of food. Some of the various forms this may take have been discussed briefly above, but actually in relatively nonmodernized societies of any scale the form of such food production in the vast majority of cases has been sedentary agriculture. Those societies whose members have depended for food primarily on nomadic husbandry, whether plants or animals, have in general been relatively small-scale ones. For societies of any considerable scale even animal husbandry is usually sedentary rather than nomadic and associated with sedentary plant husbandry. One of the great problems of the all-conquering Mongols lay in the fact that they really had only two choices in handling the territories they conquered. They could literally wipe out the existing population and turn over the lands to grazing land, or they could govern the existing population on a basis different than that on which they were accustomed to govern themselves. They could not govern sedentary agrarian populations on the basis of social structures adapted to one of the

[3] This subject is a major one in and of itself. One further implication would be that the proportion of income spent on communications always increases with modernization regardless of declines in cost per unit of communication, however those may be currently measured. The problems of centralization of governments and of modernization in general as special problems in the more general field of information theory have hardly been touched on. They will become increasingly critical questions for all persons concerned with public policy.

more radical forms of nomadism. Indeed, once the areas controlled were large enough and their own people increased sufficiently, they would not have been able to govern even those by the old laws. For all the destruction they visited on others, the further they pushed their conquests and tried to hold them, the more certainly they destroyed their own society.

One of the inevitable corollaries of modernization has been the declining proportion of the population engaged in food production. Even when food production remains or increases as an important proportion of the total national income, the personnel involved in its production declines radically with modernization. The earlier applications of inanimate sources of power and radically productive tools to manufacture in the narrow sense has led to a lag of thinking in which, somehow, food production, even under the most modernized circumstances, is regarded as less industrialized than activities carried out in factory buildings. Nothing could be more naïve. To consider our cities as the symbol par excellence of the state of our modernization is to overlook obvious gambits in the gamesmanship of world affairs. Latecomers to modernization find it far easier to reproduce our urban centers with their manufacturing productivity than to reproduce the manufacturing productivity of our agrarian production.

In this sphere it is not so much the productivity of labor which is the special mark of modernization, but rather the productivity per acre. Prior to modernization, no societies in world history have ever had structures of production such that one could expect long-run increases in productivity per acre more or less indefinitely projected into the future; virtually all such increases were sporadic and relatively long separated in time. With high levels of modernization such increases can be systematic and relatively rapid. For reasons which are by no means clear, developments in the modernization of food production is the basis of one distinction which has split relatively neatly along the increasingly outmoded distinction between capitalistic and socialistic societies. So far even the most highly developed of the so-called socialistic societies have been spectacularly less remarkable in these developments than the United States which is perhaps the epitome in these ideological terms of a so-called capitalistic society. The same contrast can be seen in a comparison of the development of agrarian productivity in China and Japan. Lack of motivation on the part of leaders in these cases cannot be argued since increase in productivity per acre of foodstuffs is usually sought by the officials controlling these developments.

For late-comers, especially, modernized production in an urban setting may be much easier to develop specifically because there is a sense in which this form of production does not replace anything but develops in an area in which there may have been little or nothing before. Relatively modernized agrarian production, however, almost inevitably replaces something in an area in which there was something before; something about which the members involved felt deeply, and something which, in its structures of organization, literally touched on, if it did not completely encompass, the entire lives of all who were concerned in it.

Nonagrarian production in all social contexts may be divided into three general types: (1) domestic or local production in terms of nonspecialized organizations, (2) production in terms of specialized small-scale units [e.g., some craft organizations], and (3) production in terms of specialized large-scale units [e.g., factories]. In all of the relatively nonmodernized social contexts a considerable part of nonagrarian production takes place in nonspecialized domestic or local units. The most obvious example of this is craft production on a nonspecialized basis in terms of a family unit. Much production of this sort is also carried out in neighborhood terms. Often, if not usually, such production is for the direct consumption of the members producing it. It is frequently a spare-time occupation. For various reasons, the emphasis on production carried out on such bases sometimes increases radically, and the products so produced are exported by the members from the social contexts in which they are produced. The so-called domestic or "putting-out" industries are obvious examples of this. Nevertheless, the organizations in terms of which these activities are carried out do not ordinarily become specialized predominantly economically oriented units. The most common of these nonspecialized units is, of course, the family. Such developments always to some extent make the members of the family concerned vulnerable to influences from without the family context, but the unit remains different from any specialized predominantly economically oriented organization. The maintenance of this difference is one of the special features of stress and strain in such social contexts. The fact that the family unit, which ideally in these cases is usually highly self-sufficient, becomes increasingly vulnerable because of its members' involvement in production for export is usually a focus for a special feeling of outrage and injury on their part. They usually have to operate in contact with specialists in exchange—i.e., *merchants*. As has been mentioned above and will be gone into in some detail below, this is one of the reasons why, ideally speaking at least, merchants have more often than not been considered marginal men regardless of how powerful they have become in actuality.

I know of no societies of any scale in which specialized units of production on a small scale do not exist. Even in the context of quite small-scale societies specialists in craftsmanship seem to develop more or less inevitably. The organizations in terms of which these individuals produce are considerably more specialized than the domestic or local units mentioned above. Even when the former are likely to be domestic or family units, as they often are, they differ from the others in that the specialized output of their members is a far greater proportion of their total production. Furthermore, the export of their finished products is overwhelmingly expected to be the source of the main proportion of the income of the members of the unit concerned. When the members of domestic or local organizations produce for export, that production is usually supplementary to some form of food production, usually sedentary agriculture, which the members of the family units concerned regard as their main occupation. The relatively specialized units of craftsmen regard their main occupation as the production of a particular good or service, e.g., doll production, blacksmithing, shoemaking, etc. Insofar as these activities are carried out in a family context the organization cannot be considered predominantly economically oriented. Even when the organization is not a family unit, one may question whether it is specialized in such a way as to be considered predominantly economically oriented. There is no doubt, however, that as far as self-conscious attitudes toward production are concerned, the attitudes of the members of those units are overwhelmingly focused on particular goods or services, that those goods or services are ordinarily disposed of to individuals who are not members of the organization in terms of which it is produced, that from the exchange involved in such disposal both new materials for further production and much of the means of living of the members of the organization are derived. For the members of such organizations the focus is on the production of the goods or services concerned.

Inseparable from this, but secondary to it from the point of view of the artisans, is the disposal of the product and the acquisition of a new supply of materials for further production. One or more members of such a unit must specialize his activities to some extent in the direction of exchange, and the members become importantly dependent upon the activities of specialists in exchange [i.e., merchants] for these reasons. The specialists in exchange have many important implications for the life of the artisans, but they are at best generally thought of as outsiders and a necessary nuisance. Once again the specialist in exchange is likely to be resented if anything goes wrong.[4]

A *factory* as that term is used here, is usually a large-scale unit. That is to say, the forms of production in which its members specialize usually involve a considerable number of individuals. I would not place the main burden of definition of a factory on the number of individuals involved, however. Either domestic, local, and craftsmen organizations may involve considerable numbers of people without becoming factories in the sense in which I would use the term. A factory is distinguished by virtue of the fact that it is a specialized unit predominantly oriented to production. In terms of its structures labor, materials, power, and tools are coordinated. In this sense factories may exist and have existed in relatively nonmodernized societies. Nevertheless, the great proliferation of factories—proliferation to such an extent that they are familiar organizations from the point of view of the general membership of the society—occurs only after change toward relative modernization has begun to gather way in a given social context. Factory units imply special sets of relationships between the members of the factory and their family members as a minimum. They also imply additional relationships of the factory members with specialists in exchange. Materials for production are imported and finished products are exported by factory members.

A factory, as the term is used here, does not have to be an organization in terms of which all activities take place under a single roof. The term refers to a particular form of social organization, not to a building. In this sense it is perfectly correct to say that in many cases there exist today factories in the field. Whatever the history of a society before the development of relatively modernized structures, factories always come into being. Even if they were present before, their proliferation and development are radically accelerated. In relatively nonmodernized societies, because of the specialized orientation of factories, they pose special problems of organization and coordination with the rest of the social structure. In such societies relatively few other social organizations are so highly specialized with regard to one of the aspects of action as are factories. The initial establishment of a

[4] There is a further element of strain inherent in the fact that the more successful any set of artisans become, the more the individual(s) among them who specializes his activities in exchange is forced into the roles appropriate to a merchant. This happens despite the fact that the role of master craftsman is usually far more prestigious.

factory in such a setting, therefore, always has far-reaching implications.

Finally, I must return to an emphasis on distribution as a special form of production. This has already been mentioned [pp. 233, 240–241]. The lower the degree of self-sufficiency and the higher the level of specialization, the greater is the importance of *distribution* as a form of production. Correspondingly, the higher the level of self-sufficiency and the lower the level of specialization, the more specialists in distribution are likely to be regarded as marginal individuals from the point of view of both producers and consumers. These specialists are always outsiders from the point of view of both producers and consumers in other contexts in relatively nonmodernized societies. This attitude is not a function of the popularity of Marxist doctrine. This element of Marxist doctrine is rather more explicable as a particularly effective distillation of an age-old attitude of distrust and distaste for specialists in exchange—an attitude that has been characteristic of the members of all save a small minority of societies.

To some extent distribution develops as a specialized form of production in every society. The development of some minimal means of communication implies this and so does the development of some governmental system. With the development of modernization, the importance of specialists in exchange increases radically if only because of increases in communication and specialization. The growing importance of such specialists is not affected materially by whether or not the society is organized on a socialistic or capitalistic basis. The distinction between capitalism and socialism may tell us a great deal about the manner in which specialists in exchange are employed, but the level of modernization achieved is more indicative of the role which will be played by such specialists than is the question of state versus private ownership.

In the history of modernization we have not only seen radical shift in the proportion of the population employed first in raw materials production, later in manufacturing, and at present "in services." The proportion of services which can be classified under the heading of distribution have increased both radically and rapidly. In the United States context this is not only reflected in the development of all sorts of specialists in communication, it is also reflected in the strategic power of the leaders of labor organizations whose members are involved primarily in services having to do with distribution such as transportation.

There is one other special feature of distribution as a form of production. In relatively nonmodernized contexts most forms of production are organized in terms of relatively nonspecialized units. This is much less likely to be the case of distribution as a form of production. Merchant firms can be, and often are, family organizations, but most of the activities of merchants and other specialists in distribution fall outside the family context. Even hawkers frequently do not hawk with other family members. There is a sense in which specialists in distribution must live on what they can charge for distribution per unit of whatever is distributed. There is thus for them a minimum viable scale of operations and constant or at least continuing pressure toward an increased scale of operations. There is also constant emphasis on thinking in terms of the possibilities of increasing scale. Specifically to the extent that the specialists in distribution are successful, their activities become less possible to organize on a relatively nonspecialized basis. Even when merchant firms are largely family firms, merchant activities tend to be separate from other family activities to an extent which is almost never the case for the activities of craftsmen or farmers in a relatively nonmodernized social context.

V

MEDIA OF EXCHANGE

In all societies there exist media of exchange, i.e., there are goods and/or services that may be exchanged for two or more different goods and/or services. *Money* is a special case of a medium of exchange. Money may be defined as something that is specifically perceived as a medium of exchange. There may be different media of exchange in a given society, but at elementary levels of development of complexity some monetary units are likely to emerge. As monetary units develop in a given social context, it is exceedingly likely that a single unit that is regarded as a *legal monetary unit,* i.e., the monetary unit controlled by the representatives of the government of the society concerned, will develop. For all of the societies of concern here, some sort of monetary unit is present. Usually there is a legal monetary unit as well, whatever other monetary units may exist. Whether there are monetary units or not, there will be other media of exchange, but the significance of other media of exchange decreases as the acceptance of a legal monetary unit becomes general, as levels of specialization and interdependency increase, and, in general, as modernization increases. There is not space here to discuss money or the social systems specialized with regard to it in any detail. These matters are considered in careful detail and sophisticated theoretical terms by highly professionalized social scientists and men of affairs—the economists. In relatively modernized social contexts money is a question about which many academics, laymen, and government officials are highly sophisticated. In many relatively nonmodernized social contexts there have also been some laymen and some governmental officials highly sophisticated in these respects.

There is not even space here to discuss in any detail the obvious, close relationship between money and government. Monetary units and social systems importantly oriented to monetary matters are rarely developed to any sophisticated degree without a vital concern with monetary matters on the part of the members of the government developing as well. Tokugawa Japan, for example, was a genuinely feudal society, but the members of the Shogun's government were much concerned with regulation and control of the monetary units used.

This is a good opportunity to draw attention to a set of considerations closely associated with the relevance of money for governments and money in other respects as well. This is a respect that we take for granted as members of relatively modernized societies. Perhaps for that reason it is not often treated explicitly. Media of exchange in general and money as a special case of such media can vary radically in the level of generalization to which they are developed. A medium of exchange has been defined here as anything which can be exchanged for two or more different things. A given medium of exchange, for example money, is relatively *more generalized* the larger the number and the greater the variety of goods and services for which it can be exchanged. The *least generalized* medium of exchange would be one which could be exchanged for only a specific pair of other things. The highest level of generalization for a medium of exchange would require something which could be exchanged for literally anything—any good or any service. For relatively modernized societies the level of generalization of the monetary units tends to be high by contrast with levels of generalization of media of exchange in past social history. An extraordinary number of things can be exchanged in such social contexts on a monetary basis.[5] Even among relatively modernized societies there are con-

[5] One may even, as a matter of speculation, consider the possibility that the reason that economics developed earlier and in a more highly generalized form than the other social sciences, qua science, lay in the fact that increases in the generalization of the media of exchange in parts of Western Europe made possible, with increasing relevance, the application of a rational model to problems of economic allocation. The fact that to some extent one could measure the most diverse forms of goods relative to one another in terms of their respective prices, regardless of whether

siderable differences in the levels of generalization of the media of exchange to which the members are accustomed. For example, in Great Britain entailed estates are not subject to purchase or sale. There are many national monuments in the United States which are not subject to purchase or sale. We need not get involved in the monetary sophistication of special blocked currencies and the like to realize that there are important variations in terms of what can be bought and sold among members of even the most highly modernized societies. Every one of those variations implies some differences in the level of generalization of the media of exchange involved.

There is a special problem connected with the level of generalization of media of exchange. We have all frequently heard or read cynics who maintain that *anything* [or anybody] has its price, that anything can be bought and sold if one has enough money. This is tantamount to alleging that the society referred to is one for which there exists a *perfectly generalized* medium of exchange, i.e., a medium such that literally anything can be exchanged for it. Cynics to the contrary notwithstanding, this has never been the case for any society in world history. If one is interested in the niceties of theoretical sociology, one can develop an argument to the effect that it cannot in fact ever be the case for any stable society. In doing so it is not necessary to rest the argument on the character inherent in the defiance of a distressed maiden who wails melodramatically, "You cannot buy my caress." There are always some things other than national monuments or a lady's virtue which cannot be bought or sold. As cynical as one might wish to be about the folkways of awarding honorary degrees in the United States, it is nevertheless true that in terms of the first-class universities of this country and probably in terms of most of the others as well it would not be possible, openly and with no avoidance of publicity, literally to purchase an A.B. degree. A recent novelist has based his work on the conception of a person who in fact wishes to buy a child despite the fact that we ostensibly have long since left the practice of slavery behind. In no open and obvious sense can an individual as such be bought and sold in the context of modern United States society. If there existed a perfectly generalized medium of exchange in a society, there could be no ethics, no

these prices reflected their true values or not, made possible such calculations. One may even speculate further that the other social sciences, as sciences, might not have developed at all had not the infant science of economics begun to bring some order into the general consideration of the patterns of allocation of goods and services on the basis of such rational models.

standards of any sort, that could not be reversed in a twinkling by the offer of sufficient accumulations of capital. Given the very extent to which men are capable of attempting to behave rationally, such a possibility would preclude the possibility of a stable social structure.

It is equally true that there has never been a society in terms of which absolutely nothing could be bought. That is to say there has never been a society in the context of which nothing could be exchanged. It is true, however, that there are [and have been] many, many societies in terms of which the generalization of media of exchange that we take for granted is simply out of the question. The works of anthropologists are full of examples of so-called primitive people who could not be easily traded with in terms of the European's beads and mirrors. Cases have even been cited in which the entering wedge of such exchange was an appeal to what the Europeans would have regarded in their own social contexts as a set of neurotics rather than the well-integrated substantial members of the society concerned.

One can generalize as follows about where within the two extremes of levels of generalization the level of generalization of a particular monetary unit in fact lies: (1) The more highly modernized the society, the more highly generalized do the media of exchange become. (2) On any given level of modernization, save some theoretical level of complete modernization, whatever that might mean, there are possibilities of variation in the level of generalization of the media of exchange. (3) For any given level of modernization, there is a level below which the generalization of the media of exchange cannot fall if the society is to remain stable. (4) There is also a level of generalization up to which it cannot rise if the society is to be stable, and that is always far short of the level of complete generalization.[6]

Increases in the level of generalization of the media of exchange have implications for the general ethical [or normative or ideal] structures of the society. The more the level of generali-

[6] These generalizations pose a problem for the general stability of relatively modernized societies. If as maintained elsewhere in this work relatively modernized societies will continue to become more highly modernized [or be instable] and if the level of centralization in long [and most short] runs always varies directly with increased modernization, then at some point the degrees of freedom inherent in the necessary increases in generalization of the media of exchange become inconsistent with the necessary level of centralization. Presumably from such a point on, either increases in direct allocation [with consequent decreases in the level of generalization of the media of exchange] and/or instability ensue.

I am indebted to P. D. Bell, A. G. Bischoff, H. P. Gassner, and J. R. Himes who, as graduate students of the Woodrow Wilson School of Public and International Affairs, forced this implication to my attention.

zation of a medium of exchange increases, the more vulnerable to exchange becomes any commodity, activity, or standard for which any goods or services are relevant. In a stable social context there are always some forms of honor that cannot be bought, but the more highly generalized a medium of exchange becomes the more vulnerable becomes honor to exchange in monetary terms. To this extent there is something in what the cynics have said. There is a corollary to this: although there can be no society whose members can be completely materialistic in this sense [i.e., bought], the more generalized the medium of exchange, the greater becomes the relevance of monetary measurement for *all other standards*. In relatively modernized social contexts it is not surprising how much monetary measurement is used as a yardstick of accomplishment or general worth. The surprising thing actually is that it is not used to an even greater degree than it is. As modernization increases, it becomes increasingly difficult to have, for example, a high-prestige occupational role whose effective incumbents receive a lower income than is received by individuals of less prestigious occupations. This is not less true of socialist than of capitalist societies. Indeed, there is a genuine sense in which socialist societies probably run far ahead of nonsocialist societies in these respects if only because of the explicitness of the planning of their leaders. Income is probably more highly correlated with social prestige in the Soviet Union than in the United States. In the United States there is a genuine sense in which the absolute pinnacles of general social prestige *cannot* go to those with the highest incomes. The very identification of an individual with such high incomes has a connotation inconsistent with the aura of self-sacrifice associated with the highest levels of prestige. The fact that the salary of the President of the United States is even a piddling one by contrast with the salary of a quite substantial number of business executives, let alone movie stars, and with no reference to gamblers and others of even lower general prestige, is a matter about which we are ambivalent. We are made uneasy by the fact that what many regard as the most important and difficult job in the world is by no means the best paid or by many standards even adequately paid. At the same time, there is a feeling of reassurance about presidential character in the feeling that no one able to get the job would ever seek it solely for the pay involved. We expect our President to be dedicated and to be more dedicated to almost anything than to his monetary income.

Regardless of the tenability of this particular speculation about the comparison of the correlation of income and social prestige in

the United States and the Soviet Union, it is still interesting to
keep in mind the assertion that, short of the upper limit already
mentioned: the more highly modernized the society becomes, the
more generalized the medium of exchange becomes; the more
generalized the medium of exchange becomes, the more accurate is likely to be the inference, ideally and/or actually, of
standings in terms of other criteria from ratings in monetary
terms. At any given level of modernization so far achieved, considerable variations in the degree of generalization of the media
of exchange and hence to some extent variations of relevance of
the monetary unit(s) to the measurement of other criteria are
possible. Nevertheless, the more highly modernized societies become, regardless of the bases from which their development took
place, the smaller is the range of variation possible among them
in these respects. Proponents and contemplators of modernization whoever they may be, may want to reflect on the prediction
that the more highly modernized a society becomes, the greater
becomes the likelihood that distributions of income will reflect
distributions of social prestige accurately, that the members of
such societies will take this for granted either consciously or un-
consciously, and that the members of these societies will increasingly come to believe that this should be the case—if they
don't already.

V I
MARKETS VERSUS TRADITIONAL EXCHANGES

A *market* has been defined above [p. 66] as any organization in
terms of which action is primarily oriented to facilitating the
exchange of goods and/or services among its members. There are
societies which are not characterized by markets in this sense, in
which the organizations in terms of which exchange takes place
are by no means primarily oriented to such an exchange. From
the point of view of exchange, I would refer to these methods of
exchange as *traditional exchanges*. Such exchanges may be exceedingly important in the structures of economic allocation of a
society. Frequently ceremonials of various sorts and especially
important *rites de passage* are attended by traditional exchanges
of this sort. Exchanges of gifts among the family members of a
bride and groom are frequent examples. Although there are certainly societies without markets, I know of no society of any
considerable scale totally lacking in markets. The presence of
even highly developed markets does not by any manner of means
imply the absence of traditional exchanges. Elements of such
exchanges remain characteristic of even the most highly modern-

ized societies, though these elements tend with modernization to become relatively insignificant in any attempt to reckon the national income. However tedious the repetition, it is characteristic of all societies that some exchange takes place in terms of family units. Such exchange is never unimportant for an understanding of general social structure, but in the sense intended here such exchanges are never market exchanges.

Markets vary widely from society to society, and they vary in many different respects. Markets may be more or less generalized, that is to say, the number and variety of items which may be exchanged in terms of the market organization may be greater or less. No completely generalized market, i.e., a market in terms of which everything or any combination of things may be exchanged for some other thing or combination of things, exists, though highly specialized markets, i.e., markets whose members specialize in dealing in even a single commodity plus some medium of exchange may and do exist. Markets also vary very widely in terms of the degree of centralization or control with which the market is organized. As indicated above [p. 68], there may be actual markets [e.g., prostitution and drugs] which ideally speaking do not exist.

From the point of view of societies in general four possibilities of allocation exist, assuming that the various subsystems that constitute a society are not completely self-sufficient—which they never are. First, there may be market structures. Second, there may be structures of traditional exchange. Third, the various exchanges of the members of the society may be planned and determined explicitly by a member(s) of a centralized authority. Fourth, there may be some combination of the first three. For societies of any considerable scale, some combination of the first three is standard. The first is never carried out to the exclusion of the second and third; the second may be for societies of small scale and great stability. The third possibility has so far in history never been successfully carried out to the exclusion of the other two. That is to say, there has never yet been a stable society in terms of which all exchange has been completely planned and determined explicitly by a member(s) of a centralized authority. To carry out such an extreme form of exchange would imply complete and perfect knowledge about the society. History has seen plenty of examples of far-reaching controls on exchange though these have by no means always been highly stable.

Amusingly, a market mechanism, which certainly does emphasize rationality in exchange, minimizes the problem of knowledge. Traditional exchanges do not accent rationality in exchange as such; they are rather ones in terms of which rational considerations are subordinate to other considerations surrounding the exchange. However the participants in terms of a given market be conceived, whether they be individuals, firms, etc., to the degree that they [or their representatives] act for themselves, to the degree that they can adjust subsequent action in terms of previous actions, reevaluate their moves etc., and to the degree that no one of them in his transactions constitutes the entire membership of the market—to that extent—the problems of knowledge are always subdivided and allocated in a special sense. The implications of irrationality for either success or failure in the market are cut down, and the risks of the implications of inescapable inadequacies of knowledge are spread. In the absence of perfect and complete knowledge on the part of the members of a central authority, operations in terms of a market mechanism, especially if regulated against excesses on the parts of individuals who participate in them, are more likely to minimize fluctuations than operations in terms of any completely centralized system. This is true, regardless of whether or not the society be considered a capitalistic or socialistic society. In both there are markets, and they will continue to exist.

In the context of relatively nonmodernized societies the proportion of exchanges that can be carried out on traditional rather than market bases is considerably higher than is conceivable in the context of relatively modernized societies. The more highly modernized societies become, the smaller the proportion of exchange carried out on a traditional basis becomes. Over the total scale of variation in modernization, particularly in some of the relatively nonmodernized segments of the scale, more complicated functions may be possible for this relationship. In general, however, they may be said to vary inversely—the more modernized the society, the smaller the proportion of exchange carried out on a traditional basis and vice versa. Insofar as traditional exchange exists in terms of a society, many problems of rationality are minimized. Not the least of the problems minimized is the problem posed by the fact that one individual or set of individuals in acting rationally may profit from far-reaching disruption and interference with the interests of others. There is also the possibility that in attempting to be rational even without deliberate disruptive intent, a given individual may make mistakes that have far-reaching implications. Exchanges carried out on a traditional basis may not maximize the possibilities of material productivity, but they are not likely to be subject to such fluctuations as emphases on rationality in exchange are likely to accompany.

There is another feature of the distinction between market exchange and traditional exchange which is of special relevance here. Structures of traditional exchange never furnish vital stimuli for systematic increases in productivity. The main focus of attention is not on the exchange of goods and/or services as such but rather on the occasion to which they are ancillary. In market exchanges, since the focus of attention is on exchange as such, there always exists the possibility that one or more individuals who are parties to the market can or will benefit from increases in productivity. There is no denying that markets can be set up in such a way as to discourage or damp down technological improvements, but on the whole it is difficult to rig a market so over long periods of time. The members of market systems are always sensitive to some degree to the implications of increases in material productivity. Markets vary in the extent to which operation in terms of the market actually stimulates technological advance, but even so market structures rather than structures of traditional exchange are far more likely to maximize the rapidity of adoption of technological improvements which arise from sources other than operation in terms of the market structure itself. Whenever there is contact with the structures of a relatively modernized society by members of a relatively nonmodernized one, the outsider makes inroads into the relatively nonmodernized social context via market mechanisms, and in this sense breaks down the structures of traditional exchanges. In addition, however, the basis of exchanges among the members of the relatively nonmodernized society themselves must always break down into an increasingly clear-cut market system [or set of market systems]. Although markets in highly organized and highly specialized forms as well as in more casual forms are taken for granted by the members of relatively modernized societies, they are not unknown or rare in relatively nonmodernized societies. Some markets exist in any relatively nonmodernized society of large scale, and some highly developed markets have existed in all cases about which we have historical records in any appreciable depth. There are, no doubt, many special and peculiar features of the sophistication of the Osaka merchants of Tokugawa Japan, but merchants who are highly sophisticated in some general respects are by no means rare in social history.

V I I
STRUCTURES OF INCOME DISTRIBUTION

The structure of income distribution characteristic of a given society and its implications are explored by economists at great length. Given the niceties of its technical development this subject is no longer a fit one for an amateur like myself. Even an amateur, however, may with some safety observe that most of the work on income distribution has been done primarily on a restricted range of societies—or for *any* society only insofar as any society approximates the criteria of the specific models used. This is a scientifically legitimate procedure, and nowadays economists in general are sophisticated about such procedures. Outside the technical literature of economics on income distribution, there is an enormous amount of discussion of distributions on the basis of status and contract, slavery and wages, class distributions, feudal systems, etc. Most of that discussion is focused on special types of societies. There are, however, some generalizations about income distribution which may be made about any societies and which have special implications in terms of the distinctions between societies of relatively small scale and relatively larger scale and between relatively nonmodernized and relatively modernized societies.

Specialized development of the economic aspects of society, while by no means unknown in relatively nonmodernized contexts, has on the whole been much rarer and much less emphasized than in the case of relatively modernized societies. This contrast has had marked corollaries. One of these has been the fact that neither individual income nor the income of the members of the society as a whole has been such a major focus of attention for the general members of any relatively nonmodernized society as it is for the general members of all relatively modernized societies. Particularly in terms of relatively nonmodernized societies of small scale, specialized orientation to income as such exists rarely if at all, despite the fact that, in such societies of any considerable scale, reckoning in terms of wealth and hence to some extent in terms of income is always commonly understood. Regardless of how much attention is placed on income as such from the point of view of the individual members of a society, an observer or social scientist may always speak of the *actual distribution of income* characteristic of any society. This may be more or less difficult to measure in different cases, but the remarks to be made here do not hang on fineness of distinction in measurement of this income. If one considers the distribution of income on either a hypothetical per capita or a hypothetical set of family members in any social context, one may distinguish among three measures of such distribution. These are quite conventional, well-understood measures. I refer to the three m's of statistical techniques: the mean, the median, and the mode. In the following discussion it will be necessary to refer to the three curves illustrated below as curves I, II, and III. These curves illustrate income distribution. The number of individuals with a given income is measured on the Y axis. The amount of income per individual is measured on the X axis.

The simplest remark about curve I is that the income distribution is such that a very large number of people have very low incomes; a very small number of people have high incomes; and very few people have incomes spread thinly in the middle income region. Such a curve is sometimes referred to as bimodal [or as

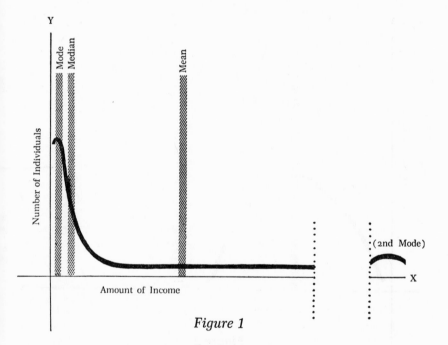

Figure 1

radically asymmetrical] in the sense that there are two important clusters of income distribution. The first is the *true mode* which is at a low income figure, and the other a slight clustering at high figures [far out to the right of the curve]. It is not difficult to envisage curves of this sort with more than two clusters. Thus trimodal or even quintimodal curves are conceivable. In curves of this sort the mean, median, and modes may fall at widely separated points on the curve. It is usually misleading to refer to curves of this sort in terms of one of these measures without any references to the other two. Many different implications may inhere in these separations of the mean, median, and mode.

Curve II pictures an income distribution such that relatively few people have very low incomes and relatively few people have very high incomes. The vast majority of incomes are bunched in the middle income range. In a sense this inverted U-shaped curve is an opposite extreme of the not so U-shaped curve I. As a curve of this shape is approached the median, the mode, and the mean of income distribution come closer and closer together. It is conceivable that an income distribution exists such that these three measures coincide exactly as in curve II. Such a curve would be a perfectly symmetrical inverted U-shaped curve. Even among curves with perfect symmetry there could still be

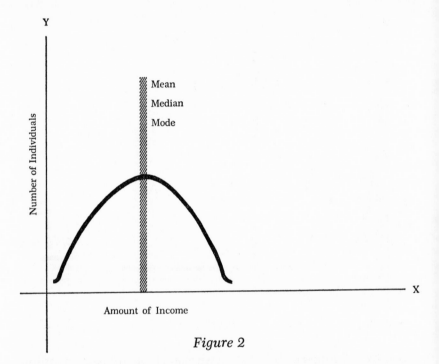

Figure 2

significant differences in terms of the spread of the curve, its height, etc. These would not necessarily be variations reflected in variations in the location in the mean, median, and modal measures.

For present purposes I would consider all cases of multimodal distribution or the like as special cases of curve I which carries with it a bimodal quality of income distribution frequently referred to in discussions of problems of economic development. It pictures an income distribution in which the vast majority of the population are relatively badly off as far as income is concerned and a small proportion of the population have very high incomes, indeed. Curve II will be referred to as a unimodal curve of income distribution. It will be considered the more nearly perfectly unimodal insofar as the three measures used here coincide. It is possible, of course, to have a unimodal distribution of income in the strictly technical sense with considerable distinction in the location of these three measures of income [see curve III for purposes of illustration].

With so much by way of nomenclature let us speculate. All income distributions in all societies may be classified as falling somewhere between the extremes of a perfectly unimodal curve

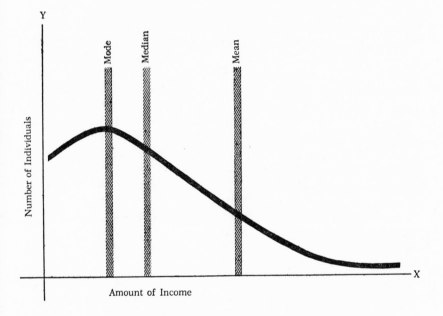

Figure 3

in the sense used here or some extreme form of curve I. Prior to the development of relatively modernized societies, virtually all societies were characterized by curves of income distribution roughly conforming to curve I. Furthermore, the main modal point of income distribution for the members of all those societies was as close to the Y axis as was consistent with survival of the populations concerned, assuming that the society did persist. That is to say, before the development of relative modernized societies the vast majority of all members of all societies lived close to the margin of subsistence. There is, perhaps, one general type of exception to this, though I doubt that this exception was ever frequent. In comparatively isolated societies of quite small scale, there may well have been income distributions of type II. Even in these small-scale societies, if they were of type II, either the societies were such that it was touch and go whether anyone would survive, given the extreme difficulties of producing a subsistence income for the members of the society, or the societies were ones characterized by a physical environment so benign from the point of view of the members that relatively little effort was involved in the collection of what the members of the society considered a quite adequate income. Examples of the former would be peoples living in stringent, sparse environments such as the Australian Bushmen, the Eskimos, etc. Examples of the latter might be peoples living on some of the more romantically described Pacific Islands. Income distributions approaching type II, however, do not characterize any societies of relatively large scale unless they are relatively modernized. Before the development of considerable levels of modernization, all societies of any scale have been ones in terms of which the vast majority of people have lived close to the subsistence margins whatever those margins may have been. A small set of elite members of those societies—never mind whether we consider those elites to have been [or to be] good, bad, or indifferent—have been, relative to virtually all other members of those societies, exceedingly well off materially. Moreover, regardless of whether they *should* have been considered elites, they were actually so considered by the other members of their societies with or without varying degrees of envy and resentment and departures from ideal structures.

I have asserted this as a historical uniformity, though in this respect as in all others I have made no attempt to produce historical data to confirm this position. As generally here, however, there are theoretical reasons for holding that this is the case. All societies of any considerable scale require some forms of specialized knowledge as has already been indicated above. In addition, some special forms of reasonably large-scale capital formation and the like are also necessary. No matter how far decentralization is carried, some centralized control exists, and so does some centralized planning. To some extent the levels of material productivity on which income production rests are a function of the existence of these specialized forms of knowledge and capital formation. In the absence of the somewhat specialized training associated with the specialized command of knowledge, neither the knowledge nor the capital formation necessary to maintain levels of productivity as they are could be maintained. Individual members in that society cannot be kept at the bare margin of subsistence and given the specialized training necessary for such forms of knowledge. Therefore, in any such social context— regardless of how wicked one may judge the relatively high income elite to be, and regardless of how much harm they may in fact do—whatever criteria of harm may be invoked— were there intervention that immediately transformed the curve of income distribution into a unimodal one approaching type II, not only would the more equal distribution of income per capita fail to improve substantially the standard of living of the general population [the more extreme the discrepancies in wealth, the less likely an equal distribution would be to improve radically the average income of the average individual], but also in subsequent income earning periods the average standard of living would probably fall further. As a result, after the initial distribution of income from the wealthy to the poor, the poor would be even worse off than they had been before. However romantic we may be about the principles of equality, and however wickedly conducted may have been the extremes of income distribution, the hard fact remains that the level of productivity actually achieved by the members of any relatively nonmodernized society of any considerable scale is importantly a function of the fact that income was [and is] actually distributed unequally among the members of the society.

In societies in terms of which the vast majority of people live at the bare margin of subsistence, whether members of private organizations or representatives of public organizations such as the government select special individuals on the basis of nepotism or predominantly universalistic, competitive examinations to receive the special education necessary to keep up the level of productivity in such societies [never mind increasing it], they will have to create of the students so selected a special elite whose income, at least in terms of the amount of resources devoted to their cultivation, will be much greater than that of the vast majority of the members of the population. The extremes of differences in income distribution for individuals need not be so radical as they frequently are, but regardless of how much income the elite may fritter away, some of the services and inevitably some of the other capital formation which account importantly for the maintenance of levels of productivity at the levels attained are functions of the special preparation which these individuals receive. No relatively nonmodernized society of any scale can continue as the system of action for members who function even at the margin of subsistence unless some proportion of the membership of that society has sufficient leisure and special command over resources to function above the generally accepted margin of subsistence. Furthermore, no matter how many other inequities may be removed, the basic form of this curve cannot be changed until the levels of material productivity characteristic of relatively modernized societies have been to some extent achieved. There may be some question as to whether income distribution will become more equitable when such levels of productivity have been achieved. Nevertheless, whether we like to face up to this picture or not, apart from circumstances made possible by subsidies from outside, the income distribution characteristic of societies in the process of modernization will remain strongly bimodal, [i.e., strongly of type I] for a considerable part of their development, whether under capitalistic or socialistic auspices.

Indeed, in the initial stages of the process, the more successful and the more rapid the modernization is, the greater is the likelihood that strategic differentials of income distribution will be maintained. Whatever our views of ethics of other standards, the distinction between capitalism and socialism has little to do with this matter. The development of modernization requires substantial capital formation and substantial specialized training for special individuals. The situation is not quite like getting "blood out of a turnip." In this case the turnip is in part the resources of the elite high-income groups. In all cases these people do have some income that from the point of view of facilitating modernization can probably be spent in more effective forms of capital formation and training than has hitherto been the case. Whatever blood does exist in this turnip, however, it is never enough without further contributions from the productive efforts of the vast majority of the members of the society to finance either the level of training or the amount of capital formation necessary for effective modernization. Not only have all developments of modernization under capitalistic direction developed by exactions from the peasant population and the laboring force in the cities, but to no lesser degree so have all developments of this sort conducted under the aegis of socialists, communists, or fascist imperialists. Indeed, one may add another generalization. The later a comer to the process of modernization, the greater is the likelihood that, apart from subsidies from outsiders, exactions from the peasants, i.e., the agrarian-based population, will have to furnish a greater proportion of such resources. This follows from the hypotheses that: (1) the vast majority of the members of all such societies will be agrarian based, (2) the later the members of a given society come into the process, the greater are the demands for performances on considerable scales both in the field of capital formation and in training, and (3) the longer the members of a society of this sort lag behind modernization which has taken place in the rest of the world, the less likely is it that the actual accumulation of wealth in the hands of the wealthy elite will amount to a sufficient accumulation to carry out these requirements without additional exactions from the vast majority at the opposite end of the income scale.

With the development of relatively modernized societies, it is possible for the first time in world history to have societies of considerable scale with curves approaching type II. Furthermore, the higher the level of modernization achieved, the greater is the possibility of approaching a perfectly unimodal distribution with adequate capital formation for maintenance and growth of the rates of productivity. The inordinate productivity of methods of organization, given the tools and sources of power characteristic of relatively modernized societies by contrast with the productivity of methods of organization characteristic of any other kind of society, has already been mentioned. Such methods of organization would not have had such implications for productivity and might not even have been feasible in the absence of such tools and sources of power. Whatever the origins, the further this process went the more it became possible for the first time in world history to produce a sufficiently high per capita income such that the mean, median, and modal incomes could approach one another without wiping out the minimal differentiation in terms of income required for the specialized knowledge and capital formation which were in turn necessary to maintain operations in terms of the society. Furthermore, these are the only societies in world history whose members have not only attained such levels of productivity and approached such distributions of income, but have also attained systematically increasing levels of productivity.[6]

Apart from relatively nonmodernized societies of relatively small scale, various elements of the productivity picture of relatively modernized societies for the first time in world history not

[6] Without pausing even to argue this assertion here, I would add that such societies cannot continue to exist stably unless the levels of productivity associated with them continue to increase. It may even be that none of them can exist stably unless these levels not only increase but continue to increase more rapidly than before. The members of such societies must not only attain some minimal velocity of productivity; they must attain some minimal rate of acceleration of productivity as well. And even so, it may not be possible for them to be stable [see pp. 783–788].

only make curves of income distribution approaching type II possible, but, historically speaking, they also make them highly probable. There are in existence, as all know, classical theories about capitalism which have broad appeal and which maintain that the longer capitalistic domination continues the greater become the discrepancies in income distribution as between the general population and the capitalist elite. This implies that the longer capitalism continues, the more the curve of income distribution takes on an extreme form of curve I. This has, of course, been neatly and precisely contradicted by the developments of history.[7] Again the distinction between capitalism and socialism has nothing whatsoever to do with the case save within narrow limits. The more highly modernized a given society, once relative modernization has been achieved, the more unimodal the income distribution in terms of it has become in every known historical case, regardless of whether it was under socialist or capitalist hegemony. Since the turn of this century the income distribution picture in the United States, which is generally considered by its own members and others to be one of the more purely capitalistic countries in the world, has been characterized more by the extent to which the mean, median, and mode of income have approached identity than by the increase in the mean of income, though that has been dramatic enough.[8] Japan is another country generally considered staunchly capitalistic. It is a country whose intellectuals and labor leaders continually talk about the bimodal distribution of income in the old sense at a period in which the trend is overwhelmingly and rapidly in the opposite direction as one may judge from the effective mass demand for heavy consumers goods which has already appeared in substantial development there. Whether the Japanese are more capitalistic than other late-comers to modernization I do not know, but of all of the non-European late-comers to relative modernization, there is absolutely no question that the Japanese are much the most highly modernized. They also ap-

[7] One of the great services of this particular formulation so often attributed to Marx lies in the sterling refutation it affords of the position held by some that nothing can be either *proved* or *disproved* in social science. This formulation is one of the few useful to social scientists because it is, to use Wilbert E. Moore's phrase, "precisely false."

[8] There are some who would make their assertion that this could not happen under capitalism true by definition by asserting that, to the extent that this has taken place, the United States is a socialistic rather than a capitalistic society. The argument need not be detained by the tautologies of the political religions of either the right or the left.

proach a unimodal distribution of income more than any of the others.

Among the nations under socialist control, which certainly has a meaning in the ideological sense regardless of whether it means what believers in either the ideology of capitalism or the ideology of socialism think it means, distinctions in the levels of modernization enable us to predict more about income distribution in terms of these curves than does anything else. Income distribution in Communist China is much more of type I than is the case of the Soviet Union which is, of course, much further along the road of modernization. China as a whole cannot yet be described as a relatively modernized society in the sense in which the term is used here.

The comparison between the United States and the Soviet Union in this respect may be speculated upon with some interest. There may be special difficulties in measuring the income of the Soviet elite, but even discounting these difficulties it is highly probable that the absolute discrepancy between the highest incomes and the lowest incomes in the Soviet Union is not so great as in the United States. It is also highly probable that there is a closer approach to identity of mean, median, and modal incomes in the United States than in the Soviet Union. Structures of automobile ownership alone suggest this unless automobile ownership is not at all closely correlated with other items in the standard of living. The vast majority of the population of the United States consider themselves radically disadvantaged if after the age of maturity they are unable to become automobile owners or to have access to automobiles as a minimum. In the Soviet Union automobile ownership or control over or access to automobiles is much more a mark of the privileged. Never mind how universalistically or justly those privileges may be gained in the one case as opposed to the other. With regard to housing, clothing, food, and many other categories the same sort of comparisons can be made despite the fact that the discrepancy between the poorest and the best housing or the cheapest and the most expensive housing in the Soviet Union may be considerably less than the corresponding discrepancy in the United States.

To close this line of speculation one additional theoretical element is necessary. I mention it only briefly here [see also below, pp. 777–790]. As far as societies of any considerable scale are concerned, not only are curves approaching type II possible only for relatively modernized societies, but the more highly modernized a society becomes, the more such curves of income distribution are required structures, if the society is to be stable. The technological possibilities opened up by action in terms of relatively modernized societies are sufficient to explain the possibility of such structures of income distribution. The levels of productivity obtained are sufficiently high that income can be allocated in such a way that there is sufficient provision for capital formation and both the freedom from other services and the means necessary for a portion of the membership to acquire the specialized intermediate forms of knowledge necessary to maintain the system without the sorts of discrepancies in income distribution illustrated in curve I. But would it not be possible, at least theoretically, for such societies to continue indefinitely with income distributions of type I pushed further and to the right? Or even not pushed further to the right? Could there not be a relatively modernized society, the vast majority of whose members stayed very poor by contrast with the elite or even stayed close to the margin of subsistence with enormous resources left over for the amusement and development of the elite and further capital formation? There could not. Not only must the mean, median, and modal incomes be pushed further to the right, that is increase in all such cases, but they must increasingly approach one another. They must do so for several reasons. First, one cannot handle people by coercion alone in terms of any society. Second, for relatively modernized societies, especially, the delicacy and fineness of adjustment of interdependencies are such that increasingly coercion, despite the radically increased efficiency of the means of coercion, cannot account for the organization of the members of such a society. Third, the adjustments of human beings to the structures characteristic of relatively modernized societies require, whatever other ways may be available, constantly increasing standards of living to keep them coordinating their activities within the limits of coercion which can be applied efficiently if necessary. Fourth, the more radically communications increase in efficiency, the less likely it is that radical discrepancies in income distributions can be kept from being generally recognized. Fifth, given the increase in generalization of the media of exchange and the increasing correlation between criteria of performance other than monetary income and monetary income distributed for those performances, if there is not an increasingly unimodal distribution of such factors, people will become just as dissatisfied as they will if their minimal incomes are not continually rising. If they become so dissatisfied, the amounts of coercion necessary to keep them functioning in terms of the system without breakdowns will rise beyond the levels of coercion consistent with such operations. Finally, as modernization increases, an increasing proportion of the members of a society must be moved away from a subsistence minimum—regardless of views of social justice, physical welfare, and human dignity—if only because of the radically increased demand for greater basic knowledge [and hence schooling] for the population in general and far more numerous highly specialized forms of intermediate knowledge for an ever increasing proportion of the total population. No doubt other reasons could also be adduced, but these will serve as a *minimal* set.

The hypothesis, the more highly modernized a society the more unimodal the allocation of income, in no way implies the limiting possibility of identical income distributed to every member of the population. On the contrary, such a distribution is quite out of the question. In connection with increasing levels of generalization of media of exchange, I pointed out that the surprising thing is not how highly merit was deemed to be correlated with income but that it is not deemed to be more highly correlated than it in fact is; that the more highly modernized a society, the more highly correlated judgments by the members of merit and income would be and would be expected to be. This does not imply that a member of such a society becomes increasingly likely to be deemed meritorious *because* he has a high income, but rather that he is more likely to have his high income attributed to his meritoriousness. Correspondingly, with regard to income distribution, insofar as members of the society continue to regard merits of whatever sort as unevenly distributed and not only to perceive differences in merit but also different degrees of merit, and given the other generalizations about increases in the generalization of the media of exchange—to that extent—discrepancies in income distribution at least sufficient to correspond to some of the discrepancies actually maintained in such judgment will be vital to operations in terms of the system. If in fact most of the members of the society without being coerced can regard all performances by their fellow men as roughly equivalent in value, the hypothesis just asserted need not hold true.

There is another point with regard to income distribution that is relevant here. Towns and villages, as those terms are generally understood, are distinguished as subsystems of all societies of considerable scale, whether relatively nonmodernized or modernized. Both towns and villages refer to types of residential systems. The members of a village are generally individuals engaged in agrarian pursuits [or fishing or the like] and some small number of additional personnel deemed necessary to provide certain services relevant to the individuals who constitute the main population of the village. Family units always exist as subsystems of villages, and most of the members of villages are organized primarily on a family basis. Towns are not only considerably larger in scale, but they also involve much greater foci of manufactured goods in the most general sense of that term used here. Most of the members of a town are not engaged in any form of raw-material production. As a minimum townspeople include ordinary workers, craftsmen, merchants or specialists in exchange of some sort, administrators or government personnel, etc. Villages, as the term is intended here, probably never involve memberships of more than a few hundred people at the very most, whereas the members of towns may vary from several hundreds to several millions.

Before the development of relatively modernized societies, a special relationship as regards the flow of goods and/or services existed between all towns and villages or between the towns and the general sedentary agrarian base of the society concerned. A substantial proportion of the income of the townsmen consisted of a flow of goods and services "exported" by the villagers. This holds true of course in an obvious sense with regard to materials such as food. From the point of view of the villagers this was considered a one-way flow of income. It has classically been received from villagers in the form of rents, taxes, interest, and profits on goods sold to the villagers. With the exception of the last item the villagers have regarded this as a one-way flow, but it has been one that, up to a point, the villagers have taken for granted as an inescapable aspect of the facts of life.

With the exception of some of the goods on which a profit is usually made, little in a tangible sense is seen by villagers as being exported by the townspeople to them. Specifically in relatively nonmodernized social contexts nothing is exported by the townspeople that systematically raises the productivity per acre of agrarian production [or corresponding productivities in activities such as fishing]. There are activities of the townspeople and even goods exported by them that certainly are relevant for the maintenance of given levels of productivity and even for occasional rises in productivity. The export to the villagers of iron tools is such an instance. In traditional China the planning and management for canals and the like and usually the direction of the actual production of such irrigation devices served from time to time to increase productivity in the agrarian areas, and the maintenance of such work certainly served to maintain productivity. Nevertheless, continuous rises in productivity, and certainly accelerated continuous rises, have never in any relatively nonmodernized social context flowed from any source at all to any other let alone from the townsfolk to the villagers. The towns, of course, were usually the focal points for the maintenance of order in the society and were the context within which governmental services were generally provided, but it was also true that the villagers of most of these societies were highly self-sufficient. In general, the more the representatives of the government left the villagers alone, the better the villagers liked it.

With the development of relatively high levels of modernization the situation changes radically. For the first time in world history there are both goods and services that (1) are produced in town environments, (2) can be exported to rural areas, and (3) can be used to raise systematically the productivity of those areas. In the context of all relatively nonmodernized societies villagers take a certain level of export to town environments as par for the course. They are accustomed to it; they do not feel themselves exploited thereby. In all such social contexts, however, if the export to the town environments is increased beyond those levels, sooner or later the members of the society do get involved in peasant revolts and the like. Only with the development of relatively modernized societies is it possible to alter the one-way flow-of-income aspect of the relationships between the townsfolk and the villagers. Usually in the early stages of modernization this is not done. The flow of goods and services from the villagers continues to be one of the main sources of capital formation for modernization. Sooner or later this situation must be changed if the relationships between townspeople and villagers are to be stable. The problem is particulary pressing if there is, as there is in most cases of relatively nonmodernized societies, the prospect of a population explosion resulting from importations of modern medical technology which drop death rates while birth rates remain high. Again, whether or not such one-way flows of income are maintainable is not a question of ethics or ideology. Quite apart from views about exploitation of peasants and the like—whether it is good, bad, or indifferent to behave so if one can get by with it—the really interesting thing is that such a procedure cannot be gotten by with indefinitely. As modernization increases, the old relationship as between villagers and townspeople must be altered in the direction of a reciprocal relationship in which the productivity in the village areas is not only maintained but systematically increased and probably systematically increased at an accelerated rate as a function of goods and services produced at least partially in a town context.

VIII
PROPERTY

I find the most sophisticated sociological treatment of the concept of *property* in the work and thought of Wilbert E. Moore. As early as 1943 he defined the concept as follows: "property consists in institutionally defined and regulated rights of persons (or other social units) in scarce values." [9] The literature concerned with property is voluminous in at least several specialized fields. The obvious fields are law, political science, economics, and sociology. Even to survey that literature would be a full-scale task in itself. Here again I shall not attempt to go into those matters treated at such length elsewhere. Despite the fact that I feel strongly that there is a profound insight implicit in the observation that a great many situations in social life can be better understood if the observer is aware of "whose ox is gored," I have not found the concept of property to be as illuminating as certain other concepts. In some of the major uses of this concept, the analysis has become so intertwined with ideology and special pleading, regardless of the point on the political compass from which the ideology or special pleading comes, that I find the reward of using the concept hardly worth the effort required to keep the analysis on the level of analysis. This no doubt, constitutes the shortcom-

[9] See, "The Emergence of New Property Conceptions in America," *Journal of Legal and Political Sociology*, vol. 1, nos. 3–4, April, 1943, pp. 34–58. This definition has many excellent aspects as a scientific concept. For one thing, it fits in well with the layman's conception of property without falling into some of the problems frequently associated with the concept from the layman's point of view. Given this definition, it is exceedingly easy to distinguish between tangible and intangible property in the layman's sense, but the concept of property as defined is easily distinguished from the physical factors in which property from the layman's point of view frequently inheres. One of the most strategic rights from the layman's point of view and from the point of view of many specialists such as economists and lawyers of the property concept is one of the rights of transference, for example, the right of sale of the property concerned. This characteristic form of transferability is in no way inconsistent with Moore's definition. In addition, however, Moore's definition is consistent with certain references to properties which are in no ordinary sense salable. The old question of entailed estates is one possible case. The reputation of a professional man is an example of a property right which Moore likes to cite as one which can be stripped from the owner but which he himself may not transfer. Good will is sometimes regarded as a property right which the owner can transfer or at least try to transfer, etc. Another implication of this definition is that the concept of property always implies a relationship. As a minimum that relationship involves the owner or possessor of the property right, the referent, whether tangible or intangible, of the property concerned, and at least one or more individuals or members of other organizations who might claim, buy, participate in or in some other way relate to the particular rights concerned.

ing of permitting certain aesthetic standards of theory construction to bias actual theory construction, but in many of these areas it is possible to go quite far in analyzing problems in terms of the interrelationships as among the members of different organizations and in terms of different aspects of their behavior without too frequent invocation of the concept of property. There are, however, a few generalizations, some of them of a rather specialized character, about property phenomena especially relevant to the arguments here.

First, there has never been a society whose members did not have some concept of property in the sense that property has been defined here, regardless of whether they attach the ownership, domination, or control of properties to specific individuals or to representatives of specific organizations. Actually, it is doubtful that there has ever been any society whose members did not attribute specific instances of property to both individuals and organizations to whom and to which they are conceived as belonging. Short of a social setting in which all goods and services are in fact free goods and services in the strict economic sense of the term one would hardly expect otherwise—and there never has been such a social setting. Indeed, even if all goods and services were in the strict definition of the term free goods by the criteria most frequently involved in that definition, if individual actors, however irrationally or arationally, acted as though any particular goods or services were in fact not a free good or service, the implications for property concepts would still inhere.

I shall distinguish three different property structures: (1) feudal structures, (2) private ownership structures, and (3) community or socialized structures. *Feudal structures* may be defined as those in terms of which the allocation of property to either individuals or members of organizations qua members of those organizations is both ideally and actually closely correlated with the allocation of power and responsibility. Feudal property is generally invested in an individual at any given point in time, but a transaction in terms of feudal property is both ideally and actually a transaction that specifically alters the political allocation. Usually societies with feudal property structures also have structures that radically restrict the purchase and sale of those properties which are most clearly defined as feudal properties. The best example of this is, of course, land. In social contexts characterized by nonfeudal property structures, at least ideally speaking and frequently actually speaking as well, there may be transfers of property without any alteration in the structure of political allocation, but this is never the case as far as feudal property is concerned. In feudal contexts political roles and ownership are closely correlated. Wherever feudal property is concerned, the allocation of loyalty, ideally speaking, is carefully correlated with the ownership of feudal property.[10]

Private ownership structures may be defined as structures in terms of which property is allocated to individuals and/or to the members of a specific organization qua members of that organization in such a way that the individuals, or the legitimate executive of the organization concerned, within considerable limits have discretion over use and transference of the instance of property concerned. Given structures of private ownership, allocations of power and responsibility may in fact be correlated with allocations of property, but ideally speaking the two are not necessarily closely correlated, and in many cases as a minimum, actually speaking, they are not. There is no such thing as a society in terms of which the allocations of private property are totally irrelevant to allocations of power and responsibility, but transference of property does not necessarily imply a transference of positions of power and responsibility in general political allocation nor is it expected to do so by many of the individuals acting within a private property context. Ideally speaking at least, the members of societies characterized by private ownership structures expect quite wide alterations in the allocations of goods and services to take place without corresponding alterations in allocations of power and responsibility. Ideally speaking the members of such societies take it for granted that all sorts of transferences of property among individuals and groups and in the name of organizations can take place without alterations in the general form or detailed substance of the government. Specifically speaking in such social contexts to use transferences of property to alter the form or effect of the actions of members of the governmental systems is to utilize property illegitimately. It is graft and corruption.

[10] I define a society as *feudal* insofar as it has the following characteristics: (1) closed social classes, (2) a well-defined hierarchy of power holders, (3) identification, at least ideally speaking, of each individual as responsible to some particular individual higher than himself in the hierarchy and related to others outside that direct line by virtue of his overlord's relation to them, (4) a distribution of goods and services, most especially land ownership and control, primarily on the basis of the ranks distinguished in the hierarchy of power and responsibility, and (5) succession to both such ranks and property, ordinarily determined on the basis of inheritance via kinship. There are, no doubt, problems about such a definition of feudal society, but it is at least more exact and considerably less misleading than the prevalent habit of referring to practically any relatively nonmodernized system, especially one which the referrer finds shocking and reprehensible, as a feudal society.

Community or *socialized structures* of property are ones such that property is not owned by individuals. It is only owned by organizations. That is to say, it is only owned in the name of organizations or by a set of individuals whose relation to the property concerned is a function of their membership in general and their specific roles in detail in the organizations concerned. In highly socialized examples of community property structures, in theory at least, the only legitimate ownership may inhere in the government as such. Any property structures will fall into one of these three categories. Community or socialized property structures always have more in common with feudal property structures than either set of structures has with the structures of private ownership. This is a result of the fact that the community or socialized organizations which are the owners of property in the third case are also usually systems that are important foci of political allocation for the members of the society in which they exist. The administrative heads of such organizations, whether they be family heads or government chiefs, in effect have major discretion with regard to the property conceived of as owned by the system. In this sense the correlation of allocations of power and responsibility and of goods and services are much more closely identified than is either actually or ideally the case given private ownership structures. Unlike the feudal structures, community and socialized structures do not necessarily involve closed classes, inheritance of office via kinship, and they need not focus discretion over property in the hands of a single individual. Discretion may volve into the hands of the members of a council of some sort, though ideally as well as actually some individual is likely to be singled out. The close coordination of the power hierarchy and discretion over property, however, is characteristic of both the feudal and the community structures.

Never has action in terms of any set of social structures succeeded in removing the political implication of allocations of goods and services, but in a peculiar sense action in terms of private ownership structures has, in fact, probably gone further in reducing those implications than any other structures of property ever realized. The amount of power associated with vast accumulations of property in the context of societies in which private ownership is institutionalized is in no way surprising. The surprising thing is that there have ever existed societies in terms of which private ownership has been carried to any considerable length and in terms of which there has been any considerable separation of allocations of goods and services and of power and responsibility. In the history of the United States, for example, it is not at all remarkable that the possessors of great wealth have sometimes succeeded in uniting their efforts in such a way as to control the government and determine the outcomes of elections at the presidential level and at lower levels. Given the inescapable relevance of allocations of goods and services for allocations of power and responsibility and vice versa, the really surprising thing about the history of the United States is that there ever should have been elections in which the possessors of great wealth were quite unable to handle matters in this fashion. There have certainly been presidential elections at least in United States history in which, despire considerable unity of opinion among the wealthy, such control has eluded them.

I X

APPROACH TO ECONOMIC SELF-SUFFICIENCY
OF A SOCIETY OR A NATION

In days gone by there were, no doubt, numerous cases of societies of some considerable scale which from the point of view of economic self-sufficiently were closed systems. The members of some of these societies had little or no contact with the members of any other societies, and insofar as they did, those contacts did not affect them substantially. In some cases these were closed systems simply because the members of the societies concerned were physically isolated from the members of all other societies. There have, no doubt, even been cases in which the closest neighbors of the members of such societies did not know of their existence. Even among those societies whose members were in constant contact with the members of other societies, there have been many cases in world history in which the individual societies concerned were to a high degree self-sufficient. As far as quite general levels of operation were concerned it would have mattered little if at all to the members of these societies had their contacts with members of other societies been totally cut off. In a setting of this sort ideas of national sovereignty and complete independence could and did develop and are quite easy to understand. Before the development of relatively modernized societies in Western Europe and the United States, a substantial number of societies were in this sense to a high degree self-sufficient. Even in cases in which members of one society were taken capitive via invasion by members of other societies and ruled by people whom they considered outsiders from the economic point of view, they may well have remained to a high degree self-sufficient, i.e., they may still have produced most of what they consumed and consumed most of what they produced. Even the early stages of imperialism did not usher in the high levels of interdependency which we take for granted nearly everywhere today. The societies of the Viking raiders about whom Veblen wrote so insightfully and with such a sense of humor were among the most extreme departures from such economic self-sufficiency.[11]

The radical decline in the possibility of such closed systems from the economic point of view is a matter of exceedingly recent history as a general phenomenon, though prior to this, all through history, there were certainly individual instances of it. The level of interdependency from the economic point of view which people take for granted today is a function of quite modern developments in the efficiency of communications. The members of Japanese society made perhaps the last and most dramatic hold-out of any considerable scale in history. After all except for a relatively small trickle of annual trade via the Dutch at Deshima in Nagasaki Harbor the Japanese from 1638 to 1853 were to all intents and purposes completely self-sufficient economically. In the economic sense as well as in others, the Japanese became importantly interdependent with the members of other societies following 1853. From the latter part of the nineteenth century on, hardly a day passed without a decline in the level of economic self-sufficiency of most of the societies of the world. Today in the economic sense, as well as in other senses, the level of self-sufficiency of individual societies, with rare exceptions, is so clearly a thing of the past that many of the arguments which developed a meaning and an appeal in an era of relatively high self-sufficiency of both societies and nations have completely lost their actual meaning except for the one imparted to them by the intense feeling associated with these conceptions as ideals of human conduct. Economic self-sufficiency is not the only element or the primary causal element involved in this change. It may not even be the most important element involved, but the increase in economic interdependency of societies, alone, is quite enough to make a special form of mockery out of the continually increasing emotional investment in the conceptions of sovereignty and complete independence which were the flowers of social philosophy of the eighteenth century. The doctrines of independence and sovereignty of that period have a high positive emotional value for me, but as they are discussed today, I know that my identification with them is primarily a matter of sentimentality—nostalgic sentimentality—by a member of a society whose earlier members

[11] See Veblen, T.: "An Early Experiment in Trusts," *The Journal of Political Economy*, vol. XII, March, 1904, pp. 270–279.

experienced such structures. It is an utterly naïve wishful sentimentality for anyone who hopes to achieve such a state of affairs
for his own nation in the future.

From the economic point of view as well as from other points
of view, there is probably not a society of any considerable scale
left anywhere in the world which approaches the degree of self-
sufficiency fairly widely achieved by the members of many different societies in the late eighteenth century. As relatively closed
social systems became increasingly less feasible with the passage
of each day and each improvement in the technology of communications, the problem facing the members of various nations in
the world has long since ceased to be a problem of protecting their
rights and their freedoms, such as they are, by the achievement of
independence and of sovereignty. The problem of maintaining
those freedoms and rights realistically becomes increasingly a
problem of whether they are compatible with the minimally necessary forms of cooperative behavior among the members of
different nations and societies. It may continue to be true as some
would maintain that it always was and always will be that "God
helps those that help themselves," but as far as rights and freedoms for the members of a given nation or society are concerned,
in the world in which we live now and are going to live in the
future, that precept will have to be modified at least to the extent
of maintaining that "God helps those who help themselves in
some sort of cooperation with others."

Insofar as the economic self-sufficiency of a given nation or
society declines, its members are involved to some extent in what
economists refer to as international trade. There is no point in
trying to handle questions of international trade in any detail
here. This is certainly a field in which immense technical sophistication exists among bankers, governmental officials of various
sorts, academic economists, general businessmen, and many
other types. There is, however, one special tool in the kit of the
economically sophisticated not generally discussed in treatments
broadly oriented to general social structure as opposed to profes-
sionally oriented to the economic analysis of international trade. I
refer to the "doctrine of comparative advantage." Any student of
international affairs or any individual charged with responsibility
in this field who is unacquainted with this doctrine had best
acquaint himself with it, and the more quickly, the better. This
imperative covers any student of public affairs, whether he thinks
he is interested in international matters or not, since increasingly
there are no problems of any importance in domestic affairs
without international implications or vice versa. The relevance of

the doctrine of comparative advantage does not depend on whether the members of a nation are aware of it or not, whether their government is fascistic, socialistic, democratic, capitalistic, or tribal. In its essence it is a simple doctrine. It maintains that as long as there are differences in the relative costs with which different goods and services are produced by the members of different countries, there is a basis for trade among the members of these countries, which can be of mutual benefit insofar as benefit can be reckoned in the maximization of goods and services per capita available from any given quantity of productive resources. The doctrine also indicates that in the absence of absolutely uniform relative distributions of resources of all sorts including skills of organization, some such differences in costs will always exist. It does not imply that the members of a given society will in fact rationally maximize the possibilities of their comparative advantages by trading internationally, but in any given case it is at least in theory possible, if one knows how to analyze situations in terms of this doctrine, to form some conclusions as to what the implications of failing to do so will be. The most rudimentary knowledge of the doctrine of comparative advantage makes absolute nonsense out of the frequently reiterated statements of highly placed statesmen that they are quite unable to compete or engage successfully in international trade because another nation's members produce everything more cheaply than the members of their nation are capable of doing. To speak in this fashion is to speak from an ignorance needless in this time and day.

Whether one likes to admit it or not, any increase in international trade is a decline in economic self-sufficiency. Any such decline increases the vulnerability of the members of a given society to the members of other societies as far as some influence is concerned. Once contacts of this sort are made, not only vulnerability but also desires relative to other societies and the products produced in terms of them are likely. Both vulnerability and desires increase as the proportion of the gross national product involved in international trade increases. The proportion of gross national product involved in international trade need not be great for the international trade to be exceedingly important in understanding the economic aspects of the society. Here again the professional economist, whether he be academic, governmental, or private, has a great deal to say. Even if only 5 per cent of the gross national product is involved in international trade, the effects of its abandonment will have far-reaching implications. As such trade continues, it is doubtful whether either the vulnerability or other desires of the people concerned can be kept from continually increasing even though the ratio of international trade to the gross national product may not increase radically.

Many years ago Fei Hsiao-T'ung in a remarkable book [12] illustrated this without full awareness of all of its implications in an exceedingly stark fashion. In a village in Eastern China somehow someone of entrepreneurial talent recruited the young girls of the village into a rudimentary factory-type organization for the reeling of silk. The venture prospered, the villagers exported the silk so produced, and not only was the standard of living of the villagers raised, but previously quite stable and strategic social structures began to alter visibly. Notably the position of women in that community began to change. Whereas formerly one married daughters off as soon after puberty as practicable, thenadays girls at that age acquired a new value as continuing members of their parental families. Marital age increased, and some marriages were put off indefinitely. The girls became independent. There were many other attendant changes. Where the silk went when it left the village, the villagers neither knew nor cared. They knew little of the outside world, and they were completely unsophisticated in the field of international trade. They were sufficiently concerned with their prosperity and the changes afoot among them without trying to understand the international scene of which they had unwittingly become a part. In 1929 the Great Depression hit. One of the first markets to suffer was, of course, the market for luxury goods in the United States. It is hard for many people to remember that such a thing ever existed, but in those days most of the best of ladies' stockings and underclothes were silk. With the radical cut-back in demand in the United States for such items, silk reeling in the small village in Eastern China suddenly became uneconomic. A depression in the United States which Chinese members of that small village neither knew nor cared about had spread to their village. The villagers not only found themselves with their incomes reduced, but more importantly in all probability they found themselves with numerous unmarried daughters, overage and out of hand. A set of remote villagers in Eastern China was tied into an interdependent set of world societies. Not a single ill-intentioned or Machiavellian hand had been raised against them, and yet their freedom and their sovereignty, such as it had been in the heyday of their higher self-sufficiency, had certainly been radically interferred with.

The degree of economic self-sufficiency of a given society always has implications for other aspects of the social organization.

[12] Fei Hsiao-T'ung, *Peasant Life in China*, E. P. Dutton and Co., Inc., New York, 1939.

This does not follow from any sort of economic determinism. The degree of economic self-sufficiency of a given society is never the sole relevant variable in understanding that society, but it is never totally irrelevant either. For that residue we are all indebted to Marx.

POLITICAL ALLOCATION

I
DEFINITION

Political allocation has been defined [p. 181] as the distribution of power over and responsibility for the actions of the various members of the social systems concerned, involving on the one hand, various forms of sanctions, of which sheer coercive force is the extreme form in one direction, and, on the other, accountability to the members and in terms of the systems concerned, or to the members of other interdependent systems. The term *power* was defined as the ability to exercise authority and control over the actions of others. The term *responsibility* was defined as the accountability of an individual (s) to another individual (s) or group (s) for his own acts and/or the acts of others. What is power from one point of view is simultaneously responsibility from another—that here again, as in the case of production and consumption, power and responsibility constitute in a sense obverse forms of one another.

I I
SPECIALIZED PREDOMINANTLY POLITICALLY ORIENTED SYSTEMS: GOVERNMENTS

In all known societies of any considerable scale there exists as a subsystem at least one specialized predominantly politically oriented organization that will be referred to here as a government.[1] All social action involves some allocations of power and responsibility, just as all social action involves some allocation of goods and services. At least three questions always arise about the allocation of power and responsibility. Those are the questions of *locus*, *definition*, and *procedure*. That is to say, it is important in analyzing any social organization to know: (1) where power and responsibility lie, (2) how they are defined [including in the question of definition whether they are defined explicitly or implicitly, etc.], and (3) what behaviors in the implementation of

[1] I would actually hold that one is able to distinguish some sort of rudimentary governmental organization in any society regardless of its scale. There is certainly no society of the scale which is a matter of general preoccupation for those concerned with public and international affairs that is not characterized by the presence of such an organization.

power and responsibility are expected and supported by the members of the various social systems concerned. No society could consist of a single subsystem or a single type of subsystem such as a family unit. Certainly in all known societies the subsystems and types of subsystems are always numerous. Given the possibility of conflict, let alone the inevitability of conflict, it is unlikely that any society could continue to exist in the absence of some organization that differed from others in that its members somehow regulate the relations among the members of other organizations when some questions are disputed among them. Thus, although *any* social organization always has some political aspects, these aspects of one type of organization can never be the sole type of political aspects for the society as a whole. In addition to the ordinary structures of political allocation that may be present in other organizations, there must be at least one additional organization characterized by structures of political allocation having to do with the regulation of behavior among the members of other organizations. Such an organization *must* be present, if the society is to be stable, but the presence of one is not a guarantee that the society will be stable. One type of organization is of special relevance from this point of view, a predominantly politically oriented organization, i.e., a *government*. It is possible that there be a society characterized by an organization somewhat different from others but not predominantly politically oriented. It is also conceivable that in fact regulation of the relationships among members of other structures when questions of dispute arise take place in terms of that organization. All societies of any scale, however, show considerably more sophisticated development in this realm than would be implied by this possibility.

When governmental units do appear, certain implications of their existence in the society are necessarily clear. They must be oriented to the regulation or supervision of relationships among the members of other units. The only conceivable exception to this would be an organization for whose members the internal allocation of power and responsibility was an end in itself, but this would not be a true exception because such an organization would not be predominantly politically oriented as that concept has been set up here. It would rather be an organization predominantly oriented to expression of a particular sort. It would actually be a specialized religiously oriented unit in which the religion concerned focused on what might be considered a political fetish. All of the known governmental units in history have to some extent been oriented to the regulation of interrelationships among the members of other membership units. Usually it is in terms of governmental structures that in the last analysis responsibility is enforced on the members of other social systems, if action in terms of the special structures of neither of those systems nor cooperative interrelationships among the members of different ones have enforced responsibility on their members. In social history, the ability of the representatives of different governments to enforce responsibility on the members of other social systems has varied widely. There have been cases of multiple governmental organizations within a given society. There have been cases in which representatives of the legitimate governmental structure have not been nearly so powerful as members acting in terms of other organizations in the society. There have also, of course, been governments in whose representatives, not only ideally but actually as well, the legitimate monopoly of power has been overwhelmingly concentrated.

Insofar as interrelationships among the members of other social organizations are regulated by members of a government and insofar as they frequently enforce responsibility on the members of other organizations, other implications follow. Governmental organizations by their mere presence always to some extent limit and define the political allocation that takes place in terms of other organizations. To some extent the activities of members of the government are always oriented to the control of behavior that is regarded as disruptive by the members of the society in general.

The importance of a balance of power and responsibility in understanding social organizations will be discussed immediately below. Here it may be pointed out that in all societies governmental organizations furnish one of the primary sources of balance for the allocation of power and responsibility in a total society, if they are actually balanced. In many cases the members of a society expect the government to be *the* primary source in this respect. This is so much the case for relatively modernized societies, and in general has been so much the case since the development in European history of relatively strong centralized states that most modern social science analysis in the field of government, either implicitly or explicitly, takes it for granted that all governments are *in fact* the primary source of such balance or that they ought to be. This is reflected in the persistent tendency to define a government or state as "having a monopoly of the legitimate use of force in the society" or in some roughly equivalent manner. Using such a definition, there are certainly many societies of considerable scale that lack governments altogether.

Most feudal societies, for example, lack governments in this special limited sense. The mistaken implications that all governments are *the* primary source of such balance, or that the members of societies characterized by such governments feel that the government should be the primary source of balance, or that the members of the government themselves feel that they should be such a source of balance—to accept those points of view, however, is to make absolutely certain that one will misunderstand a considerable part of social history as far as government is concerned.

Various forms of governments will be discussed to some extent below [pp. 436–502]. It will not, however, there or here be necessary to go into the details of governmental organization at any great length. Many of the critical questions are thoroughly and carefully investigated by professional treatises of varying sorts. The pedigree of the discipline of political science itself is an ancient and honorable one. The field of public administration is highly developed, and the literature widely produced by, of, and for governmental leaders, administrators, and employees in general is increasingly abundant. The treatment of the structures of political allocation here will refer importantly to governments but it will also be concerned with the patterns of political allocation in the society generally.

I I I
BALANCES OF POWER AND RESPONSIBILITY

A. GENERAL HYPOTHESIS

It has been indicated above that power and responsibility refer to the same phenomena looked at from different points of view. In this sense there is always as much or as little power as responsibility in any relationship. It does not follow that the power that is or can be exercised in terms of a given system is balanced by the responsibility that is or can be assessed on the members either in terms of the system itself or in terms of another system. It also does not follow that the members within a given system necessarily have power either gained in terms of that system itself or in terms of some other system to execute the performances for which they are held responsible. Thus any given individual may be a locus of power that is not balanced by responsibility, or he may have responsibilities without being endowed with corresponding powers. Cases of power without balancing responsibility are a characteristic of TV Westerns. The villain par excellence of such Westerns is often a man of considerable power who, until the hero appears, cannot be brought to book by anyone. The true or unvarnished TV Western, as distinguished from the psychologically sophisticated or TV Western *manqué*, is one in which the villain is not responsible to anyone nor is he responsible to any code which he imposes on himself. Most cases described as "arbitrary exercises of power" are cases of power not balanced by responsibility. Cases of responsibility not correspondingly balanced by power are equally familiar to any readers of modern fiction from soap opera to the *New Yorker* short story. This is the classic case of the individual who has laid upon him, never mind how, an obligation that he cannot hope to fulfill. All such fictions have endings somewhere on a triangular scale with apices of neurosis, psychosis, and mayhem.

The balance of power and responsibility in a sense referred to above is relevant for the analysis of organizations because of the following hypothesis: Any organization for which the locus of power is not balanced by the locus of responsibility is inherently instable. The balance, if one exists, may be a function of the interrelationship of the members of one organization with those of another, but the larger the scale of an organization the more likely and the more important it becomes that a considerable proportion of the balances of power and responsibility be *internal*[2] to the organization. It is essential that no one jump to the conclusion that, because imbalances of power and responsibility are inherently instable, balances of power and responsibility are inherently stable. The latter hypothesis in no way follows from the former.

The sources of instability from an imbalance of power and responsibility are of two sorts. First, individuals who possess power without responsibility for the exercise of that power always raise the possibility of exercises of power that are capricious as

[2] A relationship or other phenomenon will be spoken of as *internal* to a given system if it involves members of a given system only in their roles as members of that system. Correspondingly a relationship or other phenomenon will be spoken of as *external* to a given system in the respects that it involves a member (s) of a system (s) other than the one. Even if only members of the given system are involved but one or more of them are involved in their roles as members of some other system as well, the relationship or phenomenon will be regarded as external to the given system to that extent. Thus, a father assessing responsibility on a son for some power the son has exercised in terms of a family system represents a balance of power and responsibility internal to the family system. Arrest by the county sheriff of the father for assessing responsibility on a son in such a way as to cause his death is a case of external balancing of power and responsibility regardless of whether the sheriff is also a son of the father arrested [see pp. 307–310 below].

far as maintaining the stability of the organization concerned and that cannot be stopped whatever their consequences may be. Sooner or later, however, there are always bound to be some capricious exercises of power if only because of lack of knowledge as to what would constitute completely rational exercises of power. With even the best worked-out balances of power and responsibility the exercise of power may well be capriciously disruptive, but if so, it is not so difficult to curb. The problem of balancing power with responsibility is always posed in an especially difficult and obvious form by highly autocratic and authoritarian systems. Enforcement of responsibility on persons with power in terms of such systems always limits the scope of their power to some extent. Failure to limit them to some extent opens the possibility that their actions may destroy the stability of the social structures in general and the very basis of their own power as well. Nero and Caligula, as ordinarily portrayed for the benefit of children, are classic examples of power figures of this sort. Modern history has already supplied an interesting number of examples of this breed, and there is as yet no indication that such figures are in short supply.

Second, responsibility that is not balanced by corresponding power is no less a potential source of instability. The implications for stability of responsibility for which an individual has not corresponding powers inhere in the extent to which the action for which he is responsible is germane to the maintenance of the system to which he belongs in the given instance. If one holds someone responsible for something that he lacks the power to execute, one can even go so far as to execute him, but that will not get the task done. Furthermore, insofar as the accomplishment of that task is relevant to the stability of the system, this stability is thereby threatened.

These generalizations about the balance of power and responsibility and stability are certainly not new. In one form or another realization of them underlies all sage advice and wise description of administrative systems. Although knowledge of the implications of capricious exercises of power in the absence of responsibility and of the bootlessness of responsibility in the absence of corresponding power is as hoary as any knowledge one may wish to speak of, it is rather surprising that systematic use of this knowledge in the analysis of governments and the like has not become an outstanding element in the general quiver of political science theory. Analysis of order and change is always germane to social phenomena and particularly to those with which students of public affairs are concerned, and the balance of power and responsibility is always germane to problems of order and change.

B. FOUR TYPES OF BALANCES

The question of balances of power and responsibility can be explored at great length. I shall explore them only briefly in terms of four ranges of variation that, if not common to all societies, are certainly common to all societies of any considerable scale and hence to any questions of general interest to men of public affairs. I shall discuss these under the following four headings: (1) hierarchical versus nonhierarchical balances, (2) empirical versus nonempirical balances, (3) specific versus diffuse balances, (4) internal versus external balances.

1. HIERARCHICAL—NONHIERARCHICAL BALANCES

A system with a *nonhierarchical balance* of power and responsibility is one in which the balances of power and responsibility are mutual and equal for all members of the system. This is the type of system in terms of which every member has the same powers and responsibilities as every other member. This type of system has been discussed briefly above [pp. 149–152] in connection with the discussion of relationships that are specifically egalitarian as far as their stratification aspects are concerned. There, however, attention was focussed on the question of hierarchy as such; here the attention is focussed on the allocation of power and responsibility. Friendship as that relationship is generally described in a country like the United States is one of the very best and one of the few examples of a balance of power and responsibility that is nonhierarchical [i.e., egalitarian] by ideal. In terms of such a system, friends are expected to have equal powers over one another and equal responsibilities to one another to the degree that the similarity of their circumstances and the degree of friendship permits. Powers and responsibilities are mutually held and mutually owed. What they do in terms of their relationships with one another certainly has implications for other spheres in which they behave, but from the point of view of the friendship relationship the primary question is the mutual relevance of what they do for one another.

Nonhierarchical political balances can never be the sole type of political structures in any society. Most, if not all, of the crucial organizations as well as the more or less strategic ones in any society *must* have institutionalized hierarchical political structures if they are to be stable. If the balances of power and responsibility in a relationship are nonhierarchical, either ideally or actually, the relationship is one that can be dissolved by any party to it. Only simultaneous desire by all the parties concerned to such a relationship can both preserve the status quo and continue action in terms of the organization. Whenever or for whatever reason that mutual desire breaks down from one side or from all sides, as a minimum the political structures change radically, and in many cases the organization characterized by those structures will be dissolved or radically changed. Organizations with such structures of political allocation are obviously not well adapted to the curbing of disruptive behavior. In the field of international relations the instability characteristic of organizations whose member nations [or other organizations] ideally speaking are equals—even when the ideal is not that the balances within the organizational context be completely nonhierarchical—has been all too obvious. The periodic collapse of such organizations and the restoration of stability in terms of the establishment of a new hierarchically organized system either by virtue of a passage of arms or a recombination of "member organizations"[3] has been seen again and again in modern diplomatic history. The instability of a subsystem with a structure of egalitarian balance is no less

[3] I have placed this phrase in quotation marks because organizations as such are not members but are rather subsystems of other organizations. Action is in fact always executed by individuals or sets of individuals. Even when one can speak of sets of individuals operating in concert or unison of some sort, one of the most important questions about them is what are the structures of action [and how do they come into being, what are the implications of one set of them as opposed to another, etc.] in terms of which the individuals in the set so behave as to be identified as a set. International organizations have a general characteristic not shared by all social systems by any means. All of the members [or a very important portion of them] of such an organization are members by virtue of representing the members of some other organization. Specifically, of course, they represent nations which are a still more specific form of organization with a whole set of special properties that need not detain us here.

The important contrast here is between organizations such as these and families, universities, business firms, boys's clubs, etc. Ordinarily none or only a quite restricted portion of the members of such organizations as the latter are members of the latter specifically because of their roles as representatives of the members of some other social system. As far as I know, this is never true of family members. It is also possible to have mixed forms. For example, some members of a government may well be members by virtue of their roles as representatives of others and some may not. Thus, senators in the United States government are members of the government by virtue of being representatives in this sense: the secretaries of those same senators are not members of this sort.

Perhaps the crudest and most obvious example of the difference such distinctions can make is the question raised as to whether a given set of remarks addressed by one representative member of an international organization to another is an exchange of personal insults or an exchange that insults the members of the systems represented as a set.

obvious, even though it exists wholly within the context of a single society rather than as the result of interrelationships among the members of two or more societies. Unlike some attempts made in the international field, however, as far as is known, there has never been a conscious attempt nor an unplanned development of a society in which, ideally speaking, the structures of political allocation rested on a nonhierarchical structure of mutual balance. The problems of rearing children and keeping them from harm would, alone, necessitate some hierarchical elements.

Not only have there been no societies organized completely on a nonheirarchical basis, but there have been few social organizations of any sort that have not to some extent been organized on a hierarchical basis. Hierarchical political structures always pose the problem of maintaining a balance of the loci power and responsibility. It is the essence of such systems that responsibility is owed from the bottom up, from the less to the more powerful members, and that power is wielded from the top down. In a hierarchical political structure responsibility is never owed directly to the individual(s) over whom power is wielded in the specific respects in which that power is wielded. This is true by definition. If the contrary were true, a mutual balance would exist, and the possibility of the interference with the exercise of power would exist at every point at which power could be wielded. Despite the obvious nature of this point, emotionally charged discussions of democracy and egalitarianism which have ignored it, especially in connection with new nations, are not pauce.

An ordinary military system is one of the most clear-cut examples of the hierarchical allocation of power and responsibility. Ideally speaking the greatest power is concentrated in the role of the highest ranking official; members of the organization at every level owe responsibility to those in the ranks above them, and have power over those in the ranks below them. It is essential that the chain of command be clearly defined. To facilitate this, uniforms and insignia of rank have their utility. For quite far-reaching purposes such insignia alone are sufficient to indicate these relationships with sufficient clarity for members of the system to operate efficiently in terms of it even if no one has been properly introduced to anyone who, ideally speaking, has power over him or to anyone over whom he has power.

All authoritarian systems are by definition hierarchically structured from the point of view of the political allocation involved in addition to whatever other hierarchical structures inhere in such systems as a minimum. Because of the intense emotion that

generally surrounds all discussions of authoritarian versus democratic structures of organization, there is a broad tendency to
regard any hierarchical arrangement as inherently undemocratic. The ontological status of concepts like "democratic" and
"authoritarian" as used in the field of political philosophy is of no
concern here. If one wishes to define any democratic organization
as inherently nonhierarchical and any hierarchically organized
system as inherently authoritarian and nondemocratic, then all
that is necessary to say here is that we must forego discussion of
democratic systems so defined. They may be pleasant to contemplate as an ethical ideal, but in that sense they are a utopian ideal
only, a type of system that for societies as a whole has never
existed and never will exist. Most of the democratic systems in
this sense that the world has seen have been essentially friendship systems, and those on the whole have not been highly stable
forms of social organization.[4] I yield to no one in my personal
sentimentality for the motto of the French Revolution but if the
term *equality* is taken literally, the slogan is an impossible ideal
for social organization in general, let alone the other two terms. If
the term *democracy* is to be meaningful as a descriptive term

[4] However hostile and aggressive it may seem to observe it, no stable
society has ever been based overwhelmingly on friendship. Neither has any
stable social system of considerable scale in any known society. No social
system common to societies in general or to any considerable set of them
apart from friendships themselves in the most literal sense have been
based on friendship either. Stable governments, for example, are never so
based although it is quite possible to have governments based on kinship.
Friendship is a genuinely peculiar form of relationship even when considered on very general levels. It is puzzling that so few social scientists
have concerned themselves with it as a form of relationship that is at one
and the same time universal or well-nigh universal and exotic. It is universal in that it seems to exist in some form at least among children, in all
known societies actually if not ideally. It is exotic in that it has little in
common with other relationships in any society. It is, for example, one of
the very few relationships that is ideally egalitarian, even if not so by definition. It always injects a note of individualism into even the least individualistically oriented contexts if only because of the emphasis placed
on individual appeal of one candidate for the relationship to the other (s)
as the major basis for the relationship. Even if one defines the relationship
by such criteria, it is interesting that there seem to be instances of such
relationships in all known societies.

The implications of friendship roles for an individual's other roles always
pose interesting problems. Ideally every individual is expected to have some
friends. Despite the irony implicit in such pleas as, "Lord protect me from
my friends; I'll take care of my enemies myself," the friendless one is an
object of pity or scorn or fear in the context of all known societies. It is
especially interesting that a type of relationship so inherently fragile as
any placing emphasis on nonhierarchical structures of power and responsibility should be so generally regarded as a strong relationship, that so
apparently fragile a relationship could be considered so important in-
tegratively, etc. Friendship is a most bizarre phenomenon.

with some utility in the description of actual social organizations, apart from egalitarian friendships of a particular type, it must refer not to nonhierarchical social systems but to hierarchically organized ones in terms of which certain rights and privileges of individuals of lower ranks in the hierarchy are protected from or guaranteed by those of higher ranks in the hierarchy.

Among hierarchical structures of political allocation there are two extremely general methods of maintaining balances of power and responsibility: either ideally or actually or both. One type of balance is that in which the power holder owes responsibility directly and explicitly for the results of his exercise of power to some other actual individual or group of individuals. It is characteristic of the military forces of the United States, for example, that the balance is maintained by the requirement of responsibility of the highest officer of the armed forces to members of the civilian government and of the members of the civilian government to the population at large via elected representatives and their appointees. The commanding officer can never be called directly to account by his subordinates, but only by his superiors, to whom the subordinates may appeal under specific rules.[5] In the last analysis the commander-in-chief of the United States armed forces is a civilian official, responsible, ideally speaking, in quite specific ways to the electorate.

2. EMPIRICALLY—NONEMPIRICALLY ORIENTED BALANCES

Balances of the sort just discussed involve an unending chain of powers and responsibilities. The method of balancing power and responsibility, ideally speaking at least, is clear in any specific case at any specific stage of its development. It is a balance such that enforcement of responsibility need not interfere with the exercise of power. I shall call such a balance an *empirically oriented balance*. It is characteristic of the kind of political hierarchy with which most of us are most familiar. There is, however, another type of political hierarchy that I shall call a *nonempirically oriented balance* of power and responsibility, that is, one in which power is balanced by responsibility by virtue of the power holder's faith in and allegiance to nonempirical entities. These entities may be ideals such as justice, honor, etc., or they may be nonempirical entities in the ordinary sense such as gods, the

---

[5] Famous novels have been woven about the theme of what happens when, even under the most extreme provocation, subordinates in such a hierarchy act in defiance of those in positions above them in the hierarchy. *Billy Budd* and *The Caine Mutiny* illustrate this theme.

spirits of ancestors, etc. The balance of power and responsibility in terms of a traditional Chinese family was of this sort. Ideally speaking, a traditional Chinese father who was the head of his family had complete power over his son, for example, and owed no responsibility directly to his son in any way. He also ordinarily owed no responsibility to the district magistrate or to anyone else for his treatment of his son. If he were not the family head, he owed responsibility only to his father and/or to the family head. A properly brought up Chinese father did, however, from his own point of view as well as that of other members of the society, owe responsibility to the ancestors for the continuation of the family line. With the possible exception of incestuous relations between father and daughter-in-law, there was *no* justification for a son resisting his father in *any* way. If the father were also the family head, no other family member was qualified to interfere, ideally speaking. On the other hand, the father knew full well that, if he acted in such a way as to destroy his son or to fail to prepare him properly for adult life and continuation of the family line, he might commit the greatest of the three unfilial sins, i.e., fail to have posterity. In modern sociological and psychological jargon all such nonempirical balances of power and responsibility should probably be described as internalized balances of power and responsibility, that is they are effective by virtue of the power holder's belief or perception of obligation to something or some ideal that as far as any scientific observer can tell would not intervene actively regardless of the behavior of the power holder. In such nonempirical balances as the one described, there was at least an empirical element in the fact that the responsibility the father owed to the ancestors for the maintenance of a family was quite clearly defined in empirical terms. Even that sort of empirical element need not be present in the case of such extreme forms of nonempirical balances as that implied in the concept of the "divine right of kings." [6] Charismatic leaders, in the sense that Max Weber intended the concept, may also be in the position of leaders whose power is balanced nonempirically in both senses intended here. I do not know what a term like internalization means in any precise scientific sense, but I do know that given nonempirically oriented balances of power and responsibility, if the power holders are not somehow carefully trained to act as though their responsibilities for those

[6] This must not be confused with the concept of the "Will of Heaven" in traditional China. As in the case of the father's responsibility to the ancestors, the emperor's fulfillment of conditions that indicated that he retained the "Will of Heaven" required that a quite definitely and explicitly empirical state of affairs be maintained.

over whom they have power were in fact empirical and as though a failure to fulfill those responsibilities would in fact bring disaster, such systems can not remain stable. It is especially difficult to ensure stable operation in terms of such a system in the case of charismatic leaders. The power of such a leader is primarily a function of the blind faith that his followers have in him. The charismatic leaders of history have by no means ordinarily been individuals carefully trained in responsibility. Organizations characterized by charismatic leaders have on the whole been highly unstable in social history.

In nonempirically oriented political balances, if the power holder is somehow motivated in such a way as to balance his exercise of power with responsibility—and here it must be kept in mind that it is not enough for him to be motivated nicely, he must also be motivated correctly [7]—the organization in terms of which he wields his power will be instable. A Chinese family head who is not properly indoctrinated with a sense of responsibility to the ancestors for the continuation of the family can in fact become a little family Caligula and literally destroy the whole basis for the continuation of the family line. Not only can he do it; there are plenty of cases in Chinese history in which he has in fact behaved so; and in the Chinese case there has rarely been any critical problem of knowledge in these respects.

There is another reason, in addition to the question already mentioned of the proper indoctrination of the power holder, to expect elements of instability in nonempirically oriented political balances. There is the question of whether or not, even if he is so indoctrinated as to try to be responsible, he knows enough to wield his power responsibly. In the case of charismatic leaders there is even a third difficulty. They are likely to develop in situations of extreme tension and dissatisfaction. Their followers in general seek a change in the status quo. One of the surest ways for a charismatic leader to undermine the basis of his power is for him to sit tight. Such political balances are certain to produce changes, though not necessarily the ones looked for by the adherents of such leaders, assuming that those adherents know what changes they look for, which, of course, they may not.

Hierarchical political balances facilitate the wielding of power by minimizing the possibility of interference by those over whom power is wielded. Their interests may be protected in many different ways, or they may not be directly protected at all. If the balance of power and responsibility is empirically oriented, it is to

[7] There is, therefore, always a critical problem of rationality involved in such balances.

that extent somewhat easier for social scientists to analyse. If their analyses are successful, such balances may, therefore, be somewhat easier to alter on the basis of some form of explicit social engineering. From the point of view of those with roles in public affairs, the distinction is important. Even assuming adequate knowledge for social engineering, if the political balances in a given social context are nonempirical, it may be necessary to convert the members to a preference for empirical balances before some specific alterations can be effected.

In the last analysis, however, some nonempirically oriented political balances must be involved in every society, if only because one of the possible ranges of variation of human behavior is the orientation of human behavior to ultimate ends. Furthermore, some such orientation seems to be present in all known cases of human society. The allocation of power and responsibility is always relevant in some respects for any action, whether, from the point of view of the actor, that action is oriented to ultimate ends or not. To the extent that this is so, political aspects inhere also in actions with nonempirical orientations. From this point of view, if a society is to be stable, that stability will vary with the degree to which the ultimate ends are identified clearly with empirical states of affairs and hence can be paralleled by an empirically oriented hierarchical political balance.

United States social structure is interesting from this point of view. The structure of checks and balances, which we learned to take for granted as children, is one of the most explicitly empirically oriented balances of power and responsibility in world history. It is not a matter of chance, however, that most Americans, nevertheless, feel that ours is a "system of checks and balances under God." Margaret Mead was quite correct when she took as a leitmotif of her description of American society, an application of the old Cromwellian edict: "Trust God and keep your powder dry." Probably most members of United States society believe fairly devoutly that we exist with God's help, but most of those also believe equally fervently that "God helps those who help themselves."

In the field of international relations the problems of the balance of power and responsibility are raised in an acute form. It is not difficult to devise a structure for the delegation of power to a world or international organization, but how can the members of such an organization be held responsible for their acts? If any member can call the other members of the organization to a halt in their exercise of power over the members of the nation he represents, the power exercised in terms of that organization cannot be effective in times of crises. It is difficult to conceive of getting an effective nonempirically oriented balance in terms of such an organization if only because of the widely different conceptions of the nonempirical held by the various potential and actual members of such an international organization. The technology of the allocation of power at specific levels of application is highly developed, indeed, in the modern world, but the technology of the allocation of responsibility at general levels in terms of large-scale organizations has not received corresponding intellectual attention, public interest, or advance. In theory, at least, there seems to be no a priori reason as to why it should be a more difficult problem.

3. SPECIFIC–DIFFUSE BALANCES

Another major range of variation in terms of which balances of power and responsibility may be discussed is variation between *specific* and *diffuse* powers and responsibilities. This range of variation is obviously closely related to the functionally specific and the functionally diffuse aspects of any relationship. The powers at the disposal of any individual may be quite explicitly defined and delimited ideally and/or actually speaking. The same may be true of the responsibilities that an individual owes. On the other hand the extent of the powers and the nature of the responsibilities may be only vaguely defined and delimited. To the extent that the balance [or lack of balance] has the former character it is called a *specific* balance here; to the extent that it has the latter, it is called a *diffuse* balance. It is this type of variation which poses one of the greatest difficulties in determining whether in fact or in fancy a balance of power and responsibility exists. Not only are many different combinations possible with many different degrees of distinction among them, but variation may be considerable from the point of view of different parties to any given relationship or different members of any given organization. To sketch only the most obvious possibilities of variation in terms of the distinction between specific and diffuse balances of power and responsibility alone, and leaving questions of degree aside, there is the following list: (1) an individual may have specific powers and specific responsibilities, (2) he may have specific powers and diffuse responsibilities, (3) he may have diffuse powers and specific responsibilities, and (4) he may have diffuse powers and diffuse responsibilities.

It is not difficult to find examples of all four of these. Ideally speaking, offices in most bureaucracies are offices whose holders have highly specific powers and responsibilities. In the actual sense, and to some extent in the ideal sense as well, a primary school teacher in most areas of the United States has specific powers and quite diffuse responsibilities. Examples of individuals with diffuse powers and quite specific responsibilities are more likely to be found as actual than as ideal cases. Frequently the confidential secretary of a person quite important in an administrative hierarchy has rather diffuse powers and quite specific responsibilities to his [or her] own employer. Finally, the case of a father-son relationship is a typical case of diffuse powers and diffuse responsibilities. Neither side of the balance is both clearly defined and clearly delimited, though many elements about it may be quite precisely defined and delimited.

At this point some of the lines of complication of this question must be mentioned. If one considers the simplest of all possible relationships, a two-person relationship, one not only has the possibilities of the four types of balances mentioned above, but, identifying the two persons as A and B, the following main lines of variation also exist: (1) from the point of view of A, his powers may be specific and his responsibilities may be specific, (2) from the point of view of B, A's balance of power and responsibility may be seen as A sees it or as any one of the other combinations that obtain with regard to A, [see p. 304 as a minimum] (3) the same is true of B, of course, from A's point of view (4) possibilities corresponding to the foregoing three [the second of which contains several summarized] exist for each of the other three combinations given above [p. 304], and (5) the ideal-actual distinction may cut across [i.e., multiply by three: *a.* ideally and actually, *b.* ideally but not actually, and *c.* actually but not ideally] each of the preceding sets of possibilities. Every one of the possible variations of the situation from A's point of view as distinguished from B's and vice versa has implications not only for operation in terms of the relationship but for any other operations that either A or B has which interrelate in any other way with other individuals or the members of other organizations in any way affected by the actions of A and B in terms of their own particular relationship. There is no space here to go into this matter, but in even the most casual analysis of power and responsibility in terms of a society or a social organization, it is important for the observer to try to ascertain whether the allocations of power and responsibility are similarly or differently defined from the point of view of different members of the relationships concerned.

Another important line of variation has to do with whether or not these political balances are specific or diffuse, not with regard to the definition of the powers and responsibilities as such, but rather with regard to the individual or individuals over whom one has power and/or to whom responsibility is actually and/or ideally owed. Thus an individual may have power over, or be responsible to, one or more specifically identified individuals. The individuals concerned may be identified either personally or by virtue of the roles they hold in various organizations. On the other hand he may have power over, or owe responsibility to, an individual or individuals who are only vaguely identified. Again the variation of relationships is complicated by the fact that the description of the political allocation of a given relationship may be perceived quite differently by the different members of the relationship.

The various permutations and combinations of specific as distinguished from diffuse balances of power and responsibility can become exceedingly complex in organizations with large numbers of members. The possibilities may even be complex in relatively restricted organizations. Probably none of the permutations and combinations are totally lacking in implications at some levels of analysis. One may give obvious examples of some of the differences such variations may make. By contrast with Mr. Johnson's position as President of the United States, we tend to assume that the position Mr. Khrushchev held in the Soviet Union was one of relatively diffuse responsibilities as well as diffuse powers. Certainly in the field of foreign affairs an individual in Mr. Khrushchev's position is capable of more rapid alterations of fundamental foreign policy than is a person in Mr. Johnson's position. It is difficult for a President of the United States to execute a complete about-face in foreign policy overnight, if that foreign policy has received any general discussion by the members of the society as a whole or even by certain segments of the membership [e.g., Congressmen]. A leader in Mr. Khrushchev's position seems less inhibited. On the other hand, if such a leader does get launched on a disaster course, it is much more difficult for others acting in terms of his society to stop him without far-reaching consequences than is the case with Mr. Johnson. Here the differences in the balances of power and responsibility have implications for the ease and freedom of maneuver in the practical arena of foreign affairs.

Variations in the specificity and diffuseness of power and responsibility are considerable from society to society and from organization to organization within a given society. Variations in the specificity and diffuseness of balances of power and responsibility probably constitute one of the major lines of variation that longest survive considerable increases in the level of modernization in societies. Although in general there is a high and increasing uniformity among relatively modernized societies, they certainly do exhibit considerable differences. Some of the most noteworthy of those structured differences have to do with allocations of power and responsibility. In the long run even those increasingly get washed out, and all such societies become more similar rather than more different, but at any given point of development so far attained, the differences in these respects may be of the greatest moment. The range of possible variation among relatively nonmodernized societies in these respects is, as one would expect, much greater.

4. INTERNAL-EXTERNAL BALANCES

The distinction between internal and external balances of power and responsibility and consequently internal as opposed to external politically oriented hierarchies are specific instances of a general form of distinction. The terms *internal* and *external* are used here as defined above [see footnote 2, p. 294]. Whether a given structure [and hence action in terms of it] is internal or external cannot be determined unless the social system(s) involved are identified. In this sense the political structures relating representatives of the United States or other members of the United States to the representatives of the United Nations or other members of the United Nations are at least in part external to United States society. Relations between a member of the Federal Bureau of Investigation and any one who has broken a law of the United States are internal to United States society, though they involve external elements from the point of view of the member of the Federal Bureau of Investigation. The terms internal and external, in this sense, cannot be used fruitfully unless one is prepared to identify the units concerned. What is internal from the point of view of members of one unit may, of course, be external from the point of view of another.

The distinction between internal and external balances of power and responsibility focuses attention on two considerations relevant to public affairs. The first has to do with the sources of stability or change in terms of a given social system insofar as its structures of political allocation are germane to stability and change. The second, but closely related matter, is that of the relationship of the members of a given organization to members of other organizations with whom they are in contact. There is a sense in which a considerable portion of the balances of power and responsibility for any society is internal to the society as such, at least ideally speaking. The more highly self-sufficient any organization is, the more likely it is to be characterized overwhelmingly by internal balances of power and responsibility. This, for example, was strikingly true of the traditional Chinese family. On the other hand the members of an enormous number of organizations depend in a genuine sense on external contacts for balances of power and responsibility. One of the aspects of nations or societies whose leaders have absolute power or some near approach to it and diffuse and rather weak responsibilities, if any, rests on these considerations. If such leaders embark on extreme courses, it may be virtually impossible for any individual or any set of individuals belonging to their own society to curb such an extreme course. In such cases the course of action may be halted by members of other societies acting on a massive scale. There is a quite genuine sense in which no members of any German organization and no individual German alone could hold Hitler accountable. It required a massive alliance and a costly war to curb the activities he set in motion.

As one would expect, given the much higher level of self-sufficiency of organizations in relatively nonmodernized societies, the extent of internal balances of power and responsibility characteristic of the subsystems of such societies is much greater than is characteristic of the subsystems of relatively modernized societies. Most of the balances for most of the subsystems of those societies depend at least in part on the specialized predominantly politically oriented organizations, i.e., various governmental systems, to afford the structures of action in terms of which the members of all sorts of other organizations are in the last analysis held responsible. In a context like that of United States society, if a father mistreats his children, the members of some governmental body will take action. If the president of a corporation misappropriates funds, representatives of the government will act, etc. There are, of course, many important internal balances of power and responsibility characteristic of organizations even in relatively modernized societies, but there can be no denying that in general the more highly modernized a society becomes, the more do the balances of power and responsibility internal to the various organizations in the society depend on external balances of which the most important are those brought into operation in terms of governmental systems.

The whole issue of internal versus external balances of power and responsibility is related in a quite obvious way to the whole question of centralization and decentralization. Before turning to that question in somewhat greater detail, one further line of generalization may be presented on this score. The greater the de-

pendency of the members of subsystems of any nation or society
on internal balances of power and responsibility, the less social
planning is required for general operations in terms of the society.
Under such circumstances, however, when centralization is desired, it is much harder to realize, and other things being equal, it
requires a much larger involvement of manpower. It is not
difficult to get students of public affairs to pay close attention to
the implications of the interdependency of various organizations
when one considers their interdependency in terms of their economic aspects. To observe that members of a given unit can be
easily and quickly brought to heel by having their food supply cut
off by members of another organization is to say something that
can be and is quickly and easily understood by any member of our
society. The implications of interdependency viewed in terms of
political allocation as such rather than the means frequently
associated are no less extreme and should be no less obvious. Any
organization the stability of which depends on a balance of the
power of its leaders by their responsibility to members of yet
another organization is no less vulnerable to those interdependencies than it is to interdependencies viewed in terms of goods
and services in the more conventional sense. If the members of
the organization to whom responsibility is owed do not enforce
such responsibilities, they open the way to capricious behavior [or
close the means of preventing misuses of power] by the leaders of
the other organization as surely as if they gave them material
means of other sorts such as weapons, for in such instances
internal balances are specifically lacking. When internal balances are lacking, and especially when the individuals concerned
are long accustomed to the lack, it is difficult under any circumstances, let alone in crises, to shift to internal balances and much
more difficult, if not impossible, to shift to internal balances
quickly enough to handle a crisis. The implications of these hypotheses emerge more strongly when an additional hypothesis is
considered, i.e., that motivation for such shifts is quite unlikely to
occur in the cases mentioned except in times of crisis when the
external balancing elements fail to work.[8] The shaman of a primitive village may be a key figure in the maintenance of the stability
of village organizations because he is considered so powerful,
given his contact with the gods and the incomprehensible forces
of nature, that he is actually looked upon as an important asses-
sor of responsibilities for individual members of the society who
cannot otherwise be held to account. To prove to one and all of

[8] Some of the phenomena associated with the Fall Affair [1962] in Ox-
ford, Mississippi, can be understood in these terms.

the members of such a village that the shaman's cures [or, worse, that his spells in general] are without sound foundation may do more than rid the village of superstitious health practices. It may rid the village organizations of stability for reasons that seem difficult to understand. There are close analogies in other fields in which we are not so quick to seek more explicitly rational structures. The patient's confidence in his doctor, whether in fact justified or not, is so vital to effective medical therapy in general that there are always several reasons not involving self-interest to justify the exceeding reluctance of doctors to testify against one another in cases where the competence of a doctor is in question. Balances of power and responsibility are critical for all organizations. The interdependencies relevant to them and vice versa are no less strategic than interdependencies viewed in economic terms, although analysis of them is much less highly developed. Pursuit of even the most laudable goals of reform ignore such interdependencies at the expense of the goals specifically sought and more.

I V
CENTRALIZATION AND DECENTRALIZATION

Centralization and decentralization have already been discussed [pp. 16–18, 55–60, and 100–107]. It will suffice here to mention three combinations of special interest in matters of public affairs: (1) cases of high decentralization and low centralization, (2) cases in which centralization is greater than decentralization but for limited purposes only, and (3) cases of high general centralization and low decentralization. All of the cases of relatively nonmodernized societies that have had any considerable pedigrees of stability have been cases of the first or second type. High general centralization and low decentralization has not been a possible basis for stable large-scale societies until relatively high levels of modernization obtained in communications as well as other respects. Most of the feudal societies of world history and large numbers of small-scale societies have been societies characterized by high levels of decentralization and low levels of centralization. In the history of feudal Europe there have been many cases in which the so-called king of a country was considerably less powerful than one or more of his vassals.[9] Anthro-

[9] It is important to note in such cases, however, that this is a high level of decentralization and a low level of centralization at what we would consider today to be the national or society level. It does not follow that the social systems associated with the lands held by a given vassal were in turn organized in an equally decentralized fashion, though this was probably frequently the case.

pologists and other students of relatively small-scale societies have from time to time reported cases in which the elements of centralization on the society level were so tenuous as to call into question whether or not any such thing as a government could be said to exist at all. The case of the Jivaro Indians of South America is a notable example of this sort.[10]

All stable societies characterized by high levels of decentralization and low levels of centralization are, as one would imagine, societies characterized by subsystems capable of high degrees of self-sufficiency. The main bases of decentralization are likely to be family and village units. There are alternatives, however. Kinship units larger in scale than family units can be the major basis of decentralization,[11] and guilds and other organizations may be important bases of decentralization. Whenever one deals with members of societies characterized by high levels of decentralization, considerable alterations may sometimes be made in such centralized organizations as exist without immediate and far-reaching results, but *any* general tampering with the organizations in terms of which decentralization takes place is likely to have implications far beyond the intention or expectation of those designing the interference.

Among relatively nonmodernized societies there have been spectacular cases of highly stable large-scale societies in which important elements of centralization have far exceeded elements of decentralization, but this predominance of centralized elements has only held true for limited purposes. Two of the most spectacular of these cases are the cases of traditional China and Tokugawa Japan. The main outlines of the social structure of traditional China were stable for close to two thousand years. Tokugawa Japan was a feudal society, but it was certainly the most stable feudal society in all world history, lasting for roughly two and a half centuries. There is absolutely no question in either case but that during most of the periods concerned the central

---

[10] See, Mathew W. Sterling, *Historical & Ethnographical Material on the Jivaro Indians,* Smithsonian Institute, Bureau of American Ethnology Bulletin 117, Washington, 1938, and R. Karsten, *Blood Revenge, War & Victory Feasts among the Jivaro Indians of Eastern Ecuador,* Smithsonian Institute, Bulletin 79, Washington 1923.

[11] In all societies, however, the family unit will be *an* important basis of decentralization. No society has been characterized by structures eliminating all major elements of discretion from the family scene. Deeply respected structures of what proper conduct in a family context should be probably limit discretion in a family context more than actual transfer of decision making to another organizational context in even the most highly centralized societies. No matter how generally inculcated such respect is, it is quite another matter than centralization.

authorities could have brought overwhelming pressure to bear on any particular segment of the population in any particular area of the land had they so wished. The members of no single family, of no single locality, of no province threatened the stability of traditional China irrevocably for two thousand years, and certainly none of these ordinary foci of decentralization could stand against the power at the disposal of any emperor at the height of vigor of any dynasty. Correspondingly no daimyo could have withstood any Shogun during the Tokugawa period, or tried to.

In neither case, however, was the day-to-day conduct of affairs on a highly centralized basis. Most of the operations in terms of most of the organizations in both societies depended on internally regulated activities of the members of the various subsystems of the societies. Both Tokugawa Japan and traditional China were spectacularly effective cases of relatively high levels of centralization restricted to quite limited purposes. Nevertheless, even though they constitute spectacular cases, this type of structure is on the whole more frequent than the structure of very high decentralization and very low centralization of the sort discussed above in connection with feudalism in general and small-scale societies like that of the Jivaro Indians in particular. In the context of societies characterized by high levels of centralization for limited purposes, especially if the centralization is sufficiently great for almost any given isolated display of power, manipulation of the organizations in terms of which centralized power is exercised is a considerably more complex matter than in the case of feudal societies or ones similar to Jivaro society. In the latter, any general tampering with the organizations in terms of which decentralization takes place is likely to have far-reaching unforseen side effects. In the former the same may be said of any tampering with the organization(s) in terms of which centralization ordinarily proceeds. In both traditional China and Tokugawa Japan, despite the fact that an enormous amount of discretion was left to individuals at the local level, changes in the focus of centralized power had far-reaching implications for the local levels. Tokugawa Japan is a case in point. Before the development of the level of centralization achieved or at least maintained by the Tokugawa Shoguns internecine warfare all over the land was rife. The elements of centralization were vital to the maintenance of peace; it in turn was vital to the fact that the warriors of Japan were one of the most peculiar military castes in world history—a set of militarists who were explicitly forbidden to engage in military exploits. Finally the forms of centralization that did exist in Tokugawa Japan account for the development of structures of *absentee administration* in terms of which no ruler administered and no administrator ruled. In general, arguments about the levels of despotism that have in a fact been maintained on a stable basis in relatively nonmodernized social contexts are exaggerated, but they have not been exaggerated in one very important sense. The implications of what went on in terms of the governments of such societies for even those organizations in terms of which members ordinarily acted on an overwhelmingly decentralized basis were far-reaching and important. Whenever and wherever high levels of centralization, even for limited purposes, can be and are attained, it is important to be skeptical about local appearances of self-sufficiency.

Here it is necessary to reiterate that stable large-scale societies characterized by very high general centralization and very low decentralization are impossible until a relatively high level of modernization of communications is reached. Most treatments of centralization hinge, either implicitly or explicitly on centralization of the political aspects of social systems and especially on centralization of the governmental systems. It is always necessary to keep in mind that the allocation of power and responsibility is by no means the only respect in which a social organization can be highly centralized. Here again the habit, characteristic of all people accustomed to thinking in terms of relatively modernized societies, of considering social systems in terms of some specialized orientation to either political, economic, or some other special aspect of social life poses difficulties for the analyst of relatively nonmodernized societies. It must also be reiterated that such societies constitute the vast majority of all the societies distinguished in world history and even of all of the societies with whose members one has to deal in international affairs. There certainly have been cases of highly centralized governments in relatively nonmodernized societies, but none of these have been stable for very long periods of time as social history goes. These cases have, however, been sufficiently rare, though spectacular, that they are not likely to pie the analysis of students of international affairs. There are, on the other hand, a large number of cases of relatively nonmodernized societies for which this point of view of analysts reared in relatively modernized social contexts is exceedingly likely to pie the analysis. These are the cases like those of traditional China and Tokugawa Japan just described above. They are examples of societies which may be quite large in scale and quite stable, although the same difficulties can arise in the case of unstable examples of such societies. These are societies characterized by important elements of centralization in the governmental subsystems of the society. They may be societies in terms of which for limited purposes in general, and almost any limited purpose in particular, members of a governmental organization can dominate any other set of members of the society regardless of the degree of decentralization in terms of which affairs may ordinarily be conducted.

There is some danger that the actual levels of despotism or authoritarianism or centralization characteristic of the governments of these societies may be taken to indicate what comparable structures would indicate in a relatively modernized social context. High levels of centralization in the political sphere go hand in hand with high levels of centralization in other spheres in a manner taken for granted by the members of highly modernized societies. Furthermore, centralization in one of these spheres is never irrelevant to other spheres in any social context. Nevertheless, in a social context like that of traditional China the government [and to that extent the general allocation of power and responsibility] may be relatively far more centralized than the allocation of goods and services. Even among highly modernized societies variations of this sort may be observed. The government of the Soviet Union is surely more highly centralized than that of the United States though in some respects the latter is the more highly centralized society overall. For example, communications, economic allocation, and entertainment are in many respects— regardless of the intentions of the members—more highly centralized in the United States than in the Soviet Union. They are certainly more completely interdependent. We run a risk, even in regard to the societies we know best, in identifying governmental centralization with centralization in general, and the less modernized the society we study, the greater is the risk. The *appearance* of overwhelming centralization, which is so frequently commented on by students of relatively nonmodernized societies, is usually explicable at least in part by virtue of the fact that the vast majority of members of the society do not ordinarily get into the act as far as the actual wielding of power by members of the government is concerned. In these circumstances the important trick of analysis is not to be deceived into thinking that the level of centralization of governmental control is carried further than it actually is. Informants high in governmental circles in such societies are not necessarily the best informants on these matters, and this, of course, further complicates the problem.

The elements of centralization achieved may be great enough, as in the case of traditional China, so that vast engineered works of irrigation, canals, etc., can be constructed and maintained.

The power of the kings or emperors of such societies to work their will, however horrible it may be, on any given individual or even on considerable sets of individuals, need not be doubted either, but neither of these observations implies the level of general centralization which, whether we like to admit it or not, is increasingly characteristic of all of the relatively modernized societies, despite the very great variations of authoritarianism in governments among those societies.

Certainly no example of governmental centralization in a relatively nonmodernized society which has remained stable over any considerable period of years has approached the level of centralization attained in some of the relatively modernized despotisms such as that of Germany under the Nazis, the Soviet Union, Japanese society in the late 1930's and early 1940's, etc. For what it is worth, so far none of those cases of extreme centralization among relatively modernized societies has yet proved to be highly stable, though certainly the Soviet Union has the longest record so far. Among relatively modernized societies the most spectacular cases of instability associated with the highly centralized governmental systems have generally been functions of the international relations among the members of these societies and other societies. Germany, Italy, and Japan were all societies whose members got involved in major wars and became societies whose leaders were held responsible, as it were, for their exercises of power by external coalitions of the members of other societies. Apart from the danger, from the point of view of the members of the society concerned, of inciting some coalition of members outside the society, the limiting problem of governmental centralization, as of any other centralization, is that of adequate knowledge for the planning that must go along with such centralization. If it is possible for the members of relatively modernized societies with highly centralized governmental organizations to avoid entanglements in war and consequent instabilities, we may have an opportunity within the next few decades to see whether or not the level of centralization outruns the knowledge at the disposal of the leaders who direct such organizations, or whether to some extent there are increases in decentralization. Presumably this increase in decentralization would be possible only if the actual degree of centralization was considerably greater in the governmental sphere than was minimally required by the level of modernization so far achieved.

Finally, in considering higher levels of centralization in political allocation in general and the government in particular, I would emphasize once again that, despite compartmentalized thinking, centralization is never solely a political phenomenon. We have exceedingly little knowledge of the kinds and degrees of variations possible. Nevertheless, it is possible to assert, first, that centralization can never be solely a matter of political or governmental centralization. Second, although such centralization always has implications for other aspects or other organizations in the society, there are quite important ranges of variation possible. There are, for example, certainly some limits within which centralization of the government can increase or even decrease while the centralization of the allocation of goods and services remains constant or even in peculiar cases varies inversely. Third, although we do not know the regularities of these variations with any clarity or precision, if we do not take the attitude that such variations are at least in principle lawful and that the laws which will enable us to describe and predict their behavior are discoverable, we must in general resign any hope for public policy based on scientific analysis.

V

LEGISLATIVE, EXECUTIVE, AND JUDICIAL ASPECTS

The distinction of legislative, executive, and judicial aspects of government is a familiar one. It is dealt with at length and in depth in at least two of the major divisions of modern knowledge, the field of law and the field of political science. The behavioral science sphere of political analysis of the problems of relatively nonmodernized societies is a recent development, and a major work in it replaces the three terms used here by the terms *rule-making, rule application,* and *rule adjudication.*[12] I would use the terms *legislative, executive,* and *judicial* to refer to aspects of behavior or organizations rather than to concrete acts or organizations. Other than that I would use the terms roughly as I understand the layman to use them. The term *legislative* pertains to the establishment of structures defining who shall wield power

---

[12] This application of a special form of the "3-r's" to the field of political science is accompanied by no new definitions of these concepts nor even by any citation of old definitions. The author asserts that these ". . . are the old functions of 'separation of powers,' except that an effort has been made to free them of their structural overtones—rule-making rather than 'legislation,' rule application rather than 'administration.'" Since I find in this contribution to concept formation no greater precision of meaning or increased fruitfulness in application, either by the author or his followers, I regard this particular set of neologisms as one of the more clear-cut cases of unjustifiable jargon in the social sciences. See G. A. Almond, "Introduction: A Functional Approach to Comparative Politics:, *The Politics of the Developing Areas* [edited by G. A. Almond and J. F. Coleman] Princeton University Press, Princeton, 1960, p. 17.

and/or bear responsibility, in what respects, and how. The term *executive* pertains to the wielding of power or bearing of responsibilities. The term *judicial* pertains to the interpretation of the structures of political allocation, the judgment of what the structures mean in specific circumstances, and the decision of when and how they apply.

It is characteristic of all of the relatively modernized societies that some form of the distinction of the legislative, executive, and judicial aspects of governments is made and to a noteworthy degree generally disseminated among the members of the society concerned. A general understanding of this set of distinctions by the members of most of these societies is furthered because some of the subsystems of the governments of such societies are usually labeled specifically as legislative, executive, or judicial organizations. In the United States context, for example, where ideally at least the doctrine of the separation of powers is strongly held by the members, we distinguish with careful exactitude among legislative, executive, and judicial bodies. In the federal government, for example, we refer to *the Executive* [or *the Administration*], *the Congress*, and *the Judiciary*. It is also true that any sophisticated observer of the United States government is perfectly well aware of the fact that there are administrative and even legislative aspects of the behavior of the members of the Judiciary, that there are executive and even judicial aspects of the behavior of the members of the Congress, and that there are judicial and legislative aspects of the behavior of the members of the Administration. Despite these obvious realities of the political aspects of life in the United States, just as one can speak of the government as being a predominantly politically oriented organization, one certainly can speak quite legitimately of the Congress as a predominantly legislatively oriented organization, of the Administration as a predominantly executively oriented organization, and of the Judiciary as a predominantly judicially oriented organization.

Such a clear-cut specialization of organizations along the lines of this distinction is relatively rare even among relatively modernized societies. One need only mention the fact that in Great Britain, for example, the executive and legislative aspects are by no means so neatly compartmentalized, even ideally speaking.[13] Such specialized organizational development is, on the whole,

---

[13] There is no point whatsoever in arguing here as to whether it is better or worse to have such a clear-cut separation of powers. For the moment the discussion is only concerned with whether such separations are empirically frequent, and what forms, if any, they take.

rare, and the extreme form exemplified in a relatively stable society like that of the United States is, perhaps, unique. Moreover, not only is such organizational specialization rare, but it is even rare for the members of the society concerned to think generally in terms of such a tripartite distinction. It is not rare in social history for an observer to distinguish these aspects of governments. They may always be distinguished by an observer, and indeed these aspects can be distinguished in the observation of any organization, though the members of many organizations devote relatively little attention to such aspects and do not distinguish among them in their own views of their organizations. It is relatively rare for members of societies, apart from relatively modernized societies, to think of these aspects as separate aspects, let alone as separate organizations, however useful it may be from the point of view of an observer to make such a distinction. Furthermore, outside some of the societies of Europe, the United States, etc., the societies generally considered as Western societies, it is especially rare for much thought to proceed in these terms.[14]

Before the development of relatively modernized societies, the members of most societies considered themselves actually governed primarily by men of good judgment rather than by law, if, indeed, they did not feel that it was right and proper that they be so governed. This in the main held true even of societies among whose members quite clear-cut conceptions of law developed. There are relatively few cases of relatively nonmodernized societies for whose members anything like so clear-cut a conception of law as that developed in terms of Roman society exists. There are, however, plenty of cases in terms of which quite generally understood and disseminated statutes exist, are generally observed, and are expected to be observed by the members. Even in many of those cases, however, few members think in terms of this tripartite division. In the highly developed bureaucratic system of traditional China the district magistrate, who was the clearest embodiment of government with whom most individuals in that society came into contact, was not conceived of as now an executive, now a legislator, and now a judge. He was considered and almost certainly considered himself as *the district magistrate* in whose activities all these aspects could but need not be distinguished. He was above all a man of good judgment fitted to govern by virtue of his knowledge of the Classics. The sedentary

[14] This may be one of the rare useful uses of the concept of Western societies.

nature of relatively nonmodernized societies and the high degree of decentralization of power and other aspects of the society, the high levels of self-sufficiency of the various organizations which make up the society—all of these factors as well as others are easily compatible with "government by men of good judgment" as opposed to "government by law." All relatively modernized societies, however, must be characterized by structures of government by law rather than by men of good judgment if they are to be stable. This in no way implies that good judgment ceases to be important in such societies.[15] The increased emphasis on law is rather an implication derived from the fact that in the context of relatively modernized societies problems of scale, the frequency of change, the high level of interdependency, and all of the other factors that have been mentioned so frequently above combine to make the conduct of the allocation of power and responsibility in terms of a governmental organization out of the question in the absence of relatively precisely defined, easily located, carefully authenticated statutes, etc. One may add another, perhaps cynical, consideration. In the context of relatively modernized societies it has so far proved exceedingly difficult if not impossible to count on a sufficient number of men of good judgment sufficiently willing to serve in governmental roles to do the job on that basis even if it were practicable or possible from other points of view.

The more highly developed government by law becomes, the greater is the likelihood of the tripartite specialization under discussion. This is true both of the distinction of these aspects by the members of the society and the actual specialization of governmental subsystems in terms of these aspects. The distinction among these aspects developed long before relatively modernized societies. Even the specialization of governmental subsystems in these terms developed long before such societies appeared on the scene, but whereas the members of relatively nonmodernized societies *can* make such distinctions, the members of relatively modernized societies *must* make them if the society is to be stable. Since thinking in such terms is by no means universally distributed among the members of relatively nonmodernized societies, the development of adeptness of thinking in these terms is likely to be a special problem of transition toward higher levels of modernization.

[15] Though in nonnegligible respects, the higher the level of modernization, the greater is the effort to reduce the area of decision based on good judgment.

V I
THE USE OF FORCE

The use of force is perhaps the most striking form taken by the allocation of power and responsibility, but the use of force is never the sole means at the disposal of the members of a government or any other organization. It is in fact only an extreme in one direction as far as procedure in terms of political allocation is concerned. The idea that any system can be maintained or understood solely in terms of the use of coercive sanctions is wildly naïve. Allegations to the effect that coercion is the sole means of maintaining order in terms of a stable organization never cope successfully with the question of who guards the guards themselves. The members of highly authoritarian systems like that of Nazi Germany certainly have carried the uses of coercion to extreme lengths, but even that society is by no means understandable solely in terms of applications of coercion. Faith in Hitler as a charismatic leader was a vital element in that society. The Nazi leaders themselves and many of their followers to some degree clearly understood the importance of elements other than sheer coercion, as have authoritarian rulers in virtually all cases in history. The Nazis relied heavily on propaganda in education in their special ideal structures for lasting support. They never hesitated to use coercion as a means of insuring the success of propaganda and education or for the maintenance of the motivation to support the regime. Opposition was frequently removed by coercion, but support was by no means completely secured in that fashion. Had coercion been the sole support of the Nazi regime, it would not only be impossible to understand that regime, but it would be impossible to understand the fact that the military defeat of Nazi Germany did not eliminate all vestiges of Nazi attitudes and ideals.

Although coercive sanctions never constitute the sole form of political procedure in terms of a society, the extreme efficiency of coercive sanctions for limited ends cannot be ignored either. The careful structuring of the use of force to secure responsibility or to eliminate disruptive individuals from whom responsibility cannot be secured is essential to some extent to the stability of any society. It is certainly essential to the extent that conformity cannot be motivated in other ways, although conformity can never be secured solely in this fashion. In the context of all societies characterized by broad ideal structures of tolerance of deviant behavior special problems arise. The civil liberties institutionalized in the United States, for example, furnish a basis of protection for individuals who may even seek to overthrow that society itself. When operation in terms of the system fails to motivate conformity or to drain off the energies of possible dissident elements in other ways, as was probably done in the past to some extent by the geographical frontier and is done to some extent today and always by frontiers of activity, deviant individuals may arise who actually threaten to use the area of tolerance as a basis to gather strength to overthrow the very structures in terms of which they operate. Even if they do not actually threaten and intend to do this, they may well be considered by other members of the society to have such intentions. If they actually intend to do so, failure to close the area of tolerance may result in a closure of it by virtue of the success of the deviant individuals and their consequent rise to power. If they are considered a threat, whether justified objectively or not, a closure of the area of tolerance may be invoked to prevent such an overthrow. In any case, societies characterized by accepted structures for such an area of tolerance are peculiarly liable to social change in the political realm from real or fancied threats. In the long run in all of these cases stability of the area of tolerance is more likely to be a function of the fact that the structures of socialization prevent the rise of genuinely dissident elements or elements conceived to be dissident by other members of the society in great strength. The areas of tolerance, whether one likes to admit it or not, in such societies are more likely to persist to the degree that they are not actually put to serious test.

The problem of maintaining structures of power and responsibility by means other than coercive ones is difficult. The whole problem of motivation and of the process of inculcation and maintenance of social structures is involved. Even the general possibilities cannot be treated here, most importantly because of ignorance, and less importantly for lack of space. The relatively easy observability of applications of coercion and their extremely dramatic character when evidenced in torture, killings, concentration camps, jails, economic sanctions, and the like have tended to preoccupy students of the political aspects of phenomena with the question of the uses of force that take place both ideally and actually in terms of all societies. Nevertheless, in the context of relatively stable societies, the essence of the problem of the allocation of power and responsibility is not how they are allocated by the uses of coercion, but rather how power and responsibility are allocated in the absence of coercive sanctions. The famous French sociologist, Emile Durkheim, was partly famous for his observation that it was impossible to understand the phenomena of contracts unless one appreciated what he dubbed the "noncontractual elements of contracts." Something of an analogy may be maintained here. The noncoercive exercises of power and responsibility must be analyzed, if a society or other organization is to be understood. It is equally tenable, however, that the noncoercive exercises of power and responsibility must be analyzed if the coercive exercises are to be understood.

The tenability of these observations is not affected by whether one refers to relatively modernized as distinguished from relatively nonmodernized societies. The enormous increase in efficiency of communications and of many of the instruments especially useful in coercion certainly does increase the level of coercion that can, at least in theory, be attained and maintained. We have at our disposal today not only weapons but elements and aspects of social organization which would make sadistic despots of less technologically developed periods of history green with envy. Tyros of coercion today can, at least in theory, perform feats which virtuosi of coercion could not perform before, but neither these technological advances nor these new developments in social organizations have cut either our governmental or our general social leaders free from the irreducible bastion of concern for the views of some individuals some of the time posed by the question "who guards the guards themselves?".[16]

V I I
SPECIAL QUESTIONS

Before leaving the discussion of generalizations about the structures of political allocation I wish to touch on four questions which do not lend themselves easily to the abstractions above.

[16] Appearances to the contrary notwithstanding, there is little cause in this observation for hopefulness for those who feel that a decent consideration for the opinions of the ruled *should be* of concern to rulers. In these very societies the radically increased efficiency of communication devices makes feasible a level of mass indoctrination never before feasible for rulers. Although there are levels of coercion which cannot be exceeded, recent history has by no means been uniform in indicating any mass reluctance on the part of members of societies when they are contacted in large numbers to accept and, in some cases at least, enthusiastically endorse quite large-scale and far-reaching invocations of coercive sanctions. There have been frequent cases of this in relatively modernized social contexts such as Japan, Germany, Italy, the Soviet Union, and even in special instances in the United States [e.g., the removal of the United States citizens of Japanese ancestry from the West Coast during World War II despite the absence of a single authenticated case of sabotage or espionage on the part of any American of Japanese ancestry in the areas concerned]. Examples of the ease of quite wide-spread public acceptance of high levels of coercion in the context of relatively nonmodernized societies as they change in the direction of modernization are practically universal today.

They are the following: (A) mass appeals, (B) bureaucratic government, (C) the relevance of the structures of economic allocation to government, and (D) the interdependence of governmental systems and the underlying political allocations of any society.

A. MASS APPEALS

1. IN GENERAL

The use of mass appeals as an extremely general device by members of governmental systems—and here the concern is so overwhelmingly with governments or with individuals trying to take over a government that I shall refer only to governments rather than to the structures of political allocation in general—is quite a modern question. It is ironic that we get the major term we use for leaders who orient most of their concern to playing on the public opinions of the masses of the members of their societies from the Greek word demagogue. The Greek demagogues were not at all what we consider demagogues to be today, anymore than the so-called democracy of the Greek city-state was what is considered to be democratic organization today. In the Greek city-state only a minority of adults had any right of participation in the government. The citizens were not the general membership of that organization, but rather an elite group among the total membership. In this context the demagogues were those who played on the emotions of the elite. Before the development of relatively high levels of modernization, rarely if ever did there exist in social history the possibility of mass appeal to the membership in general of societies of any scale. With the increase of modernization and the radical increase in the efficiency of communications which is both possible and necessary for such a development, a radically different situation obtains. In the context of relatively modernized societies, it is not only possible to have mass appeals, it is impossible to avoid them. Any ruler of any relatively modernized or any increasingly modernized society who attempted to avoid all uses of mass appeals himself or by members of his government would submit himself to the risk that mass appeals would be used by others who would eventually unseat him. Today, General de Gaulle is one of the few powerful public leaders who has shown himself capable of surviving the epithet aloof, but he has mass appeal despite the extent to which he cultivates his air of aloofness. As far as relatively modernized societies are concerned, it is not a question of whether there will or will not be mass appeals that are vital to the understanding of the actions taken in the name of governmental organizations and hence are vital to an understanding of the societies concerned. There will be; it is only a question of how the mass appeals will be conducted, who will control them, etc. In the lore and literature associated with relatively nonmodernized societies one of the most persistent tales of revered leaders who sought to improve their rule and the lot of their people is the tale of the leader who simply puts on modest clothes, leaves his retinue, and moves unperceived among his people to observe what his millions do and how and why his people prosper or suffer. Without the use of an adept make-up artist and a dramatic coach to teach him to avoid his typical gestures, hardly a single modern political leader could hope to move abroad in such easy anonymity. Radio, television, picture magazines, and newspapers guarantee that the masses of the members of their societies will know him on sight and by sound.

There are two special problems associated with mass appeals of special relevance here. One is the problem of mobs, and the other is the problem of parties.

2. MOBS

I would define a *mob* as a peculiar form of social organization. A mob is a social system characterized by a minimum of explicit, planned organization, involving a sizable group of members [for arbitrary purposes let us say not fewer than several tens of individuals, and in most cases relevant here, several hundreds or several thousands of individuals] who are, in general, not acquainted with one another, who interact on relatively short notice in a manner not generally foreseen in advance in an atmosphere highly charged with emotion—most notably the emotions described by the terms hate, anger, and fear. By this definition the Nazi storm troopers were certainly not members of a mob. The storm troops were much too carefully and explicitly organized. The large aggregations of highly disciplined demonstrators frequently marshalled to display disapproval by throwing ink, carrying signs, smashing windows, etc., of a hated embassy in a given country are usually not mobs either. On the other hand, in Iran under the leadership of Mossadegh, the mass demonstrations incited and executed against the properties, policies, and personnel associated with an oil company as the hated symbol of imperialism were certainly examples of mob action in the sense intended here.

As structures of political allocation, mobs are interesting social systems. The members of a government or other individual members of a society can in a genuine and realistic sense *give* the members of a mob power. This can be done by the careful use of mass appeals to attract a large aggregation of individuals who are potential members of the mob one seeks to endow with power. One can incite the individuals so gathered, work them up to what is generally referred to as a frenzy, until in some sense the mob is formed, and its members begin to move in some concert. Finally, if one has behaved as previously indicated and if one has coercive power at his disposal and does not invoke it to stop the concerted action of the members of the mob at this point, then he has endowed the members of that mob with power.

At that point it is *his* very own mob, and at that very same point it ceases to be his since he cannot endow its members with effective responsibility. If he has sufficient determination and sufficient force at his disposal, he may find it possible to stop the activities of the members of the mob, and he may even be able to punish them in some sense. In the nature of the case, however, the effective life of a mob is one of short duration. Mobs are among the most volatile of social systems. The activities of the members of the mob are not only unpredicted in detail, but they are usually also unpredicted in quite general respects. Even if one has in the most carefully calculated sense incited the members of the mob and endowed them with power, he cannot count with certainty on what the members will do with the power which he has so painstakingly given them. They may be aroused to wreck a store and end by wrecking a government. After they are done, they can, of course, be punished, but this does not constitute effective responsibility. Such punishment in no way constitutes any sort of restoration of the effects of their exercise of power, nor is such punishment likely to be a deterrent to future mobbists. Like crimes of passion, mobbish acts are not primarily deterred by the individual mobbist's estimates in any rational fashion of what the consequences of his behavior may be.

Action on any considerable scale by members of a mob always to some extent calls into question the stable allocation of power and responsibility in terms of any government within the jurisdiction of whose representatives the members of the mob act. Mobbists do not inevitably bring about the downfall of a government, but there is a sense in which such a potential always exists for them.

Mob action may threaten governmental stabilities in many ways. It may lead to chaos in which new leaders take power, or it may paralyze or destroy important facilities for production and hence spell economic disaster. In any case, however carefully calculated the formation of a mob and the endowment of mob-bists with power may be, short of being stopped, the members of the mob know no effective control. It follows, therefore, that the attempt to use the development of mob action as an instrument of policy is, in this sense at least, always folly from the point of view of the members of the government in power, if the members of that government have any interest in staying in power and in the continuing stability of the government of which they are mem-bers. On the other hand, deliberate resort to the incitement of mobbists by individuals or members of organizations who are out of power and wish to create a situation in which the opportunities for an increase of their power are good, regardless of what other immediate costs may be—for any such individuals—the attempt to create a mob and endow its members with power may be rational even though ruthless. Incidentally, I would add that, from the point of view of such individuals, the particular focus of attention of the members of a mob is not of the essence of the matter as long as the individuals desiring to use activity in terms of the mob are not likely to become targets themselves. Especially if they are out of power, it is not difficult for these individuals to keep out of the way, as it were, of the members of the mob once they begin to move, especially since to the extent that they have participated in the creation of the situation they have some fore-warning. Even so, there is always some risk of being hoist by one's own mobbists.

In the world today with its increased facilities of communi-cation, the creation of mobs as a deliberate policy is easier than it once was. Especially in areas where stresses and strains are likely to be at a high pitch, as in the case of areas whose inhabitants are undergoing modernization, the emotional climate of the popula-tion is likely to be relatively favorable for the development of mobs. In situations of stress and strain mob action has an addi-tional appeal. Vilfredo Pareto cited as one of the six residues, which were for him what might be described in a loose sense as "forms taken by the well-springs of human action," the "need of expressing sentiments by external acts [activity, self-expres-sion]." [17] Whether one wishes to go as far with this idea as Pareto was prepared to go need not bother us here, but insofar as there was anything in his point of view at all, one should expect the actions of the members of the mob to be satisfying to them from this point of view. After all, one of the major techniques of inciting the members of the mob is in some form or another to

[17] Vilfredo Pareto, *The Mind and Society*, Harcourt, Brace and Co., New York, 1935, 4 vols, Vol II, p. 517.

urge the potential mobbists, "Don't just stand there, do something!," as anyone who has ever watched the villain of a TV western create a lynch mob knows perfectly well.

The utility of the action of mobbists as a technique of creating instability, and consequently the threat such action represents to the stability of a government whose members are in power, is quite well known. It is alleged by many, and as far as I know, it is probably correct, that the members of Communist Parties in societies in terms of which the members of the Communist Party do not control the government are always willing and anxious to create, or aid in the creation, or stimulate in other ways the development of mobs. It would be quite rational of them to aid and abet the formation of mobs focused on almost any subject, though if the mobs can be so developed that its members are more likely to attack the specific enemies of the members of the Communist Party or to carry the banners and slogans of that Party, so much the better. These allegations may or may not be exaggerated, but there is absolutely no doubt about the fact that no members of the Communist Party have so far knowingly encouraged or aided in the development of mobs in the societies in terms of which the members of the Communist Party were in control of the government. In all the societies dominated by Communists the use of mass appeals are carefully organized. The members of Communist governments make effective use of mass demonstrations, but the better organized those demonstrations are, the more disciplined the individuals involved, and the more predictable the actions taken, the better do the leaders like it.

For many reasons, ideological and otherwise, mass demonstrations and mass audiences have great appeal for political leaders of all sorts including members of the government in power as well as leaders who aspire to governmental positions of considerable power. Unless such mass demonstrations and mass audiences are carefully disciplined, and perhaps even if they are, there inheres in them the possibility of the development of mobs. As indicated above, this potentiality may be a virtue rather than a drawback of such audiences and demonstrations for leaders who are not members of the government in power [or who are not in power in terms of that government]. This potentiality may also be a virtue from the point of view of governmental leaders who do not care what happens to their government. For those leaders who do care what happens to their government, mass audiences and mass demonstrations are more ticklish phenomena than they may realize. Especially if these leaders specialize in emotional appeals, there exists always the possibility that mass enthusiasm once worked up may result in the development of a mob and the development of further consequent difficulties. In some cases such leaders may even feel that they can use a mob without fear of the consequences to themselves or for their governments. Such may have been the attitude of Premier Mossadegh of Iran. It seems that he deliberately attempted to make use of mobbists in his struggles and that he utilized the Anglo-Iranian Oil Company as a symbol at least. His regime did not survive that usage, and there is a serious question as to whether the price paid for what resulted was a bargain—quite apart from whether one looks at this from the point of view of Mossadegh, the Iranians in general, the British, or the owners of the Anglo-Iranian Oil Company.

3. POLITICAL PARTIES

The problem of political parties is another of the special problems of mass appeals. I would distinguish *predominantly politically oriented parties* from *predominantly politically oriented cliques* of various sorts. Probably no society has ever existed in which some of the members did not form some sort of organization, however loosely organized, in terms of which those members attempted to influence the allocation of power and responsibility in general and the activities carried out in terms of the government in particular. As long as the members of such organizations, seeking to influence the various activities carried out in terms of the government, are drawn from relatively restricted elite groups, whatever the basis of their elitism, I consider them here to be predominantly politically oriented cliques. If the membership in such organizations is potentially at least a mass membership, if ideally and/or actually the aim of the members of such organizations is to involve as large and as broad a segment of the population [or at least the adult population] as possible in their organization, and if the orientation of the members of that organization is toward governmental influence, via elections or what not, I consider such organizations to be predominantly politically oriented parties. Given this definition, there are obviously different degrees of development of such parties. I suspect that most parties grew out of predominantly politically oriented cliques, but regardless of origins in the history of societies like the United States and Great Britain, there were clearly periods in history in which the actual membership of what might here be called predominantly politically oriented parties, and perhaps even the ideal membership, were restricted to much smaller segments of the adult population than is the case today. In both countries today certainly predominantly politically oriented parties exist in the fullest sense of the term used here. In this sense one may wish to question whether the Communist Parties in countries controlled by the Communists are in fact predominantly politically oriented parties in this sense. There is certainly no doubt about the orientations of their members, but it is alleged by some, whether correctly or falsely I do not know, that the leaders of such organizations neither seek nor desire a full mass membership in their particular organizations. Insofar as they do not seek, ideally at least, to generalize the membership of their organization beyond the alleged and presently restricted limits, those parties differ importantly from what I have here defined as predominantly politically oriented parties.

Predominantly politically oriented parties in the sense that the term is used here are also quite modern phenomena. Developments in this direction have certainly existed in the context of relatively nonmodernized societies, and relatively highly politically oriented parties certainly exist in many such societies today. Before the development of relatively modernized techniques of communication, however, the kind of mass contacts necessary for predominantly politically oriented parties in this sense to be of great moment in a general social context were not generally available. Such parties *can* exist as subsystems in relatively nonmodernized societies today specifically because these techniques can be introduced even though the general level of modernization has not advanced very substantially.

Implicitly or explicitly predominantly politically oriented parties represent an attempt to generalize participation in and influence on governmental affairs beyond any presently possible limits of highly developed knowledge about these matters. Such parties, if highly developed, always involve the implication that many people will develop strong views about and attempt to influence policies as well as selections of personnel about which they cannot possibly have expert knowledge. The development of political parties, therefore, always poses problems of the participation of individuals in areas in which they are not experts. Since such parties cannot develop until some levels of modernization are relatively highly developed or until they are being developed, there is a sense in which participation of nonexperts increases at just the point that the importance of expert knowledge for members of governments increases.[18] This is no place to argue the

[18] I have suggested that one of the important implications of degrees of freedom in a market is that the operation in terms of a market may mitigate inadequacies of knowledge—that the market mechanism in fact serves as an alternative to knowledge. Just the opposite inheres in opera-

virtues of mass participation in governmental affairs from the point of view of how desirable democratic participation might or might not be. Whatever our views on that sort of value question may be, there is no escaping the fact that any general attempt to involve large portions of the population in active influence and participation in the operations in terms of their governmental organization or in actions highly relevant to such operations is always to some extent a matter of exciting interest and action in spheres in which adequate knowledge is in exceedingly short supply. There are many implications of this. It may be that one of the major problems involved is that of inciting participation and interest up to but not beyond a particular level. Even if we could be absolutely clear-cut about our evaluative criteria, it is still an exceedingly difficult matter to calculate the optimum location and nature of such a level of participation.

There are further special problems posed by the existence of predominantly politically oriented parties in relatively nonmodernized societies, especially if those societies exist in the world today. By importation of techniques of mass communications, it is certainly possible to develop general participation in predominantly politically oriented behavior on a mass basis to the point at which a fairly high level of development of predominantly politically oriented parties can be said to exist. In such cases there exists not only all of the problems mentioned immediately above, but also an additional special set of problems. In these cases the development of predominantly politically oriented parties is likely to disseminate influence and interest not only beyond the levels of existing expertise but also well beyond the possibilities of control and direction from other points of view. In such cases, for example, the development of predominantly politically oriented parties may radically alter the general levels of self-sufficiency and insularity to which the members of the society are exceedingly well adjusted in other respects. The development of such parties in areas in which ordinary individuals have not interacted with anyone much beyond the confines of their villages or some particular kinship unit may not only set in operation particular activities relative to which adequate knowledge and means of controls are not in existence. Such developments may also con-

---

tions in terms of predominantly politically oriented parties. Operations in terms of them magnify problems of irrationality and arationality. Part of this difference inheres in the greater probability of various nonrational elements in the one context than in the other. It is conceivable, perhaps, that predominantly politically oriented parties be so devised as to have effects more like markets in these respects but neither motivation nor creativity about how to do so seems high.

tribute to the breakdown of previously existing structures of control—again regardless of whether or not new or alternative structures have developed.

B. BUREAUCRACY

Government in terms of bureaucratic organizations is not confined to relatively modernized societies, but it is always necessary in such societies. Not only that but the level of bureaucratization always continues to increase in relatively modernized social contexts, and bureaucratic organizations are always and everywhere increasingly carried out on the basis of highly specialized personnel. In the context of relatively nonmodernized societies the members of the bureaucracy may, at least on entry, be relatively nonspecialized in their qualifications. As government largely or solely on the basis of men of good judgment becomes increasingly impossible with the development of modernization, bureaucratic organizations whose members are relatively nonspecialized personnel also become increasingly impossible. Even in the context of relatively nonmodernized societies, however, whatever the recruitment system, whether by civil-service examinations, whether by civil service by adoption, civil service by usury, etc.,—to some extent the members of the bureaucracy in the course of their services always become relatively highly specialized.

One of the special problems always posed in a bureaucratically organized government is the problem of the insulation or separation of the members of the government from influences viewed as in conflict with the interests proper to their offices. There is always the possibility that these individuals may use their offices to serve themselves or others rather than to realize the purposes that operation in terms of their bureaucratic roles is supposed to serve. As has been indicated above, either ideally or actually, kinship considerations are always likely to be important in this connection. In essence one may handle this problem in one or some combination of three different manners. First, one may simply attempt to insulate or separate members of the bureaucracy from possible conflicting influences. This was the route taken in traditional China. The Chinese forbade a member of the bureaucracy to serve in the province in which his family resided, for example. Second, one may attempt to so unify the interest associated with all other interests which may impinge upon the individual office holder that a divergence of the two sorts of interest is unlikely. To some extent this was attempted and realized in the peculiar bureaucracy of Tokugawa Japan. As mentioned above in that bureaucracy most offices were inherited and the office holder's obligation to his family members was great. His obligation to his overlord and hence to the bureaucracy in which he served, however, not only took precedence over his obligations to his family members, but one of the greatest disgraces which he could bring upon his family members was a reputation for putting their interests before those of his overlord. Third, one may attempt to erect a set of ideal structures such that the individual is not supposed to be influenced by any other interests save those consistent with his office. Actually such ideals are never completely realized, and a relatively high degree of realization of them is only to be found in social contexts in which there exists a large number of highly specialized and highly differentiated organizations in terms of which the average member of the society operates habitually. Such situations never exist save in relatively modernized social contexts. In those social settings to some extent, and particularly insofar as these relatively specialized and differentiated organizations are concerned, the average individual is expected to operate in terms of a predominantly universalistic ethic. Such radical separation of one sphere of activity from another cannot be realized to any significant extent at all unless the general membership of the society is to a high degree used to such behavior. Even in this case problems always inhere. Notable among them is how the individual handles the implications that are relevant to what happens to him in other specialized contexts or in the context of his nonspecialized organizations, notably his family organization.

In all these cases there are not only the problems of how a given individual separates [or has separated for him] various and possibly conflicting contexts in terms of which he acts. There is also the problem of how he is able to switch back and forth among these various contexts. Not only must he keep them distinct, but he must in a sense combine them in his own behavior. After all, as a minimum, the average member of a bureaucracy in such a society goes from his home to his office and from his office back to his home. He is neither, ideally speaking, away from home while he is in office in the full sense characteristic of traditional China nor is he primarily concerned with the performance of his office even while he is at home should these two interests come into conflict as was expected of him in Tokugawa Japan. In this connection one must bear in mind an additional special difficulty of all who are late-comers to modernization. They must and do develop modern bureaucratic governmental systems before the general development of highly specialized bureaucratic organizations is carried very far. For most of them, no other import is more foreign.

C. THE RELEVANCE OF STRUCTURES OF ECONOMIC ALLOCATION TO GOVERNMENTAL SYSTEMS

However much one may think of a governmental system as a predominantly politically oriented organization, the structures of economic allocation in the society in general and in the government in particular are never irrelevant to other aspects of a governmental system. Because we are so accustomed to such specialized orientations we think of the United States Government, for example, as a political organization [instead of as our more cumbersome predominantly politically oriented organization], but the United States Government is overwhelmingly the organization in terms of which the greatest known allocation of goods and services takes place. The annual budget of the United States Government alone, let alone the capital value of the assets held in its name, is out of all scale with the budget of any other organization in the world. It certainly has no competition in this sense from any other subsystem of United States society. It has no competition from any other in world history either unless one considers the Soviet Union in terms of which, given the ideals of socialist organization, literally all economic allocation associated with the members of that society can be said to take place. From the general considerations already mentioned one would expect economic and political aspects always to be highly relevant to one another, if only because they are different ways of looking at the same thing. There is no actual allocation of power and responsibility that does not involve some allocation of goods and services and vice versa, anymore than there is a concrete instance of either that involves no role differentiation, etc. In no simple sense, however, can concrete economic allocations be said in general to cause political allocations. The obverse determinism is equally meaningless or untenable. Although variations in the allocation of goods and services are always to some extent relevant to variations in political allocation and vice versa, many variations in political allocations are possible within a constant state of economic allocations and many variations in economic allocations possible within constant political allocations, at many important levels of consideration. Furthermore, some of the most important policy questions, as well as some quite important theoretical insights into human behavior, may well hinge on what sort of variations in economic allocation may take place within what sort of constant political allocations and vice versa. And, of course, similar questions may be raised about both of these allocations and role differentiations, solidarities, and states of integration and expression as well.

From the point of view of problems of government the interrelationship between economic and political aspects poses many problems. A large number of these such as the problem of taxes have been handled at exhaustive length in generally available treatises. The problem of taxes is in one form, of course, the problem of how the members of a given government get the goods and services vital for operation in terms of the government. There is, however, one special problem posed by the relevance of economic and political allocation for one another that is not generally treated explicitly. This is the problem implicit in the attempt to separate completely the general economic allocation of the members of a society from the political allocation carried out in terms of the government. This state of affairs exists when in some sense highly relevant allocations of goods and services are regarded, ideally at least, as in some sense illegitimate or nonlegitimate. When, for example, members of the government are not expected in any way to "dirty their hands" with trade, and merchants, ideally speaking, are considered as so marginal a group as to have no legitimate standing vis-à-vis members of the government, this sort of situation exists. But the operations of the specialists in exchange is always to some extent highly relevant to the operation of the members of the government, and the allocations of power and responsibility at the disposal of the members of the government is always to a high degree relevant to the operations of the merchants—even if the latter seek only to protect themselves from what they may regard as arbitrary expropriations. Whenever such separations are attempted, there will exist a situation of graft and corruption. The merchants will seek to influence the government officials for protection, for profit, or for aesthetic reasons, and some of the governmental officials will seek in some way to benefit from the activities of the merchants. No social engineering can make economic and political allocation irrelevant to one another on any such scale as this. Any social engineering that appears to make them irrelevant to one another or that makes any interaction among people whose interests are more or less specialized in one or the other sphere illegitimate will not eliminate such interactions. Such structures will simply guarantee that they continue on an illegitimate basis and on a basis fraught with important elements of instability. What the ideal structures have ordered asunder, the actual structures will unite. From the point of view of the governmental organization, the important element of that instability is likely to be the undermining of the ideal structures other than, but interdependent with, those directly violated. It is not just that a district magistrate may get a rake-off for designating a given contractor. That contractor may build an inefficient irrigation works. It is not just that one man buys freedom from punishment, but that the general administration of justice may be called into question, etc.

D. INTERDEPENDENCE OF GOVERNMENTAL SYSTEMS AND THE UNDERLYING STRUCTURES OF POLITICAL ALLOCATION

Until quite recently, so preoccupied have individuals generally been with governments and associated organizations as the major vehicles of political allocation that it has been standard procedure for most discussions of the political aspects of phenomena by both laymen and social scientists to ignore a considerable portion of the structures of political allocation in the societies concerned. Especially experts reared in terms of the relatively modernized societies discussed these matters as if the allocation of power and responsibility in a society started and ended with governments and their associated organizations. Most individuals were not conceived to participate in such matters until they reached adulthood, and at that level somehow, more or less magically, they became political individuals. This is certainly one of the greatest prices that has been paid for thinking of the political as a separate set of things or an entirely separate and disparate field or sphere of action from others such as the economic. Wherever governments appear, they are, of course, major foci of allocation of power and responsibility, and the members of many of the societies in which they appear generally expect that a government will be *the* major focus of allocation of power and responsibility. This attitude is frequently conveyed by a clause which appears in a large number of definitions of governments. This clause usually defines governments [or states], at least in part, as "organizations that have a monopoly of the legitimate use of force in a society."

No society ever existed with so sharply demarcated a political sphere, of course. However overwhelmingly attention may be focused on the government as far as allocation of power and responsibility is concerned, the members of the government always operate in terms of a more general set of structures of political allocation. There are, after all, structures of allocation of power and responsibility characteristic of every known organization in every known society, and the government is never the sole organization of any known society. Societies vary enormously from one another in the extent to which organizations other than the governmental organization are major foci for the allocation of power and responsibility as well as in the kind of structures characteristic of such organizations. However much they vary, these other organizations are always relevant to governments and vice versa. Although predominantly economically oriented organizations may be of great significance in these respects, they are by no means the only significant ones, and from many points of view they are not necessarily the most significant ones by any manner of means. On the whole their importance has been so obvious and intellectually clouting as to pie the general analysis of these phenomena.

In every known society the family organizations are especially relevant to these phenomena. It is characteristic of all societies that the average member of the society learns some [even most] of his [or her] initial responses to structures of power and responsibility within the context of some particular family organization. Action in terms of structures of allocation of power and responsibility is not, after all, something the individual in the United States can be left to learn at the age of twenty-one simply because that is the age at which voting is permissible in most of the states of the union. Most of the relevant attitudes in these respects have long since been formed. One's reactions to the details of substantive issues may change radically later in life, but general reactions to structures of power and responsibility almost certainly are as deeply ingrained as structures of eating, speaking, sleeping, and emotional display. Even in so rapidly changing a social context as that of the United States, reactions to many of the details of substantive issues seem to get fixed early in life in a family context. There is neither time nor space here to go into all of the various ways in which pressure groups lobbies, and many other nongovernmental organizations are relevant to understanding operations in terms of a government. These matters have been written on at great length. The remarks made here about the relevance of family organizations to government are made as examples of the kind of relevance of activity in terms of other organizations which until quite recently have been ignored for the most part in standard treatments by political scientists and other social scientists as well.

There is a sense in which for all known societies experiences in family terms have more relevance for the general setting as viewed from the political point of view than have any others. This generalization would hold true if only because initial learning of behavior in terms of structures of power and responsibility has always been in family settings. The only exceptions to this are, of course, the small number of people, relatively speaking, who have been reared outside family contexts, and most of those have been reared in some form of pseudo family contexts. Moreover, the relevance of family experience goes much further than is implied in this point of initial learning. In one way or another throughout most of world history the exercise of rule in governmental terms has in one fashion or another depended on the stability of family organizations. For most if not all of the relatively nonmodernized societies the final unit of decentralization of power and responsibility has been the family rather than the individual. This has been the case despite widespread variations from society to society of the actual position of the family unit in the general social structure. A member of traditional Chinese society would take it for granted that a considerable amount of discipline would be exercised in terms of requiring that the head of a given family make sure that the behavior of his family members accorded with the desires of governmental officials. The same was true in the last analysis in Tokugawa Japan, despite the fact that the family in that society was not the overriding major focus of concern for individual orientation as in traditional China. This is not to say that these societies lacked means or structures of controlling individuals as such. The representatives of the government could control individuals as such and did so in many cases, but ordinarily control was exercised in terms of family units, and there was a preference for such behavior. Given the extent to which most relatively nonmodernized societies are family oriented this should not be surprising. There is an important sense in which in most of these societies for most of their history one could find more about the interrelationships of members of nongovernmental and governmental organizations by an examination of geneological tables than one could learn by examining the account books of such organizations. There is apparently no society lacking in some conceptions of family or kinship influence—whether deemed good or bad—in governmental circles if a government exists. Increasingly with the development of modernization, however, governmental representatives never can rule through families either ideally or actually. Despite all ambivalent references to possible dynastic interests of the relatives of the past President of the United States, both ideally and actually, family interest could not rule there; the President might have been able to help his brothers succeed to the Presidency if they sought to, but he could not leave it to them. Moreover, if the members of the family who held governmental office slipped at all importantly from justification of their positions through works into maintenance of their positions by nepotism alone, their careers would have been short-lived and might have endangered his to boot.

The limitation of modern governments, however, is not merely a matter of the increasing improbability of inheritance as the structure of succession to major governmental positions. The members of modern governments ordinarily cannot exercise power through family units. There are many reasons for this. Some of them have to do with the nature of the family units which characterize such societies. More important than the change in family units in this respect, however, is the fact that increasingly in terms of these societies individuals have to be treated on predominantly universalistic bases in many contexts. Governmental officials increasingly have to deal with individuals on the basis of what they can do or have done rather than on the basis of who they are. Given the past history of mankind, the surprising thing about modern governmental organizations in the most highly modernized societies is not how much family connections still count, but how little they have come to count.

In relatively modernized social contexts, just as in relatively nonmodernized ones, initial training and habituation to structures of political allocation continues to be in family terms. Thus in terms of all societies there has always existed and always will exist some question of the relationship among individuals considered in the family context and individuals considered in the governmental context. In cases where these are supposed to be relevant to one another, accommodations are built into the system, if the system is stable. In feudal contexts, for example, one's place in the political hierarchy is inherited for life, and this in a sense is true for everyone from the top of the hierarchy to the bottom. It is in relatively modernized social contexts in which this sort of relationship as between the governmental and the family organizations is specifically not supposed to exist [19] that the mutual influence as between persons considered in their family context and persons considered in the governmental context poses its greatest problems. In all such contexts there is not only the problem posed by virtue of the fact that the family is no longer an instrument for the exercise of governmental power, ideally speaking, nor is it likely to be, actually speaking either, save for juveniles in cases considered trivial. There is also the

[19] Either ideally by the members of the society or actually by many of the social scientists analyzing it.

problem of just how one does interrelate organizations that are in fact of enormous relevance to one another but that ideally speaking are supposed to exist in entirely separate spheres. There are specific problems of this sort in all sorts of areas. For example, there is no relatively modernized society without a system [or set of systems] of public education. Public education, particularly at the elementary and secondary school levels, is education in which other family members as well as the children are most intimately involved. Virtually all children enrolled in the elementary schools are in fact living in a family context, most of their time. They leave the family environment for certain periods of the day, a certain number of days per week, to participate in schooling. They return to the family environment after school. With rare exceptions among the members of such societies, there is a general expectation that there be public schooling, and therefore that the schooling be conducted via governmental organizations. Other family members are expected to feel strongly about the operation of the schools on a governmental basis. Especially to the degree that broad expression of opinion is freely permitted, any considerable change in the structures of public schooling is likely to result in a storm of indignant parents raising questions for the members of the governments. It is characteristic of most such societies that the professional politician, at least, would much rather deal with indignant citizens in general than with indignant parents.

In all of the relatively modernized societies the increasing bureaucratization of governmental organizations increases the separation of governmental interests and the interests of specific sets of family members. There are also changes in general family structures that are highly relevant. In recent decades there has been much comment on the fact that in some of the most highly modernized contexts psychiatrists and others detect an increasing tendency for parents to award or withhold affection on increasingly universalistic grounds. Some apprehension about the possible effects of this on the children has been expressed. There is neither space nor basis for arguing here whether the effects of such treatment in terms of increased insecurity on the part of the child, etc., are good, bad, or indifferent. I would raise one question, however. Given the fact that increasingly the average child as he moves increasingly outside a family context will in fact be met with increasingly universalistic treatment, would he adjust to such treatment by others better or with greater difficulty if within his family context he encountered no treatment on such a basis whatsoever? The older he becomes the greater is the likelihood that he will move increasingly in a governmental context in which he must be so treated and so treat others. Regardless of the causal explanation of such changes, the mutual relevance of modern family structures and those of modern governments is hard to ignore.

INTEGRATION AND EXPRESSION

I
INTRODUCTORY DEFINITIONS

The structures of *integration* of any society or of any other social organization consist of those structures operation in terms of which makes for the adaptation of the members or members-to-be of the organization to the structures that constitute the organization. Unfortunately this is not a simple matter. Few, if any, structures are perfectly integrative. Therefore, those which are spoken of as more or less integrative may also have important malintegrative aspects. The use of the term *integrative* to describe a given structure will imply that its adaptive implications outweigh its maladaptive ones. The difficulties of measurement involved in this concept are too obvious to require comment here.

The concept of *expression* denotes the type and limits of reaction, symbolic or otherwise, on the part of the individuals who belong to a given organization to the various phenomena with which they come into contact. One of the most obvious forms of expression is emotional or affective expression. What sort of emotional displays are the members of a given organization expected to indulge in under given circumstances? As indicated above [pp. 25 and 183–184] the aspects of integration and expression constitute a catch-all category. I am not pleased with it, but under this heading it is possible to refer to aspects of societies which cannot and should not be ignored.

I I
INTEGRATION AND EXPRESSION
A. INTEGRATION

1. SOCIALIZATION

What are the structures in terms of which the ordinary individual in every society learns to act as a member of that society? I assume that the behavior of an individual as a member of a society is never adequately explicable without reference to the interaction of the individual concerned with other human beings. There are methods of educating new-born infants associated with all societies. To some extent associated with every sub-system within every society there are some explicit structures, as well as some implicit ones, in terms of which new members learn how to behave as they are expected to behave, ideally and/or actually, and how to inculcate such behavior on others. I would define these as the structures of *socialization*. It is characteristic of all known societies that a considerable part of the socialization of all individuals is carried out in family terms. Even in the context of the most highly modernized of societies where the amount of socialization in general and education in particular that is carried out in terms of a variety of nonfamily organizations is great, it remains true that far more of an individual's initial basic learning from practically every point of view, including especially interaction with others, takes place in family terms than in terms of any other organization.

Apart from this generalization about socialization which applies to any and all societies, the socialization that takes place in terms of units other than family organizations must be considered. These units may be divided into two general types. The first consists of relatively unspecialized units such as friendship units, neighborhood units, etc., and the other consists of specialized units such as schools, business firms, governmental organizations, etc. For all societies, including the most highly modernized, considerable amounts of socialization take place in terms of organizations which are not particularly specialized with regard to one of their aspects as opposed to another. A given individual learns something from his interaction with friends, from his interaction in terms of neighborhood organizations of various sorts, etc. These organizations, however, are not specialized either with regard to education or socialization or anything else necessarily. In this respect they share some of the characteristics of socialization or education in family terms. This is socialization which goes along with action in terms of the organization, but is not necessarily thought of as a specialized form of activity. In this sense learning by doing has a very hoary tradition indeed.

It is not true that all societies are characterized by highly specialized organizations such as business firms, schools, etc. It is probably true that a government of some sort exists in all known societies and certainly in all societies of any considerable scale, but apart from this, specialized organizations need not be highly developed at all. In all relatively modernized societies such specialized organizations become increasingly important, and in all known societies of any considerable scale, whether relatively modernized or not, to some extent specialized organizations of this sort do exist. From the point of view of socialization or education these specialized organizations may be divided into two categories: (1) organizations specialized with regard to socialization or education, and (2) organizations specialized with regard to something other than education or socialization [e.g., predominantly economically oriented organizations]. Schools are the example par excellence of the first category. Schools, as that term is ordinarily used, have many other important aspects, but they are as predominantly oriented to education as governments are to political allocation. In most of the relatively nonmodernized societies some schools have developed, if the societies were of any considerable scale, but for the vast majority of the population, little if any socialization or education took place in terms of schools. Overwhelmingly in these societies such education as takes place in terms of schools is education of the elite. In relatively modernized societies schooling in this sense must become well-nigh universal. As a minimum it is not only true that universal schooling is an ideal in such societies, but also that many of the elements of basic knowledge are taught in school contexts rather than in any other organizational context. In such societies more basic elements of education continue to be carried out in family terms than in terms of any other organization, but it is also true that for the average individual some other important forms of basic learning are carried out in terms of schools. This is not true of any relatively nonmodernized society. Never until modernization was well advanced was any basic, as distinguished from intermediate knowledge, taught to the membership of any society in terms of a specialized predominantly educational oriented organization. Prior to this, schools in such societies were devices for inculcating intermediate knowledge. One of the special phenomena possible for late-comers to modernization is that for them schools can be used to inculcate new or old forms of basic knowledge for the members of the society before modernization has proceeded far in other respects.

Whenever specialized organizations exist, to some extent regardless of their orientation, their members must receive special training if they are to learn to behave in terms of them. Thus members of a government must know how to operate in terms of the governmental organization in terms of which they serve, and the same is true of members of school systems, business firms, churches, etc. Unlike relatively nonspecialized organizations, however, the specialized nature of these makes it the more difficult to prepare the members for their roles in them in completely different contexts. Therefore, no specialized organizations ever lack education as one of the functions which must be carried out in terms of the organization. Unlike schools, however, and like the relatively nonspecialized units mentioned above, education and socialization in terms of these organizations is incidental to their other operations. As in the case of nonspecialized organizations, some of the socialization and education carried out in terms of these organizations is always implicit rather than explicit. There is an important difference, however, between specialized organizations not predominantly oriented to education or socialization and nonspecialized organizations in these respects. The very preoccupation with specialization in general which is so characteristic of the members of these organizations is likely to result in the development of a specialized subsystem of these organizations oriented to socialization or education. Although in these organizational contexts as in all others, some socialization and education of members always takes place in ways that neither they nor their fellow members understand, increasingly an effort is made by the members to put training on as explicit a basis as possible. Thus unlike the socialization or education ubiquitously associated with relatively nonspecialized organizations, the socialization or education associated with specialized organizations not specifically oriented to socialization or education tends increasingly to take place in terms of subsystems of such organizations developed specifically with these purposes in mind. In this sense, schools of some sort tend to emerge as subsystems of all specialized organizations.

For all peoples in and out of history the learning [and hence socialization] curve has no doubt been steepest in the early years. Apart from that, the shape of the curve varies with the type of society and the roles of the individual member. One of the unusual features of relatively modernized societies is the extent to which for an increasing proportion of members there are steep climbs of the curve after infancy and childhood. The structures of these societies is such that there can even be steep rises for the aged for whom the curve has probably been at its flattest for most of mankind ere now.

2. MOTIVATION

The structures of socialization or education have to do with the inculcation of knowledge and the general learning of reactions. *Motivation* is concerned with the establishment of the ends of action, whether these ends of action be empirical or nonempirical, intermediate or ultimate—whatever they may be. How are individuals brought to desire or to seek those ends that would permit the maintenance of a society or other organization, or that will result in the dissolution or change of the organizations in terms of which they act for that matter? As in the case of learning, motivation is apparently not adequately explicable in terms of human heredity and the nonhuman environment. To some extent, given the present state of our knowledge, the ends men seek in terms of all known societies are a function of the interaction of men with one another. This is not a realm in which I feel much at home, but it is necessary to point out that there are structures of motivation in all known societies and that there cannot be societies without them. This brings up the distinction between *ultimate ends* on the one hand and *intermediate ends* on the other. For present purposes I would define *ends* or *goals* as future states of affairs toward which action is oriented.[1] *Ultimate ends* may be defined as those ends or goals of action which are regarded as ends in themselves by the individuals who seek them or in other respects orient action toward them. They are not justified as means to any further end. They are regarded as good or worthwhile in and of themselves. *Intermediate ends* may be defined as any future state of affairs regarded as a means to still further future states. Whether these future states of affairs in fact exist or are only conceived to exist by the individuals who orient their behavior to them need not detain the discussion here. From the point of view of the individuals they are ends of his action in some relevant sense if he so conceives them regardless of whether an observer views the situation this way or not. Discussion of ultimate ends in relation to motivation carries the discussion into the realm of religious aspects. *Religion* may be defined as aspects of action directly oriented to ultimate ends. Such a definition is both broader and narrower than the ordinary use of this term. Therefore, if this usage is disturbing, another word should be substituted for the word religion as that is used here. It is broader than much ordinary usage because religion in the sense defined here need not involve conceptions of superhuman deities or the like. The belief that man is good in and of himself and that man should prosper on this earth for the sake of that prosperity alone—that belief is as much a religious belief in the sense intended here as many of the beliefs associated with what we generally refer to as the organized religions. Furthermore, in this sense Nazism, Communism, as well as Catholicism, Judaism, and Taoism are religions. The definition is narrower than the

[1] In doing so I follow the lead given in the early work of Talcott Parsons, *The Structure of Social Action*, McGraw-Hill Book Company, Inc., New York, 1937, p. 44.

ordinary referent of the term in the sense that to pray for the recovery of a loved one from illness is not predominantly religiously oriented action as the term is used here. The recovery of that loved one is not, ordinarily speaking, an end in itself but a means to further ends and as such is not encompassed by the term as defined here. In the sense of the term used here all societies are characterized by structures of religion. These religions may be divided into at least two categories. One of these may be called *ethical religions* and the other *supernatural religions*. This distinction is based on whether or not the orientations involved are characterized by a belief in supernatural elements. Thus Epicureanism and Humanism in some of their forms might be considered ethical religions. Judaism, Mohammedanism, Buddhism, Christianity, etc., are supernatural religions in this sense. Most if not all of the societies in world history have been characterized by supernatural religions. Quite a number of societies have been characterized by what are here called ethical religions in addition to supernatural religions, and the members of some of the societies currently existing in the world insist publicly that in the long run supernatural religions will disappear from their societies altogether. This argument need not detain us here. The ultimate questions of neither ethical nor supernatural religions are subject to solution in purely scientific terms.

Organizations predominantly oriented to religious action will be called *predominantly religiously oriented systems*. Such organizations are not necessarily present in any society. Predominantly religiously oriented actions may be carried out in terms of organizations not predominantly oriented to them. Nevertheless, such organizations do exist quite commonly in social history. The ordinary term for such organizations is the term *church*. That term may be used here. Though not necessarily ubiquitous, churches are extremely common organizations in social history. Churches, like schools, may have as members only a relatively small portion of the members of the general society.

Another distinction is useful for understanding of public affairs. This is the distinction between what may be called *exclusivist* and *nonexclusivist religions*. *Exclusivist religions* are those whose adherents believe that one may believe in one and only one religion at any given point in time without being considered a hypocrite. *Nonexclusivist religions* are those whose adherents have never raised the question or believe that one may believe in an indefinite number of different religions without any insincerity being implied. Most European or American reared scholars and laymen tend to think overwhelmingly in terms of exclusivist religions. Catholicism, and all the other sects of Christianity, Judaism, Mohammedanism, and the like are exclusivist religions. One cannot believe in two or more of them at the same time, ideally speaking. On the other hand, Buddhism, Taoism, Confucianism, Shintoism, etc., are nonexclusivist religions. For many societies there may actually be a single religion, but when the members of such a society come in contact with other religious structures, they may not regard it as insincere to participate in two or more religious beliefs at once. Quite apart from whether or not one has missionary interests, some implications of this distinction for understanding interrelationships among people who tend to look at these matters differently should be obvious.

The difference between exclusivist and nonexclusivist religions has implications for stability and change. From the point of view of stability, a single exclusivist religion has certain obvious advantages. It permits all or none answers to problems affecting the broadest framework of motivation since competing ultimate ends are eliminated. As such, it tends also to freeze the structures of intermediate motivation at least insofar as they are deemed relevant to the ultimate ends. On the other hand, exclusivist religions may interfere seriously with operations in terms of a society for whose members fairly high rates of change are important ends. If the exclusivist religion concerned is incompatible with such an emphasis on change, one or the other will have to give way.

Perhaps the major source of instability associated with exclusivist religions arises, however, from the cases of societies whose members believe in more than one religion of which at least one is an exclusivist religion. Here conflicts among adherents of the different sets of religious ideas are much in the realm of possibility if not probability. Social history is replete with many examples of such conflicts—including some of the bloodiest wars in all that history.[2] There is another source of conflict. Especially in the context of relatively modernized societies exclusivist religious ideas with which members are preoccupied are likely to be those associated with supernatural religions. These are likely to ignore ethical religious ideas which are important elements of the societies concerned. Nationalism in many cases is just such an ethical religion. Unless the interests and direction of attention of the adherents of the exclusivist religions correlate neatly with those of the not fully appreciated ethical religions concerned, poten-

[2] The substantive content of the religious ideas is curiously irrelevant to the probability or extent of the violence associated with such conflicts. True believers in some of the most pacifistic and spiritual of creeds have been known to fall on others and on one another with vim and vigor. See: Eric Hoffer, *The True Believer,* Harper & Brothers, New York, 1931.

tials of all sorts of conflicts both among the members of given churches and elsewhere in other contexts inhere.

The nonexclusivist religions are not so likely to be a source of instability by virtue of the possibility of conflicts carried out in religious terms. Religiously oriented conflicts *are* likely to inhere in a conversion of a given religion from a nonexclusivist one to an exclusivist one. On the other hand, the presence of nonexclusivist religions in a society makes the inculcation and maintenance of the basic value orientations characteristic of the society, and hence its general structures of motivations, somewhat more vulnerable to change than is the case with exclusivist religions. One should be cautious about such statements, however. Traditional Chinese society was characterized by relatively nonexclusivist religions, and despite this fact remained highly stable in its general social outlines for upward of two thousand years—the longest pedigree of such stability of any known society of very large scale. Societies characterized by exclusivist religions, on the other hand have been much more vulnerable to change at many points in history than has traditional China.

In the definition of motivation attempted roughly above, I made reference to nonempirical as well as empirical ends. Whether one regards individuals as in fact trying to get to Heaven or merely as believing that this is what they seek to do, from the point of view of a scientific observer, they are orienting their behavior to nonempirical ends. After all, no conceivable scientist could verify whether a given individual in fact achieved such an end or not. On the other hand, ends such as success in business, education of one's children, achievement of a given position in the social hierarchy—these are all empirical ends. They may be complicated ones. It may be difficult to measure whether they are in fact achieved or not, but at least in principle it is conceivable that we find a way of measuring the degree of achievement of such ends with accuracy. Throughout social history a large proportion of the members of the general population have at least thought of their action as being oriented to nonempirical ends part of the time. Insofar as this is the case, a peculiarity exists. If these nonempirical ends are in fact to be relevant to an understanding of behavior, they must to some degree be identified by the individuals who orient to them with certain empirical factors. Either the individuals who believe in such ends, with or without realizing it, equate some specific empirical state of affairs with those ends, or at least they conceive of some specific forms of actions as conducive to those ends. Even if the individual believes the nonempirical ends are completely inscrutable, some empirical elements are involved, since only inaction or relatively unstructured action could result from motivation to seek completely inscrutable ends. After all, the opening words of the *Tao Te Ching* attributed to the sage Lao Tze when literally translated carries such inscrutability to the ultimate possible lengths. This opening passage can be rendered "The way that can be known is not the true way." [3] Perhaps no one has ever defined inscrutability more rigorously than this, but belief in the principle embedded in even that text had implications for the behavior of Lao Tze and for many subsequent generations of devout Taoists. Many of them, at least, interpreted this as implying that for the true believer as little involvement with the affairs of the present world as possible is implied by this doctrine. Whether the true believer likes to think of it as so or not, this implies some identification with empirical affairs of even such an inscrutable end as seeking the true way so defined. In the early history of Protestantism, some of the members of certain sects took the doctrine of the complete unknowability of God's will, the doctrine of predestination, and the injunction to work out God's will on earth quite literally and followed them to conclusions considered logical. The result was an almost random experimentation with all sorts of actual behavior including demonstrations with or without clothes. These demonstrations as a minimum got the devotees of such principles branded as disturbing to the general social order. The concept of Nirvana in Hinduism and Buddhism is as thoroughly nonempirical an end as any, perhaps, and yet it, as in the case of ascetic Taoism, comes to be identified with action oriented to as little involvement with the empirical aspects of ordinary life as possible. From the point of view of observers or individuals who must deal with believers in such ultimate nonempirical ends, the result may be as close an approach as possible to pure apathy, complete avoidance, and withdrawal by means of trances, etc., from other forms of action and other forms of involvement with human beings. Such behavior has important implications for the action of the believers, for their relations with others, and for anyone who has any responsibilities with regard to planning or administration of social organizations to which such individuals belong, regardless of whether those individuals consider themselves as belonging to the organizations concerned or not.

This sort of consideration is not, however, only significant because of the fact that one may have to deal in any given society with highly ascetic individuals. The number of rigorously ascetic members of any society is relatively small in proportion to the

[3] Literally in Chinese, Tao k'o tao fei ch'ang tao.

total population. Genuine ascetic virtuosity is rare. Certainly there is no a priori reason to assume that the incidence of virtuosity in asceticism is higher than that of any other form of virtuosity. Even in periods of history in which large numbers of individuals have flocked to monasteries, it cannot be inferred that the monasteries of those periods were highly ascetic organizations for all or even most members.

The relevance of this extreme consideration for much broader spheres of action is directly connected with the role of a particular kind of leadership generally referred to, after Max Weber, as *charismatic leadership*. There are important elements of nonempirical sort in the general motivation of the members of any society. As a minimum, the ultimate ends of the members of a given society as well as a large number of the more or less intermediate ones are likely to contain important nonempirical elements by *lack of specification* if not by specific ideals. In the case of the Taoists the nonempirical element is a specific ideal. When, however, an individual orients his behavior to, say, "working out God's Will on earth," or to the "greater glorification of the German Reich," or to the achievement of an anarchist's "paradise on earth," or to the "fullest realization of the human spirit," or the achievement of a "just and equitable democracy," etc., there may remain an important element of nonempiricality or its equivalent by virtue of the fact that neither the individual himself nor anyone else can in any neatly provable form state exactly what those ends cover and what they do not cover in empirical terms. There is as always *some* relatively undefined element in any statement of such broad goals as these.

A *charismatic* leader may be defined as a leader in whom his followers have blind unquestioning faith. In the eyes of a true follower of a true charismatic leader, as that term is defined here, the fact that the leader says that a given thing is right is enough to make it right. The tremendous impact of such leaders on social structure may in part be interpreted as a result of the fact that in the eyes of their followers such leaders are specifically individuals qualified to identify infallibly certain empirical action or behavior as identical with or conducive to these broad goals to which the followers orient their behavior. Insofar as charismatic leadership develops, no matter how stable that society may have been in the past, for a time at least the charismatic leader may produce a situation in which radical social change is rapid. His reign may be short-lived, since what he does in the course of it may make any stability impossible. Nevertheless, whilst he leads, he can institutionalize change with great rapidity as far as his followers are concerned. Thus, for example, a Hitler can tell the Nazi faithful what new behaviors are to be identified with their end, "greater glorification of the German Reich," whether these be a new invasion, a pact with the previously damned Russian Communists, a new attitude toward illegitimate conceptions induced by warriors, etc. A government characterized by charismatic leadership is a government characterized by enormous flexibility in policy formation—for a time at least. A charismatic leader may shift with ease and rapidity from one course violently supported by his followers to another supported with equal vehemence, despite the fact that the two seem radically incompatible from the point of view of a nonbeliever in that leader's charisma.

From the point of view of the general student of public affairs, there are two main implications of lack of definition or inscrutability in ultimate ends or even in intermediate ends held to be of great significance to broad segments of the membership of a given society or social organization. If those ends, whether rigorously defined as nonempirical or simply left in part undefined with any precision, are radically inscrutable and a powerful focus of orientation, the result is always to some degree either apathetic behavior or a radical and rigorous withdrawal from participation in ordinary daily affairs, i.e., radical asceticism. Such behavior on the part of any considerable portion of the membership of a society or any other social organization dooms the persistence of the organization concerned. On the whole, apathy is more likely to be a general condition posing problems of this sort than rigorous radical withdrawal. An apathetic state of affairs can be produced in individual actions from sources other than this. Thurber's story, "The Secret Life of Walter Mitty," is from this point of view not only a creation of literary genius, it is also the sophisticated embodiment of a level of social insight and commentary that probably deserves to rank with any of the last century. No one has described with greater depth of insight, clarity, or economy of means the type of apathetic withdrawal under circumstances of extreme frustration that Thurber chronicled through Walter Mitty.

The flexibility involved in the lack of complete definitions of ultimate ends in easily verifiable empirical terms is of the greatest importance in understanding the freedom for adjustment of the members of a given system to unanticipated daily events. It is also relevant to the adjustment of the members of a given system to social change. Both ideally and actually social change is built into the relatively modernized societies, and whether the members of any given relatively nonmodernized society like it or not, those societies are going to change, and they are going to change in the direction of the structures characteristic of the relatively modernized societies. To the extent that the ultimate ends or basic value orientations of the members of a society or of any other organization are not, from the point of view of those members, tightly tied to known and understood empirical states of affairs, room is left open for the reinterpretation of older orientations as an important basis for the legitimization of new departures. Even in terms of societies whose members pride themselves on the attitude that change is good in itself, older statements of value of this sort are frequently cited as a source of legitimacy. In the context of United States society today the words of the writers of the Constitution and the Declaration of Independence are often cited as evidence of far-sighted prevision on the part of the Founding Fathers to meet just the situation that the person citing them has in mind. In the context of Russian society today nothing gives greater legitimacy than to be able to maintain that just such a policy was exactly what Marx and Lenin meant. No matter how sharp the breaks with the past may be, there must be some elements of continuity. The greater the extent to which easy reinterpretations of the implications of older standards of value can be made, the greater is the ease with which modern changes can be stimulated and even engineered. The clarity with which the average member of traditional Chinese society knew what the ideal structures of that society meant in actual empirical terms was probably a major factor in the poor success of the Chinese in early moves toward modernization. A major redefinition of quite general goals was probably required on quite a far-reaching basis before modernization could proceed efficiently. Whether one approves of their means or not, the Communists in China would certainly seem to have accomplished this if only by completing the destruction of alternatives. On the other hand, Tokugawa Japan had a more or less built-in equivalent of charisma. The belief that all individuals who counted in power questions were supposed to do what their overlords told them was carried over and focused on the restored position of the Emperor. The belief in the sacredness of the Emperor meant that any statement which could be authentically attributed to the Emperor or believed to be authentically attributed to the Emperor automatically became a statement that identified empirically the proper ideals for all proper Japanese. The modernization of Japan cannot be understood without an understanding of the importance of the position of the Emperor in that modernization and the part played by the carryover of the previous orientation to the hierarchy of overlords to the role that was to be played by the Emperor once he was restored to a central position in governmental affairs. Even if the term religion is used more conventionally than it is here, it would be difficult to understand this phenomenon in purely political terms without any reference to the religious aspects involved.

By no means all of the motivational structures of a society are phrased in terms of ultimate ends. The set of ultimate ends constitute a framework in terms of which social action takes place. Motivation in terms of intermediate ends is no less relevant for an understanding of social behavior. It is, in fact, in terms of intermediate ends that the vast proportion of all activity takes place. Intermediate ends are to a high degree capable of being classified as empirical. To some extent even when they contain important nonempirical elements, they also contain empirical ones. For example, prayer may be an end of some activities and the means for further ones from the point of view of the individual at least. However much prayer may be regarded as a specific way of putting oneself in contact with a given deity, and to that extent not adequately analyzable in scientific terms, prayer does, after all, also involve empirical behaviors such as kneeling, standing silently with bowed head, etc. The fact that intermediate ends are themselves means to other ends makes it quite feasible to analyze action in terms of intermediate ends as either predominantly rational or predominantly traditional. Insofar as the intermediate ends are empirical ones, it is possible to judge whether or not the means chosen to reach them and those ends, when they become means for something else, are rationally employed or not. From the strict scientific point of view, choices among ultimate ends may be considered a matter of taste. From a strict scientific point of view choices among intermediate ends, given certain choices of ultimate ends, is by no means a matter of taste in all cases. It is quite possible to indicate quite objectively that some intermediate ends are not in fact conducive toward the achievement of more distant ends to which they are conceived to be related.

From the point of view of social change as well as from the point of view of the maintenance of stability of social organizations, one of the most significant aspects of motivation in terms of intermediate ends is that much of such motivation must be maintained on a voluntary basis. The use of coercive sanctions to maintain motivation is always to some extent an indication of malintegration. As a minimum it indicates that from the point of view of the individuals exercising the sanctions, some other members of their organization are not behaving as they should. Furthermore, the actual extent to which pure coercion may be relied upon by the members of any social organization is strictly limited. Only those uses of coercion that will motivate subsequent voluntary conformity will contribute to the integration of a society or other social organization—and the limitations on the use of coercion even for these purposes are considerable. Spanking a child for bullying other children may stop that action and may convince the child that he should not do it in the future, regardless of whether subsequent spankings will ensue. This will increase the adjustment of the child in terms of a society whose members contemn bullying, provided that such spanking itself does not have unanticipated consequences which will decrease the child's adjustment. There may be psychiatrists who will take either side of this argument, but I doubt that today one can find a psychiatrist anywhere who will maintain that such methods of child rearing can be pursued safely without let.

The problem of intermediate motivation is a ticklish one from another point of view, since motivation in terms of the various organizations of the society cannot be mutually incompatible without limits—if stability is to result. Furthermore, to the extent that motivations in terms of different organizations are relevant to one another, if there is to be any considerable level of stability, the motivations in terms of the different organizations that make up a society must on the whole reinforce one another. The more highly involved and complicated the development of differentiated social organizations, the more highly involved and complicated must be the general structures of motivation. For all of the complexity of traditional Chinese society, from this point of view it was relatively simple. Two types of social organization were of overwhelming importance in that society; one was the traditional Chinese family and the other the Imperial bureaucracy. Radically subordinated in interest to one or the other of these two, if not to both of them, were organizations such as friendship units, neighborhood units, etc. Few members of the society carried out many of their operations in such a sphere that conflict between these two major types of organizations could arise. As was well understood in the doctrine of the Will of Heaven in traditional China, as far as social stability was concerned, the real problem of motivation was to ensure that no situation could exist such that family interest could contradict that of the members of the other organizations concerned. From the point of view of the members, things were well in that society when action in family terms and family interests were such that one could not do ill in other spheres. Though a somewhat extreme case, the case of traditional Chinese society in these respects is roughly the order of the case for all other relatively nonmodernized societies of any considerable degree of stability.

The contrast of the relative simplicity of this picture with the problem in any relatively modernized social context—with the enormous proliferation of highly specialized, highly interdependent social organizations—is not difficult to understand, even though many of the details of the discrepancy might be exceedingly difficult to state with precision. In such societies, many of these organizations, though specifically insulated from one another, are absolutely crucial for one another. Membership in them is highly mobile both ideally and actually. Orientation of the members to many of these organizations ideally speaking, is finely detailed and strictly limited—perhaps more finely detailed and more strictly limited than the members are capable of carrying out as an actual compartmentalization of their personalities. In such cases concentration on any standard of loyalty as simple as that of family loyalty would have catastrophic implications. Concentration on the individual mobility necessary for many of these organizations may create substantial problems for family stability. Inculcation on the children of belief in predominantly universalistic criteria for all sorts of selections, including some for affection and intimacy, is no doubt absolutely essential if they are to be prepared for the type of occupational sphere characteristic of any relatively modernized society. It is doubtful, however, that such emphases can be obtained effectively without an increase in the fragility of family units in general and of the bonds between parents and children and the bonds among siblings in particular. To the extent that participation of the average individual in highly interdependent, highly specialized organizations as well as in some relatively unspecialized organizations increases, the structures of intermediate motivation must also increase in actual complexity, regardless of what the ideal may be for the members of the society concerned.

There must be some indeterminacy in the sets of ultimate and intermediate ends. If some general principles such as family loyalty, etc., were not inculcated on the members of the society, no society could exist. Complete determinacy of all intermediate and ultimate ends would be like the problem of complete knowledge; indeed, it would involve complete knowledge. Every individual would have to know exactly what to do in every situation. No society or organization has ever existed, for whose members the element of judgment has been completely eliminated. Highly coercive situations tend to minimize it, but every time the problems of individual judgment are minimized, the problems of some sort of social planning are to that extent increased. Correspondingly, the problems of socialization and education, whether carried out in terms of specialized or unspecialized organizations are increased.

This problem of indeterminacy with regard to motivation is closely related to another matter already stressed above. The increased development of bureaucracies in every relatively modernized society has as a lower limit the level of coordination and control necessary to keep such a society in operation and as an upper limit a level of organization not in excess of the possibilities of knowledge necessary to plan the organization. Exactly the same upper and lower limits in terms of motivation may be asserted. In addition, for given types of societies it is important that sooner or later we go a great deal further in specifying what types of indeterminacy can [or will probably] exist with what types of implications. For example, a relatively modernized society may be compatible with considerable indeterminacy and variation in motivation as to how increases in material productivity are to be utilized. Such societies are not nearly so flexible with regard to whether or not increases in material productivity must be motivated. Such societies can not survive without increases in material productivity being motivated continuously. Morever, although relatively nonmodernized societies may exist in terms of which the emphasis on achievement as such for the average individual is quite a modest one, with increases in modernization the motivation of the average individual to achieve in manners that can be judged more or less objectively by other members of the society must increase continuously. The details of what constitutes such achievement may change, but more and more people must be motivated to seek achievements that can be recognized with increasing objectivity by an increasing segment of the membership of the society.

Finally with regard to motivation, areas of social behavior in which specific motivational structures are lacking are often quite as significant as those in which such structures are present. Since, whether we like it or not, students as well as men of responsibility in public affairs are increasingly concerned with questions of planning in general and planned social change in particular, areas of behavior in which motivational structures have not been developed may be the essence of many concerns. In such areas there always arises—in terms of any society, any time, anywhere—the question of whether or not other existing structures of motivation can be utilized to cover this situation or whether new structures have to be developed.

3. UNCERTAINTY AND RELATED QUESTIONS

B. Malinowski was perhaps more famous for his explanation of magic than for any other single contribution. *Magic,* defined as the use of nonempirical means for empirical ends, Malinowski held, developed in social situations characterized by high levels of uncertainty. He did this in a classic case of comparative analysis in which he pointed out that some people he was studying used magical practices in connection with deep-sea fishing but not in connection with lagoon fishing. Deep-sea fishing was dangerous, uncertain in yield and important to the people concerned. Lagoon fishing was safe, highly certain with regard to its yield, and also important to the people concerned. Malinowski also pointed out that these people distinguished with great precision between the effects they regarded as due to bad workmanship and those which they attributed to improperly performed magic. Malinowski thought that the practice of magic enabled the people concerned to adjust themselves to these important situations characterized by high levels of uncertainty.[4] Professor O. K. Moore has added to this picture by his hypothesis that those forms of magic that have the same effect as rational behavior would have under the circumstances diffuse more rapidly from one set of peoples to another than do other forms of magic.[5] There are societies totally lacking in practices of this sort. On the other hand, in relatively modernized social contexts, the emphasis on rationality is likely to become so great, ideally speaking, that magical practices are themselves a specific source of stress and uncertainty.

Another form of behavior highly relevant to uncertainty situations may be described as faddism. *Faddism* is defined here as the relatively rapid and intense alteration and application of means

[4] See B. Malinowski, *Magic Science and Religion and other Essays,* The Free Press, Glencoe, Ill., 1948, pp. 11–16.

[5] Moore points out that, for example, for a given set of island peoples a magical practice that in effect randomizes the direction in which one sets off in search for fish is the best solution the people concerned could possibly find in the absence of more detailed specific knowledge of just where to look for fish. Such practices as muttering prayers and throwing a feather in the air and going out to seek fish in the direction pointed to by the large end of the quill would in effect randomize the search for fish. See: O. K. Moore, "Divination—A New Perspective," *American Anthropologist,* vol. 59, no. 1, Feb. 1957, pp. 69–74.

for relatively fixed ends. Such action may be highly rational over limited periods of time which is not the case of magical action. The rapid alteration of fashions in clothing in many social contexts, of some of the techniques of therapy in modern medical practice, of recreational forms, etc., are all examples of faddism. Uncertainty elements are usually marked in situations in which fads are frequent. The element of novelty is the essence of fads, and integration to uncertainty via faddism is in terms of the faith of the actors that the new method may serve to secure or maintain an old end. That end may be social prestige, restoration of health, etc. In a field like medicine, fads may result in either greater or lesser use of a given technique of therapy than is in fact medically justified. This may enable doctors better to adjust to situations in which the level of uncertainty is high, in which some of the participants react with intense emotions, and in which there is great pressure on the physician to do something. In the field of medicine it is also possible to combine some types and levels of faddism with a high level of emphasis on rationality. The use of a given drug or a given technique may in fact be a fad, but the physicians using it may firmly believe at the time that its use is scientifically justified. Faddistic behavior is not confined to members of relatively modernized societies, but it is likely to increase in relatively modernized social contexts for at least two reasons. First, it by no means follows that uncertainty declines in relatively modernized social contexts, despite the radical increases in scientific knowledge. Second, as a form of integration to uncertainty situations, faddism is much less vulnerable to emphases on rationality than are magical practices.[6]

The problem of integration to uncertainty is one frequently commented upon by social scientists. There is, however, another problem of equal importance, much less frequently treated. This is the problem of integration to *certainty* situations. Thomas and Znaniecki treat it explicitly when they speak of the desire for new experience as characteristic of all people.[7] Nevertheless, boredom has been on the whole a much less glamorous subject for social scientists than uncertainty. Some types of activity, however, are probably not explicable save in terms of the problem of integration to certainty situations, i.e., the problem of boredom and the problem of avoiding the certain for other reasons. The most

[6] This view of the relevance of faddism to uncertainty in the medical context first came to my attention in Talcott Parsons' lectures more than twenty years ago. He has since referred to this in *The Social System*, Free Press, Glencoe, 1951, pp. 467–470.

[7] W. I. Thomas and F. Znaniecki, *The Polish Peasant in Europe and America*, Boston, 1918, vol. 1, p. 73.

notable of these is gambling. Perhaps the outstanding aspect of gambling as a special form of activity is the deliberate creation of uncertainty in a situation in which otherwise the outcome would be a great deal more certain. I refer here, of course, to honest gambling. The outcome of a horse race that has not been fixed is highly uncertain for even the most expert judges of horseflesh. By wagering money or anything else on the outcome of a horse race, one makes a specific allocation of goods or services uncertain to the extent that the outcome of the race is uncertain. To some extent the gambler always feels that the result of his wager may be a windfall gain, though he is certain there will be no such gain from any other source. It is not a matter of chance that both magic and fads are closely associated with gambling wherever it appears in world history.

Faddism has been described as a technique of integration to uncertainty situations, but it may also be a technique of integrating to certainty situations by destroying the certainty of those situations. Again, the essence of faddism is novelty, and the essence of certainty is the absence of novelty. The short-run contributions at least that can be made by faddism to situations of boredom are patent enough. Unlike magical practices, which do not seem highly appropriate as a form of integration to certainty situations, faddistic behavior may integrate simultaneously to both elements of certainty and uncertainty. In modern medical practice, for example, faddistic procedures may exist in spheres in which it is certain that established techniques will be of little use and the uncertainty which attends doing nothing is difficult to bear.

In any case it is well to keep in mind the fact that elements of both certainty and uncertainty pose problems of adjustment for human beings. Human beings are alike everywhere in the sense that there have never been social settings in which humans were incapable of being anxious, or bored, or both. Magic, gambling, and fads are closely associated with such problems. Social engineers and social reformers would do well to be sure of the parts played by such practices in integration before attempting to change them. In the attempt to design new social structures we must keep in mind that certainty as well as uncertainty poses problems of adjustment. As the levels of centralization and social planning increase, as they do characteristically in all of the relatively modernized social contexts, there is a sense in which, despite the vast areas of ignorance of social phenomena, problems of certainty are likely to increase more rapidly than problems of uncertainty. It is hard to conceive of any element of social planning or increased centralization which does not have in it, implicitly if not explicitly, a decrease in the degrees of uncertainty in the social situation. As modern men we are extremely fond of pointing to the high level of boredom which we feel must have inhered in an enormous number of situations in the context of highly sedentary relatively nonmodernized societies. We are also fond of pointing to the great sources of uncertainty that characteristically pose problems for the members of those societies—problems which are not problems for us with our inordinately productive sciences. It is, nevertheless, unlikely that we shall ever know enough to eliminate uncertainty situations. As the discussion above [pp. 79–81] of the problems of socialization for an unknown future indicates, accelerated change always carries elements of uncertainty with it.[8] We may, however, come to know quite enough to increase boredom, assuming that any accurate measurements are possible.

B. EXPRESSION

My lack of expertise makes the category of *expression* as much a problem as that of *integration*. Unlike many of the spheres referred to under the headings of economic and political allocation, these are not matters adequately and fully treated in the general literature of social science on the level of societies in general or even on the level of the types of social organizations most frequently encountered as subsystems of societies. Despite the fact that I am unable to treat them to my satisfaction, I feel these categories cannot be ignored because they are all too often ignored by students of the social sciences and men of responsibility in the field of public affairs. Recreation, for example, is not usually considered at any great length or seriously in these contexts apart from ethnographic treatments carried out on a largely descriptive level—possibly because, for modern man acting in terms of highly modernized societies, one of the aspects of great specialization has been that the term recreation has acquired a connotation of frivolity and superficiality. I shall try to point out below that it is quite possible for recreational aspects to have quite far-reaching implications for the allocations of power and responsibility. I have also heard quite recently a highly sophisticated representative of Mexico point to the fact that the great development of modern art in Mexico influenced by Picasso and others was of enormous practical signifance in the Mexican pro-

[8] It is also not a matter of chance that so much faddism is associated with the educational periods of the young members of relatively modernized societies.

gram of economic development, if only because of its attractiveness as a stimulus for tourism. If I understood him correctly, he would go so far as to counsel the representatives of most relatively nonmodernized societies or nations to pay special attention to the cultivation of their artists as a major strategy of economic development. I would not rest the justification of these considerations on their implications for the allocation of goods and services and power and responsibility. It is one of the firmest contentions of this entire treatment that, although men in any considerable organizational context are never indifferent to either bread or power, they never live by bread and power alone.

The treatment of expression here is divided into a brief treatment of recreation, artistic activities, other emotional reactions, and politics and recreation.

1. RECREATION

Recreation as the term is used here refers to a specific aspect of behavior. Insofar as given behavior is viewed as furnishing relaxation and release from the usual duties and concerns of daily life, they will be considered as at least in part *recreational*. Games, gossip, dancing, many forms of reading, drinking, feasting, vacationing, and a variety of other similar and related phenomena certainly contain aspects of recreation. One of the most obvious significances of activities with strong recreational aspects is the extent to which the actual activities involved do provide a release from the tensions and strains of everyday life and hence contribute to the general adjustment of the individual to his environment. One of the first distinctions to raise with regard to recreation has to do with the point just mentioned. Most of the social scientists and most of the men of responsibility in public affairs, who comment on these matters, are so used to thinking in terms of relatively modernized social structures that recreation is generally thought of as a separate thing just as economic activities and political activities are thought of as separate things. In relatively modernized social contexts there is a considerable development of what might be called predominantly recreationally oriented activities and organizations, just as one can distinguish with the greatest of ease predominantly economically oriented organizations and activities, etc. One of the most general distinctions is that among societies or organizations within societies in which recreational aspects are combined simultaneously with the usual duties and concerns of everyday life and those in which the two are sharply separated from one another. The contrast between relatively nonmodernized and relatively modernized societies is sharp in these respects. Both types of situations exist in both cases. In traditional Chinese society, for example, there certainly existed relatively specialized predominantly recreationally oriented activities and organizations. Attendance at opera and the telling and listening to stories were activities by no means confined to a small elite.[9] On the other hand, the most dedicated of executives and professional men in our own society are frequently described as finding in their work their main, if not their sole, recreation. This again is one of those distinctions in which, despite the fact that there are vast differences in emphases as between relatively nonmodernized and relatively modernized societies, there are enough elements common to both so that mutual understanding between their members is not necessarily difficult. Over a decade and a half ago in a song sometimes still played [10] a hypothetical nonliterate savage states that he has no desire to seek the delights of civilization since civilized people seem to him to suffer most of the year in order to practice for two weeks the delights he pursues day in and day out.[11] The song, no doubt, distorts both the life of nonliterate savages and life in a highly

[9] In this there is one of the intriguing hook-ups between recreational aspects and other aspects of social organization. The vast majority of peasant members of traditional Chinese society were illiterate, but to a degree probably seldom equalled by members of other large-scale societies, these illiterate peasants were, on the whole, surprisingly well informed about the past history and the traditions of China. Their knowledge was certainly not scholarly, but it was not pauce either. The role of the story teller, itinerant and otherwise, the role of opera troupes, etc., were of great significance in this respect. A considerable portion of the stories and the operas and the like were built around incidents of Chinese history and themes of the Chinese classics. Though slow and leisurely, as methods of mass indoctrination go today, these phenomena have some interesting implications for the number of people who are preoccupied with what has come to be called "mass culture" and is generally treated as something quite modern and perhaps even a little gross.

[10] Popular songs constitute an interesting phenomenon in any social context. Relative to a society like our own whose members generate an enormous number of popular songs with a rapid turnover, there is hardly a single point in social theory which, however abstruse, cannot be aptly illustrated for purposes of general communication [though perhaps in a somewhat oversimplified form] in terms of the lyrics of some popular song. I tried for many years to give students a precise grasp of the distinction between biological kinship and social kinship without any notable success despite the development of some fairly highly refined concepts. The revival and popularity of the old song entitled "I'm My Own Grandpa" [Lonzo and Oscar and the Winston County Peapickers, Dwight Lathan—Moe Jaffe #20–2563A, R.C.A. Victor records], solved the problem neatly since it is quite easy to convey to students via that song that, although this situation is conceivable in terms of social kinship, it is quite out of the question as a matter of biological kinship.

[11] Hear: *Civilization* (Bongo, bongo, bongo), words and music by Bob Hilliard and Carl Sigman, Edmond H. Morris and Co., New York, 1947.

modernized social setting, but there can hardly be any doubt that in general the daily routine of the members of modernized societies is from their point of view something to be escaped from in a sense that is probably not true of the daily routine in many relatively nonmodernized situations. Romantic pastoralism to the contrary notwithstanding, probably most of the members of the relatively nonmodernized societies have been miserable a good part of the time, but it is nevertheless doubtful that they drew the kind of sharp line of demarcation between working and living that is so frequently drawn by the members of relatively modernized societies. The phenomenon of vacation [with pay] during which the individual seeks to differentiate his behavior as much as possible from his usual behavior is certainly not the center of emphasis in any relatively nonmodernized social context that it is increasingly in relatively modernized social settings. In some of the relatively nonmodernized societies, if not most of them, such structures may be altogether absent.

Insofar as the members of a given society think in terms of specialized predominantly recreationally oriented activities, and so much so that they tend not to recognize recreational aspects in other activities, important consequences follow. The essence of recreation considered as an aspect of activities is certainly not the restfulness of those activities in the sense of lack of expenditure of energy. Many of the most highly prized forms of recreation in any social context, notably games, sports, dances, etc., are often exceedingly vigorous activities from the physical point of view. The essence of the difference lies rather in the fact that to be worn out by a day at the office is considered highly unpleasant and sometimes even productive of insomnia whereas physical exhaustion from a day's recreation is usually considered both pleasant and conducive to a good night's sleep. Insofar as an individual's attitude toward activities is that they are highly recreational, the integration of the individual to the usual duties and concerns of daily life may be presumed to be increased. If this aspect is considered by the members of the society to be built in, as it were, into those duties and concerns themselves, the motivational structure necessary to maintain them may be presumed to be bolstered to that extent. If the activities viewed as recreational are sharply differentiated from the usual duties and concerns of daily life, it may be increasingly difficult for the activities viewed as recreational to have the effect of such increased integration. If the distinction reaches the point at which a considerable proportion of the members of the society conceive of themselves as living only in the relatively restricted periods which they regard as overwhelmingly recreational, some of the motivational support for all the other forms of activity comes to hang increasingly on the extent to which behavior in nonrecreational periods makes possible the activities seen as overwhelmingly recreational. Under such circumstances recreation, as such, becomes the major goal of other behaviors.

Such a situation has apparently been reached in some relatively modernized social contexts. The requirements of highly mechanized mass production and many associated occupations such as secretarial work and the like are such as to call for unremitting attention and effort. Even conversation with fellow workers may be highly disruptive under such conditions. It is not accidental that cliques and special personal freedoms are so jealously guarded by and play so important a role in the morale of industrial workers.[12] Recent years have witnessed an enormous preoccupation of many leaders of organizations with attempts to provide facilities which have a high recreational content and which do not interfere with unremitting attention and efforts. Musical programs piped into plants and many other stratagems have been devised. Such stratagems are regarded successful to the extent that they are enjoyed, do not interfere with, and even increase productivity.

To the extent that activities and organizations become highly specialized recreationally, they pose exactly the same problems from the point of view of general social organizations posed by other forms of specialization. These are the two problems of how one can specialize these aspects out of what were formerly unspecialized contexts, and how, having specialized them, one can interrelate the activities carried out in terms of the specialized forms with other specialized forms of activity as well as with the activity of the individuals concerned in terms of their relatively nonspecialized social organizations.

Closely related to the question of whether or not the members of a given society consider recreation as a relatively undifferentiated component of many of their daily activities or whether they consider it to exist only when it exists in highly specialized forms is the distinction between *escapist* and *nonescapist* recreation. The distinguishing mark of *escapist recreation,* as the concept is used here, is what might be termed the nonreality of the activities as far as the individual conceived of as recreating is concerned. Recreation is escapist to the extent that the recreational value of

---

[12] The pioneering work of F. J. Roethlisberger and W. J. Dickson, *Management and the Worker,* and the subsequent work of many others is illustrative of this point.

an activity from the point of view of the individual lies in the fact that the individual is able to identify himself in part or in whole with a state of affairs that is actually not his own and by that identification lose to some extent contact with his own state of affairs. Some of the uses of drugs and alchohol are an extreme example of almost purely escapist recreational structures. The action of these substances is sometimes such as to take the user out of effectual contact with the empirical world as far as his own consciousness is concerned, and to give him at least temporarily either a feeling of ease and content or a state of oblivion. A less extreme form of escapist recreation is recreation via the role of spectator. Spectators at sport events, for example, in many cases appear to gain a considerable amount of relaxation and enjoyment from vicarious participation in the events they witness. Motion picture and television viewing are remarkably widely diffused forms of escapist recreation from this point of view, but a considerable portion of attendance at serious theatre, performances of string quartets, etc., also consists of varying forms of escapist recreation. On the other hand, actual participation in sports and games, amateur painting, participation in amateur theatricals, etc., are *nonescapist* forms of recreation from this point of view. This distinction might perhaps more aptly be described as a distinction between *vicarious* and *participant recreation*.

It is difficult to discuss a distinction of this sort and avoid evaluations. The term *escapist* itself has evaluative overtones for many people, especially in our own social context. Regardless of how good or bad the movies or television may be from the point of view of a given set of artistic standards, the recreational impact of such performances may be high, and they may have important implications for the adjustment of the individuals who enjoy vicariously the experiences portrayed specifically in part because they are not necessarily high art. For example, there are individuals, even individuals of sensitive and sophisticated taste, who find a considerable amount of enjoyment in TV westerns specifically because, in a world in which a distinction between virtue and vice is often difficult to discern, in that medium one can absolutely count on the fact that the bastards of this world will get their just deserts within the half hour or the hour.

As far as social stability is concerned, there are radically different implications of escapist as opposed to nonescapist forms of recreation. Activities with important elements of nonescapist recreation have signal possibilities for the direct reinforcement of daily routines at the same time that they afford relaxation from them. Participation in competitive sports, for example, in the United States clearly emphasizes predominantly universalistic criteria of selection and many other standards of the greatest significance in other activities.[13] Childhood participation in competitive sports in probably one of the most important educational elements in United States society. At an early age it inculcates an understanding and faith in predominantly universalistic criteria. His experience in sports tempers the highly particularistic treatment of the child as a family member and prepares him in part for the increasingly great emphasis that others with whom he will come into increasing contact as he matures are likely to place on such criteria in selecting or rejecting him for an extremely wide range of relationships. Activities with a strong nonescapist recreational component may play vital educational as well as other supportive roles in many spheres of activity.

Activities with a strong escapist recreational component make their contribution to social stability, insofar as they do contribute to social stability, in that they remove the individual at least temporarily from the whole realm in which tensions and conflicts arise. The malintegrative implications of nonescapist recreational activities inhere in the possibility that absorption with them may interfere with the level of attention necessary to other activities. The malintegrative implications of activities with a strong escapist recreational component inhere primarily in the possibility that they may fail to buttress other forms of activity in any explicit sense. Secondarily, if tensions are sufficiently high and the activities are sufficiently compelling forms of escape, those activities may become a goal of such primacy that the individual no longer operates effectively in terms of his other roles at all. Alcoholism, insofar as it can be considered as an activity with strong escapist recreational aspects, is a clear-cut though extreme case of this possibility.

Activities may, of course, combine escapist and nonescapist recreational components. The most romantic movies may picture more or less correctly the ideal structures of a society while, at the same time they distort the actual structures. Viewing them may thus at one and the same time reinforce the ideal structures and

[13] All sorts of symbols are closely associated with this. It is practically obligatory that the chief executive of the United States be an active participant in some form of sports. Franklin Delano Roosevelt, despite his infirmity, was an ardent fisherman and sailor. Harry Truman is a brisk walker. Dwight Eisenhower is an enthusiastic golfer and hunter. John F. Kennedy, until his problems with his back, was an ardent participant in touch football as well as several other sports. President Johnson is, of course, a horseman. Such brisk participant sports reassure the public that these men will not hesitate to do something.

offer the movie goer escape into that fairyland in which the discrepancies between reality and ideals is not a source of anxiety. The complexity of these possibilities is no argument against attempts at social engineering in the recreational sphere. It is simply an argument to the effect that social engineering with regard to recreation is not necessarily a simple or trivial matter. The problems of social engineering in this sphere are no less complicated than those associated with economic or political allocation—and no less serious either. Reform of recreational structures in conformity with sophisticated standards of art and ethics may be desirable, but on the other hand it may not be. Even if there is agreement on what the goals of reform should be, the rational choice of means to those goals is by no means simple or obvious in the context of any known society.

2. ARTISTIC ACTIVITIES

The term *artistic* as used here has reference to such forms of expression as sculpture, painting, literature, music, drama, etc. Artistic aspects of behavior, especially in the case of the enjoyment of the results of artistic efforts, certainly contain major recreational aspects as well. Relaxation, pleasure, and relief from the usual duties and concerns of everyday life are certainly involved. Activities usually classified as predominantly artistic, however, place a special emphasis on other factors. Most notable, perhaps, is the emphasis placed on the skill of execution within the medium chosen, the ability of the use made of the chosen medium to stimulate the observer emotionally, and the handling of the medium concerned in terms of new and distinctive ideas. It is difficult to separate the terms *artistic* and *creative* and retain any of the major elements ordinarily associated with the term *artistic*. Given the recreational aspect of art, it is possible to make the distinctions made above with regard to recreation in general. Artistic aspects may be built into daily activities, or they may be sharply separated from them in the context of different societies or even within different contexts of a single society. Escapist and nonescapist forms of artistic expression may be distinguished with some of the same types of implications already sketched above. The accent on creativity, however, makes it quite well worth while to separate artistic expression from recreation in general and consider it on the same level of generality. Since art emphasizes skill of execution, the ability to produce emotional responses, and treatment in terms of new ideas, attention is always focussed on what special or unique qualities are contributed by the artists regardless of whether they make their contributions in a spectacularly individualistic fashion or as an anonymous group. Focusing attention on the quality of creativity, the following questions arise: (1) is the creativity expected to exist within a rigidly and narrowly defined framework, (2) is the latitude of expression which does exist regarded favorably or unfavorably, or (3) is creativity considered to be a matter of spectacularly individualistic performance or as a product of a group of individuals, each of whom remains more or less anonymous? Perhaps it should go without saying that the greater the emphasis on latitude of expression from the artistic point of view the greater the possible implication of the effect of artistic production in other spheres of social life either insofar as those effects may be viewed as tending to support or alter the status quo—but it doesn't.

3. OTHER EMOTIONAL REACTIONS
[AFFECTIVE EXPRESSION]

The difficulty of the concept of affects or emotions has already been stressed above. I shall not attempt to go into this genuinely formidable problem in any depth. It requires neither great depth nor great knowledge in general to maintain that some regulation of the expression of emotions is absolutely necessary if any society or any social organization is to persist. There has never been a society whose members were perfectly free to express themselves emotionally in any way they might choose at any time. In this respect one can distinguish a range of variations between the extreme poles of complete repression and complete freedom of expression. Neither pole can be fully realized by the members of any society or of any subsystem of one. Different emphases, however, are quite possible. I would distinguish between an emphasis on *repression* of emotional reactions and an emphasis on *permissive expression* of emotional reactions. Given this distinction, there are two main lines of variation. The first has to do with the location of general emphasis. Is emphasis placed toward the one extreme or the other? It is at least in theory possible to rank societies with regard to whether or not their members tend to repress overt shows of emotion or permit them to be expressed freely. No society can exist whose members are precisely neutral on the matter of repression versus permissiveness, nor can there be one whose members are purely repressive or purely permissive about affective displays. The second main line of variation has to do with the fact that societies vary from one another, and there is considerable variation within a given society or other social organization, as to what emotions are more or less repressed or more or less freely expressed, how they are expected to be re-pressed or more or less freely expressed, and why they are expected to be repressed or more or less freely expressed by the members of the society or the social organization concerned.

If overt affective expression is to be highly repressed, there must exist highly elaborate, rigidly defined structures that will cover actions in situations likely to have strong affective effects on the individuals concerned. It is not enough merely to forbid certain forms of overt affective expressions, if it is in fact to be repressed. In such situations elaborate structures of overt affective expression must be inculcated on the individual regardless of whether these particular forms of expression in any specific case are sincerely felt or not. Elaborate sets of honorific expressions such that the very habits of speech formalize overt affective expression constitute a frequent structure with such effects in social history. I have specifically refrained from referring to such structures as a device or mechanism, since there need not be any self-conscious contriving of the structures with such effects in mind. When such structures are well and generally accepted, relatively slight breakdowns in conformity are highly noticeable. Social systems so characterized may be precariously balanced. A hydraulic theory of emotions, i.e., that emotional repression must find some outlet sooner or later, may not be tenable. It is, how-ever, at least plausible to hold that not *all* forms of affective expression can be so rigidly repressed or rigidly defined for the general membership of any society. It is probably not even pos-sible to maintain such structures all of the time even for a single individual. In all such straitly defined social contexts, there are usually quite specific phenomena that can be interpreted as out-lets. Abandonment of ordinary formalities while drinking, feast-ing, and dancing are frequent examples of this sort. At one period in Japanese history, the Japanese, who by our standards at least were relatively impassive as far as emotional displays were concerned in public, were reported as engaging in veritable orgies of sentimental weeping in darkened movie houses. If it is reason-able to expect that such outlets will exist in the context of straitly defined systems, and insofar as they actually do exist, social changes affecting the outlets may have quite dramatic conse-quences for other apparently unrelated ranges of behavior.

Another element of some significance in societies in which overt affective expression is rigidly regulated is the likelihood that the members of such societies or organizations will behave as if radically cut loose from affective regulations if they find them-selves in situations in which their habitual standards of judging behavior and of having their behavior judged have little if any reference. Again, Japanese history affords an example. The behavior in Nanking of Japanese soldiers must certainly have contained elements of this sort. The type of emotional display that took place in the non-Japanese setting of Nanking would have been out of the question in Japan proper at that time. In the usual Japanese context crimes involving personal violence, especially those of a sexual sort, are far rarer than in the United States. There is no question but that a considerable number of crimes of violence were committed by a considerable number of American soldiers during World War II, but the sort of mass berserker phenomena reported at Nanking was certainly not reported about the atrocities of either American or German soldiers.[14] The structures of affective expression characteristic of United States society permit more markedly violent displays in daily life than do the structures of Japan. Nevertheless, because of the emphasis on predominantly universalistic rather than particularistic standards of affective display, for a well-indoctrinated American of this period of history, by contrast with a correspondingly well-indoctrinated Japanese, there were no social situations that could be considered as thoroughly undefined. The more particularistically defined structures of the Japanese left situations far more open to individualism by default in the absence of what, from the Japanese point of view, constituted a qualified judge of behavior.

For the members of societies or organizations characterized by highly permissive structures of affective expression the problem of maintaining outlets for affective expressions is not great, though the problem of controlling the outlets may be. The contrast between standards emphasizing predominantly particularistic as opposed to predominantly universalistic elements in affective expression is interesting here. In the context of systems that are characterized by highly repressive structures, strait positive definitions of affective expression are of the greatest importance. Regardless of the causal explanation, the structures of such systems are characterized by a trend to emphasis on predominantly particularistic elements in the standards of affective

---

[14] Quite interesting inferences about affective expression may be drawn from a consideration of the atrocities reported in World War II. United States atrocities, for example, were on the whole highly individualistic; German atrocities tended to be carefully disciplined "by-the-numbers" performances; Japanese atrocities tended to be either highly disciplined performances or berserker performances, etc. A study of the structures of atrocious behavior in military or quasi-military situations might be valuable to students of national character.

expression. Affective expressions, after all, refer to a way of looking at reactions to what has been done at some time or other. Restrictions on such reactions in terms of who the persons involved are makes possible the formalization of specific forms of affective expression independent to a high degree of what has been done. Predominantly universalistic standards, emphasizing as they do what is done, tie affective expression to detailed variations in what has been done or what the individual thinks has been done. Since the range of variation of action actually open to an individual is always greater than the range of variation of the ideal definitions of his roles, the potential flexibility of predominantly universalistic standards is always much greater than that of predominantly particularistic ones.

It would be quite difficult, if not silly, to maintain that affective expression is more important in relatively modernized than in relatively nonmodernized social contexts. The variation of situations in which the ordinary individual acts, the number and variety of others with whom he interacts, etc., however, are certainly increased radically in relatively modernized social contexts. The relevance of such increases to the increased probabilities of emotional reactions in far more varied less predictable contexts may be as important an element in understanding the increasing emphasis on predominantly universalistic criteria characteristic of such societies as the quite obvious relations of such emphases to the efficiency of performances having to do with the production of goods and services in situations in which inanimate sources of power and extremely productive tools are involved. Predominantly universalistic criteria not only increase the flexibility of adjustment of given relationships to given purposes; they also increase the flexibility of reaction in emotional terms to an increased range of experience.

Usually in societies or other large-scale organizations there exists an extremely complex structured mixture of emphases on repressed emotional expression and permissive emotional expression. Displays of anger may be repressed and expressions of love encouraged; expressions of grief may be highly formalized. In all social contexts variation in these terms has to do with four major criteria. First, there is variation in what emotions may be more or less freely expressed. Second, there is variation in who may express them. Third, there is variation in what is considered a legitimate stimulus for such expression. Fourth, there is a range of variation in the socially acceptable procedures of expressing such reactions.

There are ranges of variation here that do not necessarily

become increasingly similar as societies become more and more highly modernized. Differences along these lines that make mutual understanding of individuals habituated to different systems extremely difficult are quite possible. For example, in the United States setting it is generally considered effeminate of a grown man to cry in public or perhaps even to cry at all unless under the most extreme circumstances of pain, grief, or anxiety. In the context of French society, which as societies go is also relatively highly modernized, the restriction of crying as a form of emotional expression by mature males is not nearly so rigid. The average American seeing a Frenchman cry, if he is charitably inclined, assumes that the situation is a very extreme one. Informed that this is not the case, he tends to assume that there is some element of effeminacy in the individual concerned. The range of variation in such forms of expression of emotions as kissing, embraces of various sorts, etc., and their differing interpretations on the part of people used to different types of structures are familiar to any individual of reasonably broad experience or reading. Although it is difficult to generalize with regard to affective expression on the basis of the distinction between relatively modernized and relatively nonmodernized societies, one generalization will certainly hold. In those spheres in which the emphasis on bureaucratization increases, in general there will be an increasing emphasis on the repression of overt affective displays. Increasingly the emphasis is on taking experiences in these contexts as they come as neutrally as possible as far as affective reactions are concerned with one exception. In such contexts an able individual is expected increasingly to make highly calculated instrumental uses of affective expression. He is expected to react in such a way that the effect of his displays of emotion on his equals, his superiors, or his subordinates is such that their behavior with regard to the maximization of what are presumed to be the goals of the members of the organization as members of that organization are maximized. In this sense in such contexts one, ideally speaking, seeks to maximize contributions to what he regards as the goals of the organization. Increasingly in all highly bureaucratized contexts affective expressions that contribute to what has come to be called *group dynamics* [a term that is much more an evaluation than it appears to be] is the approved form of affective expression.

4. POLITICS AND RECREATION

From a careful theoretical point of view these considerations probably should have been taken up under the general discussion of recreation above. They are of sufficient practical importance to be worth treating separately here. Reference will be made to these matters again in Part III, Chapters 2 and 5. So hard and fast has our thinking become in terms of highly specialized organizations that we do not ordinarily associate politics and recreation. We tend to associate the two relatively slightly despite political picnics, political dinners, etc. Even though the recreational elements in political dinners are increasingly minimized, there remain remnants in everyday language which refer to political figures. These remnants bespeak a different attitude of an earlier period. We speak of political virtuosi who love politics, for whom politics is a game, etc. Nevertheless, we tend not to think of politics as recreation or of recreation as politics. There is, however, a sense in which a new and different political history of the United States could be written about the theme that one of the most important changes in United States society has been the shift from an emphasis on politics as recreation to an emphasis on recreation as politics. One has only to read or look at the pictures of the types of gatherings that took place in the early and middle nineteenth century at which political orators by custom spoke for two or three hours at a stretch. Perhaps nothing is more often commented upon than the fact that Lincoln's Gettysburgh Address was so short, whereas Mr. Edward Everett's far longer one was at the time considered a more proper political address under the circumstances. People gathered in considerable crowds to listen to political oratory, and they made of it a festive occasion. This was, after all, one of the first periods in history in which most of the able-bodied males above the age of adulthood had the franchise. In that day, there were relatively few highly specialized forms of recreation for the average member of society. The right to listen to one's prospective political leaders, assess what they said, and choose among them was for the average man a novelty—a novelty in all social history. There was a certain zest about it. These were major recreational occasions for the participants. Remnants of this attitude persist in the United States today. One may judge this from occasional shouts such as "give 'em hell, Harry," from the interest in the Nixon-Kennedy television debates, and from the great attention which focused on the first occasions on which the national conventions were televised. On the whole today, however, the average member of United States society is really quite cynical about politics and is usually quite bored by political oratory. Unless great effort is expended, it is easier to see instances of recreational experts such as movie stars and the like devoting themselves to politics or to see various forms of entertainment viewed as political expressions than to regard politics as such as entertaining.

The point of view of those who can be thought of as late-comers to modernization is more likely to be akin to that which obtained in the United States in the nineteenth century. Politics is a major form of recreation for the members of the relatively nonmodernized societies in process of modernization. I have heard a great deal of discussion in terms of political ideologies and in terms of other political clichés about the so-called political demonstrations by the members of various African nations in which the persons demonstrating chant "Freedom! Freedom!," and about such demonstrations as those of laborers and the members of the students' organization in Japan [the Zengakuren]. Insofar as I have actually viewed such phenomena or seen films of them, I would assert that one may learn more from consideration of their recreational aspects than from the ordinary terms in which they are discussed. Whether they fully understand what they are doing or not, persons of extremist [from our point of view] political persuasions, i.e., Communists, Nazis, etc., have made far more sophisticated use of the consideration of politics as recreation than have the representatives of the less extreme [from our point of view] political ideologies. Since the vast majority of the people living in the world today live in social contexts in which the importance of politics as recreation is likely to be extremely high for some decades to come at least, this is something to think about.